Craig.
Happy 35th and
keep following your bliss
in the clear skies.

I love you, always
Dad

Richard Bach

FLYING

THE AVIATION TRILOGY

Stranger to the Ground

•

Biplane

•

Nothing by Chance

SCRIBNER CLASSICS

NEW YORK   LONDON   TORONTO   SYDNEY   SINGAPORE

SCRIBNER
1230 Avenue of the Americas
New York, NY 10020

First Scribner Classics Edition 2003

SCRIBNER and design are trademarks of Macmillan Library Reference USA, Inc.,
used under license by Simon & Schuster, the publisher of this work.

For information regarding special discounts for bulk purchases, please contact
Simon & Schuster Special Sales at 1-800-456-6798 or business@simonandschuster.com

These titles were previously published separately by Macmillan Publishing Company.

DESIGNED BY KYOKO WATANABE

Set in Stempel Garamond

Manufactured in the United States of America

1   3   5   7   9   10   8   6   4   2

Library of Congress Cataloging-in-Publication Data
Bach, Richard.
Flying: the aviation trilogy/Richard Bach.—1st Scribner Classics ed.
p. cm.
Contents: Stranger to the ground—Biplane—Nothing by chance.
1. Aeronautics—Popular works. 2. Airplanes—Piloting—Popular works.
3. Bach, Richard. 4. Aeronautics—Flights. 5. Air pilots—United States—Biography.
I. Bach, Richard. Stranger to the ground. II. Bach, Richard. Biplane.
III. Bach, Richard. Nothing by chance. IV. Title.
TL546.5.B23 2003
629.13'092—dc21
[B]
2003041619

ISBN 0-7432-4747-7

Contents

FLYING

STRANGER
TO THE GROUND

CHAPTER ONE

THE WIND TONIGHT is from the west, down runway two eight. It pushes gently at my polka-dot scarf and makes the steel buckles of my parachute harness tinkle in the darkness. It is a cold wind, and because of it my takeoff roll will be shorter than usual and my airplane will climb more quickly than it usually does when it lifts into the sky.

Two ground crewmen work together to lift a heavy padlocked canvas bag of Top Secret documents into the nose of the airplane. It sags awkwardly into space normally occupied by contoured ammunition cans, above four oiled black machine guns, and forward of the bomb release computers. Tonight I am not a fighter pilot. I am a courier for thirty-nine pounds of paper that is of sudden urgent interest to my wing commander, and though the weather this night over Europe is already freakish and violent, I have been asked to move these pounds of paper from England into the heart of France.

In the bright beam of my flashlight, the Form One, with its inked boxes and penciled initials, tells me that the airplane is ready, that it carries only minor shortcomings of which I already know: a dent in one drop tank, an inspection of the command radio antenna is due, the ATO system is disconnected. It is hard to turn the thin pages of the Form One with gloves on, but the cold wind helps me turn them.

Form signed, gun bay door locked over the mysterious canvas bag, I climb the narrow yellow ladder to my dark cockpit, like a high-booted mountain climber pulling himself to a peak from whose snows he can stand and look down upon the world. My peak is the small cockpit of a Republic F-84F Thunderstreak.

The safety belt of the yellow-handled ejection seat is wide nylon web, heavy and olive-drab; into its explosive buckle fits the nylon harness from over my shoulders and the amber steel link that automatically opens my parachute if I should have to bail out tonight. I surround myself with the universal quiet metallic noises of a pilot joining himself to his airplane. The two straps to the seat cushion survival kit, after their usual struggle, are captured and clink softly to my parachute harness. The green oxygen mask fits into its regulator hose with a muffled rubbery snap. The steel D-ring lanyard clanks as it fastens to the curved bar of the parachute rip-cord handle. The red-streamered ejection seat safety pin scrapes out of its hole drilled in the trigger of the right armrest and rustles in the darkness into the small pocket on the leg of my tight-laced G suit. The elastic leg strap of my scratched aluminum kneeboard cinches around my left thigh, latching itself with a hollow clank. My hard white fiberglass crash helmet, dark-visored, gold-lettered 1/LT. BACH, fits stiffly down to cover my head, its soft sponge-rubber earphones waiting a long cold moment before they begin to warm against my ears. The chamois chinstrap snaps at the left side, microphone cable connects with its own frosty click into the aircraft radio cord, and at last the wind-chilled green rubber oxygen mask snugs over my nose and mouth, fitting with a tight click-click of the smooth chromed fastener at the right side of the helmet. When the little family of noises is still, by tubes and wires and snaps and buckles, my body is attached to the larger, sleeping body of my airplane.

Outside, in the dark moving blanket of cold, a ghostly yellow auxiliary power unit roars into life, controlled by a man in a heavy issue parka who is hoping that I will be quick to start my engine and taxi away. Despite the parka, he is cold. The clatter and roar of the big gasoline engine under his hands settles a bit, and on its voltage dials, white needles spring into their green arcs.

From the engine of the power unit, through the spinning generator, through the black rubber snake into the cold silver wing of my airplane, through the marked wires of the DC electrical system, the power explodes in my dark cockpit as six brilliant red and yellow warning lights, and as quick tremblings of a few instrument pointers.

My leather gloves, stamped with the white wings and star of Air Force property, go through a familiar little act for the interested audience that watches from behind my eyes. From left to right around the cockpit they travel; checking left console circuit breakers in, gun heater switch *off*, engine screen switch *extend*, drop tank pressure switches *off*, speed break switch *extend*, throttle *off*, altimeter, drag chute handle, sight caging lever, radio compass, TACAN, oxygen, generator, IFF, inverter selector. The gloves dance, the eyes watch. The right glove flourishes into the air at the end of its act and spins a little circle of information to the man waiting in the wind below: checks are finished, engine is starting in two seconds. Now it is throttle on, down with the glove, and starter switch to *start*.

There is no time to take a breath or blink the eye. There is one tiny tenth-second hiss before concussion shatters icy air. Suddenly, instantly, air and sparks and Jet Propellant Four. My airplane is designed to start its engine with an explosion. It can be started in no other way. But the sound is a keg of black powder under the match, a cannon firing, the burst of a hand grenade. The man outside blinks, painfully.

With the blast, as though with suddenly opened eyes, my airplane is alive. Instantly awake. The thunderclap is gone as quickly as it came, replaced by a quiet rising whine that peaks quickly, very high, and slides back down the scale into nothingness. But before the whine is gone, deep inside the engine, combustion chambers have earned their name. The luminous white pointer of the gage marked *exhaust gas temperature* pivots upward, lifting as thermocouples taste a swirling flood of yellow fire that twists from fourteen stainless steel chambers. The fire spins a turbine. The turbine spins a compressor. The compressor crushes fuel and air for the fire. Weak yellow flames change to businesslike blue torches held in their separate round offices, and the ghostly power unit is needed no more.

Flourish with the right glove, finger pointing away; away the power, I'm on my own.

Tailpipe temperature is settled and at home with 450 degrees of centigrade, tachometer steadies to note that the engine is turning at 45 percent of its possible rpm. The rush of air to the insatiable steel engine is a constant rasping scream at the oval intake, a chained banshee shrieking in the icy black air and the searing blue fire.

Hydraulic pressure shows on a dial, under a pointer. Speed brake switch to *retract,* and the pressure pulls two great slabs of steel to disappear into the smooth sides of my airplane. Rainbow lights go dark as pressure rises in systems for fuel and oil. I have just been born, with the press of wind at my scarf. With the wind keening along the tall swept silver of my rudder. With the rush of wind to the torches of my engine.

There is one light left on, stubbornly glowing over a placard marked *canopy unlocked.* My left glove moves a steel handle aft. With the right I reach high overhead to grasp the frame of the counterbalanced section of double-walled Plexiglas. A gentle pull downward, and the smooth-hinged canopy settles over my little world. I move the handle forward in my left glove, I hear a muffled sound of latches engaging, I see the light wink out. The wind at my scarf is gone.

I am held by my straps and my buckles and my wires in a deep pool of dim red light. In the pool is all that I must know about my airplane and my position and my altitude until I pull the throttle back to *off,* one hour and twenty-nine minutes and 579 airway miles from Wethersfield Air Base, England.

This base means nothing to me. When I landed it was a long runway in the sunset, a tower operator giving taxi directions, a stranger waiting for me in Operations with a heavy padlocked canvas bag. I was in a hurry when I arrived, I am in a hurry to leave. Wethersfield, with its hedges and its oak trees that I assume are part of all English towns, with its stone houses and mossed roofs and its people who watched the Battle of Britain cross the sky with black smoke, is to me Half Way. The sooner I leave Wethersfield a smudge in the darkness behind, the sooner I can finish the letter to my wife and my daughter, the sooner I can settle into a lonely bed and mark another day gone from the calendar. The sooner I can take myself beyond the unknown that is the weather high over Europe.

On the heavy black throttle under my left glove there is a microphone button, and I press it with my thumb. "Wethersfield Tower," I say to the microphone buried in the snug green rubber of my oxygen mask. I hear my own voice in the earphones of my helmet, and know that in the high glass cube of the control tower the same voice and the same words are this moment speaking. "Air Force Jet Two Niner Four Zero Five; taxi information and standing by for ATC clearance."

It still sounds strange. Air Force Jet. Six months ago it was Air Guard Jet. It was one weekend a month, and fly when you have the spare time. It was the game of flying better than Air Force pilots and shooting straighter than Air Force pilots, with old airplanes and with a full-time civilian job. It was watching the clouds of tension mushroom over the world, and knowing for certain that if the country needed more firepower, my squadron would be a part of it. It was thirty-one pilots in the squadron knowing that fact, knowing that they could leave the squadron before the recall came; and it was the same thirty-one pilots, two months later, flying their worn airplanes without inflight refueling, across the Atlantic into France. Air Force Jet.

"Roger, Zero Five," comes a new voice in the earphones. "Taxi runway two eight; wind is two seven zero degrees at one five knots, altimeter is two niner niner five, tower time is two one two five, clearance is on request. Type aircraft, please."

I twist the small knurled knob near the altimeter to set 29.95 in a red-lit window. The hands of the altimeter move slightly. My gloved thumb is down again on the microphone button. "Roger, tower, Zero Five is a Fox Eight Four, courier: returning to Chaumont Air Base, France."

Forward goes the thick black throttle and in the quickening roar of startled, very hot thunder, my Republic F-84F, slightly dented, slightly old-fashioned, governed by my left glove, begins to move. A touch of boot on left brake and the airplane turns. Back with the throttle to keep from blasting the man and his power unit with a 600-degree hurricane from the tailpipe. Tactical Air Navigation selector to *transmit and receive.*

The sleeping silver silhouettes of the F-100's of Wethersfield Air Base sweep by in the dark as I taxi, and I am engulfed in comfort. The endless crackle of light static in my earphones, the intimate weight of my helmet, the tremble of my airplane, rocking and slowly pitching as it rolls on hard tires and oil-filled struts over the bumps and ridges of the taxiway. Like an animal. Like a trusted and trusting eager heavy swift animal of prey, the airplane that I control from its birth to its sleep trundles toward the two-mile runway lulled by the murmur of the cold wind.

The filtered voice of the tower operator shatters the serene static in the earphones. "Air Force Jet Two Niner Four Zero Five, clearance received. Ready to copy?"

My pencil springs from flight jacket sleeve to poise itself over the folded flight plan trapped in the jaws of the clipboard on my left leg. "Ready to copy."

"ATC clears; Air Force Jet Two Niner Four Zero Five to the Chaumont Airport . . ." I mark the words in scrawled shorthand. I have been cleared to fly the route I have planned. ". . . via direct Abbeville, direct Laon, direct Spangdahlem, direct Wiesbaden, direct Phalsbourg, direct Chaumont." A route detoured before it begins; planned to avoid the mass of storms and severe weather that the forecaster has marked in red squares across the direct route to my home base. "Climb in radar control to flight level three three zero, contact Anglia control . . ." The clearance comes in through the earphones and out through the sharp point of the pencil; whom to contact and when and on which frequency, one hour and twenty-nine minutes of flying pressed onto a four-inch square of penciled paper bathed in dim red light. I read the shorthand back to the tower operator, and tap the brakes to stop short of the runway.

"Roger, Zero Five, readback is correct. Cleared for takeoff; no reported traffic in the local area."

Throttle forward again and the airplane swings into takeoff position on runway two eight. The concrete is wide and long. The painted white stripe along its center is held at one end by my nosewheel, at the invisible other end by the tough nylon webbing of the overrun barrier. A twin row of white edge lights converges in the black distance ahead, pointing the way. The throttle moves now, under my left glove, all the way forward; until the radium-caked tachometer needle covers the line marked *100 percent*, until the tailpipe temperature is up by the short red arc on the dial that means 642 degrees centigrade, until each pointer on each dial of the red-soaked instrument panel agrees with what we are to do, until I say to myself, as I say every time, Here we go. I release the brakes.

There is no instant rush of speed, no head forced against the headrest. I feel only a gentle push at my back. The stripe of the runway unrolls, lazily at first, beneath the nosewheel. Crackling thunder twists and blasts and tumbles behind me, and, slowly, I see the runway lights begin to blur at the side of the concrete and the airspeed needle lifts to cover 50 knots, to cover 80 knots, to cover 120 knots (go/no-go speed checks OK) and between the two white rows of blur I see the barrier waiting in the darkness at the end of the runway and the control stick tilts easily back in my right glove and the airspeed needle is covering 160 knots and the nosewheel lifts from the concrete and the main wheels follow a half second later and there is nothing in the world but me and an airplane alive and together and the cool wind lifts us to its heart and we are one with the wind and one with the dark sky and the stars ahead and the barrier is a forgotten dwindling blur behind and the wheels swing up to tuck themselves away in my seamless aluminum skin and the airspeed is up to one nine zero and flap lever forward and airspeed two two zero and I am in my element and I am flying. I am flying.

The voice that I hear in the soft earphones is unlike my own. It is the voice of a man concerned only with business; a man speaking while he has yet many things to do. Still it is my thumb down on the microphone button and my words screened through the receiver in the tower. "Wethersfield Tower, Air Force Jet Two Niner Four Zero Five departing on course, leaving your station and frequency."

My airplane climbs easily through the strange clear air over southern England, and my gloves, not content to accept idleness, move across the cockpit and complete the little tasks that have been assigned to them. The needles of my altimeter swing quickly through the 5,000-foot mark, and while my gloves work at the task of retracting the engine screens, pressurizing the drop tanks, loosing the D-ring lanyard from the rip cord, setting the pneumatic compressor into life, I notice suddenly that there is no moon. I had hoped for a moon.

My eyes, at the command of the audience behind them, check once again that all the small-dialed engine instruments have pointers properly under their arcs of green paint on the glass. The right glove, conscientious, pushes the oxygen lever from *100 percent* to *normal,* and sets the four white numbers of the departure control frequency in the four black windows of the command ultrahigh-frequency transmitter.

The strange voice that is mine speaks to the radar control center guiding my departure. The voice is capable of doing the necessary talking, the gloves are capable of moving throttle and control stick to guide the slanting climb of my airplane into the night. Ahead of me, through the heavy angled glass of the windscreen, through a shrinking wall of clear air, is the weather. I can see that it hugs the ground at first, low and thin, as if uncertain that it is over the land that it has been assigned to cover.

The three white hands of the altimeter swing through 10,000 feet, sending my right glove into another, shorter, series of menial tasks in the cockpit. It dials now the numbers *387* into the pie-slice of window on the radio compass control panel. In the soft earphones are the faint Morse letters *A-B:* the Abbeville radio beacon.

Abbeville. Twenty years ago the Abbeville Boys, flying Messer-schmitt 109's with yellow-spiral spinners around their propeller-hub cannon, were the best fighter pilots in the German Luftwaffe. Abbeville was the place to go when you were looking for a fight, and a place to avoid when you carried canvas sacks instead of machine-gun bullets. Abbeville on one side of the Channel, Tangmere and Biggin Hill on the other. Messerschmitt on one side and Spitfire on the other. And a tangle of white contrails and lines of falling black smoke in the crystal air between.

The only distance that lies between me and a yellow-nosed ME-109 is a little bend of the river called time. The wash of waves on the sands of Calais. The hush of wind across chessboard Europe. The spinning of one hour hand. Same air, same sea, same hour hand, same river of time. But the Messerschmitts are gone. And the magnificent Spitfires. Could my airplane tonight carry me not along the river, but across the bend of it, the world would look exactly as it looks tonight. And in this same air before them, in another block of old air, the Breguets and the Latés and One Lonely Ryan, coming in from the west, into the glare of searchlights over Le Bourget. And back across the confluences of the river, a host of Nieuports and Pfalzes and Fokkers and Sopwiths, of Farmans and Bleriots, of Wright Flyers, of Santos-Dumont dirigibles, of Montgolfiers, of hawks circling, circling. As men looked up from the ground. Into the sky just as it is tonight.

The eternal sky, the dreaming man.

The river flows.

The eternal sky, the striving man.

The river flows.

The eternal sky, the conquering man.

Tonight Tangmere and Biggin Hill are quiet lighted rectangles of concrete under the cloud that slips beneath my airplane, and the airport near Abbeville is dark. But there is still the crystal air and it whispers over my canopy and blasts into the gaping oval intake a gun's length ahead of my boots.

It is sad, to be suddenly a living part of what should belong to old memory and faded gun-camera films. My reason for being on the far shore of the Atlantic is to be always ready to mold new memories of the victory of Us against Them, and to squeeze the trigger that adds another few feet to history's reel of gun-camera film. I am here to become a part of a War That Could Be, and this is the only place I belong if it changes into a War That Is.

But rather than learning to hate, or even to be more uncaring about the enemy who threatens on the other side of the mythical iron curtain, I have learned in spite of myself that he might actually be a man, a human being. During my short months in Europe, I have lived with German pilots, with French pilots, Norwegian pilots, with pilots from Canada and from England. I have discovered, almost to my surprise, that Americans are not the only people in the world who fly airplanes for the sheer love of flying them. I have learned that airplane pilots speak the same language and understand the same unspoken words, whatever their country. They face the same headwinds and the same storms. And as the days pass without war, I find myself asking if a pilot, because of the political situation under which he lives, can possibly be a totally different man from all the pilots living in all the political systems across the earth.

This man of mystery, this Russian pilot about whose life and thoughts I know so little, becomes in my mind a man not unlike myself, who is flying an airplane fitted with rockets and bombs and machine guns not because he loves destruction but because he loves his airplane, and the job of flying a capable, spirited airplane in any air force cannot be divorced from the job of killing when there is a war to be fought.

I am growing to like this probable pilot of the enemy, the more so because he is an unknown and forbidden man, with no one to bear witness of the good in him, and so many at hand to condemn his evils.

If war is declared here in Europe, I will never know the truth of the man who mounts the cockpit of a red-starred airplane. If war is declared, we are unleashed against each other, like starved wolves, to fight. A friend of mine, a true proven friend, neither imagined nor conjured out of possibilities, will fall to the guns of a Russian pilot. Somewhere an American will die under his bombs. In that instant I will be swallowed up in one of the thousand evils of war; I will have lost the host of unmet friends who are the Russian pilots. I will rejoice in their death, take pride in the destruction of their beautiful airplanes under my own rockets and my own guns. If I succumb to hate, I will myself become certainly and unavoidably a lesser man. In my pride I will be less worthy of pride. I will kill the enemy, and in so doing will bring my own death upon me. And I am sad.

But this night no war has been declared. It seems, in the quiet days, almost as if our nations might learn to live with each other, and this night the eastern pilot of my imagining, more real than the specter he would become in wartime, is flying his own solitary airplane into his own capricious weather.

My gloves are at work again, leveling the airplane at 33,000 feet. Throttle comes back under the left glove until the engine tachometer shows 94 percent rpm. The thumb of the right glove touches the trim button on the control stick once and again, quickly, forward. The eyes flick from instrument to instrument, and all is in order. Fuel flow is 2,500 pounds per hour. Mach needle is resting over .8, which means that my true airspeed is settling at 465 knots. The thin luminous needle of the radio compass, over its many-numbered dial, pivots suddenly as the Abbeville radio beacon passes beneath my airplane, under the black cloud. Eyes make a quick check of transmitter frequency, voice is ready with a position report to air traffic control, left thumb is down on the microphone button at 2200 hours, and the audience behind the eyes sees the first faint flash of lightning in the high opaque darkness ahead.

CHAPTER TWO

"FRANCE CONTROL, Air Force Jet Two Niner Four Zero Five, Abbeville." Empty static for a moment in the soft earphones, and I see, very clearly, a man in a large square room cluttered with teletypes and speakers and frequency dials and round grey radar screens. At an upholstered swivel chair, the man leans forward to his microphone, setting aside a glass of red wine.

"Four Zero Five, France Control, go ahead." The accent in his English is barely noticeable. That is rare. He reaches for a pencil, from a jar bristling with pencils.

The microphone button is down again under my left thumb, and I hear again the sidetone, just as the man on the ground is hearing it. The engine in the sidetone is a quiet and businesslike roar, a waterfall of purposeful sound that is a background for my message. My words are filtered through the tubed body of the transmitter to become impersonal and faraway, the voice of someone I know only as a casual acquaintance. "France Control, Zero Five is over Alpha Bravo on the hour, flight level three three zero, assigned instrument flight rules, estimating Lima Charlie at zero niner, Spangdahlem." Good old France. The only country in Europe where you never say the name of a reporting point, but only its initials, with a little air of mystery as you do. The familiar pattern of the position report is rhythmic and poetic; it is a pattern of pure efficiency that is beautiful to speak.

There are thousands of position reports spoken and heard every hour across the earth; they are as basic a part of instrument flying as the calls for landing information are a basic part of fair-weather flight. Position reports are part of a way of life.

"Roger, Zero Five, on your position. Report Lima Charlie." The pencil stops, the whine is lifted.

With his last word, the man at France Control has ceased to exist. I am left alone again with the night and the stars and the sounds of my airplane.

In every other fighter airplane, cruise is a time of quiet and of smooth unvarying sound. The pilot hushes along on his tamed fall of sound and knows that all is well with his engine and his airplane. But not with this airplane, not with my F-84F. My airplane is a clown. Its engine sounds more like a poorly tuned, poorly muffled V-8 than a smoothly efficient dynamo spinning on pressure-oiled bearings. I was warned when I began to fly the Thunderstreak that if the engine ever stopped vibrating I would be in trouble. It is true. Strange sounds come from nowhere, linger for a while in the body of the airplane, then die away.

Now, behind my left shoulder, a low whine begins. Intrigued by the new tone that my harlequin airplane has discovered, I listen attentively. The whine rises higher and higher, as if a tiny turbine were accelerating to tremendous speed. My left glove inches the throttle back an inch and the whine calms a fraction; throttle forward and it regains its spinning song. In another airplane the whine would be cause for serious and concerned interest; in my airplane it is cause for a slight smile under the green rubber oxygen mask. I had once thought that I had heard all the noises that it was possible for this airplane to make. After a moment, the whine dies away by itself.

Thud. There is the smallest tremor in the throttle, and a sound as if a hard snowball had hit the side of the fuselage. In an F-100 or an F-104, in the new airplanes, the thud would bring a sudden stiffening of pilot and a quick recheck of the engine instruments. In another airplane the thud would likely mean that the engine has thrown a turbine blade, and that a host of unpleasant consequences are to follow. In my '84, though, a thud is just one more sound in the kaleidoscope of sounds that the airplane offers to its pilot, another evidence of an unconforming personality hidden in the metal.

My airplane has a great variety of individual quirks; so many that before we arrived in France it was necessary to arrange a little meeting with the control tower operators, to tell them about the airplane. The boom of the engine start could send the uninitiated scrambling for the fire alarm. When the engine is idling on the ground, turning a modest 46 percent of her available rpm, she hums. She hums not quietly to herself, but an amplified, penetrating, resonant distracting MMMM that makes the crew chiefs point painfully to their ears, reminding pilots to advance the power, to increase the rpm past the point of resonance. It is a very precise and human hum she makes, and there is no doubt over all the air base that an F-84F is preparing to fly. Heard from a comfortable distance, the airplane is setting the note for the song of her higher thunder. Later, in the sky, there is usually no trace of her resonance, though the cockpit is filled with the other sounds of her engine.

Every once in a while, though, I fly an airplane that hums in the air, and the cockpit is a finely engineered box of torture. Back on the throttle after takeoff, to cruise cross-country, to stay on a leader's wing. MMM . . . Back a little more on the throttle. MMM . . . The resonance ripples through me as if I were a metal servomotor bolted to the fuselage. I shake my head quickly. It is like trying to disperse a horde of hungry mosquitoes with a toss of the head. I open my eyes wide, close them, shake my head again. Futile. Soon it is difficult to think of flying formation, of cruising, of navigation, of anything but the all-pervading hum that makes the airplane tremble as with a strange malady. Speed brakes out, halfway. Throttle open to 98 percent rpm. The hum subsides with the increased power, replaced by the tremble of air blasting against the speed brakes. To fly two hours in a badly humming airplane would reduce its pilot to a hollow-eyed automaton. I would not have believed that such a simple thing as sound and vibration could erode a man so quickly. When I wrote one airplane up for severe engine resonance, I discovered that it was most often caused by a loose tailpipe connection, allowing the eight-foot tube of stainless steel to rest lightly against the airframe like a tuning fork against a water glass. The perfect tool of a saboteur in wartime would be a wrench with which to loosen, ever so slightly, the tailpipe mounting bolts on enemy airplanes.

Other things. The airplane has a hundred little jokes to play. A hundred little things that seem to indicate that Something Is Wrong, when nothing at all is amiss. Just before takeoff, during the engine run-up on the runway, grey smoke floods into the cockpit, geysering from the air vents. Engine fire? A broken oil line in the engine compartment? No. The cockpit air temperature control is set too cold, and the moist outside air is turned to instant fog by the obedient cooling system. Press the temperature control to *hot* for a moment, and the smoke disappears. And the airplane chuckles to herself.

The same moment, run-up. Smoke, real oil smoke, streams from the fuselage, blasting down from a hidden orifice onto the runway, splashing up to wreathe the airplane in grey. Normal. Just the normal oil-mist from the pressure-lubricated bearings, venting overboard as designed.

In flight, after an hour of low-level. Fuel suddenly streams from the leader's airplane, flying back like a great white banner of distress. Broken fuel lines? An indicator of turbine blades spinning from the red-hot wheel and an engine coming to pieces? Imminent fire and a burst of scarlet in the sky? No. Quite normal, this streamer of fuel. As the drop tanks feed the last of their fuel, and as the internal tanks join to feed their own fuel, there is for a moment too much JP-4 in the main fuel tank, and it overflows, as designed, harmlessly overboard. The airplane chuckles with an old joke.

Takeoff. Heavy laden at low airspeed, close to the ground, bailout a marginal thing before the flaps are up, and a brilliant yellow light flares on the instrument panel. Suddenly. I see it from the corner of my eye, and I am stunned. For a half second. And the yellow light, all by itself, goes out. Not the yellow overheat-warning light I saw at that critical moment when fire could be disaster, but the mechanical advantage shift light, telling me, when I have recovered my composure, that the stabilator hydraulic system is going about its task as its destiny demands, changing the response of the flight controls as the landing gear locks up. And the airplane chuckles.

But once in a very long while the turbine buckets do break free and slice red-hot through the fuel lines, the fire warning light really does come on with flame at its sensors, the cockpit does fill with smoke. Once in a while. And an airplane screams.

Tonight I cruise. The steady play of whines and thuds and rumbles and squeals, and through it all the luminous needles at 95 percent rpm and 540 degrees tailpipe temperature, and 265 knots indicated airspeed. Cruise is the long radium hands of the altimeter drifting slowly back and forth across the 33,000-foot mark and other shorter needles captured by arcs of green paint on their glass dials. There are twenty-four round dials on the panel in front of me in the red light. The fact is empty and unimpressive, although I feel, vaguely, as if it should be startling. Perhaps if I counted the switches and handles and selectors . . .

At one time I would have been impressed by the twenty-four dials, but tonight they are few and I know them well. There is a circular computer on the clipboard strapped to my leg that tells me the indicated airspeed of 265 knots is actually moving my airplane over the land between Abbeville and Laon at a speed of 465 knots, 535 miles per hour. Which is not really fast, but for an old Guard airplane it is not really slow, either.

Cruise. Hours neatly shortened and diced into sections of time spent flying between city and city, radio beacon and radio beacon, between one swing of the radio compass needle and the next. I carry my world with me as I fly, and outside is the familiar, indifferent Other World of fifty-five below zero and stars and black cloud and a long fall to the hills.

From the light static in the earphones comes a quick and hurried voice: "Evreux Tower radio check Guard channel; one-two-three-four-five-four-three-two-one Evreux Tower out."

There is someone else in the world at this moment. There is a tower operator six miles below me, dwindling at 465 knots, who is this second setting his microphone back in its cradle, glancing at his runway held in a net of dim white lights and surrounded by blue taxiway lights that lead to a parking ramp. From his tower he can look down on the tall rhythmic triangles that are the vertical stabilizers of his base's transport airplanes parked. At this moment he is beginning a lonely stretch of duty; his radio check was as much to break the silence as it was to check the emergency transmitter. But now he is assured that the radio works and he settles down to wait the night through. He is not aware that I have passed over his head. To know, he would have to step out to the catwalk around his tower and listen carefully and look up through the last hole in the clouds, toward the stars. He would hear, if his night was a quiet one, the tiny dim thunder of the engine that carries me and my airplane through the sky. If he carried his binoculars, and if he watched at precisely the right moment, he would see the flashing dots of red and green and amber that are my navigation lights, and the white of my fuselage light. And he would walk back into his tower in the first drops of rain and wait for the coming of the dawn.

I remember that I wondered, once, what flying a fighter airplane would feel like. And now I know. It feels just the same as it feels to drive an automobile along the roads of France. Just the same. Take a small passenger sedan to 33,000 feet. Close the walls around the driver's seat, cut away the roof, and cap the space with Plexiglas. Steer with a control stick and rudder pedals instead of with a wheel. Put twenty-four gauges on the instrument panel. Wear a sage-green set of many-pocketed coveralls and a tight-laced zippered G suit and a white crash helmet with a dark Plexiglas visor and a soft green rubber oxygen mask and a pair of high-topped black jump boots with white shroud-line laces and a pistol in a leather shoulder holster and a heavy green flight jacket with a place for four pencils on the left sleeve and sew your squadron emblem and your name on the jacket and paint your name on the helmet and slip into a parachute and connect the survival kit and the oxygen and the microphone and the automatic parachute lanyard and strap yourself with shoulder harness and safety belt into a seat with yellow handles and a trigger and fly along above the hills to cover eight miles a minute and look down at the growing wall of cloud at your right and watch the needles and pointers that tell you where you are, how high you are, and how fast you are moving. Flying a fighter airplane is just the same as driving an automobile along the roads of France.

My airplane and I have been in the air now for thirty-one minutes since we left the runway at Wethersfield Air Base. We have been together for 415 flying hours since we first met in the Air National Guard. Fighter pilots are not in the cockpits of their airplanes a tenth as long as transport pilots are on the flight decks of theirs. Flights in single-engine airplanes rarely last longer than two hours, and new airplanes replace old models every three or four years, even in the Guard. But the '84 and I have flown together for a reasonably long time, as fighter pilots and their airplanes go. We have gotten to know each other. My airplane comes alive under my gloved touch, and in return for her life she gives me the response and performance that is her love.

I want to fly high, above the cloud, and she willingly draws her own streamer of tunneled and twisting grey behind us. From the ground the tunnel of grey is a contrail of brilliant white, and the world can see, in the slash across the blue, that we are flying very high.

I want to fly low. In a roar, flash, a sweptwing blur, we streak across the wooded valleys. We rustle the treetops in the pressure of our passing and the world is a sheetblur in the windscreen with one point fixed: straight ahead, the horizon.

We enjoy our life together.

Every once in a while as an idle hour catches me thinking of the life I lead, I ask why the passion for speed and for low-level flying. For, as an old instructor told me, you can do anything you want in an airplane without the slightest danger, until you try to do it near the ground. It is the contact with the ground, with that depressingly solid other world, that kills pilots. So why do we fly low and fast occasionally just for the fun of it? Why the barrel rolls off the deck after a pass on the army tanks in the war games? Why the magnetism of the bridge, the silent patient dare that every bridge makes to every pilot, challenging him to fly beneath it and come away alive?

I enjoy the color and the taste of life a very great deal. Although death is an interesting sort of thing on the path ahead, I am content to let it find me where it will rather than hasting to meet it or deliberately searching it out. So I ask myself, why the rolls, the lower-than-necessary passes at high speed? Because it is fun, the answer says, throwing up a screen that it hopes will be accepted as self-sufficient. Because it is fun. There. No pilot will deny that. But like a child experimenting with words, I ask, why is it fun? Because you like to show off. Aha. The answer begins to be seen, slipping into a doorway a half second too late to escape my attention. And why do I like to show off? The answer is caught in a cross fire of brilliant spotlights. Because I am free. Because my spirit is not shackled by a 180-pound body. Because I have powers, when I am with my airplane, that only the gods have. Because I do not have to read about 500 knots or see it in a motion picture from a drone airplane or imagine what it would feel like. In my freedom I can *live* 500 knots—the blur of the trees the brief flash of the tank beneath me the feel of the stick in my right hand and the throttle in my left the smell of green rubber and cold oxygen the filtered voice from the forward air controller, "Nice show, Checkmate!" Because I can tell the men on the ground that truth that I discovered a long time ago: Man is not confined to walk the earth and be subject to its codes. Man is a free creature, with dominion over his surroundings, over the proud earth that was master for so long. And this freedom is so intense that it brings a smile that will not cede its place to mature, dignified impassiveness. For, as the answer said in part, freedom is fun.

She is responsive, my airplane. She does not care that she drinks fuel at low level as a fall drinks water. She does not care that the insects of the forest are snapped into sudden flecks of eternity on her windscreen. She flies at the tops of the trees because that is where I want to fly, because she is a sensitive and responsive airplane. Because I have moved a gloved hand to give her life. Because I paint her a name on the forward fuselage. Because I call her "she." Because I love her.

My love for this airplane is not born of beauty, for a Thunderstreak is not a beautiful airplane. My love is born of a respect for quality of performance. My airplane, in the life that I bring to her, expects that I fly her properly and well. She will forgive me the moments that make it necessary to force her where she would not smoothly go, if there are reasons for the moments. But if I continually force her to fly as she was not meant to fly, overspeed and overtemperature, with sudden bursts of throttle, with hard instant changes of flight controls, she will one day, coldly and dispassionately, kill me.

I respect her, and she in turn respects me. Yet I have never said "We landed" or "We tore the target to pieces"; it is always "I landed," "I knocked out that tank." Without my airplane I am nothing, yet I claim the credit. What I say, though, is not egocentric at all.

I step into the cockpit of my airplane. With shoulder harness and wide safety belt I strap myself to my airplane (I strap on my wings and my speed and my power) I snap the oxygen hose to my mask (I can breathe at altitudes where the air is very thin) I fit the radio cable to the black wire that comes from the back of my fitted helmet (I can hear frequencies that are unheard by others; I can speak to scores of isolated people with special duties) I flick the gun switch to *guns* (I can cut a six-ton truck in half with a squeeze of my finger I can flip a 30-ton tank on its back with the faint pressure of my thumb on the rocket button) I rest one hand on the throttle, one on the contoured, button-studded grip of the control stick (I can fly).

The swept aluminum wings are my wings, the hard black wheels are my wheels that I feel beneath me, the fuel in the tanks is my fuel which I drink and through which I live. I am no longer man, I am man/airplane; my airplane is no longer merely Republic F-84F Thunderstreak, but airplane/man. The two are one, the one is the "I" that stops the tank holding the infantry in its foxholes, that strikes the enemy man/airplane out of the blind sky. The I that carries the wing commander's documents from England to France.

Sometimes I stand on the ground or lie back on a soft couch and wonder how it is possible for me to become wide-awake and a part of an airplane, to climb into that fantastically complex cockpit and go through all the procedures and do all the alert thinking that is necessary to fly in formation with other airplanes or around a gunnery pattern for score or to put a cluster of rockets on a target. This thought has stuck with me for long minutes, while I zip the legs of my G suit, while I slide into my mae west, while I strap myself into the little cockpit. It is a dull lethargy that says, "How can I do everything right?" and wants only to withdraw into itself and forget about the responsibility of flying a high-performance airplane through a precise pattern. But one of the strange features of the game is that as soon as my finger presses the starter switch to *start,* the lethargy vanishes. In that moment I am ready for whatever the mission will require. I am alert and thinking about what has to be done and knowing just how it must be done and taking the flight one step at a time and taking each step surely and correctly and firmly. The feeling of trying to accomplish the impossible disappears with the touch of the switch to my glove and does not reappear until I am again off guard and unalert and resting before the next flight. I wonder if this is common, this draining of aggressiveness before a flight. I have never asked another pilot about it, I have never heard another pilot speak of it. But as long as the touch of the switch is an instant cure, I am not concerned.

Switch pressed, in the airplane, I asked how I ever found the thought that flying single-engine airplanes is a complicated job. I cannot answer. It just seemed as if that should be, before I start the engine, and long ago, before I understood the twenty-four dials and the switches and the handles and the selectors. After I sit in one little space for 415 hours I come to know it rather well, and what I don't know about it at the end of that time is not of great importance. Where did the thought of complication begin?

At the air shows, friends who do not fly climb the yellow ladder to my airplane and say, "How complicated it all is!" Do they really mean what they are saying? A good question. I think back, before the day I knew an aileron from a stabilator. Did I once consider airplanes complicated? I think back. A shocking answer. Terribly complicated. Even after I had begun to fly, each new airplane, each larger airplane, looked more complicated than the one I'd flown before. But a simple thing like knowing the purpose of everything in a cockpit dissolves the word *complicated* and makes it sound foreign when someone uses it to describe my airplane.

This dim red panel in front of me now, what is complex about it? Or the consoles at the left and right? Or the buttons on the stick grip? Child's play.

It was a shattering disillusion, the day I landed from my first flight in the F-84. The Thunderstreak was considered then the best airplane in the Air Force for air-to-ground warfare. It could deliver more high explosive on target than any other tactical fighter airplane flying. I was hurt and disillusioned, because I had just gone through fifteen months of marching and studying and flying and Hit One, Mister, to prepare for an airplane that my wife could walk out to and fly any day of the week. I could settle her in the cockpit, put the harness over her shoulders and buckle the seat belt about her and tell her that the throttle is for fast and slow, the stick is for up and down and left and right, and there's the handle that brings the wheels up and down. Oh, and by the way, sweetheart, a hundred and sixty knots down final approach.

There goes the feeling that some magic day I would wake to find myself a superman. My wife, who had spent the last fifteen months taking letters in shorthand, could step into that little cockpit and take it through the speed of sound; could drop, if she wanted, an atomic bomb.

Divorced from my airplane I am an ordinary man, and a useless one—a trainer without a horse, a sculptor without marble, a priest without a god. Without an airplane I am a lonely consumer of hamburgers, the fellow in line at a cash register, shopping cart laden with oranges and cereal and quarts of milk. A brown-haired fellow who is struggling against pitiless odds to master the guitar.

But as "The Speckled Roan" falls to the persistence of an inner man striving with chords of E and A minor and B7, so I become more than ordinary when the inner man strives with the material that he loves, which, for me, has a wingspan of thirty-seven feet six inches, a height of thirteen feet seven inches. The trainer, the sculptor, the priest, and I. We all share a preference for string beans, and distaste for creamed corn. But in each one of us, as in each of all humanity, lives the inner man, who lives only for the spirit of his work.

I am not a superman, but flying is still an interesting way to make a living, and I bury the thought of changing into a steel butterfly and stay the same mortal I have always been.

There is no doubt that the pilots portrayed in the motion pictures are supermen. It is the camera that makes them. On a screen, in a camera's eye, one sees from without the airplane, looking into the cockpit from over the gunports in the nose. There, the roar of the guns fills the echoing theater and the sparkling orange flames from the guns are three feet long and the pilot is fearless and intense with handsome narrowed eyes. He flies with visor up, so one can see his eyes in the sunlight.

It is this view that makes the superman, the daring airman, the hero, the fearless defender of the nation. From the other side, from alone inside the cockpit, it is a different picture. No one is watching, no one is listening, and a pilot flies in the sun with his visor down.

I do not see gunports or orange flames. I squeeze the red trigger on the stick grip and hold the white dot of the gunsight on the target and I hear a distant sort of pop-pop-pop and smell gunpowder in my oxygen mask. I certainly do not feel like a very daring airman, for this is my job and I do it in the best way that I can, in the way that hundreds of other tactical fighter pilots are doing it every day. My airplane is not a roaring silver flash across the screen, it is still and unmoving about me while the ground does the blurring and the engine roar is a vibrating constant behind my seat.

I am not doing anything out of the ordinary. Everyone in a theater audience understands that this gauge shows how much utility hydraulic pressure the engine-driven pumps are producing; they know perfectly well that this knob selects the number of the rocket that will fire when I press the button on top of the stick grip; that the second button on the grip is a radar roger button and that it is disconnected because it is never used; that the button that drops the external fuel tanks has a tall guard around it because too many pilots were pressing it by mistake. The audience knows all this. Yet it is still interesting to watch the airplanes in the motion pictures.

The ease of flying is a thing that is never mentioned in the motion pictures or on the recruiting posters. Flying a high-performance military airplane is exacting and difficult, men, but maybe, if you take our training, you will become a different person, with supernatural power to guide the metal monster in the sky. Give it a try, men, your country needs fine-honed men of steel.

Perhaps that is the best approach. Perhaps if the recruiting posters said, "Anyone walking down this street, from that ten-year-old with his schoolbooks to that little old grandmother in the black cotton dress, is able to fly an F-84F jet fighter airplane," they wouldn't attract exactly the kind of initiate that looks best on a recruiting poster. But just for fun, the Air Force should train a ten-year-old and a grandmother to fly quick aileron rolls over air shows to prove that the tactical fighter pilot is not necessarily the mechanical man that he is so often painted.

There is little to do. I have another six minutes before the wide needle of the TACAN will swing on its card to say that the little French city of Laon has been pulled by beneath me. I drag my tiny cone of thunder behind me for the benefit of the hills and the cows and perhaps a lonely peasant on a lonely walk through the cloudy night.

A flight like tonight's is rare. Normally, when I fit myself into the cockpit of this airplane, there is much to be done, for my job is one of being continually ready to fight. Each day of the week, regardless of weather or holidays or flying schedule, one small group of pilots wakes earlier than all the others. They are the Alert pilots. They awaken and they report to the flight line well before the hour that is Target Sunrise. And each day of each week a small group of airplanes are set aside to wait on the Alert pad, power units waiting by their wing. The airplanes, of course, are armed for war.

After the innocuous flying of the Air National Guard, it is chilling at first to spend the dawn checking the attachment of thousands of pounds of olive-drab explosive under my wings. The Alert procedure sometimes seems an impossible game. But the explosive is real.

The day wears on. We spend an hour studying the target that we already know very well. The landmarks about it, the conical hill, the mine in the hillside, the junction of highway and railroad, are as familiar to us as the hundred-arch viaduct that leads to Chaumont. We have in our minds, as well as on the maps stamped SECRET, the times and distances and headings to the target, and the altitudes we will fly. We know that our target will be as well-defended as anyone's, that there will be a massive wall of flak to penetrate and the delicate deadly fingers of missiles to avoid. Oddly enough, the flak does not really bother us. It does not make a bit of difference whether the target is defended from every housetop or not at all . . . if it is necessary to strike it, we shall go along our memorized route and strike it. If we are caught by the screen of fire, it will be one of those unfortunate happenings of war.

The siren blows, like a rough hand jerking sleep away. My room is dark. For more than a second, in the quick ebb of sleep, I know that I must hurry, but I cannot think of where I must go. Then the second is past and my mind is clear.

The Alert siren.

Hurry.

Into the flight suit, into the zippered black jump boots, into the winter flying jacket. A hurried toss of scarf about throat, leave the door swinging closed and open again on my tousled room and join the rush of other Alert pilots in a dash down the wooden stairs and into the waiting Alert truck. The square wooden buildings of Chaumont Air Base are not yet even silhouettes against the east.

There is a husky comment in the darkness of the rattling truck: "Sleep well, America, your National Guard is awake tonight."

The truck takes us to the airplanes that wait in the dark. The maintenance Alert crew has beaten us to the airplanes, and the APUs are roaring into steely life. I climb the ladder that is chipped lemon in the daytime and invisible in the night, a feel of aluminum rungs more than a ladder-being. "Power!" The lights blaze in the cockpit, undimmed by the little night-shields that close off most of their light for flying in the dark. The light from them shows me the parachute straps and the safety belt ends and the belt release lanyard and the G suit and oxygen hoses and the microphone cables. Helmet on, oxygen mask on (how can rubber get so icy cold?), radio on. Night-shields down on the warning lights, twist the rheostats that fill the cockpit with a bloody glow. "Hawk Able Two," I say to the microphone, and if my flight leader has been faster strapping in than I, he will know that I am ready to go.

"Roj, Two." He is fast, my flight leader.

I do not know whether this is a real-thing alert or another practice. I assume it is another practice. Now I tend to the finer points of getting ready to go; checking circuit breakers in, bomb switches set in *safe* positions, gunsight properly set for the delivery that we will use.

"Hawk Able Four."

"Roj, Four."

Check the battle damage switches all down where they should be. Turn the navigation lights on to *bright flash*. We will turn them to *dim* as we approach the target.

"Hawk Able Three." Three was awake too late last night.

"Roj, Three. Parsnip, Hawk Able flight is ready to go with four."

In the combat operations center, the time is checked as we call in. We checked in well before the maximum time allowed, and this is good.

"Hawk Able, Parsnip here. This is a practice alert. Maintain cockpit alert until further notified."

"Roj."

So much meaning can be packed into three letters. Hawk Able Leader didn't just acknowledge the notice, he told the combat operations center that this is a ridiculous dumb stupid game to be played by grown men and good grief you guys it is THREE O'CLOCK IN THE MORNING and you had just better have orders from high headquarters to call this thing at this hour or you will not be getting much sleep tomorrow night.

"Sorry," says Parsnip, into the silence. They must have had the orders from high headquarters.

So I close the canopy and lock it against the eternal cold wind and I settle in the red light to wait.

I have waited fifteen minutes in the cockpit for the alert to be canceled. I have waited three hours for it. After the three-hour wait, I had climbed stiffly down from the cockpit with the perfect torture for recalcitrant prisoners of war. You take them and strap them by safety belt and shoulder harness to a soft, comfortable armchair. Then you walk away and leave them there. For the incorrigible prisoners, the real troublemakers, you put their feet into tunnels, sort of like rudder-pedal tunnels in a single-engine airplane, and put a control stick in the way so that they don't have room to move either foot into a different position. In a very few hours the prisoners will become docile, tractable, eager to mend their ways.

The sun isn't up yet. We wait in our cockpits. I drift idly in the great dark river of soft-flowing time. Nothing happens. The second hand on my watch moves around. I begin to notice things; as something to do. I hear a quiet tik . . . tik . . . tik . . . very regular, slow, metronomic. Tik . . . tik . . . tik . . . And the answer comes. My navigation lights. Without the engine running and with the canopy closed to keep out the rustle of the wind, I can hear the opening and the closing of the relays that control the flashing of the lights on wingtip and tail. Interesting. Never would have thought that I could hear the lights going on and off.

Outside is the efficient high-speed *pokpokpok* of the APU. What a truly efficient thing that power unit is. It will stand there all night and through all tomorrow if it has to, pumping a constant stream of electricity to power the radio and keep the cockpit bathed in scarlet light.

My airplane rocks slightly. I think someone has climbed to the wing and wants to talk to me, but there is no one there. The wind, that gentle cold wind, rocks this massive hard airplane. Every once in a while, and faintly, the wind moves the airplane on its landing gear struts. Thirty feet to my right the airplane of Hawk Able Leader waits, lights on, tikking silently to itself. The bloodlight of the cockpit reflects from the foam-white enameled helmet of the pilot just as it would reflect if we were cruising now at 30,000 feet. Canopy is closed and locked, the air inside the cockpit is still and cold, and I wish that someone would invent a way to pipe warm air into the cockpit of an airplane that waits in the cold of a very early day. I can feel my warmth being absorbed in the cold metal of the instrument panel and the ejection seat and canopy rails and rudder-pedal tunnels. If I could only be warm and move around a bit and have someone to talk to, sitting cockpit alert would not be too bad a thing.

I have made a discovery. This is what Lonely is. When you are walled up where no one can come inside and talk to you or play a game of cards or chess with you or share a joke about the time over Stuttgart when Number Three mistook the Moselle River for the Rhine and . . . Insulated from the outside. A truck that I know is a noisy line truck that clatters and squeaks and needs a new muffler glides noiselessly by on the road in front of my revetment. The locked canopy seals away the sound of its passing. It seals me in with my thoughts. Nothing to read, no moving things to watch, just a quiet cockpit and the tik of the nav lights and the *pok* of the APU and my very own thoughts.

I sit in an airplane that is mine. The commanders of Wing and Squadron have given it to me without question, trusting utterly in my ability to control it and guide it as they want it guided. They are depending on me to hit the target. I remember a line from the base newspaper that I read during a gigantic war game of a few weeks ago: "Yesterday the Wing saw action while it flew in support of the Army. . . ." The Wing did not see any such action. It was me that saw that action, arcing low and fast with simulated ordnance across the troops on the tanks, trying to streak low enough to make the troops jump into the mud but not low enough to take the whip antenna off the tanks.

Not the Wing making them jump.

Me.

Egoistical? Yes. But then the Wing did not take the chance of mis-judging and driving its twelve tons of airplane into the side of a 50-ton armored tank. So this is me sitting Alert, in my airplane, and if it were a real Alert, it would be me who came back or did not come back from the flak and the missiles over the target. They trust me. That seems odd, that anyone should trust anyone else with so much. They give me an airplane without question and without thinking twice about it. The number of the airplane comes up by my name on the scheduling board and I go out and fly it or sit in its cockpit and be ready to fly it. It is just a number on the board. But when I sit in it I have a chance to see what a remarkably involved, what an intricately fashioned thing it is, and what power the commanders have given me by putting that number next to my name.

The crew chief, heavy-jacketed, steel-helmeted, appears abruptly on the aluminum ladder and knocks politely on the Plexiglas. I open the canopy, grudging the loss of my pocket of still air, however slightly heated, to the cold wind, and pull one side of my helmet away from my ear so I can hear him. Red light paints his face.

"D'ymind if we climb in the truck and wait . . . be out of the wind a little bit if it's OK with you. Flash your taxi light if you need . . ."

"OK." And I resolve to discipline my thought and go over again the headings and the times and the distances and the altitudes to my target. And the great dark river of time moves slowly on.

As I sometimes have long moments for thought on the ground, so every once in a while there is a long cross-country flight that allows a moment to think and be alone with the sky and my airplane. And I smile. Alone with the airplane that has been called "the unforgiving F-84."

I have been waiting to fly the airplane that is unforgiving. There must be such an airplane somewhere that is so very critical that it must be flown exactly by the book or crash, for the word *unforgiving* appears often in the magazines racked in the pilots' lounges. But just when I think that the next type of airplane I am to fly has such high performance that it will be unforgiving, I learn to fly it. I learn its ways and its personality, and suddenly it is a forgiving airplane like all the others. It might be a little more critical on its airspeeds as I fly it down final approach to land, but as our acquaintance grows I discover that it has tolerances to either side of the best airspeed and that it will not spin into the ground if I am one knot too slow turning to the runway.

There is always a warning of danger, and only if a pilot fails to heed his airplane's warning will it go ahead and kill him.

The red fire-warning light comes on after takeoff. It could mean many things: a short circuit in the fire-warning system; too steep a climb at too low an airspeed; a hole in a combustion chamber wall; an engine on fire. Some airplanes have so much difficulty with false fire warnings that their pilots practically disregard them, assuming that the warning circuit has gone bad again. But the F-84F is not one of these; when the light comes on, the airplane is usually on fire. But still I have time to check it—to pull the throttle back, to climb to minimum ejection altitude, to drop the external stores, to check the tailpipe temperature and tachometer and fuel flow, to ask my wingman if he wouldn't mind taking a little look for smoke from my fuselage. If I am on fire, I have a few seconds to point the airplane away from the houses and bail out. I have never heard of an airplane that exploded without warning.

Jet airplanes are unforgiving in one common respect: they burn great quantities of fuel, and when the fuel is gone the engine stops running. Full tanks in a four-engine propeller-driven transport airplane can keep it in the air for eighteen hours nonstop. Twin-engine cargo airplanes often have enough fuel aboard for eight hours of flying when they take off on a two-hour flight. But when I take off on an hour-forty-minute mission, I have enough fuel in the tanks of my '84F to last through two hours of flying. I do not have to concern myself with long minutes of circling in the air after the mission while other airplanes take off and land.

Occasionally I fly into the landing pattern with three hundred pounds of JP-4 in the tanks, or enough for six minutes of flying at high power. If I were seven minutes from the runway with three hundred pounds of fuel, I would not make it home with the engine running. If I were ten minutes from the runway, my wheels would never roll on that concrete again. If an airplane is disabled on the runway after I enter the landing pattern with six minutes of fuel, there had better be a fast tow truck waiting to pull it out of the way, or a second runway ready to be used. I will be coming to earth, in an airplane or in a parachute, within the next few minutes.

With the engine stopped, my airplane does not sink like a streamlined brick or a rock or a block of lead. It glides smoothly down, quietly down, as an airplane is designed to glide. I plan a dead-stick pattern so that my wheels should touch halfway down the runway, and I hold the landing gear retracted until I am certain that I am within gliding range of the field. Then, on final approach, with the runway long and white in the windscreen, it is gear down and flaps down and speed brakes out and emergency hydraulic pump on.

Though it is a hidden point of pride to have shut down the engine after a flight with two hundred pounds of fuel remaining, tactical fighter pilots rarely give the required minimum fuel notice to the tower when they have less than eight hundred pounds remaining. The red low-level warning light may be blazing on the instrument panel near a fuel gauge needle swinging down through four hundred pounds, but unless it looks as if he will be delayed in his landing, the pilot does not call minimum fuel. He has pride in his ability to fly his airplane, and an unimportant thing like eight minutes of fuel remaining is not worthy of his concern.

A transport pilot once cut me out of the landing pattern by calling minimum fuel, receiving a priority clearance to land immediately. I had a full ten minutes of JP-4 in my main fuselage tank, so didn't mind giving way to the big airplane that needed to land so quickly. A week later I learned that the minimum fuel level set for that transport was thirty minutes of flying time; my engine could have flamed out three times over in the minutes before his fuel would have been really critical.

I respect the fact that my airplane burns fuel and that each flight ends without a great deal of fuel remaining, but it is a point of pride that I do this every day and that when I become concerned with the amount of fuel in my tanks, it is something that deserves concern.

It is a little, more than a little, like playing hooky from life, this airplane-flying business. I fly over the cities of France and Germany at ten o'clock in the morning and think of all the people down there who are working for a living while I pull my contrail free and effortlessly above them. It makes me feel guilty. I fly at 30,000 feet, doing what I enjoy doing more than anything else in all the world, and they are down there in the heat and probably not feeling godlike at all. That is their way. They could all have been fighter pilots if they had wished.

My neighbors in the United States used to look upon me a little condescendingly, waiting for me to grow out of the joy of flying airplanes, waiting for me to see the light and come to my senses and be practical and settle down and leave the Air Guard and spend my weekends at home. It has been difficult for them to believe that I will be flying so long as the Guard needs men in its airplanes, so long as there is an Air Force across the ocean that is training for war. So long as I think that my country is a pretty good place to live and should have the chance to go on being a pretty good place.

The cockpits of the little silver dots in front of the long white contrails are not manned only by the young and impractical. There is many an old fighter pilot still there; pilots who flew the Jugs and Mustangs and Spitfires and Messerschmitts of a long-ago war. Even the Sabre pilots and the Hog pilots of Korea are well-enough experienced to be called "old pilots," and they are the flight commanders and the squadron commanders of the operational American squadrons in Europe today. But the percentage changes a little every day, and for the most part the line pilots of NATO fighter squadrons have not been personally involved in a hot war.

There is a subtle feeling that this is not good; that the frontline pilots are not as experienced as they should be. But the only difference that exists is that the pilots since Korea do not wear combat ribbons on their dress uniforms. Instead of firing on convoys filled with enemy troops, they fire on dummy convoys or make mock firing passes on NATO convoys in war games a few miles from the barbed-wire fence between East and West. And they spend hours on the gunnery ranges.

Our range is a small gathering of trees and grass and dust in the north of France, and in that gathering are set eight panels of canvas, each painted with a large black circle and set upright on a square frame. The panels stand in the sun and they wait.

I am one of the four fighter airplanes called Ricochet flight, and we come across the range on a spacing pass in close formation, echelon left. We fly a hundred feet above the dry earth, and each of the pilots of Ricochet flight is concentrating. Ricochet Lead is concentrating on making this last turn smoothly, on holding his airspeed at 365 knots, on climbing a little to keep from scraping Ricochet Four into the next hill, on judging the point where he will break up and away from the other airplanes to establish a gunnery pattern for them to follow.

Ricochet Two is concentrating on flying as smoothly as he can, to give Three and Four the least amount of difficulty in flying their formation.

Ricochet Three flies watching only Lead and Two, intent on flying smoothly so that Four can stay in close to fly his position well.

And as Ricochet Four I think of staying in formation and of nothing else, so that the flight will look good to the range officer in his spotting tower. I am acutely conscious that every other airplane in the flight is doing his best to make the flying easy for me, and to thank them for their consideration I must fly so smoothly that the credit will be theirs. Each airplane flies lower than Ricochet Lead, and Four flies closer to the ground than any of them. But to take even a half second to glance at the ground is to be a poor wingman. A wingman has complete total unwavering unquestioning faith in his leader. If Ricochet Lead flies too low now, if he doesn't pull the formation up a little to clear the hill, my airplane will be a sudden flying cloud of dirt and metal fragments and orange streamers of flame. But I trust the man who is flying as Ricochet Lead, and he inches the formation up to clear the hill and my airplane clears it as though it were a valley; I fly the position that I am supposed to fly and I trust the Leader.

As Ricochet Four, I am stacked back and down to the left so that I can see up across the formation and line the white helmets of the other three pilots. That is all I should see and all I care to see: three helmets in three airplanes in one straight line. No matter what the formation does, I will stay with it in my position, keeping the three white helmets lined on each other. The formation climbs, it dives, it banks hard away from me, it banks toward me; my life is dedicated to doing whatever is necessary with the throttle and the control stick and the rudder pedals and the trim button to stay in position and keep the helmets in line.

We are over the target panels and the radio comes to life.

"Ricochet Lead breaking right." The familiar voice that I know well—the voice, the words, the man, his family, his problems, his ambitions—is this instant the sudden flash of a swept silver wing pitching up and away to begin a pattern of gunnery practice, to develop a skill in a special brand of destruction. And I have only two helmets to line.

When Lead pitches away, Ricochet Two becomes the formation leader. His helmet flicks forward from watching the first airplane to look straight ahead, and he begins to count. One-thousand-one, one-thousand-two, one-thousand-*break*! With his own sudden flash of smooth metal wing, Ricochet Two disappears, and I have the luxuriously simple task of flying formation on only one airplane. Whose pilot is now looking straight ahead. One-thousand-one, one-thousand-two, one-thousand-*break*! The flash of wing happens to Three, only a few feet from my own wing, and I fly alone.

My head locks forward with Three's break, and I count. One-thousand-one isn't it a pretty day out today there are just a few clouds for a change and the targets will be easy to see. It is good to relax after that formation. Did a good job, though, Two and Three held it in well one-thousand-two good to have smooth air this morning. I won't have to worry about bouncing around too much when I put the pipper on the target. Today will be a good day for high scores. Let's see; sight is set and caged, I'll check the gun switch later with the other switches what a lonely place for someone to have to bail out. Bet there's no village for ten miles around one-thousand-*break*!

In my right glove the control stick slams hard to the right and back and the horizon twists out of sight. My G suit inflates with hard air, pressing tightly into my legs and stomach. My helmet is heavy, but with a familiar heaviness that is not uncomfortable. The green hills pivot beneath me and I scan the brilliant blue sky to my right for the other airplanes in the pattern.

There they are. Ricochet Lead is a little swept dot two miles away turning onto base leg, almost ready to begin his first firing run. Two is a larger dot and level, following Lead by half a mile. Three is just now turning to follow Two; he is climbing and a thousand feet above me. And away down there is the clearing of the gunnery range and the tiny specks that are the strafing panels in the sun. I have all the time in the world.

Gun switch, beneath its red plastic guard, goes forward under my left glove to *guns,* sight is uncaged and set to zero angle of depression.

The *gunfire* circuit breaker is pushed down under my right index finger. I twist the thick black throttle with my left glove to bring the computed range for the gunsight down to one thousand feet. And my grip on the control stick changes.

With the gun switch off and the gunfire circuit breaker out, I fly formation holding the grip naturally, right index finger resting lightly on the red trigger at the front of the contoured plastic. Now, with guns ready to fire, the finger points straight ahead toward the instrument panel in an awkward but necessary position that keeps glove from touching trigger. The glove will stay off the trigger until I swing my airplane in a diving turn that brings the white dot on the sight reflector glass over the black dot painted on the strafing panel.

It is time to put the finishing touches on my attitude. I tell the audience behind my eyes that today I am going to shoot better than anyone else in this flight, that I will put at least 70 percent of my bullets into the black of the target, with the other 30 percent left to be scattered in the white cloth. I run through a picture of a good strafing attack in my mind; I see the black dot growing larger under the white dot of the gunsight, I see the sight-dot stay smoothly in the black, I feel the right index finger beginning to squeeze on the red trigger, I see the white now fully inside the black, I hear the muffled harmless sound of the guns firing their 50-caliber copperclad, and I see the powdered dust billow from behind the square of the target. A good pass.

But caution. Careful during the last seconds of the firing run; don't become too concerned with putting a long burst into the cloth. I remember for a moment, as I always do before the first gunnery run of the day, the roommate of cadet days who let his enthusiasm fly his airplane a second too long, until his airplane and its target came sharply together on the ground. That is not a good way to die.

Power to 96 percent on the base leg, airspeed up to 300 knots, watch Three go in on his target.

"Ricochet Three's in, white and hot." And down he goes, a twisting silhouette of an '84F.

It is interesting to watch a firing pass from the air. There is no sound from the attacking airplane as it glides swiftly toward its target.

Then, abruptly, grey smoke breaks noiselessly from the gunports at the nose of his airplane, streaming back to trace the angle of his dive in a thin smoky line. The dust of the ground begins to spray the air as the airplane breaks away, and a thick brown cloud of it billows at the base of the target when he is gone and climbing.

Now the only untouched target is target number four.

The warning panel on the ground by the spotting tower is turned red side down, white side up; the range is clear and safe for my pass. I note this, and fly along the base leg of the pattern, at right angle to my target. It is a mile away on the ground to my right. It drifts slowly back. It is at one o'clock low. It is at one-thirty low. I recheck the gun switch to *guns.* It is at two o'clock low and slam the stick whips to the right under my hand and my airplane rolls like a terrified animal and the sky goes grey with the g of the turn and the G suit inflates to press me in a hard vise of trapped air. Beneath the canopy is pivoting blurred ground moving. It is the beginning of a good firing pass. The microphone button is down under my left thumb: "Ricochet Four is in, white and hot."

White and hot. The target is clear and the guns are ready to fire. Airspeed is up to 360 knots in the dive, and my wings roll level again. In the windscreen is a tiny square of white cloth with the speck of a black dot painted. I wait. The white dot called the pipper, the dot that shows on the windscreen where my bullets will converge, bounces in lazy slow bounces as it recovers from the sharp turn that began the pass. It settles down, and I touch the control stick back very gently in the dive so the pipper ambles up to cover the square of the target. And the target changes swiftly, as I wait, to become all things. It is an enemy tank waiting in ambush for the infantry; it is an antiaircraft gun that has let its camouflage slip; it is a black and puffing locomotive moving enemy supplies along a narrow-gauge track. It is an ammunition dump a fortified bunker a truck towing a cannon a barge in the river an armored car and it is a white square of cloth with a black spot painted. It waits, I wait, and all of a sudden it grows. The spot becomes a disk, and the white pipper has been waiting for that. My finger squeezes slowly down on the red trigger. A gun camera starts as the trigger is half-closed. Guns fire when the trigger is all the way down.

Like a rivet gun finishing a last-minute sheet metal job on the nose of the airplane, the guns sound; there is no earsplitting roar and thunder and confusion in the cockpit. Just a little detached *tututut* while beneath my boots hot brass shell casings shower down into steel containers. I smell powder smoke in my oxygen mask and idly wonder how it can find its way into a cabin that is supposed to be sealed and pressurized.

In ultraslow motion I watch the target on the ground; it is serene and quiet, for the bullets have not yet arrived. The bullets are on the way, somewhere in the air between the blackening gunports on the nose of my airplane and the pulverized dust on the range. I once thought of bullets as being such fast things, and now I wait impatiently for them to touch the ground and verify my gunsight. Finger is off the trigger; a one-second burst is a long burst of fire. And there is the dust.

The ground comes apart and begins throwing itself into the air. A few feet short of the target the dust flies, but this means that many bullets will have found their way to the meeting point shown by the white dot in the center of the gunsight. The dust is still flying into the air as my right glove pulls back on the many-buttoned stick and my airplane climbs in the pattern. As my airplane and its shadow flick across the square of canvas, the bullets that are able to tear a concrete highway to slabs of broken rock still whip the air and rain on the ground. "Ricochet Four is off."

I bank to the right in the pattern and look back over my shoulder at the target. It is quiet now, and the cloud of dust is thinning in the wind and moving to the left, covering Three's target with a tenuous cloud of brown.

"Ricochet Lead is in."

I fired low that time, short of the target. There goes my 100 percent score. I must move the pipper up a little next time; place it on top of the disk of black. I smile at the thought. It is not very often that the air is smooth enough to let me think of placing the pipper inches high or inches low on the black spot of the target. I am normally doing very good to keep the pipper somewhere on the square of the strafing panel. But today is a good day for gunnery. Let the tanks beware the days of calm.

"Ricochet Two is in."

"Lead is off."

I watch Two, and in the curved Plexiglas of the canopy I see myself reflected as I watch; a Martian if I ever saw one. Hard white helmet, smooth-curved glare visor down and looking like a prop for a Man in Space feature, green oxygen mask covering all the face that the visor does not cover, oxygen hose leading down out of sight. No indication that there is a living thinking creature behind the hardware. The reflection watches Ricochet Two.

There it is, the grey wisp from the gunports in the nose. The target is still and waiting as though it will stand a year before seeing a sign of motion. Then, suddenly, the thick fountain of dust. To the left of the panel a twig on the ground jumps into startled life and leaps into the air. End over end, slowly it turns, shifting after its first instant into the familiar slow motion of things caught in the swift rain of machine-gun bullets. It twists two full turns above the fountain and sinks gracefully back beneath the thick cloud of it. The concrete highway is torn to rock and the twig survives. That should carry a moral.

"Two is off." Smoke disappears from gunports. The airplane turns its oval nose to the sky and streaks away from the target.

"Three is in."

What is the moral of the twig? I think about it and I turn sharply into the base leg of the pattern, rechecking the gunsight, right index finger pointing forward at the altimeter. What is the moral of the twig?

The wisp of smoke trails from the gunports of the smooth aluminum nose of Ricochet Three, and I watch his pass.

There is no moral. If the target were a pile of twigs, the hail of copper and lead would turn it into a scattered blanket of splinters. This was a lucky twig. If you are a lucky twig, you can survive anything.

"Three is off."

The safety panel is white, the gun switch is at *guns,* and slam the stick whips to the right under my glove and my airplane rolls like a terrified animal to the right and the sky goes grey with the G of the turn and the G suit inflates to press me in a hard vise of trapped air.

I have never been so rushed, when I fly my airplane, that I do not think. Even in the gunnery pattern, when the airspeed needle is covering 370 knots and the airplane is a few feet from the ground, the thinking goes on. When events happen in split seconds, it is not the thinking that changes, but the event. Events fall obediently into slow motion when there is a need for more thought.

As I fly tonight, navigating with the TACAN locked firmly onto the Laon transmitter, there is plenty of time for thought, and obligingly, events telescope themselves so that seven minutes will pass in the moment between the haunted land of Abbeville and the TACAN transmitter at Laon, France. I do not pass time as I fly, time passes me.

The hills slip away. There is a solid layer of black cloud from the ground to within a thousand feet of my airplane. The ground is buried, but in my chariot of steel and aluminum and Plexiglas I am carried above, and the stars are bright.

In the red light, on the windowed face of the radio compass, are four selector knobs, one switch, and one coffee-grinder tuning crank. I turn the crank. It is as old-fashioned in the cockpit of a fighter plane as would be a hand-wound telephone in an atomic research center. If it were much more quiet and if I wore no helmet, perhaps I could hear the crank squeak as it turned. I turn the handle, imagining the squeaks, until the frequency needle comes to rest over the number 344, the frequency of the Laon radio beacon.

Turn up the volume. Listen. Crank the handle a little to the left, a little to the right. Static static crank *dih-dih*. Pause. Static. Listen for *L-C. Dah-dih-dah-dih. . . . Dih-dah-dih-dih. . . .* That is it. My right glove turns the selector from *antenna* to *compass,* while the left has the unnatural task of holding the control stick grip. The slim luminous green radio-compass needle spins majestically from the bottom of its dial to the top—a cross-check on the TACAN—Laon radio beacon is ahead. A little adjustment with the crank, an eighth of an inch, and the radio compass is locked strong on Laon. Turn down the volume.

The Laon radio beacon is a solitary place. It stands alone with the trees and the cold hills in the morning and the trees and the warm hills in the afternoon, sending its *L-C* into the air whether there is a pilot in the sky to hear it or whether there is nothing in the sky but a lone raven. But it is faithful and ever there. If the raven had a radio compass, he could find his way unerringly to the tower that broadcasts the *L-C.* Every once in a long while a maintenance crew will go to the beacon and its tower and check its voltages and perform some routine tube-changing. Then they will leave the tower standing alone again and jounce back the rough road the way they came.

At this moment the steel of the tower is cold in the night and the raven is asleep in his stony home on a hillside. The coded letters, though, are awake and moving and alive, and I am glad, for the navigation is working out well.

The wide TACAN needle shares the same dial with the radio compass needle, and they work together now to tell me that Laon is passing beneath my airplane. The radio compass needle is the most active of the two. It twitches and quivers with stiff electronic life, like some deep-sea life dredged and placed on a microscope slide. It jerks to the left and right; it quavers at the top of the dial, swinging in wider and wider arcs. Then, in one decisive movement, it swings all the way around, clockwise, and points to the bottom of the dial. The Laon radio beacon has passed behind. The TACAN needle swings lazily five or six times around the dial and finally agrees with its more nervous companion. I am definitely past Laon.

That part of my thought that paid serious attention to navigation classes guides my glove to tilt the stick to the left, and the crowd of instruments in the center of the panel swings into an awareness of the seriousness of my action. Heading indicator moves on tiny oiled bearings to the left, turn needle leans to the left a quarter of an inch. The miniature airplane on the attitude indicator banks to the left against its luminous horizon line. Airspeed needle moves down a knot, altimeter and vertical speed needles drop for just a second, until I see their conspiracy and add the thought of back pressure through the right glove. The errant pair rise again into line.

Once again, the routine. Ready with the position report, thumb down on microphone button.

Though the cloud is almost at my flight level, and very dark, it looks as if the forecaster has once again gone astray, for I have not seen a flash of lightning since over the Channel. Whatever severe weather is afoot tonight over France is keeping itself well hidden. I am not concerned. In fifty minutes I shall be landing, with my precious sack of documents, at Chaumont.

CHAPTER THREE

"FRANCE CONTROL, Air Force Jet Two Niner Four Zero Five, Laon." There is quiet static in the soft earphones. I wait. Perhaps my call went unnoticed.

"France Control, France Control, Jet Two Niner Four Zero Five, how do you read on frequency three one seven point eight." There is no answer.

It is not at all unusual for a radio to break down in flight, for radios are temperamental things. But it is never a comfortable feeling to fly at night above weather without some way of talking to the people on the ground. My glove moves to the right, to the frequency selector of the UHF command radio. I do not bother to watch it work, for it is simply changing a sliding square knob one click, from *manual* to *preset*. An indicator on the instrument panel juggles numbers in small windows, and finally decides to present the number 18, in small red-lit figures. In that one click I am aligned with a different set of people, away from the busy hub of the France Control Center to the quiet and pastoral surroundings of Calva Radar. I know that the stereotype is not a valid one, for radar stations are only smaller places than traffic control centers, and are often far more rushed and busy. Yet whenever I call a radar site, I feel a little more at ease, and imagine a small red brick building set in a field of brilliant green grass, with a cow grazing not far away.

"Calva Radar, Calva Radar, Air Force Jet Two Niner Four Zero Five, how do you read channel one eight." There is perhaps one chance in three that the UHF will work on this frequency when it did not work on the frequency for France Control. The cow outside the brick building is asleep, a sculptured boulder in the dark of the grass. A light is in the window of the building, and a man's shadow moves across the glass as he reaches for his microphone.

". . . ero Five . . . d you . . . arbled . . . Calva?"

The UHF is definitely on its way out of commission. But even if it goes completely out, I am still cleared to maintain flight level 330 all the way to the Chaumont TACAN holding pattern. There are occasional moments like this when I wish that the airplane had just one more communication radio installed. But the F-84F was built for fighting, not for talking, and I must make do with what I have.

"Calva Radar, Four Zero Five unable to contact France Control, was Laon at one zero, flight level three three zero assigned instrument flight rules, estimating Spangdahlem at two eight, Wiesbaden." A wild try. A shot in the dark. But at least the information was said, and I have made the required report. I hear Calva's microphone button go down.

". . . ive . . . ort . . . mly garb . . . come up . . . point zero . . ."

Calva is suggesting another frequency, but by the time I can understand all of his message I will be too far away for it to matter. Trying to send a position report with a radio in this condition is like trying to shout a message across a deep and windy chasm; difficult and frustrating. I give my report once again to comply with the rules, click back to *manual* and forget the matter. Too bad. It would have been good to hear the latest weather report along my route, but simply getting my request understood would have been a major problem, to say nothing of receiving a reply. The weather is of only academic interest anyway, for there would have to be a pilot report of a squall line with severe turbulence and heavy icing to 40,000 feet before I would consider turning back.

I look back over my left shoulder as I turn to the heading that will take me to Spangdahlem.

I am pulling a contrail.

In a sweeping turn behind me, following like a narrow wake of a high-speed racing boat, is a twisting tunnel of glowing grey mist in the starlight that is the path that I have followed. Clearly and precisely in texts on atmospheric physics, contrails are explained by the men who spend their time with radio balloons and diagrams of the upper air.

Contrails are like fireflies. If I desire, I can find pages of explanation about them in books and in specialized magazines. But when I see one close at hand, it is alive and mystic and greyly luminous. Watching the con as I turn, I can see the rise and fall of it where I made small changes to keep my airplane at flight level 330. It looks like a very gentle roller-coaster, one for people who do not like excitement. That is where I have been. No air aside from the rolling tunnel of mist can say that it has felt my passage. If I desire, I can turn now and fly through exactly the same air that I flew before. And I am alone. As far as I can see, and that is a long distance about me, there is no other contrail in the sky. I am the only person in all the world to fly above the clouds in the hundreds of cubic miles that make the world of high altitude between Abbeville and Spangdahlem this evening. It is a solitary feeling.

But there is work to be done. Back to the coffee grinder. Squeak squeak to frequency 428. Volume up. Static. And no second thoughts, no mistaking this one. An *S* and a *P* and an *A*. A city with its thousands of people, with the cares and the joys that they share, people, with me. I am alone and six miles above their earth, and their city is not even a light grey glow in the black cloud. Their city is an *S* and a *P* and an *A* in the soft earphones. Their city is the needlepoint at the top of the dial.

The frequency selector knob of the TACAN set clicks under my right glove to channel 100, and after a moment of indecision, the modern, smooth-working mileage drum spins to show 110 miles to the Spangdahlem beacon. Except for the failure of the UHF radio, my flight has gone very smoothly. There is a faint flicker in the rising hills of cloud far ahead to my right, as if someone is having difficulty striking an arc with a gigantic welding rod. But distances at night are deceiving, and the flash of light could be over any one of four countries.

*   *   *

As a pilot, I have traveled and seen millions of square miles of land and cloud above land. As a recalled Guard pilot in Europe I have rolled my wheels on hundreds of miles of asphalt and concrete runways in seven countries. I can say that I have seen more of the continent than many people, yet Europe is a much different place for me than it is for them. It is a patterned country, broad and wide in the sunlight, wrinkled in the south by the Pyrenees and in the east by the Alps. It is a country over which someone has spilled a great sack of airports, and I seek these out.

France is not the France of travel posters. France is Etain Air Base and Châteauroux Air Base and Chaumont and Marville. It is the patchwork of Paris about its beloved river, a patchwork that flows like crystallized lava around the tictactoe runways of Orly Field and Le Bourget. France is the repetition of walking over the concrete to Base Operations and being aware, as I walk, of tiny villages outside the perimeter fence and hills everywhere.

Europe is a pitifully small place. From 37,000 feet above the Pyrenees I can see the cold Atlantic at Bordeaux and the shores of the French Riviera on the Mediterranean. I can see Barcelona, and in the haze, Madrid. In thirty minutes I can fly over England, Holland, Luxembourg, Belgium, France, and Germany. My squadron flies nonstop to North Africa in two and a half hours; it patrols the border between West and East in Germany; can fly to Copenhagen for the weekend. So this was a school for mankind. A small schoolyard.

But I rarely get firsthand, visual evidence of the postage stamp that is Europe, for much more often than not the land is covered by tremendous decks of cloud, seas of white and grey that stretch without a rift from horizon to horizon. It is the weather in Europe, as in the United States, that reminds me now and then that, although I can span continents in a single leap, I am not always so godlike as I feel. Some clouds in summer tower past my airplane to 50,000 feet, and some boil up and build faster than my airplane can climb. Much of the time I am correct in saying that mine is an over-the-weather airplane, but clouds are watch-keepers over arrogant men; they remind me, just often enough, of my actual size.

The swirling masses of white cumulus will some days harbor only the mildest of turbulence along my path. Another day I may penetrate the same type of cloud and come out of it grateful to the man who designed the crash helmet. Tight as safety belt and shoulder harness can be, it is still in the province of a few clouds to snap my helmet sharply against the canopy and flex the steelspar wings that I once swore could never be forced an inch.

I was once constantly wary of the hardest-looking clouds, but I have learned that, despite the snap of helmet on canopy, their turbulence is rarely strong enough to really damage a fighter airplane. Every once in a while I read of a multiengine airplane that lost its windshield or radome in the hail, or has taken a bolt or two of lightning, for these instances are duly reported and photographed in detail for the pilots' magazines. There are a few airplanes that have taken off into bad weather, into thunderstorms, and have been found days later or weeks later scattered across a lonely stretch of earth. The reasons are unknown. The storm might have been unusually powerful; the pilot could have lost control; he could have been caught in a web of vertigo and dived from storm into ground. So, although my airplane has a six-layer bulletproof windscreen designed for worse than hail and an airframe stressed to withstand twice the force that would tear the wings from larger airplanes, I respect thunderstorms. I avoid them when I can; I grit my teeth and hold on to the control stick when I can't. So far, I have been knocked about by a few small thunderstorms, but I have not seen them all.

There are procedures, of course. Tighten the safety belt and shoulder harness, pitot heat and defrosters on, cockpit lights to full bright, airspeed down to 275 knots, and try to hold the airplane level. In the vertical air currents of a thunderstorm, altimeters and vertical speed indicators and even airspeed indicators are practically useless. They lag and they lead and they flutter helplessly. Though the '84F tends to yaw and roll a bit in turbulence, I must try to fly by the little airplane on a two-inch gyrostabilized horizon set ahead of me on the instrument panel: the attitude indicator. I fly to hold my attitude straight and level through the storm. So I am prepared. I always have been.

* * *

In the darkness of the French night, my airplane flies easily along the continuous stream of miles between Laon and Spangdahlem, through air as smooth as polished obsidian. I tilt my white helmet back against the red ejection seat headrest and look up from the thick dark layer of cloud to the deeper, bright layer of stars overhead, that have so long guided men across the earth. The constant, eternal stars. The reassuring stars. The useless stars. In an airplane like mine, built to work at its best through a pilot's eyes and a pilot's direction, the stars have become only interesting spots of light to look out upon when all is going well. The important stars are the ones that draw the luminous needles of the radio compass and the TACAN. Stars are nice, but I navigate by the *S* and the *P* and the *A*.

Tactical fighter pilots have traditionally been on marginal terms with the thought of weather flying, and only by superhuman efforts has the Air Force brought them to accept the thought that nowadays even fighter airplanes must fly in weather. The official emphasis takes the form of motion pictures and ground schools and instrument schools and required minimum hours of instrument and hooded flight every six months. Each successive fighter airplane becomes more capable of operating in all-weather conditions, and today interceptor pilots in their big delta-wings can fly a complete interception and attack on an enemy airplane without ever seeing it except as a smoky dot of light on their attack radar screen.

Even the fighter-bomber, long at the mercy of the low cloud, is today capable of flying a low-level attack through the weather, using sophisticated radar systems in order to avoid the hard mountains and identify the target. Beyond the official emphasis and the pressure of regulations, tactical fighter pilots of the newest airplanes must learn all there is to know about weather flying simply to keep up with their airplane, to be able to use it as it was meant to be used. But weather is still an enemy. The cloud robs me of the horizon and I cannot see outside the cockpit. I am forced to depend completely on seven expressionless faces in glass that are my flight instruments. There is, in weather, no absolute up or down. There is only a row of instruments that say, *this is up, this is down, this is the horizon.* When so much of my flying is done in the clear world of air-to-ground gunnery, it is not easy to stake my life on the word of a two-inch circle of glass and radium paint, yet that is the only way to stay alive after my airplane sinks into cloud. The feel and the senses that hold the pipper steady on the tank are easily confused when the world outside is a faceless flow of grey.

After a turn, or after the harmless movement of tilting my head to look at the radio set as I change frequencies, those senses can become shocked and panic-stricken, can shout *you're diving to the left!* although the gyro horizon is a calm and steady guide on the instrument panel. Caught in the contradiction, I have a choice: follow one voice or follow the other. Follow the sense that marks me *expert* in strafe and rocket and high-angle dive-bomb, or follow the little bit of tin and glass which someone has told me is the thing to trust.

I follow the tin, and a war is on. Vertigo has become so strong that I have had to lean my helmet almost to my shoulder in accord with its version of up and down. But still I fly the instruments. Keep the little tin airplane level in its glass *you're banking hard to the right* keep the altimeter and vertical speed needles steady *look out, you're starting to dive . . .* keep the turn needle straight up and the ball in the center of its curved glass tube *you're rolling! you're upside down and you're rolling!* Keep cross-checking the instruments. One to the next to the next to the next.

The only common factor between combat flying and instrument flying is one of discipline. I do not break away from my leader to seek a target on my own; I do not break away from the constant clockwise cross-check of the seven instruments on the black panel in front of me. The discipline of combat is usually the easier. There I am not alone, I can look out and see my leader and I can look up and back to see the second element of my flight, waiting to go in and fire on the enemy.

When the enemy is an unresisting grey fog, I must rely on the instruments and pretend that this is just another practice flight under the canvas instrument hood over the rear cockpit of a T-33 jet trainer, that I can lift the hood any time that I would like, and see a hundred miles of clear air in all directions. I am just not concerned with lifting the hood. Weather, despite the textbook familiarity that ground schools give and that experience reinforces, is still my greatest enemy. It is difficult to predict exactly, and worse, it is completely uncaring of the men and the machines that fly into it. It is completely uncaring.

"Air Force Jet Two Niner Four Zero Five, France Control with an advisory." Like a telephone ringing. My radio. There is not the slightest flaw in its operation. How can that be when only a minute ago . . . but it is working now and that is all that matters. Microphone button down. Professional voice.

"Roger, France; Four Zero Five, go."

"Four Zero Five, Flight Service advised multiengine aircraft reports severe turbulence, hail, and heavy icing in vicinity of Phalsbourg. Also T-33 reported moderate turbulence at flight level three zero zero, light clear icing."

Button down. What about that. Sounds as if there might be a thunderstorm or two in the stratus ahead. That was in the textbook, too. But still it is rare to have very large thunderstorms in France. "Roger, France, thank you for the advisory. What is the current weather at Chaumont?"

"Stand by one."

I stand by, waiting while another man in a white shirt and loose tie riffles through his teletyped weather reports looking for the one out of hundreds that is coded LFQU. With one hand he sorts and moves the weather from the Continent over; he shuffles through rain and haze and fog and high cloud and winds and ice and blowing dust. He is at this moment touching the sheet of yellow paper that tells him, if he wants to read it, that Wheelus Air Base, Libya, has clear skies with visibilities to twenty miles and a 10-knot wind from the southwest. If he wants to know, a line on the paper tells him that Nouasseur, Morocco, is calling high broken cirrus, visibility fifteen miles, wind west-southwest at fifteen knots. He thumbs through weather from Hamburg (measured 1,200-foot overcast, visibility three miles in rain showers, wind from the northwest at ten knots), from Wiesbaden Air Base (900-foot overcast, visibility two miles, wind from the south at seven knots), from Chaumont Air Base.

"Jet Two Niner Four Zero Five, Chaumont is calling a measured one-thousand-one-hundred-foot overcast, visibility four miles in rain, winds from the southwest at one zero gusting one seven." The weather at Chaumont is neither good nor bad.

"Thank you very much, France." The man clicks his microphone button in reply. He lets the thick sheaf of yellow paper pile upon itself again, covering with its weight the weather of hundreds of airports across the Continent. And cover the report from Phalsbourg Air Base (measured ceiling two hundred feet, visibility one-half mile in heavy rain showers, wind from the west at twenty-five gusting thirty-five knots. Cloud-to-cloud, cloud-to-ground lightning all quadrants, one-half-inch hail).

I drift along above the slanting cloud as if reality were all a dream with fuzzy soft edges. The starlight falls and soaks into the upper few feet of the mist, and I relax in a deep pool of red light and look out at the cold idyllic world that I called, when I was a boy, heaven.

I can tell that I am moving. I do not have to accept that with my intellect as the radio compass needle swings from one beacon to the next and the mileage drum of the distance measuring equipment unrolls. I see smooth waves of cloud pull darkly silently by a few hundred feet beneath my airplane. A beautiful night to fly.

What was that? What did I say? Beautiful? That is a word for the weak and the sentimental and the dreamers. That is not a word for the pilots of twenty-three thousand pounds of tailored destruction. That is not a word to be used by people who watch the ground disintegrate when they move their finger, or who are trained to kill the men of other countries whose heaven is the same as their own. Beautiful. Love. Soft. Delicate. Peace. Stillness. Not words or thoughts for fighter pilots, trained to unemotion and coolness in emergency and strafe the troops on the road. The curse of sentimentality is a strong curse. But the meanings are always there, for I have not yet become a perfect machine.

In the world of man/airplane, I live in an atmosphere of under-statement. The wingman pulling a scarlet contrail in the sunset is kinda pretty. Flying fighters is a pretty good job. It was too bad about my roommate flying into his target.

One learns the language, what is allowed to be said and what is not. I discovered, a few years ago, that I was not different from all the other pilots when I caught myself thinking that a wingman and his contrail in the last light of the sun is not a single thing but beautiful, or that I love my airplane, or that my country is a country for which I would gladly lay down my life. I am not different.

I learn to say, "Single-engine flying is all right, I guess," and any other pilot in the Air Force knows exactly that I am as proud to be a jet fighter pilot as anyone is proud of any job, anywhere. Yet nothing could be more repelling than the term *jet fighter pilot. Jet.* Words for movie posters and nonpilots. *Jet* means glamour and glory and the artificial chatter of a man who wishes he knew something of fighter airplanes. *Jet* is an embarrassing word. So I say *single-engine,* for the people I speak with know what I mean: that I have the chance to be off and alone with the clouds every once in a while, and if I want, I can fly faster than sound or knock a tank off its tracks or turn a round-house into a pile of bricks and hot steel under a cloud of black smoke. Flying jets is a mission for supermen and superheroes, dashing handsome movie actors. Flying single-engine is just a pretty good job.

The white jagged fence of the Alps was not a fence to a Fox Eight Four, and we had ambled across them at altitude almost as uncaring as the gull that floats above the predators of the sea. Almost. The mountains, even under their tremendous blanket, were sharp, like great shards of splintered glass on a snowy desert. No place at all for an engine failure. Their spiny tops jutted above the stratus sea in the ancient way that led one pilot to call them "islands in the sky." Hard rock islands above soft grey cotton sea. Silence on the radio. I flew wing silently, watching the islands drift below. Three words from the flight leader: "Rugged, aren't they?"

We have together been watching the islands. They are the most tortured masses of granite and pending avalanche in the world. Raw world upthrust. A virgin treacherous land of sliding snow and falling death. An adventure-world for the brave and the superhumans who climb because they are there. No place at all for a bewilderingly human thing called an airplane pilot and depending on a great many spinning steel parts to go on spinning in order that he might stay in the sky. That he loves.

"Roj," I say. What else was there to say? The mountains were rugged.

It is always interesting. The ground moves below, the stars move overhead, the weather changes, and rarely, very rarely, one of the ten thousand parts that is the body of an airplane fails to operate properly. For a pilot, flying is never dangerous, for a man must be a little bit insane or under the press of duty to willingly remain in a position that he truly considers dangerous. Airplanes occasionally crash, pilots are occasionally killed, but flying is not dangerous, it is interesting.

It would be nice, one day, to know which of my thoughts are mine alone and which of them are common to all the people who fly fighter airplanes.

Some pilots speak their thoughts by long habit, some say nothing at all of them. Some wear masks of convention and imperturbability that are very obvious masks, some wear masks so convincing that I wonder if these people are not really imperturbable. The only thoughts that I know are my own. I can predict how I will control my own mask in any number of situations. In emergencies it will be forced into a nonchalant calm that is calculated to rouse admiration in the heart of anyone that hears my unruffled voice on the radio. That, for one, is not strictly my own device. I talked once with a test pilot who told me his way of manufacturing calm in emergencies. He counts to ten out loud in his oxygen mask before he presses the microphone button to talk to anyone. If the emergency is such that he does not have ten seconds to count, he is not interested in talking to anyone; he is in the process of bailing out. But in lesser emergencies, by the time he has counted to ten, his voice has accustomed itself to a background of emergency, and comes as smoothly over the radio as if he were giving a pilot report on the tops of some fair-weather cumulus clouds.

There are other thoughts of which I do not speak. The destruction that I cause on the ground. It is not in strict accord with the Golden Rule to fly down an enemy convoy and tear its trucks to shreds with six rapid-fire heavy machine guns, or to drop flaming jellied gasoline on the men or to fire twenty-four high-explosive rockets into their tanks or to loft an atomic bomb into one of their cities. I do not talk about that. I rationalize it out for myself, until I hit upon a certain reasoning that allows me to do all these things without a qualm. A long while ago I found a solution that is logical and true and effective.

The enemy is evil. He wants to put me into slavery and he wants to overrun my country, which I love very much. He wants to take away my freedom and tell me what to think and what to do and when to think and when to do it. If he wants to do this to his own people, who do not mind the treatment, that is all right with me. But he will not do that to me or to my wife or to my daughter or to my country. I will kill him before he does.

So those legged dots streaming from the stalled convoy beneath my guns are not men with thoughts and feelings and loves like mine; they are evil and they mean to take my way of life from me. The tank is not manned by five frightened human beings who are praying their own special kind of prayers as I begin my dive and put the white dot of the gunsight pipper on the black rectangle that is their tank; they are evil and they mean to kill the people that I love.

Thumb lightly on the rocket button, white dot on black rectangle, thumb down firmly. A light, barely audible swish-swish from under my wings and four trails of black smoke angle down to converge on the tank. Pull up. A little shudder as my airplane is passed by the shock waves of the rocket explosions. They are evil.

I am ready for whatever mission I am assigned. But flying is not all the grim business of war and destruction and rationalized murder. In the development of man/machine, events do not always conform to plan, and flight shacks and ready rooms are scattered with magazines of the business of flying that point up the instances when man/machine did not function as he was designed.

Last week I sat in a soft red imitation-leather armchair in the pilots' lounge and read one of those well-thumbed magazines from cover to cover. And from it, I learned.

A pair of seasoned pilots, I read, were flying from France to Spain in a two-seat Lockheed T-33 jet trainer. Half an hour from their destination, the pilot in the rear seat reached down to the switch that controls his seat height, and inadvertently pressed the release that fires a blast of high-pressure carbon dioxide to inflate the one-man rubber life raft packed into his ejection seat cushion. The raft ballooned to fill the rear cockpit, smashing the hapless pilot tightly against his seat belt and shoulder harness.

This had happened before with life rafts, and in the cockpits of the airplanes that carry them is a small sharp knife blade to use in just such emergencies. The rear-seat pilot reached the blade, and in a second the raft exploded in a dense burst of carbon dioxide and talcum powder.

The front-seat pilot, carrying on the business of flying the airplane and unaware of the crisis behind him, heard the boom of the raft exploding and instantly his cockpit was filled with talcum powder, which he assumed to be smoke.

When you hear an explosion and the cockpit fills with smoke, you do not hesitate, you immediately cut off the fuel to the engine. So the front-seat pilot slammed the throttle to *off* and the engine stopped.

In the confusion, the pilot in back had disconnected his microphone cable, and assumed that the radio was dead. When he saw that the engine had flamed out, he pulled his ejection seat armrests up, squeezed the steel trigger and was blown from the airplane to parachute safely into a swamp. The other pilot stayed with the trainer and successfully crash-landed in an open field.

It was a fantastic train of errors, and my laugh brought a question from across the room. But as I told what I had read, I tucked it away as a thing to remember when I flew again in either seat of the squadron T-33.

When my class of cadets was going through flying training, just beginning our first rides in the T-33, our heads were filled with memorized normal procedures and emergency procedures until it was not an easy thing to keep them all straight. It was bound to happen to someone, and it happened to Sam Wood. On his very first morning in the new airplane, with the instructor strapped into the rear cockpit, Sam called, "Canopy clear?" warning the other man that a 200-pound canopy would be pressed hydraulically down on the rails an inch from his shoulders.

"Canopy clear," the instructor said. Sam pulled the canopy jettison lever. There was a sudden, sharp concussion, a cloud of blue smoke, and two hundred pounds of curved and polished Plexiglas shot forty feet into the air and crashed to the concrete parking ramp. Sam's flight that day was canceled.

Problems of this sort plague the Air Force. The human part of the man/airplane has just as many failures as the metal part, and they are more difficult to troubleshoot. A pilot will fly 1,500 hours in many kinds of airplanes, and is said to be experienced. On the landing from his 1,501st flight hour, he forgets to extend his landing gear and his airplane slides in a shower of sparks along the runway. To prevent gear-up landings there have been many inventions and many thousands of words and warnings written.

When a throttle is pulled back to less than minimum power needed to sustain flight, a warning horn blows in the cockpit and a red light flares in the landing gear lowering handle. This means "Lower the wheels!" But habit is a strong thing. One gets used to hearing the horn blowing for a moment before the wheels are lowered on each flight, and gradually it becomes like the waterfall that is not heard by the man who lives in its roar. There is a required call to make to the control tower as the pilot turns his airplane onto base leg in the landing pattern: "Chaumont Tower, Zero Five is turning base, gear down, pressure up, brakes checked." But the call becomes habit, too. Sometimes it happens that a pilot is distracted during the moment that he normally spends moving the landing gear lever to the down position. When his attention is again fully directed to the job of landing his airplane, his wheels should be down and he assumes they are. He glances at the three lights that show landing gear position, and though not one of them glows the familiar green, though the light in the handle is shining red and the warning horn is blowing, he calls,

"Chaumont Tower, Zero Five is turning base, gear down, pressure up, brakes checked."

The inventors took over and tried to design the human error out of their airplanes. Some airspeed indicators have flags that cover the dial during a landing approach unless the wheels are down, on the theory that if the pilot cannot read his airspeed he will be shocked into action, which here involves lowering the gear. In the deadliest, most sophisticated interceptor in the air today, that carries atomic missiles and can kill an enemy bomber under solid weather conditions at altitudes to 70,000 feet, there is a landing gear warning horn that sounds like a high-speed playback of a wide-range piccolo duet. The inventors deduced that if this wild noise would not remind a pilot to lower his landing gear, they were not going to bother with lights or covering the airspeed indicator or any other tricks; he would be beyond them all. When I see one of the big grey delta-wing interceptors in the landing pattern, I am forced to smile at the reedy tootling that I know the pilot is hearing from his gear warning horn.

Suddenly, in my dark cockpit, the thin luminous needle of the radio compass swings wildly from its grip on the Spangdahlem radio beacon and snaps me from my idle thoughts to the business of flying.

The needle should not move. When it begins to swing over Spangdahlem, it will first make very small left-right quivers on its card to warn me. The left-rights will become wider and wider and the needle will finally turn to point at the bottom of the dial, as it did passing Laon.

But the distance-measuring drum shows that I am still forty miles from my first German checkpoint. The radio compass has just warned me that it is a radio compass like all the others. It was designed to point the way to centers of low-frequency radio activity, and there is no more powerful center of low-frequency radio activity than a fully grown thunderstorm. For years I have heard the rule of thumb and applied it: stratus clouds mean stable air and smooth flying. In an aside to itself, the rule adds (except when there are thunderstorms hidden in the stratus).

Now, like a boxer pulling on his gloves before a fight, I reach to my left and push the switch marked *pitot heat.* On the right console is a switch with a placard *windscreen defrost* and my right glove flicks it to the *on* position, lighted in red by hidden bulbs. I check that the safety belt is as tight as I can pull it, and I cinch the shoulder harness straps a quarter of an inch tighter. I have no intention of deliberately flying into a thunderstorm tonight, but the padlocked canvas sack in the gun bay ahead of my boots reminds me that my mission is not a trifling one, and worth a calculated risk against the weather.

The radio compass needle swings again, wildly. I look for the flicker of lightning, but the cloud is still and dark. I have met a little rough weather in my hours as a pilot, why should the contorted warning feel so different and so ominous and so final? I note my heading indicator needle steady on my course of 084 degrees, and, from habit, check it against the standby magnetic compass. The gyro-held needle is within a degree of the incorruptible mag compass. In a few minutes the cloud will reach up to swallow my airplane, and I shall be on instruments, and alone.

It is a strange feeling to fly alone. So much of my flying is done in two- and four-ship formations that it takes time for the loneliness to wear from solo flight, and the minutes between Wethersfield and Chaumont Air Base are not that long a time. It is unnatural to be able to look in any direction that I wish, throughout an entire flight. The only comfortable position, the only natural position, is when I am looking forty-five degrees to the left or forty-five degrees to the right, and to see there the smooth streamlined mass of the lead airplane, to see the lead pilot in his white helmet and dark visor looking left and right and up and behind, clearing the flight from other airplanes in the sky and occasionally looking back for a long moment at my own airplane. I watch my leader more closely than any first violin watches his conductor, I climb when he climbs, turn when he turns, and watch for his hand signals.

Formation flying is a quiet way to travel. Filling the air with radio chatter is not a professional way of accomplishing a mission, and in close formation, there is a hand signal to cover any command or request from the leader and the answer from his wingman.

It would be easier, of course, for the leader to press his microphone button and say, "Gator flight: speed brakes . . . now," than to lift his right glove from the stick, fly with his left for a second while he makes the thumb-and-fingers speed brake signal, put his right glove back on the stick while Gator Three passes the signal to Four, put his left glove on the throttle with thumb over sawtooth speed brake switch above the microphone button, then nod his helmet suddenly and sharply forward as he moves the switch under his thumb to *extend.* It is more complicated, but it is more professional, and to be professional is the goal of every man who wears the silver wings over his left breast pocket.

It is professional to keep radio silence, to know all there is to know about an airplane, to hold a rock-solid position in any formation, to be calm in emergencies. Everything that is desirable about flying airplanes is "professional." I joke with the other pilots about the extremes to which the word is carried, but it cannot really be overused, and I honor it in my heart.

I work so hard to earn the title of a professional pilot that I come down from each close-formation flight wringing wet with sweat; even my gloves are wet after a flight, and dry into stiff wrinkled boards of leather before the next day's mission. I have not yet met the pilot who can fly a good formation flight without stepping from his cockpit as though it were a swimming pool. Yet all that is required for a smooth, easy flight is to fly a loose formation. That, however, is not professional, and so far I am convinced that the man who lands from a formation flight in a dry flight suit is not a good wingman. I have not met that pilot and I probably never will, for if there is one point in which all single-engine pilots place their professionalism in open view, it is in formation flying.

At the end of every mission, there is a three-mile initial approach to the landing pattern, in close echelon formation. In the thirty-five seconds that it takes to cover those three miles, from the moment that the flight leader presses his microphone button and says, "Gator Lead turning initial runway one niner, three out with four," every pilot on the flight line and scores of other people on the base will be watching the formation. The flight will be framed for a moment in the window of the commander's office, it will be in plain sight from the Base Exchange parking lot, visitors will watch it, veteran pilots will watch it. It is on display for three miles. For thirty-five seconds it is the showpiece of the entire base.

I tell myself that I do not care if every general in the United States Air Force in Europe is watching my airplane, or if just a quail is looking up at me through the tall grass. The only thing that matters is the flight, the formation. Here is where I tuck it in. Every correction that I make will be traced in the grey smoke of my exhaust and will be one point off the ideal of four straight grey arrows with unmoving swept-silver arrowheads. The smallest change means an immediate correction to keep the arrow straight.

I am an inch too far from the leader; I think the stick to the left and recover the inch. I bounce in the rough afternoon air; I move it in on the leader so that I bounce in the same air that he does. Those thirty-five seconds require more concentrated attention than all the rest of the flight. During a preflight briefing, the leader can say, ". . . and on initial, let's just hold a nice formation; don't press it in so close that you feel uncomfortable," but every pilot in the flight smiles to himself at the words and knows that when that half minute comes, he will be just as uncomfortable as the other wingmen in the closest, smoothest formation that he can fly.

The tension in those seconds builds until I think that I cannot hold my airplane so close for one more second. But the second passes and so does another, with the green glass of my leader's right navigation light inches from my canopy.

At last he breaks away in a burst of polished aluminum into the landing pattern, and I begin the count to three. I follow him through the pattern and I wait. My wheels throw back their long plumes of blue smoke on the hard runway and I wait. We taxi back to the flight line in formation and we shut down our engines and we fill out the forms and we wait. We walk back to the flight shack together, parachute buckles tinkling like little steel bells, waiting. Occasionally it comes. "Looked pretty good on initial today, Gator," someone will say to the lead pilot.

"Thanks," he will say.

I wonder in an unguarded moment if it is worth it. Is it worth the work and the sweat and sometimes the danger of extremely close formation flying just to look good in the approach? I measure risk against return, and have an answer before the question is finished and phrased. It is worth it. There are four-ship flights making approaches to this runway all day long, seven days a week. To fly one approach so well that it stands out in the eye of a man who watches hundreds of them is to fly an outstanding piece of formation. A professional formation. It is worth it.

If day formation is work, then night formation is sheer travail. But there is no more beautiful mission to be found in any air force.

Lead's airplane melts away to join the black sky and I fly my number three position on his steady green navigation light and the faint red glow that fills his cockpit and reflects dimly from his canopy. Without moon or starlight, I can see nothing whatsoever beyond his lights, and take the thought on slimmest faith that there is ten tons of fighter plane a few feet from my cockpit. But I usually have the starlight.

I drift along on Lead's wing with my engine practicing its balky V-8 imitation behind me and I watch the steady green light and the dim red glow and the faint faint silhouette of his airplane under the stars. At night the air is smooth. It is possible, at altitude and when Lead is not turning, to relax a little and compare the distant lights of a city to the nearer lights that are the stars around me. They are remarkably alike.

Distance and night filter out the smallest lights of the city, and altitude and thin clear air bring the smallest of stars into tiny untwinkling life. Without an undercast of cloud, it is very difficult to tell where sky ends and ground begins, and more than one pilot has died because the night was perfectly clear. There is no horizon aside from the ever-faithful one two inches long behind its disk of glass on the panel with its twenty-three comrades.

At night, from 35,000 feet, there is no fault in the world. There are no muddy rivers, no blackened forests, nothing except silver-grey perfection held in a light warm shower of starlight. I know that the white star painted on Lead's fuselage is dulled with streaks of oil rubbed by dusty rags, but if I look very closely I can see a flawless five-pointed star in the light of the unpointed stars through which we move.

The Thunderstreak looks very much as it must have looked in the mind of the man who designed it before he got down to the mundane task of putting lines and numbers on paper. A minor work of art, unblemished by stenciled black letters that in day read FIRE INGRESS DOOR and CRADLE PAD and DANGER—EJECTION SEAT. It looks like one of the smooth little company models in grey plastic, without blemish or seam.

Lead dips his wing sharply to the right, blurring the green navigation light in a signal for Two to cross over and take the position that I now fly on Lead's right wing. With Four floating slowly up and down in the darkness off my own right wing, I inch back my throttle and slide gently out to leave an '84-size space for Two. His navigation lights change from BRIGHT FLASH to DIM STEADY before he begins his crossover, for it is easier for me to fly on a steady light than a flashing one. Although this procedure came out of the death of pilots flying night formation on flashing lights, and is a required step before Two slides into position, I appreciate the thoughtfulness behind the action and the wisdom behind the rule.

Two moves slowly back eight feet, begins to move across behind the lead airplane. Halfway to his new position, his airplane stops. Occasionally in a crossover an airplane will catch in the leader's jet-wash and require a little nudge on stick and rudder to break again into smooth air, but Two is deliberately pausing. He is looking straight ahead into the tailpipe of Lead's engine.

It glows.

From a dark apple-red at the tip of it to a light luminous pink brighter than cockpit lights at their brightest, the tailpipe is alive and vibrant with light and heat. Tucked deep in the engine is the cherry-red turbine wheel, and Two is watching it spin.

Like the spokes of a quick-turning wagon wheel it spins, and every few seconds it strobes as he watches and appears to spin backward. Two is saying to himself, again, "So that is how it works." He is not thinking of flying his airplane or of crossing over or of the seven miles of cold black air between his airplane and the hills. He is watching a beautiful machine at work, and he pauses in Lead's jet-wash. I can see the red of the glow reflected in his windscreen, and on his white helmet.

Lead's voice comes softly in the tremendous quiet of the night. "Let's move it across, Two."

Two's helmet turns suddenly and I see his face clearly for a moment in the red glow of the tailpipe. Then his airplane slides quickly across into the space that I have been holding for him. The glow disappears from his windscreen.

In all the night formation missions, it is only when I fly as Two that I have the chance to see an engine soaked in its mystical light. The only other time that I can see a fire in the fire-driven turbine engines is at the moment of engine start, when I happen to be in one airplane parked behind another as the pilot presses his start switch upward. Then it is a weak twisting yellow flame that strains between the turbine blades for ten or fifteen seconds before it is gone and the tailpipe is dark again.

Newer airplanes, with afterburners, vaunt their flame on every takeoff, trailing a row of diamond shock waves in their blast that can be seen even in a noon sun. But the secret spinning furnace of a Thunderstreak engine at night is a sight that not many people have a chance to see, almost a holy sight. I keep it in my memory and think of it on other nights, on the ground, when there is not so much beauty in the sky.

The time always comes to go back down to the runway that we left waiting in the dark, and in the work of a night formation descent there is little chance for thoughts of the grace and the humble beauty of my airplane. I fly the steady light and try to make it smooth for Four on my wing and concentrate on keeping my airplane where it belongs. But even then, in the harder and more intense business of flying twenty thousand pounds of fighter a few feet from another precisely the same, one part of my thought goes on thinking the most unrelated things and eagerly presenting for my consideration the most unlikely subjects.

I move it in just a bit more on Two and pull back just a bit of power because he is turning toward me and keep just a little more back stick pressure to hold my airplane up at its lower airspeed and should I let my daughter have a pair of Siamese kittens. Steady burns the green navigation light in my eyes and I press forward with my left thumb to make certain that the speed brake switch is all the way forward and add another second of power here, just a half percent and pull it back right away and do they really climb curtains like someone told me? There will be absolutely no cats if they climb curtains. Little forward on the stick, little right bank to move it out one foot they certainly are handsome cats, though. Blue eyes. Fuel in a quick glance is one thousand three hundred pounds, no problem; wonder how Four is doing out there on my wing, shouldn't be too difficult for him tonight, sometimes it's better to fly Four at night anyway, you have more reference points to line on. Wonder if Gene Ivan is taking the train to Zurich this weekend. Five months I've been in Europe and I haven't seen Zurich yet. Careful careful don't slide in too close, take it easy move it out a foot or two. Where's the runway? We should be coming up on the runway lights pretty soon now. Fly Two's wing here as he levels out. No problem. Just stay on the same plane with his wings. Add a bit more power . . . now peg it there. Hold what you have. If he moves an inch, correct for it right away. This is initial approach. Tuck it in. There is probably not a soul watching, at night. Doesn't matter. All we are is a bunch of navigation lights in the sky; move it in on Two's wing. Smooth now, smooth now for Four. Pardon the bounce, Four.

"Checkmate Lead is on the break." There goes Lead's light breaking away into the pattern. Been flying on that little bulb all night long, it seems. Move it in a little more on Two. Hold it in there just another three seconds.

"Checkmate Two's on the break." There we go. No more strain. Just the count to three. Almost over, Four. Few minutes and we can hang ourselves up to dry. Microphone button down.

"Checkmate Three's on the break." Don't care what kind of eyes they have, they don't live in my house if they climb curtains. Gear down. Flaps down. Lead's over the fence. Sometimes you can trick yourself into thinking that this is a pretty airplane. Button down. "Checkmate Three is turning base, three green, pressure and brakes."

Check the brakes just to make sure. Yep. Brakes are good. This airplane has good brakes. Look out for the jetwash in this still air. Better tack on another three knots down final in case it's rough. There's the fence. Hold the nose up and let it land. Wonder if all runways have fences at the end. Can't think of any that don't. Little jetwash. We're down, little airplane. Nice job you did tonight. Drag chute handle out. Press the brakes once, lightly. Rollout is finished, a bit of brake to turn off the runway. Jettison the chute. Catch up with Lead and Two. Thanks for waiting, Lead. Pretty good flight. Pretty. If I have to be in the Air Force, wouldn't trade this job for any other they could offer. Canopy open. Air is warm. Nice to be down. I am wringing wet.

Over Luxembourg now, the distance-measuring drum unrolls smoothly, as though it were geared directly to the second hand of the aircraft clock. Twenty-eight miles to Spangdahlem. My airplane grazes the top of the cloud and I begin to make the transition to instrument flying. There is another few minutes, perhaps, before I will be submerged in the cloud, but it is good to settle down to the routine of a cross-check before it is really necessary. Airspeed is 265 indicated, altitude is 33,070 feet, turn needle is centered, vertical speed shows a hundred-foot-per-minute climb, the little airplane of the attitude indicator is very slightly nose-high on its horizon, heading indicator shows 086 degrees. The stars are still bright and unconcerned overhead. One nice thing about being a star is that you never have to worry about thunderstorms.

The radio compass needle twists again to the right, in agony. It reminds me that I must not be certain of the smoothest flying ahead. Perhaps the forecaster was not completely wrong, after all. A distant flicker of lightning glitters in the southeast, and the thin needle shudders, a terrified finger pointing to the light. I remember the first time I heard of that characteristic of the radio compass. I had been astonished. Of all the worst things for a navigation radio to do! Fly the needle as I am supposed to fly it and I wind up in the center of the biggest thunderstorm within a hundred miles. Who would design navigation equipment that worked like that? And who would buy it?

Any company that builds low-frequency radios, I learned, is the answer to the first question. The United States Air Force is the answer to the second. At least they had the honesty to tell me of this little eccentricity before they turned me loose on my first instrument cross-country flight. When I need it most, in the worst weather, the last thing to count on is the radio compass. It is better to fly time-and-distance than to follow the thin needle. I am glad that the new-comer, the TACAN, is not perturbed by the lightning.

Perhaps it is well that I do not have a wingman tonight. If I did near the edge of a storm, he would not have an easy time holding his position. That is one thing that I have never tried: thunderstorm for-mation flying.

The closest thing to that was in the air show that the squadron flew shortly before the recall, on Armed Forces Day. Somehow you can count on that day to have the roughest air of the year.

Every airplane in the squadron was scheduled to fly; a single giant formation of six four-ship diamonds of Air Guard F-84F's. I was sur-prised that there were so many people willing to drive bumper to bumper in the summer heat to watch, above the static displays, some old fighters flying.

Our airplanes are arranged in a long line in front of the bleachers erected for the day along the edge of the concrete parking ramp. I stand uncomfortably sunlit in front of my airplane at parade rest, watching the people waiting for the red flare that is the starting signal. If all those people go through the trouble of driving hot crowded miles to get here, why didn't they join the Air Force and fly the air-plane themselves? Of every thousand that are here, 970 would have no difficulty flying this airplane. But still they would rather watch.

A little *pop* and the brilliant scarlet flare streaks from the Very pis-tol of an adjutant standing near the visiting general in front of the reviewing stand. The flare soars up in a long smoky arc, and I move quickly, as much to hide myself from the gaze of the crowd as to strap myself into my airplane in unison with twenty-three other pilots, in twenty-three other airplanes. As I set my boots in the rudder pedal wells, I glance at the long straight line of airplanes and pilots to my left. There are none to my right, for I fly airplane number twenty-four, as the slot man in the last diamond formation.

I snap my parachute buckles and reach back for the shoulder harness, studiously avoiding the massive gaze of the many people. If they are so interested, why didn't they learn to fly a long time ago?

The sweep second hand of the aircraft clock is swinging up toward the 12, moving in accord with the second hands of twenty-three other aircraft clocks. It is a sort of dance; a unison performance by all the pilots who make solo performances on their spare weekends. Battery ON. Safety belt buckled, oxygen hoses attached. The second hand touches the dot at the top of its dial. Starter switch to START. The concussion of my starter is a tiny part of the mass explosion of two dozen combustion starters. It is a rather loud sound, the engine start. The first rows of spectators shift backward. But this is what they came to hear, the sound of these engines.

Behind us rises a solid bank of pure heat that ripples the trees on the horizon and slants up to lose itself in a pastel sky. The tachometer reaches 40 percent rpm, and I lift my white helmet from its comfortable resting place on the canopy bow, a foot from my head. Chinstrap fastened (how many times have I heard of pilots losing their helmets when they bailed out with chinstrap unfastened?), inverter selector to *normal.*

If the air were absolutely still today, I would even so be thoroughly buffeted by the jetwash of the twenty-three other airplanes ahead of me in flight. But the day is already a hot one, and the first airplane in the formation, the squadron commander's, will itself be stiffly jolted after takeoff into the boiling air of a July noon. In the air I will depend upon my flight leader to avoid the jetwash by flying beneath the level of the other airplanes, but there is no escaping the jetwash that will swirl across the runway as I take off on Baker Blue Three's wing, after all the other airplanes have rolled down the mile and a half of white concrete on this still day. After the squadron commander's takeoff, and because of the jetwash from his airplane and his wingman's, each successive takeoff roll will be just a little longer in the hot rough air that has been spun through rows of combustion chambers and stainless steel turbine blades. My takeoff roll will be the longest of all, and I will be working hard to stay properly on Three's wing in the turbulence of the airy whirlpools. But that is my job today, and I will do it.

To my left, far down the long line of airplanes, the squadron commander pushes his throttle ahead and begins to roll forward. "Falcon formation, check in," he calls on twenty-four radios, in forty-eight soft earphones, "Able Red Leader here."

"Able Red Two," his wingman calls.

"Three."

"Four."

A long succession of filtered voices and microphone buttons pressed. Throttle comes forward in cockpit after cockpit, fighter after fighter pivots to the left and swings to follow the polished airplane of the squadron commander. My flight leader takes his turn. "Baker Blue Leader," he calls, rolling forward. His name is Cal Whipple.

"Two." Gene Ivan.

"Three." Allen Dexter.

I press my microphone button, at last. "Four." And it is quiet. There is no one left after the slot man of the sixth flight.

The long line of airplanes rolls briskly along the taxiway to runway three zero, and the first airplane taxies well down the runway to leave room for his multitude of wingmen. The great formation moves quickly to fill the space behind him, for there is no time allowed for unnecessary taxi time. Twenty-four airplanes on the runway at once, a rare sight. I press my microphone button as I roll to a stop in position by Baker Blue Three's wing, and have a private little talk with the squadron commander. "Baker Blue Four is in."

When he hears from me, the man in the polished airplane, with the little cloth oak leaves on the shoulders of his flight suit, pushes his throttle forward and calls, "Falcon formation, run it up."

It is not really necessary for all twenty-four airplanes to turn their engines up to 100 percent rpm at the same moment, but it does make an impressive noise, and that is what the people in the stands would like to hear this day. Two dozen throttles go full forward against their stops.

Even with canopy locked and a helmet and earphones about my

head, the roar is loud. The sky darkens a little and through the massive thunder that shakes the wooden bleachers, the people watch a great cloud of exhaust smoke rise from the end of the runway, above the shining pickets that are the tall swept stabilizers of Falcon formation. I jolt and rock on my wheels in the blast from the other airplanes, and notice that, as I expected, my engine is not turning up its normal 100 percent. For just a second it did, but as the heat and pressured roar of the other airplanes swept back to cover my air intake, the engine speed fell off to a little less than 98 percent rpm. That is a good indicator that the air outside my small conditioned cockpit is warm.

"Able Red Leader is rolling." The two forwardmost pickets separate and pull slowly away from the forest of pickets, and Falcon formation comes to life. Five seconds by the sweep second hand and Able Red Three is rolling to follow, Four at his wing.

I sit high in my cockpit and watch, far ahead, the first of the formation lift from the runway.

The first airplanes break from the ground as if weary of it and glad to be back home in the air. Their exhaust trails are dark as I look down the length of them, and I wonder with a smile if I will have to go on instruments through the smoke of the other airplanes by the time I begin to roll with Baker Blue Three.

Two by two by two they roll. Eight; ten; twelve . . . I wait, watching my rpm down to 97 percent now at full throttle, hoping that I can stay with Three on the roll and break ground with him as I should. We have the same problem, so there should be no difficulty other than a very long takeoff roll.

I look over toward Three, ready to nod OK at him. He is watching the other airplanes take off, and does not look back. He is watching them go . . . sixteen; eighteen; twenty . . .

The runway is nearly empty in front of us, under a low cloud of grey smoke. The overrun barrier at the other end of the concrete is not even visible in the swirl of heat. But except for a little bit of sudden wing-rocking, the earlier flights get away from the ground without difficulty, though they clear the barrier by a narrower and narrower margin.

... twenty-two. Three looks back to me at last and I nod my OK. Baker Blue Lead and Two are five seconds down the concrete when Three touches his helmet back to the red ejection seat headrest, nods sharply forward, and we become the last of Falcon formation to release brakes. Left rudder, right rudder. I can feel the turbulence over the runway on my stabilizer, through the rudder pedals. It is taking a long time to gain airspeed and I am glad that we have the full length of the runway for our takeoff roll. Three rocks up and down slightly as his airplane moves heavily over the ripples in the concrete. I follow as if I were a shining aluminum shadow in three dimensions, bouncing when he bounces, sweeping ahead with him, slowly gaining airspeed. Blue Lead and Two must be lifting off by now, though I do not move my eyes from Three to check. They have either lifted off by now or they are in the barrier. It is at this moment one of the longest takeoff rolls I have seen in the F-84F, passing the 7,500-foot mark. The weight of Three's airplane just now finishes the change from wheels to swept wings, and we ease together into the air. A highly improbable bit of physics, this trusting twelve tons to thin air; but it has worked before and it should today.

Three is looking ahead and for once I am glad that I must watch his airplane so closely. The barrier is reaching to snag our wheels, and it is only a hundred feet away. Three climbs suddenly away from the ground and I follow, pulling harder on the control stick than I should have to, forcing my airplane to climb before it is ready to fly.

The helmet in the cockpit a few feet away nods once, sharply, and without looking, I reach forward and move the landing gear lever to up. There is the flash of the barrier going beneath us, in the same second that I touched the gear handle. We had ten feet to spare. It is good, I think, that I was not number twenty-six in this formation.

The landing gear tucks itself quickly up and out of the way, and the background behind Three changes from one of smooth concrete to rough blurred brush-covered ground; we are very definitely committed to fly. The turbulence, surprisingly enough, was only a passing shock, for our takeoff is longer and lower than any other, and we fly beneath the heaviest whirlpools in the air.

A low and gentle turn to the right to join on Blue Leader and Two as quickly as possible. But the turn is not my worry, for I am just a sandbagger, loafing along on Three's wing while he does all the juggling and angling and cutting off to make a smooth join-up. The worry of the long takeoff roll is left behind with the barrier, and now, takeoff accomplished, I feel as if I sat relaxed in the softest armchair in the pilots' lounge.

The familiar routine of a formation flight settles down upon me; I can hold it a little loose here over the trees and away from the crowd. There will be plenty of work ahead to fly the slot during the passes over the base.

There in the corner of my eye drifts Blue Leader and Two, closing nicely above and back to Three's left wing. Around them are the silver flashes and silhouettes that make the mass of swept metal called Falcon formation, juggling itself into the positions drawn out on green blackboards still chalked and standing in the briefing room. The wrinkles in the monster formation have been worked out in a practice flight, and the practice is paying off now as the finger-fours form into diamonds and the diamonds form into vees and the vees become the invincible juggernaut of Falcon formation.

I slide across into the slot between Two and Three, directly behind Baker Blue Leader, and move my airplane forward until Lead's tailpipe is a gaping black hole ten feet ahead of my windscreen and I can feel the buffet of his jetwash in my rudder pedals. Now I forget about Three and fly a close trail formation on Lead, touching the control stick back every once in a while to keep the buffet on the rudder pedals.

"Falcon formation, go channel nine."

Blue Lead yaws his airplane slightly back and forth, and with the other five diamonds in the sky, the four-ship diamond that is Baker Blue flight spreads itself for a moment while its pilots click their radio channel selectors to nine and make the required cockpit check after takeoff.

I push the switches aft of the throttle quadrant, and the drop tanks under my wings begin feeding their fuel to the main fuselage tank and to the engine. Oxygen pressure is 70 psi, the blinker blinks as I breathe, engine instruments are in the green. I leave the engine screens extended, the parachute lanyard hooked to the rip cord handle. My airplane is ready for its air show.

In this formation there are probably some airplanes that are not operating just as they should, but unless the difficulties are serious ones, the pilots keep their troubles to themselves and call the cockpit check OK. Today it would be too embarrassing to return to the field and shoot a forced landing pattern on the high stage before an audience so large.

"Baker Blue Lead is good."

"Two."

"Three."

I press the button. "Four."

Normally the check would have been a longer one, with each pilot calling his oxygen condition and quantity and whether or not his drop tanks were feeding properly, but with so many airplanes aloft the check alone would take minutes. It was agreed in the briefing room to make the check as usual, but to reply only with flight call sign.

Six lead airplanes rock their wings after my call and the six diamonds close again to show formation. I do not often have the chance to fly as slot man in diamond, and I tuck my airplane in close under Lead's tailpipe to make it look from the ground as if I had flown there all my life. The way to tell if a slot man has been flying his position well is to look at his vertical stabilizer as he lands. The blacker his stabilizer and rudder with Lead's exhaust, the better the formation he has been flying.

I move up for a moment into the position that I will hold during our passes across the base. When I feel that it is correct, the black gaping hole of Lead's tailpipe is a shimmering inky disk six feet forward of my windscreen and a foot above the level of my canopy. My vertical stabilizer is solid in his jetwash, and I ease the weight of my boots from the rudder pedals to avoid the uncomfortable vibration in them. If it were possible to move my boots completely off the pedals, I would, but the slanting tunnels that lead down to them offer no resting-place, and I must live with the vibration that means that the stabilizer is blackening in burnt JP-4. I can hear it, a dull heavy constant rumble of twisted forced air beating against the rudder. The airplane does not fly easily in this, and it is not enjoyable to fly with the tail, like a great dorsal fin, forced into the stream of heat from Baker Blue Lead's turbine. But that is the position that I must fly to make Baker Blue flight a close and perfect diamond, and the people who will watch are not interested in my problems. I move the throttle back an inch and ahead again, touch the control stick forward, sliding away and down into a looser, easier formation.

Two and Three are using the time that Falcon formation spends in its wide turn to check their own positions. The air is rough, and their airplanes shudder and jolt as they move in to overlap their wings behind Lead's. To fly a tight formation, they must close on the leader until their wings are fitted in the violent wake of Lead's wing. Although that air is not so rough as the heat that blasts my rudder, it is more difficult to fly, for it is an unbalanced force, and a changing one. At 350 knots the air is as solid as sheet steel, and I can see the ailerons near their wingtips move quickly up and down as they fight to hold smoothly in formation. During normal formation flying, their wings would be just outside the river of air washing back from their leader's wing, and they could fly that position for a long time with the normal working and coaxing and correcting. But this is a show, and for a show we work.

Two and Three are apparently satisfied that they will be able to hold a good position for the passes across the base, for they slide out into normal formation almost simultaneously. Still they watch nothing but Baker Blue Lead, and still they bounce and jar in the rough air. Every few seconds the flight slams across an invisible whirlwind twisting up from a plowed field, and the impact of it is a solid thing that blurs my vision for an instant and makes me grateful for my shoulder harness.

This is summer on an air base: not blazing sun and crowded pool and melting ice cream, but the jarring slam of rough air when I want to tuck my airplane into close formation.

The wide circle is completed, and Falcon formation begins to descend to its 500-foot flyby altitude.

"Close it up, Falcon," comes the voice of the man who is Able Red Leader. We close it up, and I lift my airplane to push the rudder again into Lead's tumbling jetwash. I glance at my altimeter when the formation is level and three miles from the crowd by the runway. One quick glance: four hundred feet above the ground. The leading vee of diamonds is at five hundred feet and we are stacked one hundred feet beneath it. As a slot man, altitude is none of my business, but I am curious.

Now, in these last three miles to the base, we are being watched by the American people. They are interested in knowing just how well the part-time Air Force can fly its airplanes.

The diamonds of Falcon formation are hard and glittering in the sun, and even from the center of Baker Blue flight the formation looks close and good. I think again the old axiom of bouncing in the same air with the leader, and I am not alone with the thought. Two and Three have placed their wings unnervingly close to Lead's smooth fuselage, and we take the ridges of the air as a close formation of bobsleds would take the ridges of hard-packed snow. Slam. Four helmets jerk, four sets of stiff wings flex the slightest bit. My rudder is full in Lead's jetwash and the pedals are chattering heavily. This rumble of hard jetwash must be loud even to the people standing by the bleachers on the flight line. Hold it smooth. Hold it steady. Hold it close.

But the people on the concrete do not even begin to hear the rumble that makes my rudder pedals dance. They see from the north a little cloud of grey smoke on the horizon. It stretches to become a quiver of grey arrows in flight, shot at once from a single bow. There is no sound.

The arrows grow, and the people on the ground talk to each other in the quiet air as they watch. The arrowheads slice the air at 400 knots, but from the ground they seem to be suspended in cold clear honey.

Then, as the silent flight reaches the end of the runway a quarter mile from the bleachers and even the visiting general is smiling to himself behind his issue sunglasses, the honey becomes only air and the 400 knots is the ground-shaking blast of twenty-four sudden detonations of high explosive. The people wince happily in the burst of sound and watch the diamonds whip together through the sky in unyielding immovable grace. In that moment the people on the ground are led to believe that Air Guard airplanes are not left to rust unused in the sun, and this is what we are trying to tell them.

In one fading Dopplered roar we flick past the stands and are to the people a line of dwindling dots, pulling two dozen streamers of tenuous grey as we go. Our sound is gone as quickly as it came, and the ground is quiet again.

But still, after we pass the crowd, we fly formation. Baker Blue flight and Falcon formation are just as present about me as they have been all morning. The brief roar that swept the people is to me unchanged and constant. The only change in Falcon formation after it crosses the field is that the diamonds loosen a few feet out and back, and the bobsleds take the ridges a tenth second apart rather than in the same instant.

During the turn to the second pass across the base, I slide with Baker Blue Lead to form a new pattern in which our diamond is the corner of a giant block of airplanes. Regardless of the position that we fly, the rough sky beats at our airplanes and the jetwash thunders over my vertical stabilizer. I think of the landing that is ahead, hoping that a light breeze has begun across the runway, to clear the jetwash out of the way by the time my airplane slides down final approach to land.

Maybe they don't want to be pilots.

Where did that come from? Of course they want to be pilots. Yet they watch from the ground instead of flying wing in Baker Blue flight. The only reason that they are not flying today instead of watching is that they do not know what they are missing. What better work is there than flying airplanes? If flying was the full-time employment of an Air Force pilot, I would have become a career officer when the chance was offered me.

We force our airplanes close again, fly the second pass, re-form into a final design, and bring it through the rocky air above the field. Then, from a huge circle out of sight of the runway, flight after flight separates from the formation, diamonds changing to echelon right, and the echelons fly a long straight approach across the hard uneven air into the landing pattern.

It is work, it is uncomfortable. The needle that measures G has been knocked to the number 4. But in the moments that the people watch this part of their standby Air Force, and were glad for it, the flight was worthwhile. Able Red Leader has completed another little part of his job.

That was months ago. These days, in Europe, our formation is not for show but for the business of fighting. A four-ship flight is loose and comfortable when it is not being watched, and the pilots merely concentrate on their position, rather than devote their every thought and smallest action to show flying. At altitude we wait for the left-right yaw of the lead airplane, and spread out even more, into tactical formation. Three and Four climb together a thousand feet above Lead and Two; each wingman sliding to a loose-angled trailing position from which he can watch the sky around as well as the airplane that he protects. In tactical formation and the practice of air ·combat, responsibility is sharply defined: wingman clears leader, high element clears low element, leaders look for targets.

Flying at the contrail altitudes, this is easy. Any con other than our own four are bogies. During a war, when they are identified, they become either bogies to be watched or bandits to be judged and, occasionally, attacked. "Occasionally" because our airplane was not designed to engage enemy fighters at altitude and destroy them. That is the job of the F-104's and the Canadian Mark Sixes and the French Mystères. Our Thunderstreak is an air-to-ground attack airplane built to carry bombs and rockets and napalm against the enemy as he moves on the earth. We attack enemy airplanes only when they are easy targets: the transports and the low-speed bombers and the propeller-driven fighters. It is not fair and not sporting to attack only a weaker enemy, but we are not a match for the latest enemy airplanes built specifically to engage other fighters.

But we practice air combat against the day when we are engaged over our target by enemy fighters. If hours of practice suffice only to allow us a successful escape from a more powerful fighter, they will have been worthwhile. And the practice is interesting.

There they are. Two '84F's at ten o'clock low, in a long circling climb into the contrail level, coming up like goldfish to food on the surface. At 30,000 feet the bogie lead element begins to pull a con. The high element is nowhere in sight.

I am Dynamite Four, and I watch them from my high perch. It is slow motion. Turns at altitude are wide and gentle, for too much bank and G will stall the airplane in the thin air and I will lose my most precious commodity: airspeed. Airspeed is golden in combat. There are books filled with rules, but one of the most important is Keep Your Mach Up. With speed I can outmaneuver the enemy. I can dive upon him from above, track him for a moment in my gunsight, fire, pull up and away, prepare another attack. Without airspeed I cannot even climb, and drift at altitude like a helpless duck in a pond.

I call the bogies to Three, my element leader, and look around for the others. After the first enemy airplanes are seen, it is the leader's responsibility to watch them and plan an attack. I look out for other airplanes and keep my leader clear. When I am a wingman, it is not my job to shoot down enemy airplanes. It is my job to protect the man who is doing the shooting. I turn with Three, shifting back and forth across his tail, watching, watching.

And there they are. From above the con level, from five o'clock high, come a pair of swept dots. Turning in on our tail. I press the microphone button. "Dynamite Three, bogies at five high."

Three continues his turn to cover Dynamite Lead during his attack on the bogie lead element in their climb. The decoys. "Watch 'em," he calls.

I watch, twisted in my seat with the top of my helmet touching the canopy as I look. The two are counting on surprise, and are only this moment, with plenty of airspeed, beginning to pull cons. I wait for them, watching them close on us, begin to track us. They are F-84's. We can outfly them. They don't have a chance.

"Dynamite Three, break right!" For once the wingman orders the leader, and Three twists into a steep bank and pulls all the back pressure that he can without stalling the airflow over his wings. I follow, seeking to stay on the inside of his turn, and watching the attackers. They are going too fast to follow our turn, and they begin to overshoot and slide to the outside of it. They are not unwise, though, for immediately they pull back up, converting their airspeed into altitude for another pass. But they have lost the surprise that they had counted on, and with full throttle we are gaining airspeed. The fight is on.

A fight in the air proceeds like the scurrying of minnows about a falling crumb of bread. It starts at high altitudes, crossing and recrossing the sky with bands of grey contrail, and slowly moves lower and lower. Every turn means a little more altitude lost. Lower altitudes mean that airplanes can turn more tightly, gain speed more quickly, pull more G before they stall. Around and around the fight goes, through the tactics and the language of air combat: scissors, defensive splits, yo-yos and "Break right, Three!"

I do not even squeeze my trigger. I watch for other airplanes, and after Three rivets his attention on one enemy airplane, I am the only eyes in the element that watch for danger. Three is totally absorbed in his attack, depending on me to clear him of enemy planes. If I wanted to kill him in combat, I would simply stop looking around.

In air combat more than at any other time, I am the thinking brain for a living machine. There is no time to keep my head in the cockpit or to watch gauges or to look for switches. I move the control stick and the throttle and the rudder pedals unconsciously. I want to be *there*, and I am there. The ground does not even exist until the last minutes of a fight that was allowed to get too low. I fly and fight in a block of space. The ideal game of three-dimension chess, across which moves are made with reckless abandon.

In two-ship combat there is only one factor to consider: the enemy airplane. I seek only to stay on his tail, to track him with the pipper in the gunsight and pull the trigger that takes close-ups of his tailpipe. If he should be on my tail, there are no holds barred. I do everything that I can to keep him from tracking me in his gunsight, and to begin to track him. I can do maneuvers in air combat that I could never repeat if I tried.

I saw an airplane tumble once, end over end. For one shocked moment the fighter was actually moving backward and smoke was streaming from both ends of the airplane. Later on, on the ground, we deduced that the pilot had forced his aircraft into a wild variation of a snap roll, which is simply not done in heavy fighter airplanes. But the maneuver certainly got the enemy off his tail.

As more airplanes enter the fight, it becomes complicated. I must consider that this airplane is friend and that airplane is enemy, and that I must watch my rolls to the left because there are two airplanes in a fight there and I would fly right through the middle of them. Midair collisions are rare, but they are always a possibility when one applies too much abandon in many-ship air combat flights.

John Larkin was hit in the air by a Sabre that saw him too late to turn. "I didn't know what had happened," he told me. "But my airplane was tumbling and it didn't take long to figure that I had been hit. I pulled the seat handle and squeezed the trigger and the next thing I remember, I was in the middle of a little cloud of airplane pieces, just separating from the seat.

"I was at a pretty good altitude, about thirty-five thousand, so I free-fell down to where I could begin to see color on the ground. Just when I reached for my rip cord, the automatic release pulled it for me and I had a good chute. I watched the tail of my airplane spin down by me and saw it crash in the hills. A couple of minutes later I was down myself and thinking about all the paperwork I was going to have to fill out."

There had been a great amount of paperwork, and the thought of it makes me doubly careful when I fly air combat, even today. In a war, without the paperwork, I will be a little more free in my fighting.

When it spirals down to altitudes where dodging hills enters the tactic, a fight is broken off by mutual consent, as boxers hold their fists when an opponent is in the ropes. In the real war, of course, it goes on down to the ground, and I pick up all the pointers I can on methods to scrape an enemy into a hillside. It could all be important someday.

The wide luminous needle of the TACAN swings serenely as I pass over Spangdahlem at 2218, and one more leg of the flight is complete.

As if it recognized that Spangdahlem is a checkpoint and time for things to be happening, the thick dark cloud puts an end to its toying and abruptly lifts to swallow my airplane in blackness. For a second it is uncomfortable, and I sit tall in my seat to see over the top of the cloud. But the second quickly passes and I am on instruments.

For just a moment, though, I look up through the top of my canopy. Above, the last bright star fades and the sky above is as dark and faceless as it is about me. The stars are gone, and I am indeed on instruments.

CHAPTER FOUR

"Rhein Control, Air Force Jet Two Niner Four Zero Five, Spangdahlem, over." From my capricious radio I do not know whether or not to expect an answer. The "over," which I rarely use, is a wistful sort of hope. I am doubtful.

"Jet Four Zero Five, Rhein Control, go ahead."

Someday I will give up trying to predict the performance of a UHF radio. "Roger, Rhein, Zero Five was Spangdahlem at two niner, flight level three three zero assigned instrument flight rules, Wiesbaden at three seven, Phalsbourg next. Latest weather at Chaumont Air Base, please." A long pause of faint flowing static. My thumb is beginning to be heavy on the microphone button.

"Roger your position, Zero Five. Latest Chaumont weather is one thousand overcast, visibility five miles in rain, winds from the west at one zero knots."

"Thank you, Rhein. How about the Phalsbourg weather?" The static is suddenly louder and there is a light blue glow across the windscreen. Saint Elmo's fire. Harmless and pretty to watch, but it turns low-frequency radio navigation into a patchwork of guesses and estimates. The radio compass needle is wobbling in an aimless arc. It is good to have a TACAN set.

"Zero Five, Phalsbourg weather is garbled on our machine. Strasbourg is calling eight hundred overcast, visibility one-half mile in heavy rain showers, winds variable two zero gusting three zero knots, isolated thunderstorms all quadrants." Strasbourg is to the left of course, but I could catch the edge of their thunderstorms. Too bad that Phalsbourg is out. Always seems to happen when you need it most.

"What is the last weather you had from Phalsbourg, Rhein?" A garbled Teletype weather report is really garbled. It is either a meaningless mass of consonants or a black jumble where one weather sequence has been typed on top of another.

"Latest we have, sir, is two hours old. They were calling five hundred overcast, visibility one-quarter mile in . . ." He pauses, and his thumb comes off the microphone button. It comes on again. ". . . hail—that might be a misprint—scattered thunderstorms all quadrants." Quarter-mile visibility in hail. I have heard that nocturnal thunderstorms can be violent, but this is the first time that I have heard the direct report as I fly on instruments in the weather. But the sequence is two hours old, and the storms are isolated. It is rare for storms to hold their violence for a long time, and I can get a radar vector from a ground station around active storm cells.

"Thank you, Rhein." The air is very smooth in the stratus, and it is not difficult to hold the new heading at 093 degrees. But I am beginning to think that perhaps my detour did not take me far enough around the severe weather.

I am well established in the routine of the cross-check now, and occasionally look forward to the liquid blue fire on the windscreen. It is a brilliant cobalt, glowing with an inner light that is somehow startling to see at high altitude. And it is liquid as water is liquid; it twists across the glass in little rivulets of blue rain against the black of the night weather. The light of it, mingling with the red of the cockpit lights, turns the instrument panel into a surrealist's impression of a panel, in heavy oil paint. In the steady red and flickering blue of the electrical fire on the glass, the only difference between my needles and the painter's is that a few of mine are moving.

Turn back.

The air is smooth. The needles, except for the wobbling radio compass needle and the rolling numbered drums of the distance-measuring equipment, move only the smallest fractions of inches as I make the gentle corrections to stay at 33,000 feet. The airplane is flying well and the UHF is back in action.

There are storms ahead, and this airplane is very small.

My cross-check goes so smoothly that I do not have to hurry to include a look at the fuel flow and quantity gauges, the pale green oxygen blinker blinking coolly at me as I breathe, the utility and flight control system pressure gauges, the voltmeter, the loadmeter, the tailpipe temperature. They are all my friends, and they are all in the green.

I will not live through the storms.

What is this? Fear? The little half-noticed voices that flit through my thought like scurrying fireflies might warrant the name of fear, but only if I stretch the definition until it applies to the thoughts that scurry before I begin to walk across a busy highway. If I reacted to the half-thoughts, I would have quit flying before I made my first flight in the light propeller-driven trainer that first lifted me away from a runway.

The Florida sky is a gay blue one, puffing with the high cumulus that prevails in southern summers. The metal of my primary trainer is hot in the sun, but before my first flight in the United States Air Force, I am not concerned with heat.

The man who settles himself in the rear cockpit of the airplane is not a big man, but he has the quiet confidence of one who has all power and knows all things.

"Start the engine and let's get out of here" are the first words that I hear in an airplane from a flight instructor.

I am not so confident as he, but I move the levers and switches that I have studied in the handbook and call, "Clear!" as I know I should. Then I touch the starter switch to *start,* and feel for the first time that strange instant awareness of my ability to do everything that I should. And I begin to learn.

I discover, as the months pass, that the only time that I am afraid in an airplane is when I do not know what must be done next.

The engine stops on takeoff. Whistling beneath my airplane is a swamp of broken trees and hanging Spanish moss and alligators and water moccasins and no dry ground for wheel to roll upon. At one time I would have been afraid, for at one time I did not know what to do about the engine failure and the swamp and the alligators. I would have had time to think, So this is how I will die, before I hit the trees and my airplane twisted and somersaulted and sank in the dark green water.

But by the time that I am able to fly the airplane by myself, I know. Instead of dying, I lower the nose, change fuel tanks, check the fuel boost pumps *on* and the mixture *rich,* retract the landing gear and wing flaps, pump the throttle, aim the airplane so that the fuselage and cockpit will go between the tree stumps, pull the yellow handle that jettisons the canopy, lock the shoulder harness, turn the magneto and battery switches off, and concentrate on making a smooth landing on the dark water. I trust the shoulder harness and I trust my skill and I forget about the alligators. In two hours I am flying another airplane over the same swamp.

I learn that it is what I do not know that I fear, and I strive, outwardly from pride, inwardly from the knowledge that the unknown is what will finally kill me, to know all there is to be known about my airplane. I will never die.

My best friend is the pilot's handbook, a different book for each type of airplane that I fly. Technical Order 1F-84F-1 describes my airplane; every switch and knob of it. It gives the normal operating procedures, and on red-bordered pages, the emergency procedures for practically any critical situation that can arise while I sit in the cockpit. The pilot's handbook tells me what the airplane feels like to fly, what it will do and what it will not do, what to expect from it as it goes through the speed of sound, procedures to follow if I suddenly find myself in an airplane that has been pushed too far and has begun to spin. It has detailed charts of my airplane's performance to tell just how many miles it will fly, how quickly it will fly them, and how much fuel it will need.

I study the flight handbook as a divinity student studies the Bible. And as he goes back time and again to Psalms, so I go back time and again to the red-bordered pages of Section III. Engine fire on takeoff; after takeoff; at altitude. Loss of oil pressure. Severe engine vibration. Smoke in the cockpit. Loss of hydraulic pressure. Electrical failure. This procedure is the best to be done, this one is not recommended.

In cadet days, I studied the emergency procedures in class and in spare time and shouted them as I ran to and from my barracks. When I know the words of the red-bordered pages well enough to shout them word for word as I run down a long sidewalk lined with critical upperclass cadets, it can be said I know them well.

The shined black shoe touches the sidewalk. Run. "GLIDE NINETY KNOTS CHANGE FUEL TANKS BOOST PUMPS ON CHECK FUEL PRESSURE MIXTURE RICH PROP FULL INCREASE GEAR UP FLAPS UP CANOPY OPEN . . ." I know the forced landing procedures for that first trainer as well today as I knew them then. And I was not afraid of that first airplane.

But not every emergency can be put in a book, not even in a pilot's handbook. The marginal situations, such as planning a flight to an airport that I know is buried in solid weather to its minimums, such as losing sight of my leader in a formation letdown through the weather, such as continuing a flight into an area of thunderstorms, are left to a thing called pilot judgment. It is up to me in those cases. Bring all of my experience and knowledge of my airplane into play, evaluate the variables: fuel, weather, other aircraft flying with me, condition of the runway, importance of the mission—against the severity of the storms. Then, like a smooth-humming computer, I come up with one plan of action and follow it. Cancel the flight until I get more rest. Make a full circle in the weather and make my own letdown after my leader has made his. Continue toward the storms. Turn back.

When I make the judgment I follow it without fear, for it is what I have decided is the best course of action. Any other course would be a risky one. Only in the insecure hours before I touch the starter switch can I see causes for fear; when I do not take the effort to be alert.

On the ground, if I concentrated, I could be afraid, in a detached, theoretical sort of way. But so far I have not met the pilot who concentrated on it.

I like to fly airplanes, so I learn about them and I fly them. I think of my job in the same light that a bridge builder on the high steel thinks of his: it has its dangers, but it is still a good way to make a living. The danger is an interesting factor, for I do not know if my next flight will be an uneventful one or not. Every once in a long while I am called to step on the stage, under the spotlight, and cope with an unusual situation, or, at longer intervals, an emergency.

Unusual situations come in all sizes, from false alarms to full-fledged emergencies that involve my continued existence as a living member of a fighter squadron.

I lower my landing gear on the turn to final approach. The little green lights that indicate wheels locked in the down position are dark longer than they should be. The right main gear locks down, showing its light. The left main locks down. But the nosewheel light is dark. I wait a moment and sigh. The nosewheel is a bother, but not in the least is it an emergency. As soon as I see that it is not going to lock down, the cautious part of me thinks of the very worst that this could mean. It could mean at worst that the nosegear is still locked up in its wheel well; that I will not be able to lower it; that I will have to land on only two wheels.

There is no danger (oh, once long ago an '84 cartwheeled during a nosegear-up landing and the pilot was killed), even if that very worst thing happens. If the normal gear-lowering system does not work after I try it a few times again; if the emergency gear-lowering system, which blows the nosegear down with a high-pressure charge of compressed air, fails; if I cannot shake the wheel loose by bouncing the main gear against the runway . . . if all these fail, I still have no cause for concern (unless the airplane cartwheels). Fuel permitting, I will circle the field for a few minutes and the fire trucks will lay a long strip of white foam down the runway, a place for my airplane's unwheeled nose to slide. And I will land.

Final approach is the same final approach that it has always been. The fence pulls by beneath the wheels as it always does, except that now it pulls beneath two landing gear instead of three, and with a gear warning horn loud in the cockpit and the red warning light brilliant in the clear plastic handle and the third green light dark and the word from the control tower is that the nosewheel still looks as if it is up and locked.

The biggest difference in the final approach is in the eye of the observer, and observers are many. When the square red fire trucks grind to the runway with their red beacons flashing, the line crews and returning pilots climb to stand on the swept silver wings of parked airplanes and watch to see what will happen. (Look at that, Johnny, turning final with no nosewheel. Heard about an 'eighty-four that cartwheeled on the runway trying this same trick. Good luck, whoever you are, don't forget to hold the nose off as long as you can.) It is interesting to them, and mildly annoying to me, for it is like being pushed onstage without having anything to perform. No flames, no eerie silence of a frozen engine, a practically nonexistent threat of spectacular destruction, no particular skill on display.

I simply land, and the twin plumes of blue rubber-smoke pout back from the main wheels as they touch the hard concrete. I slow through 100 knots on the landing roll, touching right rudder to put the narrow strip of foam between the wheels. Then, slowly and gently, the unwheeled nose of the airplane comes down.

At that moment before the metal of the nose touches the runway and I tilt unnaturally forward in my cockpit and the only sight in the windscreen is the fast-blurred strip of white foam, I am suddenly afraid. This is where my control ends and chance takes over. A gust of wind against the high rudder and I will surely cartwheel in a flying swirling cloud of brilliant orange flame and twisted metal; the airplane will tumble and I will be caught beneath it; the hot engine will explode when the cold foam sprays up the intake. The ground is hard and it is moving very fast and it is very close.

Throttle *off*, and the nose settles into the foam.

White. Instant white and the world outside is cut away and metal screams against concrete loudly and painfully and I grit my teeth and squint my eyes behind the visor and know in a surprised shock that my airplane is being hurt and she doesn't deserve to be hurt and she is good and faithful and she is taking the force of a 90-knot slab of concrete and I can do nothing to ease her pain and I am not cartwheeling and the scream will never end and I must have slid a thousand feet and

I am still slammed hard forward into the shoulder harness and the world is white because the canopy is sprayed with foam and get that canopy open now, while I'm still sliding.

The foam-covered sheet of Plexiglas lifts as I pull the unlock lever, as smoothly as if nothing were the least unusual and there is the world again, blue sky and white runway sliding to a stop and grass at the side of the concrete and visor up and oxygen mask unsnapped and it is very quiet. The air is fresh and smooth and green and I am alive. Battery *off* and fuel *off*. As quiet as I have ever heard. My airplane is hurt and I love her very much. She didn't somersault or cartwheel or flip on her back to burn and I owe my life to her.

The advancing roar of fire truck engines and soon we'll be surrounded by the square monsters and by talking people and say, Why couldn't you get the nosewheel down and That landing was a pretty good one, boy, and You should have seen the foam spray when your nose hit. But before the people come, I sit quietly in the cockpit for a second that seems a long time and tell my airplane that I love her and that I will not forget that she did not trap me beneath her or explode on the runway and that she took the pain while I walk away without a scratch and that a secret that I will keep between us is that I love her more than I would tell to anyone who asks.

I will someday tell that secret to another pilot, when he and I happen to be walking back from a night formation flight and the breeze is cool and the stars are as bright as they can get when you walk on the ground. I will say in the quiet, "Our airplane is a pretty good airplane." He will be quiet a second longer than he should be quiet and he will say, "It is." He will know what I have said. He will know that I love our airplane not because she is like a living thing, but because she truly is a living thing and so very many people think that she is just a block of aluminum and glass and bolts and wire. But I know and my friend will know and that is all that must be said.

Though it had its moment of fear and though it opened the door of understanding a little wider, the nosegear failure is an incident, not an emergency. I have had a few incidents in the hours that I have spent in the little cockpit, but so far I have never experienced a real emergency or been forced to make the decision to pull the yellow ejection seat handles, squeeze the red trigger, and say a quick farewell to a dying airplane. Yet that sort of thing is what the newspapers would have me believe happens every day in the Air Force.

At first, I was ready for it. When the engine sounded rough during those first hours alone, I thought of the ejection seat. When a tailpipe overheat light came on for the first time in my career, I thought of the ejection seat. When I was nearly out of fuel and lost in the weather, I thought of it. But the part of my mind that is concerned with caution can cry wolf only so many times before I see through its little game and realize that I could easily fly through my entire career without being called upon to blast away from an airplane into a cold sky. But still it is good to know that a 37-millimeter cannon shell is waiting just aft of the seat, waiting for the moment that I squeeze the trigger.

If I ever collide with another airplane in the air, the seat is waiting to throw me clear. If I lose all hydraulic pressure to the flight controls, it is waiting. If I am spinning and have not begun to recover as the ground nears, the seat is waiting. It is an advantage that conventional aircraft and transport pilots do not have, and I feel a little sorry for them at their dangerous job.

Even without passengers to think about, if they are hit in the air by another airplane, transport pilots do not have a chance to crawl back to the trapdoor on the floor of the flight deck and bail out. They can only sit in their seats and fight the useless controls of a wing that is not there and spin down until their airplane stops against the ground.

But not the single-engine pilot. Climbing or diving or inverted or spinning or coming to pieces, his airplane is rarely the place that he dies. There is a narrow margin near the ground where even the ejection seat is a game of chance, and I am in that margin for five seconds after the end of the runway has passed beneath me. After that five seconds I have accelerated to a speed that allows a climb to a safe ejection altitude; before that five seconds I can put my airplane back down on the runway and engage the nylon webbing and steel cable of the overrun barrier. When I engage that barrier, even at 150 knots, I drag a steel cable and the cable drags a long length of anchor chain and no airplane in the world can run on forever with tons of massive chain trailing behind it. The five seconds are the critical ones. Even before I retract the flaps after takeoff, I can eject if the engine explodes. And no engine explodes without warning.

Flying is safe, and flying a single-engine fighter plane is the safest of all flying. I would much rather fly from one place to another than drive it in that incredibly dangerous thing called an automobile. When I fly I depend upon my own skill, not subject to the variables of other drivers or blown tires at high speed or railroad crossing signs that are out of order at the wrong moments. After I learn my airplane, it is, with its emergency procedures and the waiting ejection seat, many times more safe than driving a car.

Four minutes to Wiesbaden. Smooth cross-check. Smooth air. I relax and drift with the smoothness across the river of time.

When I was a boy I lived in a town that would last from now to now as I fly at 500 knots. I rode a bicycle, went to school, worked at odd jobs, spent a few hours at the airport watching the airplanes come and go. Fly one myself? Never. Too hard for me. Too complicated.

But the day came that I had behind me the typical history of a typical aviation cadet. I did not make straight A's in my first college year and I thought that campus life was not the best road to education. For a reason that I still do not know, I walked into a recruiting office and told the man behind the desk that I wanted to be an Air Force pilot. I did not know just what it was to be an Air Force pilot, but it had something to do with excitement and adventure, and I would have begun Life.

To my surprise, I passed the tests. I matched the little airplanes in the drawings to the ones in the photographs. I identified which terrain was actually shown in Map Two. I wrote that Gear K will rotate counterclockwise if Lever A is pushed forward. The doctors poked at me, discovered that I was breathing constantly, and all of a sudden I was offered the chance to become a United States Air Force Aviation Cadet. I took the chance.

I raised my right hand and discovered that my name was New

Aviation Cadet Bach, Richard D.; A-D One Nine Five Six Three Three One Two. Sir.

For three months I got nothing but a life on the ground. I learned about marching and running and how to fire the 45-caliber pistol. Every once in a while I saw an airplane fly over my training base.

The other cadets came from a strangely similar background. Most of them had never been in an airplane, most of them had tried some form of higher education and did not succeed at it. They decided on Excitement and Adventure. They sweated in the Texas sun with me and they memorized the General Orders and Washington's Address and the Aviation Cadet Honor Code. They were young enough to take the life without writing exposés or telling the squadron commander that they had had enough of this heavy-handed treatment from the upper class. In time we became the upper class and put a stripe or two on our shoulder boards and learned about being heavy-handed with the lower class. If they can't take a little chewing out or a few minutes of silly games, they'll never make good pilots.

LOOK HERE MISTER DO YOU THINK THIS JOKE'S A PROGRAM? ARE YOU SMILING, MISTER? ARE YOU SHOWING EMOTION? MAINTAIN EYE-TO-EYE CONTACT WITH ME, MISTER! DON'T YOU HAVE ANY CONTROL OVER YOURSELF? GOD HELP THE UNITED STATES OF AMERICA IF YOU EVER BECOME AN AIR FORCE PILOT!

And then, suddenly, Preflight Training was over and we were on our way to become the lower class at a base where we began to learn about airplanes, and where we first breathed the aluminum-rubber-paint-oil-parachute air of an airplane cockpit and where we began to get a tiny secret idea, shared in secret by every other cadet in the class, that an airplane is actually a living thing, that loves to fly.

I took the academics and I loved the flying and I bore the military inspections and the parades for six months. Then I left Primary Flight School to become part of the lower class in Basic Flight School, where I was introduced to the world of turbine and speed and spent my first day in Basic Single-Engine Flight School.

Everything is new fresh exciting imminent tangible. A sign: *Cadet Club*; rows of tar-papered barracks; close-cut brown grass; weedless sidewalks; hot sun; bright sun; blue sky, ceilingless and free above my polished hatbill and stripeless shoulder boards. A strange face above white-banded boards and a set of white gloves. "Fall in, gentlemen."

A flight of four sun-burnished silver jet training planes whistle over the base. Jets. "Let's expedite, gentlemen, fall in."

In we fall. "Welcome back to the Air Force, gentlemen, this is Basic." A pause. Distant crackle of full throttle and takeoff. "You tigers will get your stripes here. It's not a lot of fun or a no-sweat program. If you can't hack it, you're out. So you were Cadet Group Commander in Primary; you let up, you slack the books, you're out. Stay sharp and you'll make it. LAIUFF, HAICE! Ho-ward, HAR!"

The B-4 bag is heavy in the right hand. Dust on shined shoes. Hot air doesn't cool as I move through it. Black rubber heels on dusty asphalt. Away, a lone jet trainer heads for the runway. Solo. I am a long way from Primary Flight School. A long way from the chug of a T-28's butter-paddle propeller. And a long way still from the silver wings above the left breast pocket. Where are the hills? Where is the green? The cool air? In Primary Flight School. This is Texas. This is Basic.

"... program will require hard work ..." says the wing commander.

"... and you'd best stay sharp in my squadron ..." says the squadron commander.

"This is your barracks," says the whitegloves. "There are T-33 pilot's handbooks in every room. Learn the emergency procedures. All of them. You will be asked. Another whitegloves will be around later to answer questions."

Questions.

"Inspections every Saturday?"

"Are the classes tough?"

"What is the airplane like?"

"When do we fly?"

A cold night in a white-collar bed. Cold twinkle of familiar stars through the window. Talk in the dark barracks.

"Just think, boy, jets at last!"

"So it's tough. They'll have to throw me out. I'll never quit because it's hard."

"... airspeed down final with the gun bay doors open is one twenty plus fuel plus ten, right?"

"Let's see, Johnny, is that 'climb to twenty-five thousand and rock wings'? Twenty-five thousand feet! Man, we're flying JETS!"

"Never thought I'd make it to Basic. We've come a long way from Preflight . . ."

Behind the quiet talk is the roar of night-flying turbines as the upper class learns, and the flash of landing lights bright for an instant on the wall opposite my open window.

Tenuous sleep. Upper-class voices by the window as they return in the night. "I never saw that before! He only had ninety-five percent and his tailpipe was bright red . . . really red!"

". . . so then Mobile told me to climb in Sector One to thirty thousand feet. I couldn't even find the field, let alone Sector One . . ."

My glowing Air Force watch says 0300. Strange dreams. The beautiful blonde looks up at me. She asks a question. "What's your airspeed turning base leg with three hundred and fifty gallons of fuel on board?" A crowded and fantastically complex instrument panel, with a huge altimeter pointing to 30,000. Helmets with visors, red-topped ejection seats, instruments, instruments.

Sleep soaks away into the pillow and the night is still and dark. What do I do with a zero loadmeter reading? Battery *off* . . . no . . . battery on . . . no-no . . . "activate electrical device" . . . Outside, the green beam and the split white beam of the beacon on the control tower go round and round and round.

But once again the days pass and I learn. I am concerned with ground schools and lectures; with first flights in the T-33; and after ten hours aloft with an instructor in the back seat, with flying it alone. Then with instruments and precise control of an airplane in any weather. With formation. With navigation.

It would all be a great deal of fun if I knew for certain that I would successfully finish Basic Training and wear at last the silver wings. But when instrument flying is new, it is difficult, and my class that numbered 112 in Preflight is now cut to 63. None has been killed in airplane crashes, none has bailed out or ejected from an airplane. For one reason or another, for academic or military or flying deficiencies, or sometimes just because he has had enough of the tightly controlled routine, a cadet will pack his B-4 bag one evening and disappear into the giant that is the Air Force.

I had expected some not to finish the program, but I had expected them to fail in a violent sheet of flame or in a bright spinning cloud of fragments of a midair collision.

There are near-misses. I am flying as Lead in a four-ship flight of T-33's. With 375 knots and a clear sky overhead, I press the control stick back to begin a loop. Our airplanes are just passing the vertical, noses high in the blue sky, when a sudden flash of blurred silver streaks across our path, and is gone. I finish the loop, wingmen faithfully watching only my airplane and working hard to stay in their positions, and twist in my seat to see the airplane that nearly took all four of us out of the sky. But it is gone as surely and as completely as if it had never been. There had not been time for reaction or fear or where did he come from. There had simply been a silver flash ahead of me in the sky. I think about it for a moment and begin another loop.

A few weeks later it happened to a lower-class cadet, practicing acrobatics alone at 20,000 feet. "I was on top of a Cuban Eight, just starting down, when I felt a little thud. When I rolled out, I saw that my right tiptank was gone and that the end of the wing was pretty well shredded. I thought I'd better come back home."

He didn't even see the flash of the airplane that hit him. After he had landed and told what had happened, the base settled down to wait for the other airplane. In a little more than an hour, one airplane of all the airplanes on mobile control's list of takeoffs failed to have an hour written in the column marked "Return." Search airplanes went up arrowing through the dust like swift efficient robots seeking a fallen member of the clan. The darkness fell, and the robots found nothing.

The base was quiet and held its breath. Cadet dining halls were still, during the evening meal. Not everyone is home tonight. Pass the salt please, Johnny. The clink of stamped steel forks on mass-fired pottery. I hear it was an upperclassman in the other squadron. Muted clinks, voices low. Across the room, a smile. He should be calling in any minute now. Anybody want some more milk? You can't kill an upperclassman.

The next day, around the square olive-drab briefing tables in the flight shack, we got the official word. You can kill an upperclassman. Let's look around, gentlemen; remember that there are sixty airplanes from this base alone in the sky during the day. You're not bomber pilots here, keep that head on a swivel and never stop looking around.

And we briefed and flew our next mission.

Then, suddenly, we had made it. A long early morning, a crisp formation of the lower class in review as we stand at parade rest, a sixteen-ship flyby, a speech by a general and by the base commander.

They return my salute, shake my hand, present me a cold set of small wings that flash a tiny beam of silver. I made it all the way through. Alive. Then there are orders to advanced flying training and the glory-soaked number that goes F-84F. I am a pilot. A rated Air Force pilot. A fighter pilot.

The German night is full around me, and in my soft earphones is solid hard static from the blue fire that sluices across the windscreen and across the low-frequency antenna in the belly of my airplane. The slim needle of the radio compass is becoming more and more excited, jerking to the right, always to the right of course; trembling for a second there, swinging back toward Spangdahlem behind me, jerking again toward my right wingtip. I am glad again for the TACAN.

The air is still and smooth as velvet glass, but I tighten again my safety belt and shoulder harness and turn up the cockpit lights. Bright light, they like to say in the ground schools, destroys night vision. Tonight it does not make any difference, for there is nothing to see outside the Plexiglas, and the bright light makes it easier to read the instruments. And in the brightness I will not be blinded by lightning. I am strapped in, my gloves are on, my helmet chinstrap is fastened, my flight jacket is zipped, my boots are firm and comfortable. I am ready for whatever the weather has to offer me. For a moment I feel as if I should push the gun switch to *guns,* but it is an irrational fleeting thought. I check again the defroster on, pitot heat on, engine screens retracted. Come and get me, storm. But the air is still and smooth; I have minute after minute of valuable weather time ticking away, adding to the requirement for an advanced instrument rating.

I am foolish. Here I am as nervous as a cat, thinking of a storm that has probably already died away off-course. And above 30,000 feet even the worst storms are not so violent as they are at lower altitudes. As I remember, it is rare to find much hail at high altitudes in storms, and lightning has never been shown to be the direct cause of any airplane crash. These elaborate precautions are going to look childish after I land in half an hour at Chaumont and walk up the creaky wooden stairway to my room and take off my boots and finish my letter home. In two hours I will be sound asleep.

Still, it will be good to get this flight over with. I would never make a good all-weather interceptor pilot. Perhaps with training I could become accustomed to hours and hours of weather and storms, but at this moment I am quite happy with my fighter-bomber and the job of shooting at things that I can see.

I have heard that interceptor pilots are not even allowed to roll their airplanes: hard on the electronic gear. What a dismal way to make a living, straight and level and solid instruments all the time. Poor guys.

I might, just a little, envy the F-106 pilot his big delta-wing interceptor. And he might, just a little, envy me my mission. He has the latest airplane and an engine filled with sheer speed. His great grey delta would make a good air combat plane, but he flies day on day of hooded attacks toward dots of smoky green light on his radar screen. My '84F is older and slower and soon to be changed from sculptured aluminum to a seamless swept memory, but my mission is one of the best missions that a fighter pilot can fly.

FAC, for instance. Pronounced *fack*. Forward Air Controller. The blast of low-level and gunsight on the truck columns of the Aggressor. FAC. "Checkmate, Bipod Delta here. I've got a bunch of troops and two tanks coming toward my position. They're on the high ground just south of the castle on the dirt road. You got 'em in sight?"

The greening hills of Germany below me, the chessboard in

another war game. What a job for a fighter pilot, to be a FAC. Stuck out with the Army in the mud with a jeep and a radio transmitter, watching your friends come in on the strikes. "Roj, Delta. Got the castle and the road in sight, not the target." A sprinkling of dots in the grass by the road. "As you were, got 'em in sight. Take your spacing, Two."

"What's your armament, Checkmate?"

"Simulated napalm and guns. First pass will be the napalm."

"Hurry up, will you? The tanks are pouring on the coal; must have seen you."

"Roj."

I melt into stick and throttle, my airplane leaps ahead and hurls itself in a sweeping burst of speed at the road. There are the tanks, feathers of dust and grass spraying long behind their tracks. But it is as if they were caught in cooling wax; I move fifteen times faster than they. Take it down to the deck, attacking from behind the tank. In its wax, it begins to turn, grass spewing from beneath its right track. I bank my wings, ever so slightly, and feel confident, omnipotent, as an eagle plunging from height to mouse. Men are riding on the tank, clutching handholds. They do not hear me, but they see me, looking back over their camouflaged shoulders. And I see them. What a way to make a living, clinging with all your strength to the back of a 50-ton block of steel hurtling across a meadow. In the time it takes me to count three, the tank, frozen in its turn, frames itself for a moment in my windscreen, and the lowest diamond of my gunsight flicks through it and my thumb has released the imaginary tanks of jellied gasoline from beneath the wings. Wouldn't be a tank driver in wartime for all the money in the world. Pull up. Hard turn right. Look back. The tank is rolling to a stop, obedient to the rules of our game. Two is snapping his black swept shadow over the hatch of the second tank. Tanks make such easy targets. I guess they just hope that they won't get caught in an air strike. "Nice job, Checkmate. Work over the troops, will you?" A friendly request, from a man who is seeing from the ground the sight that so often has been caught in his forward windscreen. In the war we would worry now about small-arms fire and shoulder-mounted antiaircraft missiles, but we would already have decided that when our time comes, it will come, and the worry would be a transient one. Down on the troops. Most unwarlike troops, these. Knowing the game, and not often having the chance for their own private and special air show, they stand and watch us come in. One raises his arms in a defiant V. I bank again, very slightly, to hurtle directly toward him. He and I have a little personal clash of wills. Low. I climb up the slope of the long meadow toward my antagonist. If there are telephone wires across the meadow, I will have plenty of clearance going beneath them. In war, my antagonist would be caught in the hail of Armor Piercing Incendiary from six Browning 50-caliber machine guns. But though this is not real war, it is a real challenge he throws to me. I dare you to make me duck. We are all such little boys at heart. I make one last tiny adjustment so that my drop tanks will pass on either side of his outflung hands if he does not duck. I see the arms begin to falter as he flicks from sight beneath the nose. If he hasn't ducked, he is due for a flattening burst of jetblast. But he does have determination, this man. Usually we scatter the troops like flocks of chicks around the hilltops. I turn on another pass from another direction, looking, from sudden height of my pull-up, for my friend. One dot looks like another.

Another pass, carried perhaps a little too low, for my friend dives for the ground even before I pass over him. That is really very profound. One dot looks like another. You can't tell good from evil when you move five hundred feet per second above the grass. You can only tell that the dots are men.

On one FAC mission near the hem of the iron curtain we were asked to fly east for two minutes in order to find our Controller. Two minutes east would have put us over the border and into Soviet airspace. Enemy airspace. The Controller had meant to say "west." The hills did not look any different on the Other Side. As we circled and turned west I had looked across into the forbidden land. I saw no fences, no iron curtains, no strange coloring of the earth. Only the green rolling of the constant hills, a scattering of little grey villages. Without my compass and map, with the East-West border heavily penciled in red, I would have thought that the villages of men that I saw in the east were just as the villages of the west. Fortunately, I had the map.

"How about a high-speed run for the troops, Checkmate?"

"Sure thing," I say, smiling. For the troops. If I were a fighter pilot marooned on the ground with the olive-drab Army, nothing would ease my solitude quite so much as the 500-knot rapport with my friends and their airplanes. So, a pass for the troops. "Open her up, Checkmate." And throttle full open, engine drinking fuel at seven thousand pounds per hour. Across the meadow, faster than an arrow from a hundred-pound bow, heading this time for the cluster of dots by the radio-jeep of the FAC. Five hundred and ten knots and I am joy. They love my airplane. See her beauty. See her speed. And I, too, love my airplane. A whiplash and the FAC and his jeep are gone. Pull up, far up, nose high in the milk-blue sky. And we roll. Earth and sky joyously twined in a blur of dwindling emerald and turquoise. Stop the roll swiftly, upside down, bring the nose again through the horizon, roll back to straight and level. The sky is a place for living and for whistling and for singing and for dying. It is a place that is built to give people a place from which to look down on all the others. It is always fresh and awake and clear and cold, for when the cloud covers the sky or fills the place where the sky should be, the sky is gone. The sky is a place where the air is ice and you breathe it and you live it and you wish that you could float and dream and race and play all the days of your life. The sky is there for everyone, yet only a few seek it out. It is all color, all heat and cold, all oxygen and forest leaves and sweet air and salt air and fresh crystal air that has never been breathed before. The sky whirs around you, keening and hissing over your head and face and it gets in your eyes and numbs your ears in a coldness that is bright and sharp. You can drink it and chew it and swallow it. You can rip your fingers through the rush of sky and the hard wind. It is your very life inside you and over your head and beneath your feet. You shout a song and the sky sweeps it away, twisting it and tumbling it through the hard liquid air. You can climb to the top of it, fall with it twisting and rushing around you, leap clear, arms wide, catching the air with your teeth. It holds the stars at night as strongly as it holds the brazen sun in the day. You shout a laugh of joy, and the rush of wind is there to carry the laugh a thousand miles.

In my climbing roll away from the FAC, I love everyone. Which, however, will not prevent me from killing them. If that day comes.

"Very nice show, Checkmate."

"Why, feel free to call on us at any time, Bravo." So this is joy. Joy fills the whole body, doesn't it? Even my toes are joyful. For this the Air Force finds it necessary to pay me. No. They do not pay me for the hours that I fly. They pay me for the hours that I do not fly; those hours chained to the ground are the ones in which pilots earn their pay.

I and the few thousand other single-engine pilots live in a system that has been called a close fraternity. I have heard more than once the phrase "arrogant fighter pilots." Oddly enough as generalizations go, they are both well-chosen phrases.

A multiengine bomber pilot or a transport pilot or a navigator or a nonflying Air Force officer is still, basically, a human being. But it is a realization that I must strive to achieve, and in practice, unless it is necessary, I do not talk to them. There have been a few multiengine pilots stationed at bases where I have been in the past. They are happy to fly big lumbering airplanes and live in a world of low altitudes and long flights and coffee and sandwiches on the flight deck. It is just this contentment with the droning adventureless existence that sets them apart from single-engine pilots.

I belong to a group of men who fly alone. There is only one seat in the cockpit of a fighter airplane; there is no space allotted for another pilot to tune the radios in the weather or make the calls to air traffic control centers or to help with the emergency procedures or to call off the airspeed down final approach. There is no one else to break the solitude of a long cross-country flight. There is no one else to make decisions. I do everything myself, from engine start to engine shutdown. In a war, I will face alone the missiles and the flak and the small-arms fire over the frontlines. If I die, I will die alone.

Because of this, and because this is the only way that I would have it, I do not choose to spend my time with the multiengine pilots who live behind the lines of adventure. It is an arrogant attitude and unfair. The difference between one pilot in the cockpit and many on the flight deck should not be enough to cause them never to associate. But there is an impassable barrier between me and the man who prefers the life of low and slow.

I ventured, once, to break the barrier. I talked one evening to a pilot in a Guard squadron that had been forced to trade its F-86H's for four-engine transports. If there ever was a common bond between single- and multiengine flying, I could see it through the eyes of this man. "How do you like multi after the Sabre?" I had asked, lights dancing on the pool beside the officers' club.

I had picked the wrong pilot. He was new in the squadron, a transfer.

"I've never flown an 'eighty-six and I have no desire to fly one," he said.

The word *eighty-six* sounded strange and foreign in his mouth, words not often said. I discovered that there had been a complete turnover of pilots in that squadron when its airplane changed from fighter-interceptor to heavy transport, and that my partner in conversation had a multiengine mind. The silver wings above his pocket were cast in the same mold that mine had been, but he lived in another world, behind a wall that has no gate. It has been months since that evening, and I have not since bothered to speak with a multiengine pilot.

Every so often a single-engine pilot is caught in a web of circumstance that transfers him from a fighter squadron into the ranks of multiengine pilots, that forces him to learn about torque pressure and overhead switch panels and propeller feathering procedures. I have known three of these. They fought furiously against the change, to no avail. For a short while they flew multiengine airplanes with their single-engine minds, but in less than a year all three had been released from active Air Force duty at their own request.

The program that switched fighter pilots into transports had once been quite active, affecting hundreds of single-engine pilots. Shortly after, perhaps by coincidence, I had read an article that deplored the loss of young Air Force pilots to civilian life. I would gladly have bet that some interesting statistics awaited the man who first probed the retention rate of fighter pilots forced to fly multiengine aircraft. The code of the Air Force is that any officer should be able to adapt to any position assigned him, but the code does not recognize the tremendous chasm between the background and attitude of single- and multiengine pilots.

The solitude that each fighter pilot knows when he is alone with his airplane is the quality that shows him that his airplane is actually a thing of life. Life exists in multiengine airplanes, too, but it is more difficult to find through the talk of crew on interphone and how are the passengers taking the rough air and crew chief can you pass me up a flight lunch. It is sacrilege to eat while you fly an airplane.

Solitude is that key that says that life is not confined to things that grow from the earth. The interdependence of pilot and airplane in flight shows that each cannot exist without the other, that we truly depend upon each other for our very existence. And we are confident in each other. One fighter squadron motto sums up the attitude of fighter pilots everywhere: *We can beat any man in any land in any game that he can name for any amount that he can count.*

In contrast, I read on the wall of Base Operations at a multiengine base: *The difficult we approach with caution. The impossible we do not attempt.* I could not believe it. I thought that it must have been someone's idea of a joke for the day. But the sign was neatly lettered and a little grey, as if it had been there for a long while. It was joy to spin the dust of that runway from my wheels and to be out again in a sky designed for fighter pilots.

It is from pride that my arrogance comes. I have a history of sacrifice and of triumph and of pride. As the pilot of my Thunderstreak, in charge of an airplane built to rocket and bomb and strafe the enemy on the ground, my history goes back to the men who flew the P-47's, the Thunderbolts of the Second World War. The same hills that are buried beneath me tonight remember the stocky, square-cut Jug of twenty years ago, and the concrete silos that were flak towers still bear the bulletholes of its low-level attack and its eight 50-caliber machine guns.

After the Jug pilots of Europe came the Hog pilots of Korea to face the rising curtain of steel from the ground. They flew another Republic airplane: the straight-wing F-84G Thunderjet, and they played daily games of chance with the flak and the rifle bullets and the cables across the valleys and the MiGs that crept past the '86's on the patrol. There are not a great many '84G pilots of Korea who lived through their games, as, if a war breaks out in Europe tomorrow, there will not be a great many '84F pilots surviving.

After me and my Superhog are the F-100D Super Sabre pilots that have waited out the years of cold war on alert all around the world. And after them, the men who fly the Ultimate Hog, the F-105D Thunderchief, who can attack targets on the ground, through weather, by radar alone.

My airplane and I are part of a long chain from the mist of the past to the mist of the future. We are even now obsolete; but if a war should begin on the imminent tomorrow, we will be, at least, bravely obsolete.

We fill the squares of our training board with black X's in grease pencil on the acetate overlay; X's in columns headed "Low-level navigation without radio aids" and "Combat profile" and "Max-load take-off." Yet we are certain that we will not all survive the next war.

Coldly, factually, it is stated that we are not only flying against the small arms and the cables and the flak, but against the new mechanics in the nose of a ground-to-air missile as well. I have often thought, after watching the movies of our ground-to-air missiles in action, that I am glad I am not a Russian fighter-bomber pilot. I wonder if there is also a Russian pilot, after seeing his own movies, with thanks in his heart that he is not an American fighter-bomber pilot.

We talk about the missiles every once in a while, discussing the fact of their existence and the various methods of dodging them. But dodging is predicated on knowing that they are chasing, and during a strike we will be concentrating on the target, not on worrying about the fire or the flak or the missiles thrown up against us. We will combine our defense with our offense, and we will hope.

Speaking factually, we remind ourselves that our airplanes can still put almost as much ordnance on the target as any other fighter available. It does it without the finesse of the F-105's radar, we say, but the fire eventually reaches the target. Our words are for the most part true, but there is a long mental battle to submerge the also-true words that our airplane is old, and was designed to fight in another era of warfare. We fly with a bravely buried sense of inferiority. As Americans, we should fly modern American airplanes. There is no older or slower ground support airplane in any NATO Air Force than ours.

The French fly F-84F's, but they are transitioning now into Mirages and Vautours built for modern sky. The Luftwaffe is flying F-84F's, but they are well into the task of converting to Maltese-crossed F-104G's. The Canadians are flying Mark VI Sabres, contemporary with the '84F, and they are changing now to their own CF-104G.

We fly our '84F's and the never-ending rumors of airplanes to come. We will get F-100D's soon. We will get F-104's soon. We will get the Navy's F4H's soon. We will be in F-105's before the year is up.

There is, somewhere, a later airplane scheduled and waiting for us. But it has not yet shown its face and we do not talk about our shortcomings. We make do with what we have, as the P-39 pilots and the P-40 pilots did at the beginning of the Second War.

The pilots in my squadron today are as varied a group of men as could be netted at a random stroke into the waters of civilian life. There is a young second lieutenant, a housewares salesman, just accumulating the first fine scratches on his golden bars. There is a major who flew Mustangs and Jugs on long-ago fighter sweeps into Germany. There is a lawyer, practice established; a computer engineer; three airline pilots; two bachelors whose only income came from Guard flying. There are the successful and the unsuccessful. The unruffled and the volatile. The readers of books and the seekers of adventure.

If you looked closely you would find constants that many share: most are within five years of thirty, most are family men, most have served their years of active duty with the regular Air Force. But one constant, without exception, they are all men of action. The most introspective pilot in the squadron leaves his book, carefully marked, in his BOQ room, and straps himself each day to twenty-five thousand pounds of fighter airplane. He leads a flight of four airplanes through patterns of bombing and strafing and rocket firing and nuclear weapon delivery. He makes wing takeoffs into 500-foot weather ceilings and doesn't see the ground again until he breaks out of the ragged cloud and freezing rain two hours and nine hundred miles from his takeoff runway. He alternates his letters to his family with an occasional review of airborne emergency procedures, and, occasionally, puts them to use when a red warning light flares in his cockpit, or his nosewheel fails to extend when it is time to land. There are those who speak loudly, and perhaps with too little humility, but those same back their words with action every time they step into an airplane. There are nights in the officers' club when whiskey glasses splinter against the rough stone walls, there are colored smoke bombs thrown into the closed rooms of sleeping comrades, there is a song, not altogether complimentary, sung of the wing commander.

But you can count on the coming of the dawn, and with it the concussion of engine start in the cold wind. Take First Lieutenant Roger Smith, for instance, who last night deftly introduced four lighted firecrackers into the wing matériel officer's room. Grounds, really, for court-martial. But in the confusion he was not identified, and this morning he flies number Two in a ground support mission against the Aggressor Force at Hohenfels. You cannot tell him, under oxygen mask and lowered visor, from Captain Jim Davidson, flight leader, calling now for radar vector to the target area. Davidson spent the night writing to his wife, and telling her, among other things, that he did not have any real reason to believe that the squadron would be released from active duty before the assigned year of duty was finished. In close formation the two swept fighters drop from altitude, indicating the same 450 knots on identical airspeed indicators. "Tank column at ten o'clock low," Davidson calls. And they turn together to the attack.

Men of action, and every day, new action. In the gloved right hand, the possibility of life and death.

The loud slurred drawl harassing the multiengine pilot at the bar belongs to a man named Roudabush, who, a year ago, against all regulations, landed a flamed-out fighter at night, without electrical power and therefore without lights, at an airport in Virginia. He refused to bail out of his airplane or even to jettison his external fuel tanks over the city of Norfolk, and was reprimanded.

"You tell yourself that you'll bail out if the thing quits at night," he said once, "but when you look down and see all the lights of the city . . . kinda changes your mind." A man like that, you don't care how he talks. You fly with him, and it makes you proud.

Johnny Blair, leaning against the mahogany bartop swirling the ice cubes in his glass and smiling faintly at Roudabush's banter, has a little scar on his jaw. Shortly past noon on one day in his life he was beginning a LABS run, 500 knots toward the target, a hundred feet in the air, when he heard a thud and the overheat and fire warning lights came on. He pulled up, heard another thud, and the cockpit filled with smoke. Without a word to his wingman, he shut down his engine, jettisoned the canopy, and squeezed the trigger on the right handgrip. For a few seconds in the afternoon he fought to release himself from the tumbling steel seat, eight hundred feet over a forest of pine. The automatic parachute release failed. That inward person immediately pulled the manual parachute release, with the world spinning green and blue about him. He swung one time in the harness before he dragged through the treetops and was slammed to the ground. He lost his helmet and mask in the bailout, and an anonymous tree branch slashed his jaw. Then it was over, the inner man subsiding, the outward man spreading the parachute canopy as a signal to the helicopters, suffering slightly from shock, and telling the story very plainly and undramatically to whoever could benefit from it. Otherwise he does not talk of it, and except for the scar, he is the sort of person who would lead you to say, "Now there is a typical high-school geometry teacher." Which, of course, is exactly what he is.

It takes a while to learn to know many of these men as friends, for many of them, in the fear of being thought braggart or self-styled superman, do not tell of narrow escapes and brushes with disaster to anyone who inquires. Gradually, with much time, the newcomer to the squadron discovers that Blair had an interesting low-altitude bailout, that Roudabush "coulda kissed that bitch" when his airplane stretched its glide, in the dark, to the Virginia runway; that Travas ran into an air-to-air target in the days when they were made of plastic rag and steel bars, and dragged seventy pounds of steel and thirty feet of polyethylene home, embedded in his wing.

And the squadron learns, gradually, that the newcomer has had his own share of experience in the world above the ground. A squadron is a swirling multicolored pool of experience, from which is painted the freewheeling sweep of life in the air, in individual brushstrokes. The brilliant shimmering brass of combat in the sun burns itself into the pilots in their cockpit; dark sky and dark sea soak their enormous blue into the man who guides his airplane between them; and, once in a very long while, the scarlet of a fireball against a mountainside glares to outshine all the other hues, in time breaking to tiny sharp sparkles of pain that never quite disappear.

I reach to my right in the red darkness and turn the volume of the radio compass as low as it will go. It reports now only fragments of the Spangdahlem call sign behind me, and has become more of a thunderstorm indicator than a navigation radio. This is not bad, with the TACAN working well, and I am glad to have a thunderstorm indicator that is so reliable. There is a dim flash in the grey to my right, a momentary suggestion of light that is instantly gone again.

Tuning down the radio compass was a short break, and the routine of the cross-check continues. Straight and level. Attitude and airspeed. Needle and ball. No swerving from the target. As if I had a Shape under my wing.

There are Shapes and there are Bugs and there are Blue Boys, all names for the form that houses a few million tightly controlled neutrons that make an atomic bomb. Or more properly, a Nuclear Device. It is always called a Device.

The first mission of many squadrons of tactical fighters is now a strategic one, and the numbers of many fighter wings are followed by the ominous letters *SD*.

SD stands for Special Delivery, and means that pilots spend hours studying targets of remote corners of the world and learning selected bits of nuclear physics and building their language to include LABS and Shape and Nuke and the meaning of the T-Zero light. They fly a strange new bombing pattern in their practice, they fly it alone, and only the first bomb counts for score. A pilot away from a fighter cockpit since Korea would not recognize a full panel of switches and lights for the nuclear weapons delivery system. But it is an important panel, today.

Part of my job is to know how to deliver a Shape, and I practice it dutifully. The placing of Device on Target begins with a swirl of charts and dividers and angles and measurements. From that emerge a few highly classified figures that are given for the nourishment of a pair of computers mounted in my airplane.

Normally, the missions are flown with only a small 25-pound practice bomb to record the effectiveness of the delivery, but once a year I am required to fly with a full-size, full-weight Shape under my left wing. This is to remind me that when I carry a real atomic bomb, I will have to hold a bit of right stick-pressure to keep the wings level on takeoff.

A practice Shape is smooth and streamlined and not unpretty. The real Device, which looks exactly the same, is the ugliest mass of metal that I have ever seen. Blunt-nosed, olive-drab and heavy, it is like a greedy deformed remora attached to the smooth swept wing of my airplane.

With every other pilot in the squadron, I joined the Air National Guard because I like to fly airplanes. With strafing and rocketing and conventional bombing, of course, our mission passes the realm of mere airplane-flying and becomes one of destroying enemy machines and enemy troops. But the mounting of a Device on the airplane is, as far as the pilots are concerned, one step too many. I do not like it at all, yet the Shape is a part of my mission, and I learn to toss it and hit a target.

Hold the right stick-pressure, and gear up and flaps up and low-level to the target. The trees flick by below, the sky is the same French sky that I have flown for months, the cockpit is the same about me, and I cannot see the Device under my wing. But the lights on its control box glimmer dully in front of me, and I am acutely aware of its nearness. I feel as if I am standing near a lightly chained gorilla as it awakens. I do not care for gorillas.

The lights tell me that the Device is awakening, and I respond by pushing up the proper switches at the proper moments. The Initial Point rushes in at me from the horizon, and I push my distaste for the monster to the back of my mind as I set another panel of switches in the last combination of steps that lead to its release. One hundred percent rpm.

The last red-roofed village flashes below me, and the target, a pyramid of white barrels, is just visible at the end of its run-in line. Five hundred knots. Switch down, button pressed. Timers begin their timing, circuits are alerted for the drop. Inch down to treetop altitude. I do not often fly at 500 knots on the deck, and it is apparent that I am moving quickly. The barrels inflate. I see that their white paint is flaking. And the pyramid streaks beneath me. Back on the stick smoothly firmly to read four G's on the accelerometer and center the needles of the indicator that is only used in nuke weapon drops and center them and hold it there and I'll bet those computers are grinding their little hearts out and all I can see is sky in the windscreen hold the G's keep the needles centered there's the sun going beneath me and WHAM.

My airplane rolls hard to the right and tucks more tightly into her loop and strains ahead even though we are upside down. The Shape has released me more than I have released it. The little white barrels are now six thousand feet directly beneath my canopy. I have no way to tell if it was a good drop or not. That was decided back with the charts and graphs and the dividers and the angles. I kept the needles centered, the computers did their task automatically, and the Device is on its way.

Now, while it is still in the air and climbing with the inertia that my airplane has given it, my job becomes one of escape. Hold the throttle at the fire wall, pull the nose down until it is well below the horizon, roll back so that the sun is over my head, and run. If the Shape were packed with neutrons instead of concrete ballast, I would need every moment I could find for my escape, for every moment is another foot away from the sun-blast that would just as easily destroy a friendly F-84F as it would the hostile target. Visor down against the glare-that-would-be, turn the rearview mirror away, crouch down in the seat and fly as fast as possible toward Our Side.

At the same moment, the Device has stopped in the air, at the very apex of its high trajectory. A long plumb line descended would pass through the center of the white pyramid. Then it falls. Subject only to the winds, impossible to halt, the bomb falls. If it were a real Device in a real war, it would be well at this time for the enemy to have his affairs in order. The hate of the enemy has been reflected in the hate of the friend, reflected through me and my airplane and the computers that it carries.

And it is too late. We may declare an armistice, we may suddenly realize that the people under the bomb suspended are truly, deeply, our friends and our brothers. We may suddenly, blindingly see the foolishness of our differences, and the means to their solution. But the Device has begun to fall.

Do I feel sorry? Do I feel a certain sadness? I have felt those from the moment I saw the first practice Shape lifted into position under my wing.

But I love my airplane more than I hate the Device. I am the lens through which the hatred of my country is focused into a bright molten ball over the home of the enemy.

Although it is my duty and my only desire in wartime to serve my country as best I can, I rationalize. We will never really use the Devices. My targets will be completely and solely military ones. Everyone who is consumed in the fire is purely evil and filled with hatred for freedom.

There is a point where even the most ardent rationalization is only a gesture. I hope, simply, that I will never have to throw one of the repellent things at living people.

The distance-measuring drum of the steady TACAN has turned down now to 006 and that is as far as it will go, for I am six miles into the deep night directly above the transmitter of the Wiesbaden TACAN station. I am a minute and a half behind schedule in a wind that came from nowhere. In thirty minutes my wheels will be touching the cold wet runway at Chaumont Air Base.

The thought would have been reassuring, but there are two quick flashes of lightning to the right, across my course.

Once again, ready the report, tilt the stick to the right, fly the instruments, fly the instruments, thumb down on microphone button.

CHAPTER FIVE

"RHEIN CONTROL, Air Force Jet Two Niner Four Zero Five, Wiesbaden." The City That Was Not Bombed.

Silence. Here we go again. "Rhein Control, Rhein Control; Air Force Jet..." I try once. Twice. Three times. There is no answer. I am alone with my instruments, and suddenly aware of my aloneness.

Click around with the radio channel selector under my right glove; perhaps I can talk to Barber Radar. "Barber Radar, Air Force Jet Two Niner Four Zero Five, over." Once. Twice. Three times. Nothing.

A flash in the clouds ahead. The air is still smooth, paving the way. Hold the heading. Hold the altitude.

A decision in my mind. If I were flying this cross-country just to get myself home tonight, I would turn back now. I still have enough fuel to return to the clear air over Wethersfield. With my transmitter out, I cannot ask for a radar vector through the storms ahead. If it were not for the sack above the machine guns, I would turn back. But it is there, and at Chaumont there is a wing commander who is trusting me to complete my mission. I will continue.

I can use the radio compass needle to point out the storms; if worst comes to worst I can dodge them by flying between the flashes. But still it is much more comfortable to be a spot of light on someone's radar screen, listening for sure direction about the white blurs that are the most severe cells of a thunderstorm. One more try, although I am certain now that my UHF radio is completely dead. Click click click to 317.5 megacycles. "Moselle Control, Moselle Control, Jet Zero Five." I have no hope. The feeling is justified, for there is no answer from the many-screened room that is Moselle Radar.

Turn back. Forget the wing commander. You will be killed in the storms.

Fear again, and it is exaggerating, as usual. I will not be killed in any storm. Someone else, perhaps, but not me. I have too much flying experience and I fly too strong an airplane to be killed by the weather.

Flash to the right, small flash to the left. A tiny tongue of turbulence licks at my airplane, making the wings rock slightly. No problem. Forty minutes from now I shall be walking across the ramp through the rain to Squadron Operations, Chaumont Air Base. The TACAN is working well, Phalsbourg is eighty miles ahead.

Friends have been killed. Five years ago, Jason Williams, roommate, when he flew into his strafing target.

I was briefing for an afternoon gunnery training mission, sitting on a chair turned backward with my G suit legs unzipped and dangling their own way to the wooden floor of the flight shack. I was there, and around the table were three other pilots who would soon be changing into airplanes. Across the room was another flight briefing for an air combat mission.

I was taking a sip of hot chocolate from a paper cup when the training squadron commander walked into the room, G suit tossed carelessly over one shoulder.

"Anybody briefing for air-to-ground gunnery?"

I nodded over my cup and pointed to my table.

"I'm going to tell you to take it easy and don't get target fixation and don't fly into the ground." He held a narrow strip of paper in his hand. "Student flew into a target on Range Two this morning. Watch your minimum altitude. Take it easy today, OK?"

I nodded again. "Who was it?"

The squadron commander looked at the paper. "Second Lieutenant Jason Williams."

Like a ton of bricks. Second Lieutenant Jason Williams. Willy. My roommate. Willy of the broad smile and the open mind and the many women. Willy who graduated number four in a class of sixty cadets. Willy the only Negro fighter pilot I had ever known. It is funny. And I smiled and set down my cup.

I was amazed at myself. What is so funny about one of my best friends flying into a target on the desert? I should be sad. Dying is a horrible and terrible thing. I must be sad. I must wince, grit my teeth, say, "Oh, no!"

But I cannot keep from smiling. What is so funny? That is one way to hit the target? The '84 always was reluctant to change direction in a dive? The odds against the only Negro fighter pilot in all the USAF gunnery school at this moment flying into the ground? Willy's dead. Look sad. Look shocked. Look astounded. But I cannot keep from smiling because it is all so very funny.

The briefing is done and I walk outside and strap my airplane around me and push the throttle forward and go out to strafe the rocks and lizards on Range Number Three. Range Number Two is closed.

It happened again, a few months later. "Did you hear about Billy Yardley?" I had not heard from Bill since we graduated from cadets. "He flew into the side of a mountain on a weather approach to Aviano." A ringing in my ears. Billy Yardley is dead. And I smile. Again the wicked unreasoning uncontrollable smile. A smile of pride? "I am a better pilot than Jason Williams and Billy Yardley because I am still alive"? Kenneth Sullivan crashed in a helicopter in Greenland. Sully. A fine man, a quiet man, and he died in a spinning cloud of snow and rotor blades. And I smile.

Somehow I am not mad or insane or warped, for I see it once in a while on the faces of others when they hear the ringing in their ears at the death of a friend. They smile, just a little. They think of a friend that knows now what we have wondered since we were old enough to wonder: What is behind the curtain? What comes after this world? Willy knows it, Bill Yardley knows it, Sully knows it. And I do not. My friends are keeping a secret from me. It is a secret that they know and that they will not tell. It is a game. I will know tonight or tomorrow or next month or next year, but I must not know now. A strange game. A funny game. And I smile.

I can find out in a minute. Any day on the range I can wait two seconds too long in the pullout from the strafing panel. I can deliberately fly at 400 knots into one of the very hard mountains of the French Alps. I can roll the airplane on her back and pull her nose straight down into the ground. The game can be over any time that I want it to be. But there is another game to play that is more interesting, and that is the game of flying airplanes and staying alive. I will one day lose that game and learn the secret of the other; why should I not be patient and play one game at a time? And that is what I do.

We fly our missions every day for weeks that become uneventful months. One day one of us does not come back. Three days ago, a Sunday, I left the pages of manuscript that is this book piled neatly on my desk and left for Squadron Operations to meet a flight briefing time of 1115. The mission before mine on the scheduling board was "Low-level," with aircraft numbers and pilots' names.

391—Slack
541—Ulshafer

Ulshafer came back. Slack didn't.

Before he was driven to Wing Headquarters, Ulshafer told us what he knew. The weather had gone from very good to very bad, quickly. There were hills ahead that stretched into the clouds. The two '84F's decided to break off the mission and return to the clear weather, away from the hills. Slack was in the lead. The weather closed in as they began to turn, and Ulshafer lost sight of his leader in the clouds.

"I've lost you, Don. Meet you on top of the weather."

"Roj."

Ulshafer climbed and Slack began to climb.

The wingman was alone above the clouds, and there was no answer to his radio calls. He came back alone. And he was driven, with the base commander, to Wing Headquarters.

The schedule board changed to:

51-9391—Slack AO 3041248
541—Ulshafer

A map was drawn, with a red square around the place where they had met the weather, southwest of Clermont-Ferrand. The ground elevation there changes from 1,000 feet to a jutting mountain peak at 6,188 feet. They had begun their climb just before the mountain.

We waited in Operations and we looked at our watches. Don Slack has another ten minutes of fuel, we told ourselves. But we thought of the peak, that before we did not even know existed, and of its 6,188 feet of rock. Don Slack is dead. We call for the search-rescue helicopters, we fret that the ceiling is too low for us to fly out and look for his airplane on the mountainside, we think of all the ways that he could still be alive: down at another airport, with radio failure, bailed out into a village that has no telephone, alone with his para- chute in some remote forest. "His fuel is out right now." It doesn't make any difference. We know that Don Slack is dead.

No official word; helicopters still on their way; but the operations sergeant is copying the pertinent information concerning the late Lieutenant Slack's flying time, and the parachute rack next to mine, with its stenciled name, *Slack,* is empty of helmet and parachute and mae west. There is on it only an empty nylon helmet bag, and I look at it for a long time.

I try to remember what I last said to him. I cannot remember. It was something trivial. I think of the times that we would jostle each other as we lifted our bulky flying equipment from the racks at the same time. It got so that one of us would have to flatten himself against a wall locker while the other would lift his gear from the rack.

Don had a family at home, he had just bought a new Renault, waiting now outside the door. But these do not impress me as much as the thought that his helmet and chute and mae west are missing from his rack, and that he is scheduled to fly again this afternoon. What arrogant confidence we have when we apply grease pencil to the scheduling board.

The friend whose parachute has hung so long next to mine has become the first recalled Air National Guard pilot to die in Europe.

A shame, a waste, a pity? The fault of the president? If we had not been recalled to active duty and to Europe, Don Slack would not be twisted against a French mountain peak that stands 6,188 feet high. Mrs. Slack could blame the president.

But if Don was not here with his airplane, and all the rest of the Guard with him, there might well have been many more dead Americans in Europe today. Don died in the defense of his country as surely as did the first of the Minutemen, in 1776. And we all, knowingly, play the game.

Tonight I am making a move in that game, moving my token five squares from Wethersfield to Chaumont. I still do not expect to fly into a thunderstorm, for they are isolated ahead, but there is always one section of my mind that is devoted to caution, that considers the events that could cost me the game. That part of my mind has a throttle in it as controllable as the hard black throttle under my left glove. I can pull the caution almost completely back to *off* during air combat and ground support missions. There, it is the mission over all. The horizon can twist and writhe and disappear, the hills of France can flick beneath my molded Plexiglas canopy, can move around my airplane as though they were fixed on a spinning sphere about me. There is but one thing fixed in war and practice for war: the target. Caution plays little part. Caution is thrown to the 400-knot wind over my wings and the game is to stop the other airplane, and to burn the convoy.

When the throttle that controls caution is at its normal position, it is a computer weighing risk against result. I do not normally fly under bridges; the risk is not worth the result. Yet low-level navigation missions, at altitudes of fifty feet, do not offend my sense of caution, for the risk of scratching an airplane is worth the result of training, of learning and gaining experience from navigating at altitudes where I cannot see more than two miles ahead.

Every flight is weighed in the balance. If the risk involved outweighs the result to be gained, I am nervous and on edge. This is not an absolute thing that says one flight is Dangerous and another is Safe, it is completely a mental condition. When I am convinced that the balance is in favor of the result, I am not afraid, no matter the mission. Carried to extremes, a perfectly normal flight involving takeoff, circling the air base, and landing is dangerous, if I am not authorized to fly one of the government's airplanes that day.

The airplane that I fly has no key or secret combination for starting; I merely ask the crew chief to plug in an auxiliary power unit and I climb into the cockpit and I start the engine. When the power unit is disconnected and I taxi to the runway, there is no one in the world who can stop me if I am determined to fly, and once I am aloft I am the total master of the path of my airplane. If I desire, I can fly at a twenty-foot altitude up the Champs-Élysées; there is no way that anyone can stop me. The rules, the regulations, the warnings of dire punishment if I am caught buzzing towns means nothing if I am determined to buzz towns. The only control that others can force upon me is after I have landed, after I am separated from my airplane.

But I have learned that it more interesting to play the game when I follow the rules; to make an unauthorized flight would be to defy the rules and run a risk entirely out of proportion to the result of one more flight. Such a flight, though possible, is dangerous.

At the other extreme is the world of wartime combat. There is a bridge over the river. The enemy depends upon the bridge to carry supplies to his army that is killing my army. The enemy has fortified his bridge with antiaircraft guns and antiaircraft missiles and steel cables and barrage balloons and fighter cover. But the bridge, because of its importance, must be destroyed. The result of destroying the bridge is worth the risk of destroying it. The mission is chalked on a green blackboard and the flight is briefed and the bombs and rockets are hung on our airplanes and I start the engine and I take off and I fully intend to destroy the bridge.

In my mind the mission is not a dangerous one; it is one that simply must be done. If I lose the game of staying alive over this bridge, that is just too bad; the bridge is more important than the game.

How slowly it is, though, that we learn of the nature of dying. We form our preconceptions, we make our little fancies of what it is to pass beyond the material, we imagine what it feels like to face death. Every once in a while we actually do face it.

It is a dark night, and I am flying right wing on my flight leader. I wish for a moon, but there is none. Beneath us by some six miles lie cities beginning to sink under a gauzy coverlet of mist. Ahead the mist turns to low fog, and the bright stars dim a fraction in a sheet of high haze. I fly intently on the wing of my leader, who is a pattern of three white lights and one of green. The lights are too bright in the dark night, and surround themselves with brilliant flares of halo that make them painful to watch. I press the microphone button on the throttle. "Go dim on your nav lights, will you, Red Leader?"

"Sure thing."

In a moment the lights are dim, mere smudges of glowing filament that seek more to blend his airplane with the stars than to set it apart from them. His airplane is one of the several whose *dim* is just too dim to fly by. I would rather close my eyes against the glare than fly on a shifting dim constellation moving among the brighter constellations of stars. "Set 'em back to bright, please. Sorry."

"Roj."

It is not really enjoyable to fly like this, for I must always relate that little constellation to the outline of an airplane that I know is there, and fly my own airplane in relation to the mental outline. One light shines on the steel length of a drop tank, and the presence of the drop tank makes it easier to visualize the airplane that I assume is near me in the darkness. If there is one type of flying more difficult than dark-night formation, it is dark-night formation in weather, and the haze thickens at our altitude. I would much rather be on the ground. I would much rather be sitting in a comfortable chair with a pleasant evening sifting by me. But the fact remains that I am sitting in a yellow-handled ejection seat and that before I can feel the comfort of any evening again I must first successfully complete this flight through the night and through whatever weather and difficulties lie ahead. I am not worried, for I have flown many flights in many airplanes, and have not yet damaged an airplane or my desire to fly them.

France Control calls, asking that we change to frequency 355.8. France Control has just introduced me to the face of death. I slide my airplane away from leader's just a little, and divert my attention to turning four separate knobs that will let me listen, on a new frequency, to what they have to say. It takes a moment in the red light to turn the knobs. I look up to see the bright lights of Lead beginning to dim in the haze. I will lose him. Forward on the throttle, catch up with him before he disappears in the mist. Hurry.

Very suddenly in the deceptive mist I am closing too quickly on his wing and his lights are very very bright. Look out, you'll run right into him! He is so helpless as he flies on instruments. He couldn't dodge now if he knew that I would hit him. I slam the throttle back to *idle,* jerk the nose of my airplane up, and roll so that I am upside down, watching the lights of his airplane through the top of my canopy.

Then, very quickly, he is gone. I see my flashlight where it has fallen to the Plexiglas over my head, silhouetted by the diffused yellow glow in the low cloud that is a city preparing to sleep on the ground. What an unusual place for a flashlight. I begin the roll to recover to level flight, but I move the stick too quickly, at what has become far too low an airspeed. I am stunned. My airplane is spinning. It snaps around once and the glow is all about me. I look for references, for ground or stars; but there is only the faceless glow. The stick shakes convulsively in my hand and the airplane snaps around again. I do not know whether the airplane is in an erect spin or an inverted spin, I know only that one must never spin a sweptwing aircraft. Not even in broad light and clear day. Instruments. Attitude indicator shows that the spin has stopped, by itself or by my monstrous efforts on the stick and rudder. It shows that the airplane is wings-level inverted; the two little bars of the artificial horizon that always point to the ground are pointing now to the canopy overhead.

I must bail out. I must not stay in an uncontrolled airplane below 10,000 feet. The altimeter is an unwinding blur. I must raise the right armrest, squeeze the trigger, before it is too late.

There is a city beneath me. I promised myself that I would never leave an airplane over a city.

Give it one more chance to recover on instruments, I haven't given the airplane a chance to fly itself out.

The ground must be very close.

There is a strange low roaring in my ears.

Fly the attitude indicator.

Twist the wings level.

Speed brakes out.

I must be very close to the ground, and the ground is not the friend of airplanes that dive into it.

Pull out.

Roaring in my ears. Glow in the cloud around me.

Saint Elmo's fire on the windscreen, blue and dancing. The last time I saw Saint Elmo's fire was over Albuquerque, last year with Bo Beaven.

Pull out.

Well, I am waiting, death. The ground is very close, for the glow is bright and the roaring is loud. It will come quickly. Will I hear it or will everything just go black? I hold the stick back as hard as I dare—harder would stall the airplane, spin it again.

So this is what dying is like. You find yourself in a situation that has suddenly gone out of control, and you die. And there will be a pile of wreckage and someone will wonder why the pilot didn't eject from his airplane. One must never stay with an uncontrolled airplane below 10,000 feet.

Why do you wait, death? I know I am certain I am convinced that I will hit the ground in a few thousandths of a second. I am tense for the impact. I am not really ready to die, but now that is just too bad. I am shocked and surprised and interested in meeting death. The waiting for the crash is unbearable.

And then I am suddenly alive again.

The airplane is climbing.

I am alive.

The altimeter sweeps through 6,000 feet in a swift rush of a climb. Speed brakes *in*. Full forward with the throttle. I am climbing. Wings level, airspeed a safe 350 knots, the glow is fading below. The accelerometer shows that I pulled seven and a half G's in my recovery from the dive. I didn't feel one of them, even though my G suit was not plugged into its source of pressured air.

"Red Lead, this is Two here; had a little difficulty, climbing back through ten thousand feet . . ."

"TEN THOUSAND FEET?"

"Roger, I'll be up with you in a minute, we can rejoin over Toul TACAN."

Odd. And I was so sure that I would be dead.

The flashes in the dark clouds north of Phalsbourg are more frequent and flicker now from behind my airplane as well as in front of it. They are good indicators of thunderstorm cells, and they do not exactly fit my definition of "scattered." Directly ahead, on course, are three quick bright flashes in a row. Correct thirty degrees left. Alone. Time for twisted thoughts in the back of the mind. "You have to be crazy or just plain stupid to fly into a thunderstorm in an 'eighty-four F." The words are my words, agreed and illustrated by other pilots who had circumstances force them to fly this airplane through an active storm cell.

The airplane, they say, goes almost completely out of control, and despite the soothing words of the flight handbook, the pilot is relying only on his airplane's inertia to hurl it through and into smooth air beyond the storm.

But still I have no intention of penetrating one of the flickering monsters ahead. And I see that my words were wrong. I face the storms on my course now through a chain of logic that any pilot would have followed. The report called them "scattered," not numerous or continuous. I flew on. There are at least four separate radar-equipped facilities below me capable of calling vectors through the worst cells. I fly on. A single-engine pilot does not predicate his action on what-shall-I-do-if-the-radio-goes-out. The risk of the mission is worth the result of delivering the heavy canvas sack in the gun bay.

Now, neither crazy nor stupid, I am at the last link of the chain: I dodge the storms by the swerving radio compass needle and the flashes of lightning that I see from the cockpit. The TACAN is not in the least disturbed by my uneasy state of mind. The only thing that matters in the world of its transistorized brain is that we are 061 miles from Phalsbourg, slightly to the left of course. The radio compass has gone wild, pointing left and right and ahead and behind. Its panic is disconcerting among the levelheaded coolness of the other instruments, and my right glove moves its function switch to *off.* Gratefully accepting the sedative, the needle slows, and stops.

Flash to the left, alter course ten degrees right. Flash behind the right wing, forget about it. Flash-FLASH directly brilliantly ahead and the instrument panel goes featureless and white. There is no dodging this one. Scattered.

The storm, in quick sudden hard cold fury, grips my airplane in its jaws and shakes it as a furious terrier shakes a rat. Right glove is tight on the stick. Instrument panel, shock-mounted, slams into blur. The tin horizon whips from an instant thirty-degree left bank to an instant sixty-degree right bank. That is not possible. A storm is only air.

Left glove, throttle full forward. My airplane, in slow motion, yaws dully to the left. Right rudder, hard. Like a crash landing on a deep-rutted rock trail. Yaw to the right. My airplane has been drugged, she will not respond. Vicious left rudder.

The power, where is the power? Left glove back, forward again, as far as it will go, as hard as it will go. A shimmering blurred line where the tachometer needle should be. Less than 90 percent rpm at full throttle.

I hear the airplane shaking. I cannot hear the engine. Stick and rudders are useless moving pieces of metal. I cannot control my airplane. But throttle, I need the throttle. What is wrong?

Ice. The intake guide vanes are icing, and the engine is not getting air. I see the intake clogged in grey ice. Flash and FLASH the bolt is a brilliant snake of incandescent noon-white sun in the dark. I cannot see. Everything has gone red and I cannot even see the blurred panel. I feel the stick I feel the throttle I cannot see. I have suddenly a ship in the sky, and the storm is breaking it. So quickly. This cannot last. Thunderstorms cannot hurt fighters. I am on my way to Chaumont. Important mission.

Slowly, through the bone-jarring shake of the storm, I can see again. The windscreen is caked with grey ice and bright blue fire. I have never seen the fire so brightly blue. My wings are white. I am heavy with ice and I am falling and the worst part of a thunderstorm is at the lowest altitudes. I cannot take much more of this pounding.

White wings, covered in shroud. Right glove grips the stick, for that is what has kept my airplane in the sky for six years. But tonight the airplane is very slow and does not respond, as if she were suddenly very tired and did not care to live. As if her engine had been shut down.

The storm is a wild horse of the desert that has suddenly discovered a monster on its back. It is in a frenzy to rid itself of me, and it strikes with shocks so fast they cannot be seen. I learn a new fact. The ejection seat is not always an escape. Bailout into the storm will be just as fatal as the meeting of earth and airplane, for in the churning air my parachute would be a tangled nylon rag. My airplane and I have been together for a long time, we will stay together now. The decision bolts the ejection seat to the cockpit floor, the Thunderstreak and I smash down through the jagged sky as a single dying soul. My arm is heavy on the stick, and tired. It will be good to rest. There is a roaring in my ears, and I feel the hard ground widening about me, falling up to me.

So this is the way it will end. With a violent shuddering of airplane and an unreadable instrument panel; with a smothered engine and heavy white wings. Again the feeling: I am not really ready to end the game. I have told myself that this day would come to meet me, as inevitably as the ground which rushes to meet me now, and yet I think, quickly, of a future lost. It cannot be helped. I am falling through a hard splintering storm with a control stick that is not a control stick. I am a chip in a hurricane a raindrop in a typhoon about to become one with the sea a mass of pieces-to-be a concern of air traffic controllers and air police and gendarmerie and coroners and accident investigators and statisticians and newspaper reporters and a board of officers and a theater commander and a wing commander and a squadron commander and a little circle of friends. I am a knight smashed from his square and thrown to the side of the chessboard.

Tomorrow morning there will be no storm and the sun will be shining on the quiet bits of metal that used to be Air Force Jet Two Niner Four Zero Five.

But at this instant there is a great heavy steel-bladed storm that is battering and crushing me down, out of the sky, and the thing that follows this instant is another just like it.

Altimeter is a blur, airspeed is a blur, vertical speed is a blur, attitude indicator is a quick-rocking blurred luminous line that does not respond to my orders. Any second now; as before, I am tense and waiting. There will be an impact, and blackness and quiet. Far in the back of my mind, behind the calm fear, is curiosity and a patient waiting. And a pride. I am a pilot. I would be a pilot again.

The terrier flings the rat free.

The air is instantly smooth, and soft as layered smoke. Altimeter three thousand feet airspeed one ninety knots vertical speed four thousand feet per minute down attitude indicator steep right bank heading indicator one seven zero degrees tachometer eighty-three percent rpm at full throttle. Level the white wings. Air is warm. Thudthudthud from the engine as ice tears from guide vanes and splinters into compressor blades. Wide slabs of ice rip from the wings. Half the windscreen is suddenly clear. Faint blue fire on the glass. Power is taking hold: 90 percent on the tachometer . . . thud . . . 91 percent . . . thudthud . . . 96 percent. Airspeed coming up through 240 knots, left turn, climb. Five hundred feet per minute, 700 feet per minute altimeter showing 3,000 feet and climbing I am 50 degrees off course and I don't care attitude indicator showing steady left climbing turn I'm alive the oil pressure is good utility and power hydraulic pressure are good I don't believe it voltmeter and loadmeter showing normal control stick is smooth and steady how strange it is to be alive windscreen is clear thud 99 percent rpm tailpipe temperature is in the green. Flash-FLASH look out to the left look out! Hard turn right I'll never make it through another storm tonight forget the flight plan go north of Phalsbourg 15,000 feet 320 knots flash to the left and behind, faint.

And strangely, the words of an old pilot's song: ". . . for I, am, too young, to die . . ." It is a good feeling, this being alive. Something I haven't appreciated. I have learned again.

Rpm is up to 100 percent. I am climbing, and 20,000 feet is below flash 21,000 feet is below. Blue fire washes across the windscreen as if it did not know that a windscreen is just a collection of broken bits of glass.

What a ridiculous thought. A windscreen is a windscreen, a solid piece of six-ply plate glass, for keeping out the wind and the rain and the ice and a place to look through and a place to shine the gunsight. I will be looking through windscreens for a long time to come.

Why didn't I bail out? Because the seat was bolted to the cockpit floor. No. Because I decided not to bail out into the storm. I should have bailed out. I definitely should have left the airplane. Better to take my chances with a rough descent in a torn chute than certain death in a crash. I should have dropped the external tanks, at least. Would have made the airplane lighter and easier to control. Now, at 32,000 feet, I think of dropping the tanks. Quick thinking.

Flash.

I flew out of the storm, and that is what I wanted to do. I am glad now that I did not drop the tanks; there would have been reports to write and reasons to give. When I walk away from my airplane tonight I will have only one comment to make on the Form One: UHF transmitter and receiver failed during flight. I will be the only person to know that the United States Air Force in Europe came within a few seconds of losing an airplane.

Flashflash. Ahead.

I have had enough storm-flying for one night. Throttle to 100 percent and climb. I will fly over the weather for the rest of the way home; there will be one cog slipping tonight in the European Air Traffic Control System, above the weather near Phalsbourg. The cog has earned it.

CHAPTER SIX

THE PEOPLE ON the ground who operate the air traffic control system are very important people, but not indispensable. The system, although it is a good one, is not an indispensable system. Airplanes were flying long before the first sign of air traffic control appeared, they will go on flying if it all suddenly disappears.

When the rules of the air were set down, there was a very wise man present who knew that cogs will slip now and then, and that the system had best be flexible. I am still in command of my airplane, and I will put it where I think that it is best for it to go, system or no system. Now I have decided that I would rather not engage another thunderstorm. I climb away from my assigned altitude of 33,000 feet to seek the clear air and smooth flying above the clouds. I am passing through altitudes that might have been assigned to other airplanes, and there is the possibility of midair collision.

Yet the chance of my colliding with another airplane is almost nonexistent. I am off course; in order to collide with me, another airplane would have to be precisely as far off course as I am.

Though I have not talked to a ground station for a long while, I have not been forgotten; I am a flight plan written on a strip of paper at all the stations along my route. Other airplanes will be told of my course and my estimated times over those stations.

I am a quarter-inch dot on the radar screens, and controllers will vector other airplanes around me.

The primary reason that I will not collide with any other airplane is that my Thunderstreak is forty-three feet three inches long, its wingspan is thirty-three feet six inches, and it flies in a block of air that is a thousand cubic miles of empty space. And so I climb.

My approach time to Chaumont will be held open for a half hour past my estimated time of arrival. I dial the familiar channel 55 on the TACAN and listen to the identifier. Chaumont. I never would have thought that a little French village could be so like Home. Bearing is 239 degrees, distance is 093 miles. Phalsbourg is drifting behind me to the left. I should have reported over the French border and over Phalsbourg. But the cog is slipping.

Thirty-eight thousand feet on the altimeter and still no top to the cloud. The blue fire is gone. Fuel is down to 2,700 pounds, and at this weight a practical ceiling for my plane will be about 43,000 feet. It is rare to have clouds in Europe that top at more than 40,000 feet, and I am not concerned. My interest is directed only over the instruments in front of me. There is now, without a radio, no other world.

The old pilots tell of days when it was "needle-ball and alcohol" through the weather: a turn-and-bank indicator and a magnetic compass their only aid in the cloud. But this is a modern age, and tonight I fly by the seven instruments in the center of the panel, and have my navigation solved second by second in the two dials of the TACAN.

If the inverter that changes the generator's DC power to AC were to fail, my gyro instruments, attitude indicator, and heading indicator would slowly run down into uselessness. But the '84F is an American airplane, and therefore has safety systems for the safety systems. In this instance, the safety factor is called the alternate instrument inverter, waiting to drive the gyros should the engine-driven generator or the main inverter fail. Should both inverters fail, I am moved back through the years to fly a fighter airplane by needle-ball and alcohol.

There is a light tremble through my airplane as I climb through 40,000 feet, and the wings begin to rock. There has been no lightning. I scan the windscreen, looking for ice. I cannot carry much ice and continue to climb. The windscreen is clear.

With no sound and with no warning, like the magician's silk from above the hawk, the cloud is gone. In one instant I am checking for ice, in the next I am looking through the glass, as through a narrow Gothic arch in steel, at two hundred miles of crystal air, floored 20,000 feet below by unruffled cloud. It is vertigo, as if I had run over a hidden cliff and discovered myself in thin air. Right glove tightens on the stick.

I have flown from a sheer wall of cloud, and it tumbles away toward the earth like the mountains south of Strasbourg tumble away to the valley of the Rhine. The giant wall swings in wide arc to my left and right, and it flickers here and there with its storms.

I am an invisible speck of dust sifting on a tiny breath of air.

A hundred and fifty miles behind me to the north, the wall becomes the smooth gentle-rising slope that I entered long ago. But this is helpless knowledge, for I can see in the starlight that the only real thing in all the world is the awesome mass of cloud around my 43-foot airplane. There is no ground, there is no steady glow of lighted city through the floor of the mist. There is not one other flashing navigation light from horizon to horizon. I am alone, with one thousand stars for company.

I rest my helmet against the ejection seat headrest and look out again at the sky. The sky is not blue or purple or merely black. It is a deep meadow of powdered carbon, a bed for the stars. Around me.

Back with the throttle, to make the engine quiet. Right glove reaches to the three knobs that control the red light of the cockpit, and my own little red world fades into the meadow.

The dust mote settles gently back toward 33,000 feet, and its voice is the barest whisper in the dimension of the night.

I am one man. Tonight, perhaps, I am Man, alive and looking out over my planet toward my galaxy, crystallizing in myself, for a span of seconds, the centuries of looking out from this little earth that Man has done.

We have much in common, we men.

Tonight I, who love my airplane with all its moods and hardships and joys, am looking out upon the stars. And tonight, twenty minutes to the east, there is another pilot, another man who loves his airplane, looking out at these same stars. These symbols.

My airplane is painted with a white star, his with a red star. It is dark, and paint is hard to see. In his cockpit is the same family of flight instruments and engine instruments and radio control panels that is in my cockpit. In his airplane as in mine, when the stick is pressed to the left, the airplane banks to the left.

I know, unquestioningly, that I would like the man in that cockpit. We could talk through the long night of the airplanes that we have known and the times that we were afraid and the places that we have been. We would laugh over the half-witted things that we did when we were new in the air. We have shared many things, he and I, too many things to be ordered into our airplanes to kill each other.

I went through flying training at a base near Dallas, he went through it at a base near Stalingrad. My flight instructors shouted at me in English, his at him in Russian. But the blue fire trickles once in a while across his windscreen as it does across mine, and ice builds and breaks over his wings as it does mine. And somewhere in his cockpit is a control panel or a circuit breaker panel or a single switch that he has almost to stand on his head to reach. Perhaps at this moment his daughter is considering whether or not to accept a pair of Siamese kittens. Look out for your curtains, friend.

I wish that I could warn him about the kittens.

Fifty miles from Chaumont. Fifty miles and Through the Looking-Glass of cloud and rain and Hi there, ace, how'd the cross-country go? Fifty miles is a very long way.

I have a not-working radio, above the clouds. Not a great problem, but enough of one so that I force my attention from the peaceful meadow of black to the task of putting my airplane back on the earth. Throttle forward at 33,000 feet, and again the rumble and whines and squeaks and moans from my comic in spinning steel.

No radio. I can fly on to the west, looking for a hole in the clouds, descend, fly back to Chaumont and land. A very poor plan for the fuel that remains in my tanks and for the vagaries of French weather.

I can fly a triangular pattern to the left, with one-minute legs. After a few patterns, a radar site will notice my path and its direction, vector an interceptor to me, and I will fly a letdown and instrument approach as his wingman. A drastic plan, but one to remember as a last-ditch, last-resort action.

I can fly a letdown at Chaumont as I had planned, hoping that the weather is not so bad that I need a Ground Controlled Approach in order to find the runway. At last report the weather was not so bad. If I do not break out of the weather at the TACAN low-approach minimum altitude, I will climb back on top and try a penetration at my alternate, Etain Air Base, ten minutes to the north. I have just enough fuel for this plan, and I shall follow it. For interest's sake, I will try my radio once more when I am directly over Chaumont. One can never tell about UHF radios.

Forty miles. Five minutes. To home. But months still to a home where there is a wife and daughter and where the people in the towns speak English.

The bulletin board in the Chaumont pilots' quarters is a mass of newspaper clippings from that older Home. On the board are charges and countercharges concerning the wisdom of recalling the Guard without a war to make it necessary. There are letters to the editors from wives and families and employers, asking questions and offering answers. The newspapers tell of poor conditions into which we were forced, of our trials and our difficulties, of the state of our morale. The picture they paint is a bleak one, but our lot is not really so bleak.

I left an interesting civilian job, flying small airplanes and writing for an aviation magazine, and was ordered back into the Air Force. It was disrupting, of course. But then I have never before been needed by the country to which I owe so much. I would be happier in the freedom of my old life, but my country has come fearfully close to war. The recall was not convenient for me or for my family, but it was a wise plan of action. The recall showed that Air Guard pilots were not merely sportsmen at government expense; a feeling that I sometimes harbored, guiltily, after pleasant weekends spent flying military airplanes, at $80 per weekend.

My squadron crossed the Atlantic in three hops. It made the crossing without air refueling, without proper air navigation stations covering the route, without an incident. We landed at Chaumont Air

Base one month after we were called to active duty, flying whenever ceilings were higher than five hundred feet.

The multiengine pilots in their tremendous airplanes brought hundreds of tons of support equipment and parts and supplies. We listened to briefings from NATO pilots about the strange new world of European air traffic control. Ammunition specialists emptied boxcars of 50-caliber machine-gun bullets and racks of olive-drab, yellow-striped high-explosive bombs and long aluminum tanks of napalm and rack on rack of slim unpainted rockets. We were assigned areas of battle and we met with the army that we were to support. We held practice alerts that began as chaos, progressed through orderly confusion, and became, finally, quick and efficient.

Though the complaints are made and duly printed, though the crisis that called us has subsided, we accomplished the task set for us. We arrived in France with all our pilots and all our airplanes. Today the Alert pilots play bridge and chess and Ping-Pong near the red telephone.

Not all without cost, of course. To date, our readiness has cost Don Slack, pilot, and the flags are still at half-mast.

For us who fly the '84F, the mobilization is one long weekend of Air Guard duty. In town the people speak a different language, and there are sentries and rolls of barbed wire surrounding the flight line, but we fly with the same friends (except one) and the same airplanes (except one) that we have always flown with, and the life is not cause for complaint (except one). We fly, and the sky of France is much the same as the sky of home. Wind and rain and sun and stars. It is its own kind of home, the sky, and for the brief hours of my flight I do not miss the other home across the sea. I do miss Don Slack.

The stars glow steadily in the darkness of their meadow, part of my world. I think, for a moment, of all that has been said of the enchantment of this cathedral of air. A million words, written and spoken and turned to photograph, in which people who fly risk the curse of sentiment, that deadly curse, to tell of what they have seen. The enchantment does not lend itself to paper and ink or to syllables, or even to sensitized film, but the people's risk of the curse is itself witness to the sight and the mood that awaits the man who travels the high land. Cloud and star and bow of color are just so many words to be laid carefully in a shallow grave of corrasable bond. The sky, in the end, can only be called an interesting place. My beloved sky.

The wide needle of the TACAN wobbles, the distance-measuring drum turns through 006, and it is time to put my set of plans into action.

I begin the left turn into the holding pattern, and my right glove half-turns the cockpit light rheostats, soaking itself in soft red. The IFF dial goes to Mode Three, Code 70. I should now be an identified and expected dot on the radar screen of Chaumont Radar. Thumb down very hard on microphone button, throttle back, speed brakes out, and the rumble of shattering air as they extend from the side of the plane. "Chaumont Approach Control, Jet Four Zero Five, high station on the TACAN, requesting latest Chaumont weather." There is a sidetone. A good sign. But there is no reply.

Fly along the pattern, recheck defrosters and pitot heat *on,* a quick review of the penetration: heading 047 degrees outbound from the holding pattern, left descending turn to heading 197 degrees, level at 3,500 feet and in to the 12-mile gate.

I level now at 20,000 feet, power at 85 percent rpm and ready in my mind for the letdown.

". . . measured nine hundred feet overcast, visibility five miles in light rain, altimeter two niner eight five."

I have never had a more capricious radio. Hard down on the plastic button. "Chaumont Approach, Zero Five leaving flight level Two Zero Zero present time, requesting GCA frequency." Stick forward, nose down, and I am through 19,000 feet, through 18,000 feet, through 17,000 feet, with airspeed smooth at 350 knots.

". . . ive, your radar frequency will be three four four point six, local channel one five."

"Roj, Approach, leaving your frequency." In the left bank of the turn, I click the channel selector to one five. And back to the instruments. Look out for vertigo. "He went into the weather in a bank, and he came out of it upside down." But not me and not tonight; I have come through worse than vertigo, and I have been warned. "Chaumont Radar, Jet Four Zero Five, how do you read on three four four point six." A pause, and time to doubt the errant radio.

"Read you five square, Zero Five, how do you read Radar?" So the radio becomes better as I descend. Interesting.

"Five by."

"Roger, Zero Five, we have you in positive radar contact one eight miles north of Chaumont. Continue your left turn to heading one three five degrees, level at two thousand five hundred feet. This will be a precision approach to runway one niner; length eight thousand fifty feet, width one hundred fifty feet, touchdown elevation one thousand seventy-five feet. If you lose communication with Radar for any one minute in the pattern or any thirty seconds on final approach . . ."

I am gratefully absorbed in familiar detail. Continue the turn, let the nose down a little more to speed the descent, recheck engine screens retracted and pneumatic compressor *off* and oxygen 100 percent and engine instruments in the green and hook again the lanyard to the D ring of the parachute rip cord. My little world rushes obediently down as I direct it. Concentrating on my instruments, I do not notice when I again enter the cloud.

The voice continues, directing me through the black with the assurance of a voice that has done this many times. The man behind the voice is an enlisted man, to whom I speak only on official business. But now I give myself and my airplane wholly to his voice, and rank is a pompous thing. Microphone button down.

"Zero Five is level . . ." No sidetone. I am not transmitting. Microphone button down hard and rocking in its little mount under the left thumb. "Zero Five is level, two thousand five hundred feet, steady one three five degrees." Flaps down. Airspeed slows through 220 knots. Left glove on the clear plastic wheel-shaped handle of the landing gear lever. A mechanical movement: pull the handle out a quarter inch and push it down six inches. At the instant that the lever slams down into its slot, the tall hard wheels of my airplane break from their hidden wells and press down, shuddering, into the rush of cloud. Three bright green lights flare at the left of the instrument panel. Speed brake switch forward.

"Zero Five has three green, pressure, and brakes." Tap the brakes.

"Roger, Zero Five, you are now one zero miles from touchdown, recheck your gear, the tower has cleared you for a full-stop landing. Turn heading one seven five, stand by this frequency for final controller." Inside the rain-spattered red-checkered Ground Control Approach van at the side of Chaumont's only runway, the search controller looks across to his companion, framed dimly in the green light of his own radar screen. "He's all yours, Tommy." Tommy nods.

"Jet Zero Five, this is your final controller, how do you read?" He already knows that I can hear him very well. The procedure is part of a time-honored ritual.

"Zero Five reads you five by." And I say with him to myself his next words, the lines assigned to him in the script for his role as GCA Final Approach Controller.

"Roger, Zero Five," we say. "You need not acknowledge any further transmissions, however there will be periodic transmission breaks on final approach which will be identified." Fuel aboard shows just under two thousand pounds on the big tank gauge. At my airplane's present weight, I should fly down final approach at 165 knots. "Repeat the tower has cleared you for a full-stop . . ."

When I am under the direction of a good GCA operator, I might just as well be on the ramp and shutting down my engine, for my landing is absolutely certain.

". . . you are thirty seconds from the glide path, correcting left to right on the centerline. Turn heading one eight zero. One eight zero. Transmission break." He lifts his foot from the microphone pedal on the floor under his screen, giving me a few seconds to speak. I have nothing to say to fill his silence, and his foot comes down again. "One eight zero is bringing you out on centerline, drifting slightly from left to right. Ten seconds to glide path. Turn one seven niner. One seven niner . . ." That is a little compliment for me. One-degree corrections are very small, very precise, and require smooth aircraft control from the pilot. I hear one-degree corrections only in still air, only when I am flying well. A smile under the oxygen mask. He should have seen me thirty minutes ago.

"On glide path, begin descent. Suggest an initial rate of descent of seven hundred fifty feet per minute for your aircraft . . ." What could be simpler than flying a GCA through the weather to the runway? There are the crossbarred pointers of the Instrument Landing System to accomplish the same job, but the ILS is not human. Technically, an ILS approach is more consistently accurate than a GCA, but I would much rather work with a good man behind a good radar, in any weather. Speed brakes out with left thumb aft on sawtooth switch. I lower the nose, visualizing as I do the long slide of the invisible glide slope in front of me. The rate-of-climb needle points on the *down* side of its scale to one thousand feet per minute, then moves back to eight hundred feet per minute.

"Rolled out nicely on glide path . . . on centerline . . . drifting now slightly left of centerline, turn heading one eight three degrees, one eight three. On glide path . . ." Airspeed is 170 knots, back on the throttle for a second, then up again. Airspeed 168. Back again and up again: 165.

"Going five feet low on glide path, adjust your rate of descent slightly . . . on centerline . . . transmission break." I think the stick back a little, think it very slightly forward again.

"Up and on glide path, resume normal rate of descent. On centerline . . . on glide path . . . on centerline . . . an excellent rate of descent . . ." Sometimes, I would bet, a GCA operator runs out of things to say. But he is required to give continuous direction to aircraft on final approach. What a boring life he must lead. But bored or not, I am very glad to hear him.

"On glide path . . . doing a nice job of it, Lieutenant . . . on centerline . . . tower reports braking action good . . ." How does he know that I am a lieutenant? I could be a major or a colonel out in the night weather to check on the standardization of GCA operators. But I am not, I am just a man happy to be through a storm and grateful to hear again a voice on my long-silent radio.

". . . you are two miles from touchdown, on glide path, going ten feet left of centerline, turn right heading one eight four degrees . . .

one eight four. On glide path correcting back to centerline . . . one eight four . . . a mile and a half from touchdown . . ."

I look up, and realize suddenly that I have been out of the cloud for seconds. The red and green and twin white rows of runway lights stretch directly ahead. Back a fraction on the throttle, slowing down.

". . . one mile from touchdown, going ten feet low on the glide path . . ." Here it comes. I know it, the final controller knows it. I drop below the glide path when I have the runway in sight. If I were to stay completely under his direction, I would touch down some six hundred feet down the runway, and that is six hundred feet I can well use. It takes normal landing distance and two thousand feet more to stop my airplane if the drag chute fails on a wet runway. And regardless of drag chute, regardless of airplane, I learned as a cadet to recite the three most useless things to a pilot: runway behind you, altitude above you, and a tenth of a second ago.

Though I listen offhandedly to the GCA operator's voice, I fly now by only one instrument: the runway. Landing lights on. Left glove reaches ahead and touches a switch down to make two powerful columns of white light pivot from beneath my wings, turning forward to make a bright path in the droplets of rain.

". . . one quarter mile from touchdown, you are going thirty feet below the glide path, bring your aircraft up . . ." I wish that he would be quiet now. I need his voice in the weather, but I do not need him to tell me how to land my airplane when I can see the runway. The columns of light are speeding over white concrete now, red lights, green lights flash below.

". . . thirty-five feet below glide path, you are too low for a safe approach, bring your aircraft up . . ."

Quiet, GCA. You should have more sense than to go to pieces when I begin the flare-out. Either I am happy with a touchdown on the first few hundred feet of runway or you are happy with my airplane landing six hundred feet along a wet runway. Stick back, throttle to *idle*, stick back, a bit of left aileron . . . I feel for the runway with my sensitive wheels. Down another foot, another few inches. Come on, runway.

Hard rubber on hard concrete. Not as smooth a touchdown as I wanted but not bad stick forward let the nosewheel down squeak of fourteen-inch wheel taking its share of nineteen thousand pounds of airplane right glove on yellow drag chute handle and a quick short pull. Glove waits on handle ready to jettison the chute if it weather-vanes and pulls me suddenly toward the edge of the runway. I am thrown gently forward in my shoulder harness by the silent pouf of a sixteen-foot ring-slot parachute billowing from the tail. Speed brakes in, flaps up, boots carefully off the brakes. The drag chute will stop me almost before I am ready to stop. I must turn off the runway before I may jettison the chute; if I stop too soon and have to taxi to the turnoff with this great blossom of nylon behind me, I would need almost full power to move at more than two miles per hour. It is an effective drag chute.

We roll smoothly to the end of the runway, and even without braking I must add a burst of throttle to turn off at the end. Boot on left pedal and we turn. Drag chute handle twisted and pulled again, as I look back over my shoulder. The white blossom is suddenly gone and my airplane rolls more easily along the taxiway.

Left glove pulls the canopy lock handle aft, right glove grips the frame and swings the roof of my little world up and out of the way, overhead. Rain pelts lightly on my face above the green rubber mask. It is cool rain, and familiar, and I am glad to feel it. Landing lights *off and retracted* taxi light *on,* ejection seat safety pin from the G suit pocket and into its hold in the armrest, UHF radio to tower frequency.

"Chaumont Tower, Jet Four Zero Five is clear the active runway, taxi to the squadron hangar."

"Cleared taxi via the parallel taxiway, Zero Five. We had no late estimate on your time of arrival at Chaumont. Did you have difficulties en route?"

Tower feels chatty this evening. "A little radio trouble, tower."

"Read you five square now, Zero Five."

"Roj."

Right glove presses the shiny fastener at the side of my mask as I glide between the rows of blue taxiway lights, pushed by the soft sigh of engine at 50 percent rpm. Cool rain on my face. We trundle together in a right turn, my airplane and I, up a gentle hill, and follow after the green letters of a Follow Me truck that appears suddenly out of the darkness.

Above this dark rain and above the clouds of its birth is a world that belongs only to pilots. Tonight it belonged, for a moment, only to me and to my airplane, and across the breadth of it to the east, to another pilot and another airplane. We shared the sky tonight, and perhaps even now he is tasting the cool raindrops as he taxies by a runway that is as much a target in my intelligence folders as Chaumont Air Base is a target in his.

And I understand, in the rain, that although tonight there has been only he and me in our airplanes, tomorrow it will be some other one of Us and some other one of Them. When my little scene is played and I am once again back in the United States and a pilot of the New Jersey Air National Guard, there will still be someone flying the European night in a white-starred airplane and one in a red-starred one. Only the faces in the cockpits change.

Share work, share dedication, share danger, share triumph, share fear, share joy, share love, and you forge a bond that is not subject to change. I'll leave Europe for America, he'll leave Europe for Russia. The faces change, the bond is always there.

Hard on the right brake, swing around into the concrete pad of a parking revetment, nose pointing out toward the taxiway and the runway beyond. Taxi light *off,* check that the ground crew from the Follow Me truck slide the chocks in front of the tall wheels.

May you have the sense and the guidance to stay out of thunderstorms, distant friend.

Throttle back swiftly to *off.* The faithful spinning buffoon in steel dies with a long fading airy sigh, pressing the last of its heat, a shimmering black wave, into the night. Sleep well.

A slap on the side of the fuselage. "Rundown!" the crew chief calls, and I check my watch. It took sixty-one seconds for the turbine and the compressor to stop their sigh. Important information, for a maintenance man, and I enter the time in the Form One.

Inverter *off,* fuel *off,* UHF radio *off,* and at last, battery *off.* There is one last heavy click in the night as the battery switch goes to *off* under my glove, and my airplane is utterly and completely still.

In the beam of my issue flashlight, I write in the form that the UHF radio transmitter and receiver operate erratically above 20,000 feet. There is no space in which to enter the fact that the Air Force is lucky to have this airplane back at all. I log forty-five minutes of night weather, one hour of night, one TACAN penetration, one GCA, one drag chute landing. I sign the form, unsnap the safety belt and shoulder harness and survival kit and G suit and oxygen hose and microphone cable and soft chinstrap.

A blue Air Force station wagon arrives, splashing light on my nosewheel, and the sack from above the guns is handed down.

I lay my white helmet on the canopy bow in front of me and climb stiffly down the yellow ladder from the lonely little world that I love. I sign a paper, the station wagon leaves me in the dark. Helmet in hand, scarf pressed again by the wind, I am back on the ground of my air base in France, with a thousand other civilians in uniform, and with thirty-one . . . no, with thirty . . . other pilots.

My airplane is quiet, and for a moment still an alien, still a stranger to the ground, I am home.

BIPLANE

CHAPTER ONE

IT IS LIKE opening night on a new way of living, only it is opening day, and instead of velvet curtains drawing majestically aside there are hangar doors of corrugated tin, rumbling and scraping in concrete tracks and being more stubborn than majestic. Inside the hangar, wet still with darkness and with two wide pools of dark underwing and evaporating as the tall doors slide, the new way of living. An antique biplane.

I have arrived to do business, to trade. As simple as that. A simple old airplane trade, done every day. No slightest need to feel unsure.

Still, a crowd of misgivings rush toward me from the hangar. This is an old airplane. No matter how you look at it, this airplane was built in 1929 and this is today and if you're going to get the thing home to California you've got to fly it over twenty-seven hundred miles of America.

It is a handsome airplane, though. Dark red and dark yellow, an old barnstormer of a biplane, with great tall wheels, two open cockpits, and a precise tictactoe of wires between the wings.

For shame. You have a fine airplane this moment. Have you forgotten the hours and the work and the money you poured into the rebuilding of the airplane you already own? That was only a year ago! A completely rebuilt 1946 Fairchild 24, as good as brand-new! Better than brand-new; you know every rib and frame and engine cylinder of the Fairchild, and you know that they're perfect. Can you say as much for this biplane? How do you know that ribs aren't broken beneath that fabric, or wingspars cracked?

How many thousand miles have you flown the Fairchild? Thousands over the Northeast, from that day you rolled her out of the hangar in Colt's Neck, New Jersey. Then from Colt's Neck more thousands to Los Angeles, wife and children seeing the country at first hand as we moved to a new home. Have you forgotten that flight and the airplane that brought your country alive in rivers coursing and great craggy mountains and wheat tassels in the sun? You built this airplane so no weather could stop it, with full flight instruments and dual radios for communication and navigation and a closed cabin to keep out the wind and rain. And now this airplane has flown you across more thousands of miles, from Los Angeles to this little land of Lumberton, North Carolina.

This is good biplane country. March in Lumberton is like June is like August. But the way home is a different land. Remember the frozen lakes in Arizona, three days ago? The snow in Albuquerque? That's no place for an open-cockpit biplane! The biplane is in her proper place this moment. In Lumberton, with tobacco fields green about her airport, with other antique airplanes sheltered nearby, with her gentle owner taking time from his law practice to tend to her needs.

This biplane is not your airplane, your kind of airplane, even. She belongs and she should belong to Evander M. Britt, of Britt and Britt, attorneys-at-law. A man who loves old airplanes, with the time to come down and take care of their needs. He has no wild schemes, he hasn't the faintest desire to fly this airplane across the country. He knows his airplane and what it can do and what it can't do. Come to your senses. Just fly home in the Fairchild and forget this folly. His advertisement for a trade should find him his coveted low-wing Aeronca, and from someplace just down the road, not a brand-new Fairchild 24 from Los Angeles, California. The biplane doesn't even have a radio!

It is true. If I make this trade, I will be trading the known for the unknown. On the other side stands only one argument, the biplane itself. Without logic, without knowledge, without certainty. I haven't the right to take it from Mr. Britt. Secretary to the local chapter of the Antique Airplane Association, he should have a biplane. He needs a biplane. He is out of his mind to trade this way. This machine is his mark of belonging to an honored few.

But Evander Britt is a grown man and he knows what he is doing and I don't care why he wants the Fairchild or how much money I've put in the rebuilding or how far I've flown in it. I only know that I want that biplane. I want it because I want to travel through time and I want to fly a difficult airplane and I want to feel the wind when I fly and I want people to look, to see, to know that glory still exists. I want to be part of something big and glorious.

This can be a fair trade only because each airplane is worth the same amount of money. Money aside, the two airplanes have absolutely nothing in common. And the biplane? I want it because I want it. I have brought sleeping bag and silk scarf for a biplane voyage home. My decision is made, and now, touching a dark wingtip, nothing can change it.

"Let's roll 'er out on the grass," Evander Britt says. "You can pull on that outboard wing strut, down near the bottom. . . ."

In the sunlight, the darks of red and yellow go bright scarlet and blazing bright flame to become a glowing sunrise biplane in four separate wing panels of cloth and wood and an engine of five black cylinders. Thirty-five years old, and this hangar could be the factory, and this air, 1929. I wonder if airplanes don't think of us as dogs and cats; for every year they age, we age fifteen or twenty. And as our pets share our household, so do we in turn share with airplanes the changing drifting sweeping household of the sky.

". . . not really so hard to start, but you have to get the right combination. About four shots of prime, pull the prop through five or six times . . ."

It is all strange and different, this cockpit. A deep leather-trimmed wood-and-fabric hole, cables and wires skimming the wooden floorboards, three knobbed stalks of engine controls to the left, a fuel valve and more engine controls forward, six basic engine and flight instruments on a tiny black-painted instrument panel. No radio.

A four-piece windscreen, low in front of my eyes. If it rains now, this whole thing is going to fill with water.

"Give it a couple of slow pumps with the throttle."

"One . . . two. OK." Funny. You never hear of cockpits filling up with water, but what happens when it rains on one of these things?

"One more shot of prime, and make the switches hot."

Click-click on the instrument panel.

"CONTACT! And brakes."

One quick downward swing of the shining propeller and the engine is very suddenly running, catching its breath and choking and coughing hoarse in the morning chill. Silence runs terrified before it and hides in the far corners of the forests around. Clouds of blue smoke wreathe for a second and are whipped away and the silver blade becomes nothing more than a great wide fan, and it blows air back over me like a giant blowing on a dandelion and the sound of it over the engine sound is a deep westwind in the pines.

I can't see a thing ahead but airplane; a two-passenger front cockpit and a wide cowling and a silver blur that is the propeller. I let go the brakes and look out over the side of the cockpit into the big fan-wind giant-wind and touch the throttle forward. The propeller blur goes thinner and faster and the engine sound goes deeper, all the while hollow and resonant, as though it were growling and roaring at the bottom of a thousand-gallon drum, lined in mirrors.

The old tall wheels begin to roll along the grass. The old grass, under the old wind, and bright old wings of another year and of this year, bound solidly together with angled old wires and forward-tilting old struts of wood, all a painted butterfly above the chill Carolina grass. Pressing on the rudder pedals, I swing the nose slowly from one side to the other as we roll, making sure that the blind way ahead is clear.

What a very long way has come the dream of flight since 1929. None of the haughty proud businesslike mien of the modern airplane hinted here. None of it. Just a slow leisurely taxi, with the constant S-turns to see ahead, pausing to sniff the breeze and inspect a flower in the grass and to listen to the sound of our engine. A quiet-seeming old biplane. Seeming, though, only seeming.

I have heard about these old airplanes, heard stories aplenty. Unreliable, these machines. You've always got to be ready for that engine to stop running. Quit on takeoff, usually, just when you need 'em most. And there's nothing you can do about it, that's just the way they are. If you do make it through the takeoff, look out for those old ones once they're in the air. Slow up just a little too much, boy, and they'll jerk the rug right out from under you and send you down in a spin. Like as not, you won't be able to recover from the spin, either. They'll just wrap up tighter and tighter and all you can do is bail out. Not too strange or unusual for the whole engine to fall out, sometimes. You just can't tell. That old metal in those old engine mounts is all crystallized by now, and one day SNAP and there you are falling backward out of the sky. And the wood in these airplanes, look out for that old wood. Rotted clean through, more than likely. Hit a little bump in the air, a little gust of wind, and there goes one of your wings folding and fluttering away, or worse, folding back over the cockpit so that you can't even bail out. But worst of all are the landings. Biplanes have that narrow landing gear and not much rudder to work with; they'll get away from you before you can blink your eyes and suddenly you're rolling along the runway in a big ball of wires and splinters and shredded old fabric. Just plain vicious and that's the only word for 'em. Vicious.

But this airplane seems docile and as trim as a young lady earnestly seeking to make a good impression upon the world. Listen to that engine tick over. Smooth as a tuned racing engine, not a single cylinder left out of the song. "Unreliable," indeed.

A quick engine run-up here on the grass before takeoff. Controls all free and working properly, oil pressure and temperature pointing as they should. Fuel valve is on, mixture is rich, all the levers are where they belong. Spark advance lever, even, and a booster magneto coil. Those haven't been built into airplanes for the last thirty years.

All right, airplane, let us see how you can fly. A discreet nudge on the throttle, a touch of left rudder to swing the nose around into the wind, facing a broad expanse of tall moist airport grass. Someone should have stamped out those rumors long ago.

Chinstrap fastened on leather helmet, dark goggles lowered.

Throttle coming full forward, and the giant blows hard twisting sound and fanned exhaust upon me. Certainly aren't very quiet, these engines.

Push forward on the control stick and instantly the tail is flying. Built for little grass fields, the biplanes. Weren't many airports around in 1929. That's why the big wheels, too. Roll over the ruts in a pasture, a racetrack, a country road. Built for short-field takeoffs, because that's where the passengers were, short fields were where you made your money.

Grass fades into a green felt blur, and the biplane is already light on her wheels.

And suddenly the ground is no more. Smooth into the sky the bright wings climb, the engine thunders in its hollow drum, the tall wheels, still spinning, are lifted. Listen to that! The wind in the wires! And now it's here all around me. It hasn't gone at all. It isn't lost in dusty yellow books with dusty browning photographs. It is here this instant, the taste of it all. That screaming by my ears and that whipping of my scarf—the wind! It's here for me now just as it was here for the first pilots, that same wind that carried their megaphoned words across the pastures of Illinois and the meadows of Iowa and the picnic grounds of Pennsylvania and the beaches of Florida. *"Five dollars, folks, for five minutes. Five minutes with the summer clouds, five minutes in the land of the angels. See your town from the air. You there, sir, how about taking the little lady for a joyride? Absolutely safe, perfectly harmless. Feel that fresh wind that blows where only birds and airplanes fly."* The same wind drumming on the same fabric and singing through the same wires and smashing into the same engine cylinders and sliced by the same sharp bright propeller and stirred and roiled by the same passage of the same machine that roiled it so many years ago.

If the wind and the sun and the mountains over the horizon do not change, a year that we make up in our heads and on our paper calendars is nothing. The farmhouse, there below. How can I tell that it is a farmhouse of today and not a farmhouse of 1931?

There's a modern car in the driveway. That's the only way I can tell the passing of time. It isn't the calendar makers who give us our time and our modern days, but the designers of automobiles and dish-washers and television sets and the current trends in fashion. Without a new car, then, time stands still. Find an old airplane and with a few pumps of prime and the swing of a shining propeller you can push time around as you will, mold it into a finer shape, give its features a more pleasant countenance. An escape machine, this. Climb in the cockpit and move the levers and turn the valves and start the engine and lift from the grass into the great unchanging ocean of air and you are master of your own time.

The personality of the biplane filters back to me as we fly. Elevator trim has to be almost full down to keep the nose from climbing when I take my hand from the control stick. Aileron forces are heavy, rudder and elevator forces are light. In a climb, I can push the throttle full forward and get no more than 1,750 revolutions per minute from the shining propeller. The horizon is balanced, in level flight, just atop the Number Two and Five cylinder heads. The airplane stalls gently, and before it stalls there is a tapping in the stick, a warning that the nose is about to drop slowly down, even with the control stick pulled back. There's nothing at all vicious about this airplane. Windy, of course, when you move your head from behind the glass windscreen, and not so quiet as modern airplanes. The wind goes quiet when the airplane is near its stalling speed; it shrieks warnings if it flies too fast. There is a great deal of airplane flying out ahead of the pilot. The forward windscreen clouds over with oil film and rocker-box grease after an hour in the air. When the throttle has been back for a moment, the engine misfires and chokes as it comes forward again. Certainly not a difficult airplane to fly. Certainly not a vicious one.

A circle over the airport now, with its great runways lying white ribbons in the grass. The most difficult time, they say, is the landing. I must look over the field carefully and make sure the runway is clear. When I am ready to land, that big nose will block the view ahead and I can only trust that nothing will wander into my path until I can slow down and begin S-turning to see. There, the field that I will land upon, the grass next to the runway. Away over to the left, the gasoline pumps and a little cluster of people watching.

We slide down a long invisible ramp in the sky, down past two giant poplar trees guarding the approach to the runway. The biplane flies so slowly that there is time to watch the poplars and see how their leaves flutter silver in the wind. Then I look out to the side as the runway appears below, look out to the side and judge the height, gauge the height of tall wheels above the grass, and with a shudder the stall and the airplane is down and rolling left-rudder right-rudder keep it straight beside the runway don't let it get away from you right-rudder now, just a touch of right rudder. And that's all there is to it. Simple as can be.

Another takeoff, another landing, another bit of knowing tucked away. Somehow, taxiing to the hanger, I'm surprised that it should be so easy to demolish the stories and the grim warnings.

"Evander Britt, you just made a deal."

The trade is completed in a day, with only an occasional rustle in the forest that shows where a misgiving lurks.

I am owner of a 1929 Detroit-Ryan Speedster, model Parks P-2A.

Good-bye, Fairchild. We have flown many hours and learned many things together. Of instruments humming and the things that happen when they cease to hum, of riding invisible radio beams over Pennsylvania and Illinois and Nebraska and Utah and California, of landings at international airports with jetliners close behind and on beaches with only a gull or a sandpiper to hurry us along. But now there is more to learn, and different problems.

The hangar doors that had opened on a new way of life close now on an old one. Into the front cockpit of the Parks go the sleeping bag and sandwiches and the jug of water, cans of sixty-weight oil and cockpit covers and C-26 spark plugs, tools and tape and a coil of soft wire.

Fill the gas tank to its five-hour brim; a last handshake from Evander Britt. From those who stand near and know where I plan to fly, a few faint words.

"Good luck."

"Take it easy, now."

"You be careful, hear?"

A newspaper reporter is interested to find that the biplane is seven years older than its pilot.

Engine started, muttering softly at the bottom of its drum, I buckle into the unfamiliar parachute harness, fasten the safety belt, and jounce slowly over the grass, fanning it back behind me, moving into position for takeoff.

It is one of those times when there is no doubt that a moment is an important moment, one that will be remembered. In that moment, the old throttle goes forward under my glove and the first second of a journey begins. The technical details are here, and crowding about: rpm at 1,750, oil pressure at 70 psi, oil temperature at 100 degrees F. The other details are here, too, and I am ready to learn again: I can't see a *thing* ahead of this airplane when it is on the ground; look how far forward the throttle will move without gaining another revolution from the engine; this is going to be a long and windy journey; note the grassblades growing at the edge of the runway; how quickly the tail is flying and we can skim the ground on the main wheels only. And we're off. A constant thunder and beating twisting wind about me, but I can hear it all as they are hearing it, on the ground: a tiny hum increasing, for a quick second loud and powerful overhead, then dwindling on down the scale to end in a tiny old biplane quiet against the sky.

CHAPTER TWO

As long as I'm so few miles from the Atlantic, I'll fly east to the ocean. Make it a more fitting triumph to have flown literally from one coast to the other; from sea, as it were, to shining sea.

We are aloft, and heading east as the sun grows into a cool setting fireball behind. The shine is gone from the railroad tracks, and shadows have washed together into a dark protecting coat for the ground. I am in daylight still, but that is night seeping up out of the ground and my new old airplane has no lights. Barely airborne, it is time to land.

Five minutes away, down and to our right, a field. A pasture. It is a quarter mile long, with only a single row of trees to make the landing approach an interesting problem. We circle the field three times, the biplane and I, watching closely for ruts and holes and tree stumps and hidden ditches. And in the circling and the watching, the quarter mile of land changes from anonymous old pasture to *my* pasture; my field, my home for the night, my airport. A few minutes ago this land was nothing, now it is my home. I know that I shall have to land well to the left, paralleling the dirt road, avoiding a jackstraw pile of pine logs near the forest.

For the briefest of moments, a frightened voice. What the devil am I doing here, sitting in a wild old biplane with the sun gone down, circling a pasture with intent to land and a good chance of overlooking one felled tree in the dark grass and adding another twenty-three hundred pounds of kindling to the pile of jackstraws? One last cautious pass. The field looks short, and it looks wet, too. But I am committed to land, short or not, wet or not, kindling or not.

Eighty miles per hour and whistling down over the row of trees. One brief sideslip to lose the last of my altitude, black grass blurring by, the pile of giant logs that were jackstraws a moment ago, and in the last second the world forward is blanked in the long wide nose of my new airplane. For better or . . . for . . . worse. The wheels . . . SLAM down. Instant geysers of high-pressure mud swallow the airplane in flying spray and I fight, I just hang on and fight to keep her straight it takes forever to stop we should be stopped by now and we're just barely beginning to slow and the mud is still roaring up from the wheels and I can feel it wet on my face and the world goes dim as it sprays my goggles and we should be stopped by n . . . BAM! what was that the tail, something has snapped in the tail and HANG ON! We finish our mud landing with a hard wrench to the right, with a great sheet of liquid brown thrown in a tenth second to be a solid storm of mud over airplane and grass for a hundred feet around. We slide to a stop with our tall wheels four inches down in the sodden ground. Switches off and the engine stops and we are forlorn and unmoving, wrapped in a blanket of deepest silence.

Across the field, a bird chirps, one time.

What a landing. Something is broken, for the Parks is twisted, her nose high in the air. So this is what it was like in the old days of flying. A pilot was on his own. If I would live the old days, I must be on my own.

It is clear, in a moment, that nothing will happen and nothing will move unless I make it happen and unless I make it move. We will sit together, the biplane and I, to freeze into mud and all eternity unless I break this silence and move around and find out what damage I have done.

So, while night oozes up out of the mud, I stir and climb over the side of my cockpit to step squishing down and look fearfully upon the tail wheel. It does not look good. Only the tip of the wheel shows round beneath the fuselage, and I am certain that the axle has been smashed and twisted beyond any hope of repair.

But, lying in the mud, pointing a flashlight, I discover that it is not so, that only a small shock cord has broken, allowing the wheel to fold backward. The cord replaced by a length of nylon rope from my front-cockpit supply depot, the wheel rotates down once again into position, ready for other fields to conquer. The work takes ten minutes.

So this is how it was. A pilot handled his own problems as they came, and he went without help wherever he felt like going.

In modern aviation there is a runway for every man, and scores of people earn their living by helping the pilot in need. And mind your conduct, pilot, when the control tower is watching.

What would they have thought, those pilots who barnstormed alone in the Parks and her sisters across the meadows and the early years of flight? Perhaps they would have seen how wonderful it all is today, at the big airports. But perhaps, too, they would have shaken their heads a bit sadly and flown back into the days when they are free and on their own.

Here, in my muddy pasture, I have followed them. This is a barnstormer's field. No control tower or runway here, no fuel-and-oil service, no follow-me truck to tell me where to park. There is not a trace of the present, there is not a hint of time in the air. If I wish, I can find reference in the papers and cards I carry to years labeled 1936 and 1945 and 1954 and May 1964. And I can burn them all. I can burn them and squash their ashes down into this black mud and press more mud over them, and there I would be, all alone, way out in the middle of now.

Darkness gathers full about us, and I spread my waterproof cockpit cover on the ground beneath the left wing, and the sleeping bag upon the cover, where it will be dry. The only sounds in the whole field, quarter mile long and rimmed in uncut forest, are the sound of a sleeping bag straightened over a canvas cockpit cover and a sound of cold chicken sandwiches unwrapped.

Stretched out beneath the wing of my airplane, I sleep, but wake later in the cold of the night. Above me the sky is moving its fresh cold dark silent way to its own secret horizons. I have watched the sky for hours uncounted and followed it, and crossed horizons with it, and still have not begun to tire. The everchanging, fascinating sky.

The airplane, of course, is the key. It makes the sky accessible. As astronomy without a telescope can be uninteresting, so the sky without an airplane. One can watch only so much before he is sated, but when he can participate, when he can move himself through the halls of cloud in the day and travel from star to star in the night, then he can watch with knowing, and does not have to imagine what it would be like to walk those halls and those stars. With an airplane, he can learn to know the sky as an old friend, and to smile when he sees it. No prodding the memory nor need to keep reminders. A glance through a window, a walk along a crowded or along a secluded street, at noon or at midnight. The sky of now is always here, moving; and we, watching, share a part of its secret.

I rest, tonight, partly beneath a white-flour moon and partly beneath a wing of wooden ribs that carries struts and wires to support another wing of wooden ribs above it. This is not happening years ago, I rest here now. The barnstormers? They live with the same moon and the same stars. Their time has not gone, it is still about us.

I wonder about my new biplane. She has spent many calendars safe in a silent hangar, and has been cared for patiently, and rarely flown. The rain did not touch her, nor the sun, nor the wind. And here she is in the mud of a cold night field, sheathed in dirt and water mixed, with dew beading on her wings. Around her no black hangar air, but the sky and stars. Knowing where she is, Evander Britt would wince and turn away. The last remaining Detroit-Parks P-2A flying, the very last, priceless; and tonight, you say, in the MUD?

I have to smile. For I truly think, with no need for guile, that she is happier here. For fields and mud she was built, with fields and mud and nights under the stars in mind she was set from designer's pen to paper. Designed to make her living flying passengers on joyrides from pastures and crossroads, from green-summer county fairs and in rainbow air circuses traveling, traveling. She was designed to be flown.

The pages of the aircraft logbook, buried now under tool kit and tie-down ropes, are a document of flight, a memory in ruled paper.

"DATE: *May 14, '32*, DURATION OF FLIGHT: *10 min.* NUMBER OF PASSENGERS: *2.*" Page after page of five-minute and ten-minute flights, just time for one takeoff, one circle of the field, one landing. Occasionally, in the REMARKS column: *"Total passengers carried to date—810."* A few pages further: *"Total passengers—975."* Between these, the column makes minor reference that all landings were not smooth. *"Propeller removed and straightened." "Wingtip repaired." "Tail-wheel replaced."* In September 1939: *"Passengers—1,233,"* and the next entry: *"Aircraft prepared for storage."*

If he had not been able to sell the airplane soon, Evander Britt had said, he was going to give her to the National Air Museum, the last aircraft of her type, and a symbol of her time.

Which would you choose, airplane, polished linoleum floors and a life secure behind purple-velvet rope, or the insecurities of mud and moonlight, of bent propellers and wingtips for repair?

A good question for the pilot, too. There can be the security of polished floors and velvet ropes for him, too. No need to be thundering about the countryside, to be tackling highly improbable odds, when he can be forever safe behind a desk. There is only one sacrifice to be made for that security. To be safe he has only to sacrifice living. In safety there are no fears to conquer, no obstacles to overcome, no wild screaming dangers stalking behind the fence of our mistakes. If we wish, velvet ropes, and a single word on the wall: "Silence."

A mist has risen from the damp earth of the field, and under the moon it is a field of spun glass glowing. What is this like? To what does it compare? I consider for a long time, to discover that it compares to nothing I have ever known. An airplane teaches many things, but always before I have learned in the air, while flying. When the airplane was on the ground, the lesson was over. But tonight, in a nameless field in North Carolina, the airplane huge above me, casting a quiet black shadow across my sleeping bag, I am still learning. Will I never stop learning from airplanes? How can there be room in tomorrow for still another lesson?

The biplane stands serene and unmoving. She seems very sure that there will be room for a lesson tomorrow.

CHAPTER THREE

ADVENTURES BEGIN with the sun. By the time the mist is gone, and the mud dry on the wings, the biplane and I begin our first full day together. The only sounds in the field are the unusual ones of cylinders 1–3–5–2–4 slowly, over and again while the bright blade flickers around.

I pace the field in front of the plane, moving blown tree branches and occasional stones aside, marking the holes that could give difficulty. This first part of the takeoff is critical, before the weight has gone from the wheels into the wings.

The 1–3–5–2–4 comes fainter and fainter as I pace, a soft sewing machine stitching quietly away to itself. If someone wanted, he could dash to the biplane, push the throttle forward, and be gone. I know that the field is deserted, but still I am glad to return and work closer to the biplane.

Sleeping bag stowed in its tight fluffy cylinder and strapped in the front cockpit, giant fan-wind whirring past once again to establish a pattern of familiar, we are ready to say good-bye to a field that has been friend and tutor.

The thought flag comes down, checkered, and a single word: Go. Center of a roaring hemisphere of 1–3–5–2–4 round and round 1,750 times a minute, moving slowly at first on heavy wheels, jouncing. Then faster. Then skipping from peak to tiny peak. Splashing mud in the first second, then spattering it, then spraying it hard, then skimming it, then leaving it smooth and untouched, casting down a shuddering black shadow.

Good-bye, field.

A railroad track points east, and so does the nose of the Parks. For the decision to fly from coast to coast, for the poor human frailty of wanting to tie things in neat packages with colorful bows just so, we fly east on our journey west. Because of an intangible unseen whim, a most seen and quite tangible old biplane whirs and thrashes through the sky, above a railroad track, reaching for the Atlantic Ocean.

Ahead, the sun rises from a golden sea. I need railroad tracks no longer, and shift my navigation from dull rails to a blinding star.

Sometimes there are so many symbols about me in the air that it is surprising I can see to fly. I become a symbol, myself. Which is a glorious sort of feeling, for there are so many meanings for me that I can inspect the meaning-bin and carefully select the one that looks best and feels best for this day and this hour. And all good meanings, and real.

What shall I be, this moment? For that part of me that keeps a cautious and uneasy distance from meanings, I am the holder of Commercial Airman's Certificate 1393604, with the privileges of flight instructor, rated for instrument flying and to control single- and multiengine land airplanes through the air and along the ground as necessary to accomplish the mission of flight. For that part of me, I am 5.27 miles from the Wilmington Omnirange, on the 263-degree radial, at 2,176 feet pressure altitude at 1118 hours Greenwich Mean Time on the 27th day of March in the 1,964th year of the Gregorian Calendar, New Style.

The fuselage of the airplane I fly is painted Stearman Vermilion, Randolph stock number 1918; the wings and tail are Champion Yellow, Randolph stock number unknown but very definitely and precisely listed somewhere in the dusty records of a forgotten drawer in a lost attic away over the horizon. A very precise airplane, every bolt and joint and stitch of it. Not only Detroit-Ryan Speedster, Model Parks P-2A, but serial number 101, registration number N499H, built December 1929, and licensed January 1930, under Aircraft Type Certificate 276.

Divorced from meanings, with labels only attached, the airplane and I become very complex and forbidding machines. Every bolt and wire of the engine and the airplane has a stock number, a serial number, a lot number. Take a magnifying glass, scrape away the varnish, and there are our numbers, stamped. And meaningless. When one surrounds oneself with meanings there are conflicts and shades of meanings and meanings whose holes are not drilled to line up and can't be bolted together. One can be safe, with serial numbers, in a land of utter quiet. No disputes. Nothing moves.

But I am moving now, and so would carefully select a tailored meaning to outfit my airplane and one to slip about my own shoulders.

Since it is a bright day, biplane, and promising fair, let us mean joy. How does that fit? Look: joy seeks the sun, and the early of the mornings. Joy moves with delight, hasting to where the ocean is golden and the air crisp and cold. Joy tastes the liquid air spraying back onto leather helmet and lowered goggles. It delights in the freedom that is only found and won away up in the sky, from which there is no falling if one only keeps moving. And in the moving, we gain, and joy is precious even in Stearman Vermilion number 1918.

Here, here, son. The practical self speaking, uneasy with symbols, the rein-holding, solemn self. Here, here. All we want to do is get this thing out over the Atlantic a foot or two, so you can say you've done it, and then we have to get along on west. Engine, you know. It *could* fail.

How is it possible, I wonder, for me to be so sure, so self-centered certain that I am in control? I do not know, but the fact remains that I am, when I fly. Those clouds, for instance. Others may pass through them, but I am the one who lends them to the world. The patterns now in the sunlight on the sea, the streaks of fire in the sunrise, the cool breeze and the warm, all of these. Mine. For surely there can be in the world no one who knows and loves these as I. There, the source of the confidence and the power. I am sole heir to these, who can lift an airplane into the sky and feel, as the cloud wheels beneath him, that he has come truly home once again.

Look up, of a morning when the sun rises through the clouds, or of an evening as it sets. A thousand slanting shafts of gold, aren't there? A brilliance, a sort of molten fire hidden? These are just the sights of my land seen from the ground, so bright and so warm and with beauty filled that the cloud cannot contain it all and splashes its overflow onto the earth as just a hint of the brilliance and the gold that exists above.

That little sound of four cylinders or five or seven, above the cloud, comes from a winged machine that is immersed in bright wonder. To be up there and fly alongside this creature is to see a vision, for the wings of an airplane in the sunrise are of beaten gold, going bright silver if you catch the proper angle, and on the canopy and along the windscreen dance the sparkle of diamonds. And within, a pilot, watching. What can you say, seeing this? You say nothing, and you share with another man in another cockpit a time of silence.

For when he sees this, when the magnificence floods over an airplane and the man who guides it, there is no speaking. Enchanted in the high land, to mention beauty and joy in the mundane surroundings of earth and city and wall and polite society is to feel gawkish and out of place. Even to his best beloved, a pilot cannot speak of the wonder of the sky.

After the sun is high and the spell fades, one's fuel is gone. The white needle is at the *E,* the little indicator cork ceases its bobbing, a red low-level-warning light glares above a fuel counter. And in a minute or five or ten, the tires thud again onto the grass or scream a blue-smoke cry against the concrete of a once-forgotten runway. Mission done, flight over. Chalk up another hour. Pencil and logbook for a moment busy. But though the earth once again spreads beneath our feet, and the unnatural quiet of an engineless world surrounds us, there is new fuel to be hosed into tanks, and another page in the log to be filled.

To a pilot, the most important thing in the world is flight. To share it is the gift without price. Therein is a key to the sometimes wild acts of young pilots. They fly under bridges, they buzz housetops, they loop and roll their airplane much closer to the ground than is safe. They are a major concern of military flight-training bases, for such action reflects a lack of discipline, and occasionally means the loss of student and airplane. But his thought is to give, to share joy with those he loves, to share a truth. For pilots sometimes see behind the curtain, behind the veil of gossamer velvet, and find the truth behind man, the force behind a universe.

In the bright thread are woven 4 billion lives. Now and again, a man will see a certain brightness beyond the curtain and go spinning away into the depths of reality. We who remain watch him go, marvel for a moment, and return to our stations at our own cross-threads in the woof and the warp of a sparkling illusion.

For even in an airplane we see too often imperfectly. With advancing invention, with cockpits closed and navigation instruments and radio and new electronics, the problem of flying has become something to be solved more and more within an arm's distance of the pilot. Drifting off course? A needle shows it, points the error, and all the pilot must do to see it is to look within a three-inch face of glass. Concerned about weather ahead? Dial a frequency on the radio, call a meteorologist and ask expert advice. Airplane slowing in the air, approaching a stall? A red light flashes on the instrument panel, a warning horn blares. We look outside to the sky only when we have time to enjoy the view, and if we don't want to be bothered with the view, we needn't look outside from takeoff till touchdown. It is this kind of flight over which the manufacturers of flight simulators can boast, "Impossible to tell our trainer from flight itself!" And so it is. Those who define flight as a series of hours spent in attention to the moving gauges of an instrument panel cannot tell the difference. The only thing that is missing is the wind. The heat of the sun. The canyons of cloud and sheer white walls rising solid at each wingtip. The sound and the sting of rain, the freezing cold of altitude, the sea of moonlight in its bed of fog, the stars untwinkling and ice-hard in a midnight sky.

So. The biplane. Is it the better way? If the Parks flies too slowly, there are no warning horns or flashing red lights. Just a shudder in the control stick and it turns into a machine unwilling to be controlled, suddenly aware that it is heavier than the air. One must be careful and alert for the shudder. One must look outside, for outside is flight itself, the moving through the air and knowing it. Especially, knowing it.

Navigation is goggles down, look over the side, down through the churning winds. The railroad: so. The river crossing: so. But the lake, there should be a lake here. Perhaps there are headwinds. . . .

A check on the weather is a constant thing. The clouds mass and grow together, lowering into the hills. Slanting columns of rain, where earlier there was no rain. What to do, pilot, what to do? Beyond the hills, the cloud may thin, or break. But then, beyond the hills, the cloud can lower to brush the grasstops ragged and soak them in rain. Hills are green coffins for the airplanes and pilots who judge wrongly. Beware the hills when the cool grey mist is pulled over your eyes.

Decide, pilot. Land now? Choose the pasture for soft touchdown and certainty of longer living? Or push on, into the grey? This is flight: decisions. And knowing that sooner or later an airplane must always come to rest.

We turn south, the Parks and I, to follow the Atlantic coastline. The beach is wide and hard and deserted, and the only sounds across it are the sounds of the wind and the waves crashing and the cry of a seagull and the brief windy passing roar of an airplane flying. The air is salt air, and salt spray leaps toward the tall wheels of the biplane. Here for a hundred miles we can fly in comfort with the wheels skimming the wave tops, for the old fliers' caution—always be able to land safely should the engine stop—is satisfied by the wide smooth expanse of sand to our right. There is no greater security for a pilot than the security of flat land nearby. Flat land equals peace of mind and serenity in any situation. Fail the engine, bring the downdraft, bring the storms with thunder rolling; with a level field nearby, the pilot has no worry. A circle once to lose altitude, a gentle lifting of the nose, and airplane and pilot are blessed with their only time without the pressure and the need for constant motion. To fly above flat fields is to fly without pressure, and is the most relaxed flying that a pilot can know. And now from horizon to horizon as far as I can see ahead is the broad flat landing beach of South Carolina.

But, oddly enough, the biplane does not feel right, as if she is not glad to be here. There is foreboding in her, a sense of caution that dampens even the assurance of the infinite beach strip ahead. What could be wrong? Why, I simply am not used to her yet, or she to me. It will take time, it will take a few hours to fly this beach and enjoy it to its full.

A brief inlet, with a single small sailboat drifting idly along. We roar over its mast, with one quick wave to the skipper at the helm, and catch his wave in return.

The shape of the land now, and of the beach, is familiar. I know that to the right there should be a swamp soon, and soon to the right there is a swamp. How can I know? A map can give no such familiarity, for ink and colored lines, unless studied and imagined, are only ink and colored lines. And this is familiar, the curve of the beach, the swamp.

Of course! I have been here before! I have flown this very stretch of beach; and the vagueness and the familiarity come from a different viewpoint. I have flown the beach before at an altitude many times higher than the biplane will ever reach, from eight miles in the air, and looked down upon these same sands and have noted with satisfaction that my ground speed was six hundred miles per hour. A different day then, and a different airplane. Fine days, those. Of strapping into thirteen-ton fighters and riding the twisting thundering heat of a turbine engine. Climb straight up, come blasting straight down through the speed of sound.

A good life, and it was sad to leave the fighters with their great speed and their brilliant glory. But I nodded my head to circumstance and the reins were snapped and the days of machmeters and gunsights faded behind me.

Yet the high land is the same no matter the vehicle. With a whirling thrashing propeller again in front of the cockpit instead of a spinning turbine behind, I discover that the only real difference is that a tank of fuel lasts three times as long, and in place of speed I am the master of time, and a new kind of freedom.

Suddenly, on the beach below a sunrise biplane in the world of now, a house. Two houses. Five, and a wooden pier stretching out into the sea. A water tower, and the name CRESCENT BEACH. We have arrived. Time for fuel and a sandwich.

Still, though, the foreboding, the reluctance in the wood and the fabric and a trembling in the control stick.

The airport is a single runway, a hard-surface runway not far from the water tower. The wind is blowing from the sea, across the runway. Official terminology: crosswind. I have heard the stories of the old pilots. Never land in a crosswind, they said, and told stories of the days when to do this was a painful and costly error.

And for a moment I forget what time it is. The airport is safe in 1964 and I am flying in 1929.

Come on, airplane, settle down. The Parks feels brittle and stiff, and I move the rudder from side to side to make her loosen up. She is trying to remind me of the stories. Crosswinds to her are like flames to a racehorse, and I am leading her, urging her into the heat and the fire, concerned only about fuel and sandwiches.

Eighty miles per hour and lined on the runway. Power back, the Parks settles lifelessly toward the ground. I am puzzled that she should feel so dead. Settle down, there, little friend. In a minute you will be drinking a tank of cool red eighty-octane.

The wheels touch the concrete smoothly at 70 mph, and, tail held high, we slow, runway blurred still at the edges. Finally the tail loses its flying speed and the tailwheel comes down to squeak on the hard surface. And we meet the inevitable. Moving at thirty miles per hour, the biplane, against her will and mine, begins to turn into the wind. Sudden full rudder against the turn has no effect, and she swings faster into the wind. Press hard opposite brake . . . but that instant when the brake could have helped is past and from the slow turn a monster grabs the biplane and slams her into an instant whiplash turnabout. With a great shriek from the tires we snap around, sliding sideways down the runway. A shriek, a horizon blurring all around, a sharp pistol-shot from the right main landing gear, all in a half-second. While I sit powerless in the cockpit, numbly holding full opposite rudder, a wheel breaks, folds beneath the airplane. A wingtip grinds suddenly down into the concrete, spraying sparks and splinters and old fabric to mix with blue burning rubber smoke. Scraping and screaming about me, the biplane is lashed once, hard, by her old enemy, the crosswind.

And then it is quiet, save for the engine panting and quickly dying as I cut the switches.

You fool.

You stupid idiot you harebrained excuse for a pilot you hamfisted imbecile. You idiot you fool you dumb stupid—you've broken her! Look at what you've done, you idiot, you fool! I climb slowly from the cockpit. It has been very quick, very sudden, and I have destroyed an airplane because I didn't heed the old warnings. Nineteen twenty-nine does not mix with today. They are separate separate worlds. You fool. The right wheel is smashed beneath the airplane and torn in two pieces. You idiot. The right wingtip is shredded, the rear wingspar cracked. You dumb stupid imbecile. I forced 1929 into the present and that force was enough to shear the carbon-steel bolts of the right main gear fittings, to twist them into little bent-clay cylinders of something once useful. You worthless clod.

A few tears of gasoline fall from the engine. It is very quiet on the runway. The crosswind sighs now, unconcerned, no longer interested.

Airport attendants, those that heard the crash, drive from the hangar with a truck and a winch and they lift the nose of the biplane, and help me guide her under a roof. A tall jack is moved in to replace the missing wheel and broken landing gear strut.

They leave me and I sit alone with the biplane. What is the lesson, airplane? What am I supposed to learn here? There is no answer. Outside, the sky goes dark, and later it begins to rain.

CHAPTER FOUR

"Is that all that's wrong?" Colonel George Carr speaking, and the words echo in the hangar. "From the way Evander talked, I thought you had hurt something! Son of a gun, boy, we'll have you flying by tomorrow noon!"

George Carr. A collection of letters that stands for a weather-beaten face below a shock of grey hair and warm blue eyes that have seen many calendars come and go, and many, many airplanes.

The call to Lumberton, this morning, had not been easy to make.

"Evander, I'm at Crescent Beach."

"You're fine, I hope," Evander Britt said. "And how's your new airplane flying? Still like it?"

I was grateful for the straight-line. "I like it fine, Van. But I don't think it's too crazy about me."

"Now how would you mean that?" If he thought from my call that something had gone wrong, he was certain of it now.

"I had a bit of a ground-loop here, trying to land in a crosswind. Lost a gear and a wheel, tore one wing up pretty bad. Wonder if you'd happen to have a spare gear and wheel around." There. I had said it. Whatever he says now I deserve. The worst thing he can say, I deserve every bit of it. I clenched my teeth.

"Oh . . . no . . ."

For a moment there was full silence on the line, when he knew that he had given his airplane to the wrong man, to a brash cocky young-ster who hadn't begun to learn how to fly an airplane or to be a pilot. The silence was not enjoyable.

"Well." He was brisk and friendly again, all business, trying to solve my problems. "I've got a spare set of landing gear all right, that you can have. And a set of wings, if you need. You broke the wheel, did you?"

"Right main wheel. Tire looks usable, but there's not a chance for the wheel."

"I don't have any wheels. Maybe Gordon Sherman, over in Asheville, might loan you one to get home on. I'll call him up now and drive over and get it if he does. . . . Don't know what we're going to do if he doesn't have one. Those big wheels scarcer than hens' teeth. I'll call George Carr the minute I hang up. He's done all the mechanic work on the Parks, and licensed it for you. If anyone can fix the Parks, he can. I'll put the landing gear and wheel in his car, if he'll drive down. I'd be down myself, but I've got a case going in court tomorrow that I just can't leave. You have the airplane in a hangar, do you?"

"Yes."

"That's good. We're having some rain up here, moving down that way. Wouldn't want to get her wet." He paused. "If you want to have your Fairchild back, I'm making the offer."

"Thanks, Van. I got my airplane right now. All I have to do is learn how to fly it."

George Carr had arrived, windshield wipers squeaking across bat-tered glass, three hours later.

"Why don't you strip the fabric off around that aileron fitting there, so we can get at it a little easier? Might pull that panel beneath the wing, too, would help."

The colonel works happily, because he likes to work on airplanes. He likes to see them come back to life beneath his hands. He is pounding with a rawhide mallet on a twisted bracket, straightening it. Pound, pound, echoing.

"... used to take my old Kreider-Reisner 31 out Sundays, land on the crossroads. People for the most part never seen an airplane up close before, let alone got in one." Pound. Pound-pound-pound. "Yeah. For a while there it was a pretty good livin'.'" Pound-pound-pound.

He talks on, as we work, of a world that I am just beginning to know. A world in which a pilot always has to be ready to repair his airplane, or it will never fly again. He speaks without nostalgia or longing for the days past, as though they weren't really past at all, as though as soon as he has the wheel back on the biplane we'll start the engine and fly to a crossroad or a pasture close to town, to begin flying the folk who have never seen an airplane up close before, let alone got in one.

"Looks like that ought to do the job." The pounded aileron fitting is straight and flat as a concrete hangar floor. "Stronger than it was before. Cold-worked, you know."

Perhaps I haven't been born too late, after all. Perhaps it isn't too late to learn. I have been brought up in a world of airplanes with the white stars of the military upon their wings, and U.S. AIR FORCE stenciled beneath gunports. Of airplanes repaired by specialists, in accordance with T.O.1-F84F-2, of flying procedures prescribed by Air Force Regulation 60-16, of conduct controlled by the Universal Code of Military Justice. There is, in all of this, no regulation that allows a pilot to repair his own airplane, for that requires a special army of technicians with a special army of serial numbers and job classifications. Airplanes and parts of airplanes in the military service are rarely repaired at all—they are replaced. Radio fading and going dim in flight? Corrective action: remove and replace. Engine operated overtemperature? Remove and replace. Landing gear strut collapse after touchdown? Class 26: aircraft removed from service.

And here is George Carr, barnstormer, mechanic, with a rawhide mallet in his hand, saying it would all be stronger than ever. I learn that the repairing or rebuilding of an airplane, or of a man, doesn't depend upon the condition of the original. It depends upon the attitude with which the job is taken. The magic phrase "Is THAT all that's wrong!" and an attitude to match, and the real job of rebuilding is finished.

"Gordon Sherman's loaning you a wheel from his Eaglerock to get home on; 'Vander Britt put it out in the trunk of the car." He is straining now over a heavy bolt on the landing gear leg. "You might run . . . the wheel . . . down to the gas station . . . and see if they can put the tire on for us."

As simple as that. Gordon Sherman is loaning you a wheel. A rare old thirty-by-five spun-aluminum wheel, the kind that aren't built now and haven't been built for thirty years and that never will be built again. On loan from a friend I never met. Perhaps Gordon Sherman had wondered how he'd feel a continent away from home, in need of a rare old wheel for his Eaglerock. Perhaps he has wheels to spare. Perhaps his basement is filled with thirty-by-five spun aluminum wheels. But Gordon Sherman is this moment silently thanked by a friend he has never met, and will be thanked, silently, for a long time after.

Colonel George Carr works on into the night, under the green fluorescent lights of the hangar at Crescent Beach, South Carolina. He works and he directs and I learn from him until 1:30 A.M. At 1:30 A.M. the biplane is patched, and ready to fly.

"You might fly her over toward North Carolina tomorrow," he says, grinning, not knowing that at one-thirty in the morning people are supposed to be dead tired and ready to drop instantly asleep, "and we'll put the finishing touches on her there. There's some fabric around the shop, and some dope. We'll put you to work doping."

And it is done. He lifts his clanking, boulder-heavy tool kit into the car, sets the torn wheel carefully beside it, and with a wave disappears into the darkness, driving back to Lumberton. Exit, for the moment, a teacher of confidence. Exit a window into what, until one knows better, one calls the past. By the time he is home, I am asleep on the hangar floor, having spent half an hour listening to the rain, thinking that there are only twenty-six hundred miles to go.

In the morning, one patched biplane, yellow fabric held together here and there with bright red tape, lifts away from Crescent Beach, following from above a river, a highway, a railroad track, and arrives again at Lumberton, North Carolina.

Turn into the wind, touch the grass, taxi to the hangar where the colonel waits, readying fabric and dope.

Evander Britt is inspecting the taped wing before the propeller has stopped turning, running his hand lightly over the tape, feeling for broken ribs.

"You got a broken rib out here, Dick."

"I know."

"And I see you welded a plate onto the main landing gear fitting. Cracked out down there, was it?"

"Little crack, where it started to give before the bolt sheared. Welded the plate on, and it shouldn't want to crack any more." As long as we are talking, the guilt on my shoulders doesn't hurt. It hurts when Evander Britt is silent, and looks at the biplane.

"If you want to trade back for your Fairchild . . ."

"Evander, I want this airplane and I know I don't deserve it. I'm going to fly it home if it takes me all year, if I have to pick it up in a box and carry it to California." That is probably the wrong thing to say. After this start, the chances of my having to pick up the pieces and carry them west are much greater than the chances of the biplane flying there under her own power. There is little doubt that the lawyer would like to have his airplane safely again in his hangar instead of chasing around the country with a novice pilot in its cockpit. There is less than little doubt. There is no doubt at all.

"Well, if you ever want to . . . ," he says, looking again at the taped wing. "Boy, you sounded miserable as a wet rooster on that telephone. Like a little old soaking-wet banty rooster. Like the whole world had just come down on your head."

"Sure wasn't very happy. That was a stupid thing, trying to land in that wind. It was really stupid."

"Well, don't feel bad about it, boy. These things happen. Come on now. Roll up your sleeves and we'll help George get her fixed better than new."

I learn about repairing wood-and-cloth airplanes. The colonel shows me how to cut a patch of Grade A cotton fabric and fray the edges, and smooth it to the wing with clear dope, let it dry and sand it smooth. Another coat of clear dope, another sanding. Then colored dope and sanding, over and over, until I can't tell the patch from the rest of the fabric around. After many patches, at last finished and better than new, it is afternoon and time to turn the nose westward, and fly.

"What do I owe you, George?" This is a hard time, when the business has to come to the front and the learning and the friendship of working together on an airplane take a backseat.

"Oh, I don't know. Didn't really do much. You did most of the work." He rummages in a tool bin, looking for his pipe tobacco.

"The devil I did. Wasn't for you, this airplane would be sitting in that hangar at Crescent Beach till the junkman came to haul her away. What do I owe you?"

A week ago, in Wichita, the tailwheel on the Fairchild had been replaced. A four-hour job, by businesslike modern-day mechanics. Cost: $90.75, parts and labor and tax included. What should it cost, then, to replace aileron fittings that had been smashed flat and immovable, install new shock cord on a main gear leg, install a new wheel, repair a wingtip and ribs and spar and cover the whole with fabric; parts, labor and tax included?

George Carr is awkward and uncomfortable and for a full twenty minutes I point out that my thanks aren't going to buy him dinner tonight or replace the dope and fabric I have used, or buy back the sleep that he missed or even the gasoline that he used driving to Crescent Beach.

"Name a figure, then," he says. "Whatever you say will be fine with me."

"Five hundred dollars is what it would cost me, assuming I could have found somebody that even knew where a spar is in a biplane."

"Don't be silly."

"I'm not being silly. When was the last time you had to pay the going rates to have some work done on an airplane, George? You're the world's best mechanic, sir, but the world's worst businessman. Come on, now. I have to get going before the sun's down. I can't leave till I pay you something. I won't be able to look at myself in the morning if I walk out of here without paying you. Honest. And I really am sorry."

A small shy voice from across the room. "Thirty, forty dollars be too much?"

I argue for a while and work him up to strike an agreement at fifty dollars, which leaves me just enough money to finish the trip across the country, but still feeling like a young and heartless overlord taking advantage of the kind and gentle people who dwell about him. And I feel at the same time, helplessly, that I am committing a sacrilege. For George Carr and I love the same machines and the same joys. I can't help but believe that in the short time we spent working together over the biplane we each earned a friend. What kind of person is it who offers blind money to a friend in return for an act of friendship?

But the others, who were not my friends, those sheer brisk businessmen repairing a tailwheel, had handsomely charged and been handsomely paid. It isn't fair.

The biplane takes her throttle well, and lifts quickly into the wind. A last wing-rocking pass over the hangar and over two tiny figures on the grass, waving, and we point our nose again into the sun, swinging swiftly down out of its high arc toward certain collision with an immovable horizon.

How many collisions, sun? How many times have you dropped from high focused white heat down through the same cooling arc and fallen into the same valley that you will fall into this evening? And across the world, every moment a sunrise, and a new day beginning.

The sun moves another tenth of a degree toward the horizon, and as I fly, the valley that would have received it becomes a little lake, all golden, a mirror of a golden sky. And then a forest of trees moves in to stand pretender to the final resting place of the sun. If I could stand still in the air, I would be able to believe that the sun truly sinks into that valley, that lake, that forest. But the biplane dispels old illusions as quickly and as firmly as she creates new ones.

One that she is working on now: the engine will run forever. Listen: 1–3–5–2–4, over and again and again and again. If there is no faltering now, there will never be a faltering. I am strong and powerful and I shall spin my bright propeller until the sun itself is weary of rising and of setting.

*   *   *

The ground now is going dark, and the surface of the land is one smooth pool of shadow. Once again the biplane reminds me that she has no lights for flying or landing. Even the flashlight is out of reach, in the front cockpit.

Fine thing this could be. Spend your time daydreaming and wake to find yourself enveloped in night. Find a place to land, son, or there will be more repairs for you to make. At 1,740 revolutions per minute, fifty-two gallons of gasoline will last five hours and six minutes. Which means, at the moment, that there are three hours and twenty-one minutes left for my brave engine. My five-cylindered companion and its faithful flashing blade will cease to turn at just the moment that the sun sets in San Francisco, and that it rises in Jakarta. Then, perhaps, twenty-five minutes of silent gliding and the end of the world. For the sky is the only world, quite literally the only world there is for an airplane and for the man who flies it. The other world with its flowers and its seas and its mountains and deserts is a doorway to dying for the craft and the man of the sky, unless they return very gently, very carefully, seeing where they touch.

It is time to land now, while I still can see. And let us see. Over the side, down through the deep wind, we have a few darkening pastures, a puzzlework forest of black pines, a little town. And look at that, an airport. Beacon going green . . . going white . . . going green . . . and a short double row of white pinpoints in the dark; runway lights. Come along, airplane, let us go down and sleep against the earth tonight.

Tomorrow will be a big day.

CHAPTER FIVE

MORNING, SUN ONCE again, and a fresh green wind stirring across the wing that shelters me. A cool wind, and so fresh out of the forest that it is pure oxygen blowing. But warm in the sleeping bag and time for another moment of sleep. And I sleep to dream of the first morning that I ever flew in an airplane. . . .

Morning, sun, and a fresh green wind. Softly softly it moves, hushing gently, curving smoothly, easily, about the light-metal body of a little airplane that waits still and quiet on the emerald grass.

I will learn, in time, of relative wind, of the boundary layer and of the thermal thicket at Mach 3. But now I do not know, and the wind is wind only, soft and cool. I wait by the airplane. I wait for a friend to come and teach me to fly.

The distant seashell hush of a small-town morning is in the air, whispering along with the early wind. You have missed much, city dweller, the words trace in smoky thought. Sleep in your concrete shell until the sun is high and forfeit the dawn. Forfeit cool wind and quiet seashell roar, forfeit carpet of tall wet grass and soft silence of the early wind. Forfeit cold airplane waiting and the footstepsound of a man who can teach you to fly.

"Morning."

"Hi."

"Get that tie-down over there, will you?" He doesn't have to speak loudly to be heard. The morning wind is no opponent for the voice of a man.

The tie-down rope is damp and prickly, and when I pull it through the lift strut's metal ring, the sound of it whirs and echoes in the morning. Symbolic, this. Loosing an airplane from the ground.

"We'll just take it easy this morning. You can relax and get the feel of the airplane; straight and level, a few turns, look over the area a bit. . . ."

We are settled in the cockpit, and I learn how to fasten the safety belt over my lap. A bewildering array of dials on the dashboard; the quiet world is shut away outside a metal-doored cabin fitted to a metal-winged, rubber-tired entity with words cast into the design of the rudder pedals. Luscombe, the words say. They are well-worn words and impartial, but flair and excitement were cast into the mold. Luscombe. A kind of airplane. Taste that strange exciting word. Luscombe.

The man beside me has been making little motions among the switches on the bewildering panel. He does not seem to be confused.

"Clear."

I have no idea what he means. Clear. Why should he say *clear*?

A knob is pulled, one knob chosen at this moment from many samelooking knobs. And there goes my quiet dawn.

The harsh rasp of metal against metal and gear against gear, the labored grind of a small electric motor turning a great mass of enginemetal and propeller steel. Not the sound of an automobile engine starter. A starter for the engine of an airplane. Then, as if a hidden switch were pressed, the engine is running, shattering stillness with multibursts of gasoline and fire. How can he think in all this noise? How can he know what to do next? The propeller has been a blur for seconds, a disk that shimmers in the early sun. A mystic, flashing disk, rippling early light and bidding us follow. It leads us, rubber wheels rolling, along a wide grass road, in front of other airplanes parked and tied, dead and quiet. The road leads to the end of a wide level fairway.

He holds the brakes and pushes a lever that makes the noise unbearable. Is there something wrong with the airplane? Is this flying? We are strapped into our seats, compressed into this little cabin, assailed by a hundred decibels running. Perhaps I would rather not fly. *Luscombe* is a strange word and it means small airplane. Small and loud and built of metal. Is this the dream of flight?

The sound dies away for a moment. He leans toward me, and I toward him, to hear his words.

"Looks good. You ready?"

I nod. I am ready. We might as well get it over with. He had said it would be fun, and had said the words with the strange soft tone he used, belying his smile, when he truly meant his words. For that meaning I had come, had left a comfortable bed at five in the morning to tramp through wet grass and cold wind. Let's get it over with and trouble me no more with your flying.

The lever is again forward, the noise again unbearable, but this time the brakes are loosed, and the little airplane, the Luscombe, surges ahead. It carries us along, down the fairway.

Into the sky.

It really happened. We were rolling, following the magic spinning brightflashing blade, and suddenly we were rolling no more.

A million planes I had seen flying. A million planes, and was unimpressed. Now it was I, and that green dwindling beneath the wheels, that was the ground. Separating me from the green grass and quiet ground? Air. Thin, unseen, blowable, breathable air. Air is nothing. And between us and the ground: a thousand feet of nothing.

The noise? A little hum.

There! The sun! Housetops aglint, and chimney smoke rising!

The metal? Wonderful metal.

Look! The horizon! I can see beyond the horizon! I can see to the end of the world!

We fly! By God, *we fly!*

My friend watches me and he is smiling.

The wind stirs the flap of my sleeping bag and the sun is already above the horizon. It is six-fifteen and time to get up and get moving. The wind is not just cool; the wind is cold. Cold! And I thought spring in the South was a languid time of liquid warm from dawn to dawn. Into the chilled flight suit and pull on the frozen boots and the icy leather jacket. The airport is flat and closed about me and the runway lights are still on. Breakfast at the next stop, then, and time now to get the engine started and warming. One must always let the old engines warm themselves well before flight. They need ten minutes running on the ground to get the cold out of their oil and life into their controls.

Despite the cold, engine start is a beautiful time of day. The routine: pull the propeller through five times, fuel valve on, mixture rich, seven shots of priming fuel, pull the prop through two more times, magneto switch on, pump the throttle, crank the inertia starter, run back to the cockpit, engage the starter and swallow exhaust and engine thunder unfiltered and loud and frozen sharp, shattering again the silence of a little airport.

How many times have I started an airplane engine, even in the few years that I have been flying? In how many airplanes? So many different ways, so many different sounds, but beneath them all the same river; they are symbols of one meaning.

"Clear!"

Pull the starter knob to send the propeller into a faltering blurred arc. Press the primer knob. And from the exhaust stacks a cloud of blue and a storm of sound. Inspect the cloud under a microscope and you would find tiny drops of oil unburned. Inspect the sound on an oscilloscope and trace a quickchanging world of harsh pointed lines under the reference grid. In neither instrument can the essence of engine start be caught. That essence is unseen, in the thought of the one who controls the bank of switches that bid an engine to life. Get the prop turning, check the oil pressure, let the engine warm up. About 900 rpm for a minute or two. Forward on the throttle until the wheels begin to roll. Taxi to the waiting runway.

How many times in the history of flight has the routine been followed? From the earliest days, when engine start was the signal for ground crew to throw themselves on the stabilizer, holding a brakeless airplane until the wave of the pilot's hand. Through the days in the sun of war when engine start was the crashing roaring climax to "Run One . . . mesh One . . ." and the steepfalling whine of the inertia starter. To the days when now and then along the line of the crew's checklist there is the softest of purring rumbles, and the only visible sign of an engine alive is the quick-rising needle of the tailpipe temperature gauge, and the first ripples of heat drifting back from smooth-cowled turbines.

But for every one, for every single one, engine start is journey start. If you would seek some of the romance of flight, watch when the engines first begin to turn. Pick any place in aviation history, in any kind of airplane, and there is a shard or a massive block of romance, of glory and glamour. The pilot, in the cockpit, readies himself and his airplane. In scores of languages, in a hundred different terms, there comes the moment when one word or one sign means: Go.

"CLEAR!"

"CONTACT!"

". . . mesh One."

". . . OK. Start One."

"Clear left."

"Light-off."

A green flare in the sky.

A flight leader's finger, drawing a quick circle in the air.

"PILOTS. START YOUR ENGINES."

"Hit it."

"Let's go."

Great black massive propellers slam suddenly around. External power carts stagger and nearly die under instant load of high amperage. The explosion of shotgun starters. Hiss and ground-shaking concussion of compressed-air starters. Rattle and clatter and labored moan of hand-cranked inertia flywheels. The snap and clack of impulse magnetos. Roar of external air to the air-driven turbine starters. Slow soft acceleration of squaretipped turboprop blades.

From stillness into motion. From death into life. From silence into rising thunder. And each a part of the journey, for every man in every cockpit.

There is sound and glory, blue smoke and thunder, for anyone who wishes. Descendants of pioneers need not mourn the passing of an untouched frontier; it waits quiet above their heads. Little difference makes the look of the machine that becomes soon a part of the pioneer. He can be on flight orders, with a military commission signed by the president of the nation, riding forty thousand pounds of thrust at twice the speed of sound, protected by inch-thick glass and an artificial atmosphere within his cockpit. Despite the restrictions of the military, he has still his taste of freedom, his sight of the sky. Or he can be on the orders of desire and conscience alone, with an airplane bought instead of a second automobile, traveling a hundred miles per hour and protected from the wind by an eighth inch of Plexiglas or by a leather helmet and a pair of goggles.

The journey has been traveled tens of thousands of times, a trail blazed by Montgolfier and Montgomery and Wright, hewn and cleared by Lincoln Beachy and Glenn Curtiss and Earle Ovington and Jack Knight, paved and smoothed and widened by every man that guided an airplane away from the earth or who spent an hour in the dream of flight. Yet, in the billions of hours that men have been aloft, not one has left a mark in the sky. Into the smooth sky we pull a tiny wake of rippled air. When our airplane is gone, the sky smooths, carefully covering every sign of our passing, and becomes the quiet wilderness that it has always been.

So call the *Clear!* and starter engaged. Breathe blue smoke and set the wheels to rolling. Oil pressure and temperature and valve the fuel and set the flaps for takeoff. Set propeller revolutions to tremble at the redline, submerge in a sea of sound and bright glory. And go the way along the path, take up the journey in solitude.

Today our task is to cross the land in giant steps, to move as far as we can westward before the sun again wins its race.

A quick engine run-up, feeling again the goodness of being a long way from home and having an engine check out precisely as it should.

Throttle forward, a cloud of early dust, and we are airborne once again. Splashing green fountains of spring trees roll below as we settle into cruising flight, to share the joy of other machines and other people who are only happy when they are moving.

The hand on the control stick, testing elevators and rudder, the fingers on the magneto switch, the voice, *"Contact!"* each a part of one who seeks horizons lost a thousand years ago. "This time," the thought. "Maybe this time." The search, always the search. On a routine trip, over lands crossed daily on Flight 388, from the crowded flight deck of a jet airliner and from the cockpit of a sport airplane, the eyes of the wanderer look down, seeking the hidden; Elysium overlooked, the happy valley undiscovered. Now and again, the wanderer stiffens quickly in his cockpit, points down for the copilot to see, banks a wing for a clearer view. But the grass is never quite green enough; those are weeds at the water's edge, a strip of barren ground between the meadow and the river. Every once in a while the ideal is mirrored in the sky. Every once in a while there is a moment's perfection: the cloud, hard and brilliant against a hard and brilliant sky. Wind and cloud and sky; common denominators in perfection, eternals. The ground you can change. Rip out the grass, level the hill, pour a city over it all. But rip out the wind? Bury a cloud in concrete? Twist the sky to the image in one man's mind? Never.

We search for one goal and find another. We search the visible, holding the polished memory of perfection that was, and in the tens and hundreds and thousands of hours that we drift through the sky we discover a much different perfection. We journey toward a land of joy, and in our search we find the way that other, earlier pilots have scouted before us. They spoke of solitude in the high places, and we find the solitude. They spoke of storms; the storms are there, glowering still. They spoke of high sun and dark skies and stars clearer than ground ever saw; all of them remain.

If I could talk now to a barnstormer or read his words on the yellowed pages of 1929, he would tell me of flying the South, on the route from Columbia, South Carolina, to Augusta, Georgia. It's the easiest thing in the world to follow a railroad, but out of Columbia there's such a twist and tangle of railroad it takes a good eye to sort the tracks that lead to Augusta from the ones that lead to Chattahoochee, to Mirabel, to Oak Hollow. Follow the wrong one, he would say, and you find yourself off in the middle of nowhere, and not much of an idea how to get back.

And it's true. *Look* at the mass of railroads down there! Maybe there's an air molecule or two around that remembers the flash of his propeller, that might chuckle at my concern, coming along so much later, over precisely the same problem that caused his concern before me. We both must find our way out of the maze, and find it by ourselves. I don't know what he did, but I look ahead to pick the sharp arrowhead of a lake on course, and fly to that and pick the railroad then, when there is clearly only one choice to make. Perhaps he had a better way. I wish he were around still; I wish that I could look out and see his Jenny or his J-1 Standard smoothing along above the twin rails. But this morning I continue alone, or at least as far as my eyes can see, alone. The history and the tradition and the old molecules are here about me every second. The barnstorming pilots said that the sky was cold and that they froze in their cockpits. I know now that they kept warm for some time by simply not believing that it could possibly be so cold over the South, where, after all, people come to flee the ice of northern winters. But at last there is no fighting left to be done; the lesson is learned. It gets terribly cold; hard, ice-freezing cold over South Carolina in the morning of a spring day. I used to smile when I heard of the early pilots huddling forward under what little shelter they could get from the windscreen, and shuffling their feet quickly back and forth in odd strange movements just for the sake of moving and keeping the cold at bay.

I am not smiling now. Instead I discover a technique on my own, over South Carolina. I won't be so brash as to think that it hasn't been discovered scores of times before, in the same air, in fact, by scores of early pilots. There is a huge imaginary crank on a shaft thrust through the center of the instrument panel. Turn it. Turn it faster and faster with the right glove, reverse it and turn it faster still with the left glove. If you turn that crank long enough and fast enough, it just barely keeps you from going numb and blue in the cold. And it makes you so tired you can hardly muster strength to look over the icy side and down to check where the winds are drifting you now.

The sun in South Carolina is timed to begin to warm the air precisely one second before the frost-covered pilot decides to call a halt to all this nonsense and land and start a gasoline fire to warm himself. Fleece-lined leather jacket, woolen flight suits and shirts and rabbit-fur gloves don't make a bit of difference. The only thing that steps in at that last second is the sun, throwing a billion BTUs into the earth, and gradually, very gradually, beginning to warm the air. Old pilots, wherever you are now, I can report that the mornings of the South Carolina spring are exactly as you left them.

Always they looked for places to land should the engine suddenly stop, and always do I. That is one of the old habits that has disappeared. The odds against a modern engine failing during any one flight are astronomical. The odds against it failing during any one moment of any one flight, while the pilot happens to be considering a place to land, is out of the realm of ordinary mathematics. So, beyond a bit of lip service, forced landings in modern airplanes are no longer practiced. Why bother, if an engine will never fail? Spins and spin recoveries have not been taught for years. We have horns and lights that warn against the conditions under which an unknowing pilot can manhandle an airplane into a spin. And if an airplane will never be spun, why bother to teach spin recoveries? Why bother to teach aerobatics? The chance that a pilot could save his life by knowing how to control an airplane when it is in a vertical bank or when it has been tossed upside down are rather remote, because unless one flies into extreme turbulence or crosses the wake of a jet transport, the chances are remote that the airplane will ever know more than a shallow bank. Besides, most modern airplanes are not licensed for aerobatics.

Gone the old skills. Don't listen to the wind to tell your airspeed, watch the airspeed indicator and hope that it is correct. Don't look over the side to gauge your altitude, trust the altimeter, and don't forget to set it properly before each flight. Make the proper numbers appear in the proper dials at the proper time, and you have a first-class automobile with wings.

But no need for bitterness, for when I say gone the old skills, I don't speak true. The old skills and the old days are there for those who would seek them out.

One hour, the end of the railroad track, and the town of Augusta. Lower into the warming air, and left-rudder-left-stick in a wide sweeping turn about the airport. There the wind sock, saying the winds are almost calm this morning. There a pattern of runways, which I disregard, and rows of grass between, to which I pay very close attention. There the red fuel pumps, with no customer so early in the morning.

No customers in the sky this morning, either. I am alone. A little more aileron, to bank the wings up vertically and drop quickly toward the grass. Grass isn't often landed upon at airports, and one must be careful to look at it closely for traces of rabbit holes hidden and gullies crossing. The biplane skims the grasstops and there is not far down to look to see the ground. It looks good for landing.

Forward on the throttle for a burst of power, a long climbing turn to the left, in a pattern that will bring us lined once again on the grass, this time to land.

In three minutes I fly the last turn to line up with the grass and have one last chance to look at it. Then, look out, rabbits. All there is ahead is a wide expanse of cherry-lemon fabric, braces and cross braces humming, a shining aluminum cowl, an oil-sprayed front windscreen, black engine cylinders, the blur of a propeller idling around, here and there a little triangle of sky peeking, to the sides a slow blur of grass flowing, and sudden hard hard rolling of the wheels on the cold ground and the brittle cold grassblades by the thousands splintering underwheel and this is the time we really go to work on the rudder pedals to keep it straight keep it straight and right about here is where we lost it in the crosswind and remember the way she just started to go around and there was nothing you could do about it left-rudder-right-rudder-left but we just about got this one wired and my gosh it sure didn't take us long to get stopped and it's a nice feeling to be under control again and able to S-turn and see ahead and move slowly along.

An easy turn around, grassblades splintering now only by the scores and if I wanted I could get out right here and walk on the grass. The biplane is no longer an airplane, but a big awkward three-wheeled teetery vehicle pulled along by the most inefficient expedient of a fan turning around on its nose.

We roll onto the concrete of a taxiway and the bumps and rills of the grass are gone. From traveling through the air of 1929, I have moved, through the process called "landing," back into the world of new concrete taxiways and will the gasoline, sir, be cash or credit?

Sometimes, when you taxi back into Modern, they're a bit too quick on the service. It takes a minute to get the roar out of your ears and you should be allowed a moment to take off your helmet and enjoy taking it off, and feel the calm and enjoy it, and unstrap the seat belt and the parachute harness knowing that any time you can get out and walk around and have a root beer or stand and warm at a heater in the flight office. You can't envy the pilots who fly the modern sky. You have to feel sorry for them, if they haven't tucked somewhere away the joy of taking off a brown leather helmet and unstrapping from an old airplane hot-engined after its return to the earth.

Bright sun. Cold, still; but bright. I am for a moment tempted to seek the warmth of the flight office, and its maps, and its telephone to the great web of information about winds and weather across the country this morning. But aside, temptation, and away, evil thought. One never leaves the needs of an antique for another to fill. A creed among those who fly old airplanes? In part. But more binding, the fact that the pilot is the only one who knows how to service his machine. A simple little thing, to fill a gasoline tank. But one day one pilot was forced to land in a pasture with his propeller standing still and straight in front of him, the pistons of the engine frozen in their cylinders. The one time that he was too cold, and passed the servicing of his old airplane to another, his oil tank was filled with gasoline, for the two tank caps were similar and close together. A stupid mistake, almost an inconceivable one, but the knowledge that it was stupid and that it was inconceivable offered little comfort to him when the propeller ceased to turn.

The truest reason that I stand this day cold, crouching between the wings, threaded through the jungle of struts and wires and holding the black python of a fuel hose to the tank, is not that I obey a creed or fear another's error. I stand here because I must learn to know my airplane and give her a chance to know me. In flight, hour on hour, it is the airplane that does the work; engine absorbing many thousand detonations each minute, and heats and pressures that I couldn't absorb for a second. The wires and the struts and the fabric on the wings are holding in the air twenty-three hundred pounds of airplane and fuel and pilot and equipment and doing it in a hundred-mile-per-hour wind. On each landing the frail landing-gear struts and the old wheels must stand fast with the strain of that twenty-three hundred pounds coming hard down at sixty miles per hour onto the earth, with its mounds and hollows that keep the force from being smooth. I have only to sit within the cockpit and steer, and even this I do while paying only half attention to the job. The other half of the attention is spent ducking forward out of the wind that keeps us in flight, turning imaginary cranks to keep warm, considering other times, other flights, other airplanes.

The least, the very least that I can do in atonement is to see to the needs of my airplane before moving selfishly after my own comfort. Were I not at least to care for her during the time that her wheels are on the ground, I would never have the right to ask a special favor of her, now and then, as she flies. The favor, perhaps, of running on though the rain is in solid walls over her engine, or of wires and struts holding fast in the sudden and furious downdrafts of the mountain winds. And perhaps the ultimate favor of tearing herself to shreds on the rocks of a desert forced landing and allowing her pilot to walk away untouched.

Stopping to think, stopping to analyze as I give her a drink of eighty-octane, I should be able to look with surprise upon myself, and scoff. Asking a favor of an airplane? Letting an airplane get to know you? You feeling all right? But it doesn't work, I can't scoff. I'm not living a fantasy; this is quite solid concrete on the quite solid earth of Augusta, Georgia; in my right glove is the hard steel of a fuel-hose nozzle, with gasoline pouring from it down into a very real fuel tank, and the sharp acid vapor of gasoline flooding over me from the tank as I peer past the nozzle to see how much more fuel the tank will hold. Below me the line boy is punching a sharp metal spout into a metal can of engine oil; the cutting scrape of the spout is quick and harsh and it sounds real enough. This doesn't seem to be a fantasy world, and if it is, it is at least the same familiar fantasy world that I've moved through for several years. Strange, that I should not be able to scoff. When I began to fly, I could have scoffed. After flying ten years and two thousand hours, one should be expected to know some of the realities about flying and about airplanes, and not to dwell in fantasy lands.

It comes with a jolt and with a bit of a shock. Perhaps I *am* beginning to know some of the realities, and those realities include something about getting to know an airplane and letting her get to know you. Perhaps it is true that a pilot's longevity depends sometimes as much upon his faith in his airplane as upon his knowledge of it, and perhaps sometimes the answer to flight isn't always found in wingspans and engine horsepower and resultants of forces plotted on engineering graph paper. And perhaps again I'm wrong. But, right or wrong, I stand and I fuel my own airplane for reasons that seem true and good to me. When the propeller stops in flight over a desert, with rocks around as far as I can see, I'll have the chance to see whether or not I should have scoffed, that morning in Augusta.

CHAPTER SIX

THERE IS A sign by the telephone:

FOR FLIGHT SERVICE, CHECK THE LINE CLEAR, PRESS
BLACK BUTTON TWO SHORT RINGS, SAY "FLIGHT SER-
VICE, AUGUSTA MUNICIPAL AIRPORT."

There are thousands of these telephones in airports across the country, and each one has its own sign with precise directions for use. It
used to be, in aviation, that a pilot could get along without any directions at all. Press black button for two short rings.

"Flight Service."

"Hi, Flight Service. Going Augusta on out around Columbus,
Auburn-Jackson-Vicksburg. What you got for weather?" I remember the advice an airline captain once gave me. Never listen to a
weatherman's forecast. The weather that's *there* is the stuff you fly
through, and you'll never know what that's like till you get there.

"Looks like a good day. Columbus is clear and twelve miles visibility, Jackson is clear and twenty, Vicksburg clear and twenty. Dallas
is clear and fifty, if you want that. Forecast will be for scattered cumulus on into the afternoon, maybe some scattered showers or thunder-
showers."

"Any winds, surface to five thousand feet?" I wait in interest, consuming a potato-chip breakfast and a bottle of Pepsi-Cola.

"Ah, let's see. Surface winds light and variable through Columbus, going west at ten by the time you get into Jackson-Vicksburg. Five-thousand-foot winds are three three zero degrees fifteen knots, all the way. Looks like it will be a good day."

"Good. Thanks for the weather."

"Can I have your aircraft number?"

"Four nine nine Hotel."

"OK. You want to file a flight plan?"

"Might be nice, but I'm a no-radio airplane."

He laughs, as though I had made some sort of mildly funny joke: an airplane with no radio. "Well then, guess there's not too much we can do for you. . . ."

"Guess not. Thanks for the weather."

Ten minutes from the moment that the telephone touches the cradle near the black button and its list of directions, a biplane is airborne once again over Georgia, flying west. The chill in the air is now a comfortable chill, and not cold. Even without Flight Service doing anything for me, it is fun to be flying. Winds from the west at altitude; those will be headwinds, and those we can do without.

We stay as low as we can, still keeping within gliding range of fields fit for landing. At times this is not very low, for the fields are scattered, intruders in the kingdom of pines that mat the earth as far as I can see. Here a road cutting through to parallel my railroad track, here a small lake and pasture, then the pines again, all around. They are old green, dark green, and among them the fresh young lime green of the leaved trees turning early to the sun, looking at it still in wonder. So many trees, so very many trees.

Along the side of a dirt road, a weathered house, a tangled yard. The shadow of the biplane flicks over its chimney and the engine noise must be loud and unusual. No door opens, though, no sign of movement. Now it is gone, and lost behind.

Who lives in the house? What memories does it have tucked into its wood; what happiness has it seen, what joys and what defeats? A full world of life, there, and sorrow and pleasure and gain and loss and interest and bright things happening day on day as the sun rises over the same pines to the east and sets over the same pines to the west. A whole world of important things happening, to real people. Perhaps tomorrow night there is a dance in Marysville, and inside the house there are gingham dresses being ironed. Perhaps a decision made to leave the house and seek a better living in Augusta or Clairmont. Perhaps and perhaps and perhaps. Perhaps there is no one in the house, and it is the body of a house, only. Whatever it is, whatever its story, it took the shadow of the biplane something less than half a second to cross it, and leave it dwindling away behind.

Come, now. Let's stay awake on our navigation. Where are we, by the way? How many miles out from Augusta and how many miles left to go into Auburn? How's that ground speed? What's our estimate over the next checkpoint? What *is* the next checkpoint? Do I even know our next checkpoint?

Listen to all those old questions. They used to be such important questions, too. Now, in the biplane, they don't matter at all. The question of finding a destination was solved before we took off; there is three hours flying to Auburn, I have five hours of fuel. I follow a railroad track. End navigation problem. At one time away off in the future it was a great game to compute estimates and ground speeds and to tell to the second when the wheels would touch at destination. But that was with a different sort of airplane and in a world where answers were important things. Miss the estimate and a host of other airplanes would have to be advised. When fuel was critical, and gallons of it burned in a minute, one kept a close watch upon headwinds and ground speeds. A headwind too strong meant that there wasn't enough fuel to reach destination and one had to land short to refuel. Critical, critical, every bit of it.

Now, in 1929, what matter? With headwinds, I'll arrive a half hour later, or an hour later, with still an hour's flying left in the tank. I am not in a hurry, for anyone who flies an old slow biplane cannot afford to be in a hurry. What matter if I do not make it to destination? I'll land sooner, at a different destination, and in the next flight pass over my first goal, to another beyond. In 1929, without radio or navigation equipment or an anxious agency waiting my arrival, I am on my own.

Seeing a smooth pasture, I can land and take time without worry, and perhaps even trade a ten-minute flight for a home-cooked meal.

I know roughly where I am. The sun rises in the east and it sets in the west; I need only follow the setting sun, without ever glancing at a map, and in time I will reach the other coast of the United States. Any town of size has an airport and fuel. Climb, then, when the fuel is getting low, find the town, fill the tank, and go on into the west.

The biplane rachets and thunders through the low sky, bright-winged, whirring, pulling a shadow ninety miles per hour across the sandy earth and through the needled treetops. Things moving, things to watch, air to drink and to slice into long ribbons with wingwires. But still the strange touch of the dream so long dreamed.

Perhaps in a few thousand years flight will become something we can accept and believe to be real. Do the gulls enjoy flying, and the hawks? Probably not. Probably they wish that they could stride along the ground, and know what it is to be held firmly down and not subject to every toss of an air current. I'd like to say, "I'll trade you, hawk," but I'd want to attach a few strings to the deal. The more I consider it, the more strings there would be to attach, until in the end I'd only want to be me, with an ability to fly. And this is what I am at this moment. I'll still take my life and my clumsy clattery way of moving through the air. For in working and striving and sacrificing for this way of flying, I can enjoy it fully; give me flight without effort and I'll turn shortly, bored, to something that challenges.

A challenge: let us invent a way that will allow us to fly. And poor earthbound man sought and dreamed and worked for a long time before he struck upon an answer. Try wings like the birds' wings, try sails like a boat's, try the flame of gunpowder rockets. Try and try and try. Kites and cloth and feathers and wood and steam engines, nets about birds and frames of bamboo. Then bamboo with cloth stretched and a cradle for the man pilot. If I build a mountain and stretch my bamboo wings at the top, and run down the side of the mountain into the wind . . . and there he had it. Man at last was flying. Months of flights from the mountaintop, but still, it should be able to last longer, I should be able to taste more fully this rare sweetness. Oars, then, and pedals and treadmills and handcranks and paddle-wheels and flapping wings and a little homebuilt gasoline engine. If we take the engine, and attach a chain drive that can turn two propellers and fit it all to the wings and perhaps the pilot can lie down on the lower wing . . . Another step made, another beginning. A beginning laid down for all mankind to work from.

At first, flying is a blind sort of fun, the challenge again, something different to do. Enjoyable to feel in control of a big metallic bird and look down on all the little buildings and lakes and ants on the road. In time, for those who persevere through the archaic accumulation of tests that lead to a pilot's license, the joy subtly switches from that of controlling the bird into that of being the bird, with eyes bright for looking down, with wings that on the ground are only wood and cloth and sheet aluminum, but in flight become so alive that one can feel feathers in the wind.

We notice first the change in the world outside us. It changes from familiar low perspective to the unfamiliar high one, and we wonder what it would feel like to fall all that way down. Fun it might be, but a timid kind of fun, for after all, we say, the air is not really our element. We don't change our mind about that for a long time.

Then come the hours when we feel uneasily at home, with time to notice the world again, when the flying takes care of itself. From this the uneasiness goes out, as we learn that we can handle many problems successfully.

And then we begin to see the earth and the sky as symbols. The mountain is not so much a mass of peaked earth to be feared as an obstacle to be conquered in pursuit of a higher goal.

And an airplane, we discover, is a teacher. A calm, subtle, persuasive teacher, for it is infinitely patient. An airplane does not question its pilot's motives, or misunderstand him, or have hurt feelings for him to soothe. Like the sky, an airplane simply *is*, offering its lessons. If we wish to learn the lessons, they are there in plenty, and can become very detailed and profound lessons.

Columbus ahead. A touch backward on the control stick to lift us from the treetops to a platform high above them. One is not allowed to cross cities at low altitude and one should not, even if there were no law. Cities do not offer many good places to land if an engine should stop, and those not interested in airplanes should not have their thought turned for an instant by the sound of cylinders firing to blur a propeller. Two thousand feet, then, over Columbus, and the flight goes for a moment less interesting. At low level there is a blurred fringe on the land speeding by. At two thousand feet, the fringe is gone and all is clear and sharp, slow-moving. There the highways leading into the city, and automobiles and trucks crowding along. There a refinery, going to a great amount of effort to the simple end that the smoke from its tall stacks should tell the pilot of a passing biplane from just what direction the wind is blowing. There, on the meadow by the river, is Columbus Municipal Airport, with many runways angled and set for many winds. A curved airplane-parking ramp, and oil spots from its passenger airplanes in front of the terminal. Columbus Municipal Airport is no place for an old radioless biplane.

From the concrete giant, for a second, there shines a green light. There. Again. From the control tower, a brilliant green pencil flashing. And behind the green, a tiny figure in the tower. He is clearing me to land. How kind of him, how very thoughtful! From two thousand feet above his airport, we have been invited to stop and have a cup of coffee and talk about the old days.

Thank you very much, friend, but I must really be on my way. Wouldn't want to disturb those airplanes that do believe in radios. We rock our wings in thanks, and rock them with a gentle wish, for his is an unusual offer. There is an interesting fellow behind the green light at Columbus Municipal, and someday I shall come through here again and ask of him.

A crossing of a river, some tall radio towers sliding below, and the country closes back in as the city has gone. Cities are always losing the battle. No matter how big they are, there is always the country; patient, like a quiet green sea about it, waiting to close back in. The ground changes quickly from Modern back to Always, after one flies over a city. A strip of motels hangs on for a moment lining the highways into town, but at last they surrender and the country takes over, and with it the quiet life and the quiet people. Again the roar of the engine drifts down to treetop height and is absorbed into green needles.

Parallel to the deserted road that will bring me to the Auburn airport is a wide field cut, and level, fit for landing. My money in the bank, that allows me play and the enjoyment of flying low.

Two tall pines ahead, a wingspan apart, swifting closer, stretching high above us until one last second and hard back on the control stick and full left aileron and in a steep climbing turn we watch the needles brush by. That's the consciousness of flying, when you can reach out and touch the ground moving by, and brush the branches of a tree as you pass. There is no place that is more fun to fly than a horizon-to-horizon meadow with trees sparsely planted. Fly down low with wheels flicking through the grass; flash by the first trees at cow-level so that they look normal and unscalable, rush toward the next that look just as haughty and then in a simple small movement of stick and rudder roar straight up and over and roll inverted and look down at its branches.

Yet how they worked, how those first to fly worked to get away from the ground! Years of their life and thought for a flight of a hundred feet, for an altitude of ten feet, for twenty seconds in the air. And today we can taste the sheer and untrammeled fun of flying the twenty seconds, then another twenty, and another. Roll the wheels in the meadow, swing them high and rolling over the top of the tallest trees. Slice the rush of air with a wingtip, with a glove, with eyes squinting. This is flying. The power to throw yourself happily through the sky, to see the familiar world from any angle at all, or not to see it, to turn one's head and spend an hour in the otherworld of the hills and plains and cliffs and lakes and meadows all built of cloud.

But take a pilot in his very favorite airplane and immerse him in his very favorite conditions: meadow with trees planted, mountains to conquer, alone in the sunset clouds. Rarely, very rarely, and then only if you watch very closely, you may see him smile. I caught myself at this and asked how could it be.

It was low-level flying over the desert, at very high speed, leading a flight of four F-86 Sabrejets to a target. All the cards were there and face up: we needed the low-level training mission to fill a squadron requirement; we were heavy on fuel and had to go full throttle to burn it away; the ground was flat and the air was caught in the stillness of early morning. At the end of the low-level flight waited the gunnery targets. I flew a good airplane, and the bet was a nickel for every bullethole in the target.

Result, then, was a needle on the airspeed indicator that settled on 540 miles per hour. Result was the need for tiny little movements of the control stick to follow the low rise and fall of the earth and for quick jumps over tall cactus. Result was three friends in loose formation to left and right, engaging all in the favorite mission of highspeed low-level, and a challenge waiting. Eight heavy machine guns, in that flight, loaded and ready to fire. Four smooth sweptwing arrows that were sheer beauty in their silver against the early desert, one rising here over a boulder, one dipping now into a hollow, banking sharply to avoid a single yucca plant. Like kids down the block playing at Jet Fighter Pilot, with great big pretty authentic official toys, splitting the air with sudden howitzer-sounds to the lizards in the sun, and not a single human ear to be disturbed or to voice complaint.

Speed and power and control; toys enjoyed to their fullest. But I wasn't smiling. I wasted a precious second of that joy distilled in concern. Why wasn't I smiling? I should be laughing, singing; were there room to dance I should be dancing.

The lesson then, handed from a different airplane, handed at a speed of 543 miles per hour, at an altitude of seven feet three inches. Inwardly, inwardly, pilot. The only important things happen within yourself. Something great and wild and different and unusual may happen outside of you, but the meaning and importance of it come from within. A smile is outward, a way of communicating. Here you can be lost in the joy and hold it all to yourself, knowing it, tasting it, feeling it, being happy. No communication required.

There, beyond the power lines, Auburn airport. Back on the stick, roaring up over the wires, seeing clearly and at once the two hard-surface runways, the two grass landing strips, a scarlet wind sock stirring softly above the gasoline pumps. Into the wind, circle the field, pick the landing strip and the part of the strip that we shall land upon. The parachute is hard; it will be good to get out and walk around.

One lonely biplane in the landing pattern, but the biplane is not aware of her loneliness and turns easily toward the bright spring grass.

A good strip, this, not even the ruts of many landings worn into it. An inviting soft place to come again to ground and a place that the biplane can turn toward as she has so many times before. Throttle back and the propeller becomes a silent windmill. Down we glide, green ahead, wind going soft in the wires, whishing gently just enough to say that it is there. Forward on the stick, forward and the trees growing tall at each side of the strip, and taller and the grass is blocked out ahead and blurred to the sides, stick back now, as we slow, and back and back . . . and with a little crash we're down and rolling on all three wheels, clattering and thudding through the unevenness from which the green grows. Left-rudder-right-rudder and here we are all of a sudden at that familiar speed at which I could hop over the side and walk. A touch of throttle and we taxi slowly toward the gasoline pumps and the few buildings clustered around. Neither old buildings nor new; one a hangar, another a flight school with windows looking out upon the runways, another hangar around back. A few people standing near the door, talking and watching the biplane as it taxis.

A burst of power and the pulsing wind beating back upon me for a moment, then left rudder to swing around near the low-octane pump and bring the red-knobbed mixture lever forward to *Idle-Cutoff.* The engine runs on for four seconds, then all at once it goes quiet and I can hear the pistons clanking softly and the propeller coasting to a stop.

Switch off.

Fuel off.

Seat belt unfastened, parachute straps unbuckled, gloves off, helmet off and feel the gentle soft wind that doesn't come from a propeller. Still sunlight. Quiet. I can have only a nodding acquaintance with the quiet, for the engine roars on in my ears; the ghost engine, the spirit of a thing that one might be tempted to call dead.

The little crowd walks over as I begin to refill the tank. They are awed a bit and look silently at the old airplane. Flight students, and they do not see many old airplanes flying. Are they aware of the biplane as a heritage, or just as a strange relic that has come wandering through? It would be good to know, but one can't ask a stranger group are you aware of this as a heritage. One can't ask that sort of a thing until one gets to know them, until they are strangers no more.

"Hi. Anyplace around here to get a sandwich?"

CHAPTER SEVEN

THE BIPLANE FLIES on, following the road west to incidents, to lessons. From small incidents, like the filling of a gasoline tank; from bigger incidents, like the spinning crash on the runway at Crescent Beach, something to learn and to apply to knowledge and future action.

The land changes subtly, the pines cut back for more and more farms to lay themselves green on the earth, under the sun. Like the Land of Oz it is becoming, and the road I follow might as well be of yellow brick. So very neat is the land, even from a short hundred feet in the air. There isn't a grassblade out of place in the pastures, even the cows are standing over *X*'s chalked on the ground by a careful director. Places, everyone! Places! Action! Roll 'em!

I feel like an intruder over the set, and the engine noise will ruin the soundman's tapes. Somewhere around here, under a giant oak, must be a soundman and a boom mike. But wait. We're part of the show. And right on cue:

Enter BIPLANE, flying east to west. Sound of BIPLANE rises from TINY WHISPER to ROAR overhead to fade into WHISPER in west. CUT to cockpit of BIPLANE. Camera holds for moment on COWS, pans forward along YELLOW BRICK ROAD, pans out to FARMHOUSE. *Note to Property Manager:*

FARMHOUSE should symbolize EMERALD CITY; symbolize neatness, spotlessness, everything in working order and moving peacefully through time, should suggest that the over-rainbow magic city often takes forms that we know best, so we cannot see the magic existing.

CUT to GIANT OAK, from whose shade we watch BIPLANE approaching again east to west, passing LOUD and ROARING through leaves overhead, dwindling and finally disappearing in the west. Dissolve to black and green letters: THE END.

Good take! Print it!

Nice that it went so well, but for the biplane, the show is still going on, and on and on. Beneath us, hundreds of directors working hidden, from canvas-backed chairs. Places! Action! BIPLANE. FARMHOUSE. EMERALD CITY. And through it all, YELLOW BRICK ROAD. This is the South in spring, 1929. Every once in a while, some children by their Saturday stream, waving, and worthy of a wave back, from a hundred feet away. And gone. People living down there. I can see them living and fishing and swimming and plowing and starting fires that lift blue smoke up through chimneys. Smoke that curls and drifts in the wind and tells me that the headwind has come now down to the ground. Not a strong wind, but enough to keep us from moving quite so quickly as we would across the earth. And the slower we fly, the more we see the earth and appreciate it. An airplane, especially an antique airplane, cannot hurry. It has only one working speed. For the biplane, I set the throttle in level flight until the tachometer needle steadies at 1,725 revolutions. A good comfortable speed where the engine sounds right, neither loafing nor straining; 1,725 becomes a good sound, a right sound in the wind. In still air, 1,725 gives something like ninety-five miles per hour; in the headwind this noon we move eighty miles per hour across the ground. We definitely will not startle the country with a new speed record on this crossing.

But we do startle ourselves with a sight of a beautiful land wheeling below. The South is supposed to be an ugly place, and on occasion, on the ground, I have seen it ugly, twisted and roiled in blind dull hatred. But from the air one cannot see hatred roiling and the South is a place with gentleness and beauty filled.

Airplanes offer pilots a balance for evil, and more than one pilot, more than ten, keeps in his mind an index of places he has seen from the air that are good. In my own file is a valley in the hills bordering the sea at Laguna Beach, California. And that valley just to the east of Salt Lake City, Utah, on the other side of the big mountain there, where down the valley a river flows and in summer it is Shangri-La perfected. There is a good place in eastern Pennsylvania, that happens even to have a little grass airstrip near it. An airline pilot told me of a place he discovered in Arizona. He had seen it from 32,000 feet on the New York–Los Angeles run, had studied it on every flight since his discovery. He said it would be a good place to go, when he retires, to be alone and quiet.

There is a plain in northern France, a hill in Germany, a beach of sand like sugar on the Gulf side of Florida. And today I add another to my file: the farms and the pastures of central Alabama. If a need comes for escape, these are waiting.

Places that are good. And, too, times that are good. Not *have been* good. Are good. For they remain, and I can savor their goodness by simply opening the file and picking one out and refeeling the thought that came from the incident. Not the incident that matters, but the learning. Not the symbol, but its meaning. Not the outside, but what happens within.

Pick a card, any card. Here is one; at the top it is marked *Pat and Lou—El Toro.* An incident.

I had been away from the 141st Tactical Fighter Squadron for a year, moved to the other side of the country from them. And one day a phone call. Patrick Flanagan and Lou Pisane, Crosscountry Aces of the New Jersey Air National Guard, scoring again. This time they were on a 2,600-mile training mission, and had landed their F-86's at El Toro Marine Air Station, thirty miles from me.

The card is written and filled with old days renewed, of the time Pat managed with a clumsy old F-84F to outfox a Royal Canadian Air Force Mark VI Sabre in the skies of France, to track him for a moment in his gunsight. A mock battle, of course, yet the Mark VI was an airplane built for air combat and the '84 was not. But Pat is a skillful pilot, and with just a little embellishing here and there and with a polished gift of the dramatic and the funny, why, the poor Maple Leaf didn't have a chance from the beginning.

And Lou; tall cool Lou, who taught me something about patience as I flew his wing one day and he stalked and finally caught a French fighter plane, to make a roaring blasting pass a yard off his wingtip to remind him that one must look around or he will be caught even by old F-84's. Lou, as formal and polite and absolutely proper as though he had been raised on etiquette from the moment he could listen; till you got to know him and he came alive, cool still, but a sharp logical mind that wouldn't stand for nonsense even from the commanding general. "Aw c'mon, General. You know and I know we don't read every single item on that checklist in the Preflight. If you want us to carry the checklist around in our hand while we make the Preflight, just say so. But don't try to give us that stuff about reading every single item on there every single time we go out to fly."

Filed under Times That Are Good, to see them again and to drive them back to the flight line at El Toro. And there, surrounded by Marine airplanes, two silver Air Guard F-86's parked together.

"Kinda sad to leave the '84's in France, but the '86 is a good airplane, too, and before long the squadron will be getting '105's. Don't you wish you were back with us?"

"Back with you characters? I had to go clear across the country to get away from you guys, and now you follow me out here, even. Good old '86. Mind if I look in your cockpit, Lou, if I promise not to touch any switches? Boy, there aren't enough wild horses left in this world to drive me back into the 141st Tac Fighter Squadron."

Look at that cockpit. Everything there, the way it used to be: armament panel, throttle, speed brake switch, flight instruments, the long-handled landing-gear switch, circuit breaker panels, the pins in the ejection seat. You guys never learn anything, a dangerous bunch to be with. "Lou, you left your checklist up here! How can you run a proper Preflight inspection without that checklist in your hand?" Never obey regulations. A hopeless bunch.

And the time is come for a last handshake in the dusk as they climb up the kicksteps to their cockpits, and strap in. The strange uncomfortable feeling that I've got to hurry to get into my airplane, or they'll take off without me. Where's my airplane? I've never had to stay on the ground while the rest of my flight makes ready to go. His helmet and oxygen mask fitted now, Pat talks for a moment on the radio, copying the instrument departure clearance in his high cockpit, reading it back to the control tower. Hey, Pat! Remember the time when Roj Schmitt was on your wing, his first time up in the weather? And he said, "Don't worry about me, just fly it like you're alone. . . ." Do you remember, Pat?

Hey, Lou! Remember back in Chaumont when you bet that the shock of a parachute landing was no more than you'd get if you jumped out a two-story window? Remember?

And Pat draws the start-engine circle in the air to Lou, and, darn it, he draws it to me, too, standing on the ramp, in a civilian business suit. Why did you do that, Flanagan? You hoop, you darn silly hoop. And FOOM-FOOM! the two engines burst together into life, the rising whine of the compressors sucking air in the intake and the rumble of the combustion chambers turning it into fire and pushing it through the turbine. I can shout now and they'll only see my mouth moving. There the wheels start to roll, and they turn to taxi by me on the way to the runway. Hidden dust sprays out of the concrete where the jet-blast catches it in a scorching storm. Pat taxis by, way up in his cockpit, looking down at me, tossing a little salute. See ya, Pat. See ya round, boy. His wingtip grazes my suit coat, the high-swept rudder sails proudly by. And twenty feet behind comes Lou, breaking regulations. You're supposed to have a hundred feet separation when you taxi, Pisane. Think you're at some kind of an air show, ace?

A salute from the cockpit, returned from a civilian in a business suit, standing on the concrete. Give the general hell for me, Lou. Not that you wouldn't, anyway.

And they're gone down the taxiway, as the blue taxilights come on in the evening. Way down at the end of the runway there's a thunderstorm of two airplanes running up their engines. What are you doing right now, Pat? Emergency fuel check? Stomp on those brakes, run the throttle up to 95 percent rpm, reach over and throw in the emergency fuel switch, let the rpm stabilize, run it on up to full throttle, cut the power back and switch over to normal fuel. And Lou? Checks done, run her up to 98 percent, hold the brakes, nod across to Pat when you're ready to roll.

The tiny little fighters at the end of the runway begin to move, trailing thin black smoke of full throttle. Together they grow, lift from the ground, together gear doors drop open, landing gear sucks back into two smooth fuselages, gear doors close, stiff and robotlike. Faster and faster they move, flying low in the air.

Locked in tight formation, they're suddenly fire-eating arrows overhead, trying to blast the air loose with sheer sound and fury, and send it in avalanche to the runway. For one long proud moment they're in side silhouette, and from the ground I can see the dots of the pilots in the cockpits. Then I see wings only, and rudders and elevators and two trails of thin black smoke.

They grow smaller and smaller toward the mountains in the east, climbing now, swiftly . . . and smaller . . . good-bye, Pat . . . and smaller . . . tuck it in there, Lou-babe . . . and gone.

Two trails of smoke in the air, twisting now in the wind.

I look down in the dead quiet to see my civilian shoes standing on the damned concrete and I can't see shoes or concrete very clearly and it's just as damn well because even with the damn floodlights on, the night comes in and blurs things. Why did you have to come back, you guys? Why'd you follow me, then leave without me, you blockheads? You hoops couldn't get me back in that damn squadron for all the damn tea in China.

Lots of times filed away, in that box, lots of incidents.

Shadows on the ground. Not long ones. Indicators only that the sun is passing me by. Inevitable, I guess. If the sun moved eighty miles an hour around the earth we'd have a pretty long day. Go on ahead, sun. About time for me to land, anyway. I can get one more hop in today; might make it to the Mississippi, with luck.

The clean clipped pastures of Oz have given way to a swampy land, and still lakes lying warm. The biplane pulls her shadow steadily along, driving it down the road to slowly slowly pass an occasional automobile. Thank heaven we're still passing the cars. There's the cutoff point between Fast and Slow. As long as you can pass the cars, you've got nothing to worry about.

Ahead, what is a thin blue circle on the map becomes Demopolis, Alabama. Not far from a river (squiggly blue on the map), ground covered nearby with reeds. A great big giant airport, in the precise and geometrical center of Nowhere. Even the town of Demopolis is a long drive down the road. During the war, the airport must have trained some kind of aviator, but now it is nearly deserted, with one tiny gasoline pump, one solitary wind sock, a weathered building nearby. Down again on the grass, airplane, and into the wind, to see what we shall find.

We shall find, strangely, a little crowd of people, appearing from hidden nowhere to see the biplane. She is an Event at Demopolis, where there is only one other airplane parked in sight, on fifty acres of concrete and two hundred acres of airport surrounding. Questions in the sun, while the fuel hoses softly into the tank.

"Where you from?"

"North Carolina."

"Where you goin'?"

"Los Angeles."

A pause. A look inside the cockpit, at the little black instrument panel. "That's a long way."

"It does seem a long way." And I think of the gallons of gasoline I still have to pump into this tank, and of the hours yet to peer around the oil-smeared windscreen, of the sun at my back in the mornings to come, and in my eyes in the evenings. It does seem a long way to go.

Inside the flight office, and time enough for a bottle of eternal Pepsi-Cola. I know that it must be very quiet here, but the engine is still firing 1–3–5–2–4 in my ears. One more flight today. Stretch one long flight, fly till the sun goes down. Perhaps the Mississippi tonight. Good to stand up, to be able to walk around. Been in the cockpit a long time today. Be nice just to stretch out on the grass and go to sleep. One more hop and I'll do it.

CHAPTER EIGHT

IT'S ALL BEGINNING to fade, and run together. I catch myself seeking to hurry. Trees growing back and crowding in about the road and as far as I can see there are treetops greening in the afternoon. There have been many hours spent this day in this cockpit, and I am tired.

Instantly, an astonished little voice. Tired? Tired of flying? Oho, so all it takes is a few hours of the wind and you're tired, ready to quit. We see at last there is a difference between the pilots of then and of now. Not even halfway across and you're breaking under the tiny strain of a few hours' flying.

All right, that's enough of that. You've not much evidence to prove that the early pilots didn't get tired, and you'll note that I had no thoughts of quitting, or even of slowing down. Not words, but action will decide whether I can stand with them. Only by living it can I discover flight.

So it is that many people travel by airplane, but few know what it is to fly. A passenger waiting in an airline terminal sees the airplanes through a twenty-foot sheet of glass, from an air-conditioned cube in which soft music plays. The sound of an engine is a muffled murmur outside, a momentary purring background for the music. In some terminals the reality is almost served to them on a silver tray, for their clothes can be whipped by the same propeller blast, that same sacred propeller blast, that whipped the coats of the great men of flight. And the airplane is right there, towering over them, that has flown many hours and will fly many more before it is replaced by one more modern. So often, though, the propeller blast is only a force that tugs at one's lapels, an annoyance; and the big airplanes are barely noticed by passengers who are concerned only with finding the entry steps as quickly as possible, to escape the wind. And the airplane, with so much to offer those who will only take the time to see, does it go unseen? The curve of its wing, that has changed the history and the highway of mankind, is it unnoticed?

Well, what do you know. Not unnoticed. There in the wind, hands in pockets, hunched against the sunny cold, the first officer, three gold stripes on his sleeves, paying no attention to the passengers, pays full attention to his airplane. He sees that there are no leaks in the hydraulic lines, that everything is neat and in order inside the giant wheel wells of the wing. The wheels themselves, and the tires, all look good. On around the airplane he walks, looking at it, checking it, enjoying it without a trace of a smile.

The picture is complete. The passengers find their cushioned seats, and will soon be on their way in a machine that so many neither understand nor care to understand. The first officer and the captain do understand, and care for their airplane, and pay her every attention. So no one is forgotten; the airplane is happy, and the flight crew, and the passengers are ready to go their way.

Still, one airplane is two very separate places. In the passenger cabin, the fear that this may be the Last Flight, the awareness of air crashes in newspaper headlines, a certain tension in the narrow air when the throttles come forward, and a hoping that there will be one more flight safely completed before the next set of headlines are splashed across the newsstands. Step forward, through the door and onto the flight deck, and tension disappears as though there were no such thing. The captain in the left seat, the first officer in the right, the flight engineer at his board of solid instruments behind the first officer. All is smooth routine, for it has been lived many times over and again. Throttles come forward all under one hand, checks and cross-checks of engine instruments and of airspeed slowly increasing, a hand on the nosewheel steering shifts to the control column when the flight controls become effective before the airplane is off the ground. The voice of the first officer, as he reads the airspeed indicator: "V-one." A little code that means, "Captain, we are committed to fly; there is not enough room left to stop the airplane without rolling off the end of the runway."

"V-R." And in the captain's hand the control wheel comes back slightly, and the nosewheel lifts from the ground. A tiny pause, and mainwheels come free and the airplane is flying. A hand, the first officer's, on the switch marked *Landing Gear—Up*, and a rumbling sheathing sound from the depths of the airplane as the gigantic heavy wheels, still spinning, move ponderously up into the wheel wells.

"V-two." Or, "At this airspeed, we can lose an engine and still be able to climb." The takeoff is marked by checkpoints saying, this is what we can do if we lose an engine now. Takeoff is the beginning, for the flight crew, of an interesting time with many little problems to solve. They are real problems, but they are not difficult, and they are the kind of problems that flight crews solve every hour, every flight. What is the estimated time of arrival over Ambrose intersection? Get a position report ready for Phoenix Center as we cross Winslow, give them a call on the number two radio, on frequency 126.7 megacycles. Transmit a report to the weather stations, telling the actual winds along our course and the turbulence and cloud tops and any icing along the way. Steer 236 degrees for a while, then add three degrees, settle on 239 degrees to correct for the winds.

Little problems, familiar ones, and friendly. Once in a while a bigger problem will come along, but that is part of the fun and keeps flying a fresh and a good way to make a living. If only the door to the passenger cabin from the flight deck weren't such an effective door, the confidence and the interest that come from thousands of flying hours might filter back and destroy the tension and the fear that there exists.

As it is, even airline pilots are often uneasy when they must fly as passengers. Each pilot would feel a little more comfortable if he were at the controls and not sitting to look at a faceless door that doesn't admit that there is anyone at all on the flight deck. Gone for pilots is the fun of flying as passenger, unknowing and fearful, unknowing and enjoying flight. There is always the creature within that is criticizing the way an airplane is being flown. Even sitting at the rear of a 110-passenger jetliner there is one lonely soul, during landing, that is saying wordlessly to the pilot, "Not now, you fool! We're rounding out too soon! East it forward, ease it on in . . . that's the way . . . too much, too much! Pull it back now! Flare out or you'll . . ." and with a thump the wheels are rolling on the concrete. "Well, all right," from the back of the passenger cabin, "but *I* could have had her down much more smoothly."

The biplane hums loudly along with the sun now low ahead, a round circle of distorted oily brightness in the forward windscreen. Not much daylight left to fly. The baseball sun, thrown high, having paused at its noon top, comes whistling down through the horizon. Though the sky goes on being happily light, the ground is not taken in. The ground is a solemn keeper of very precise time, and when the sun is down it dutifully smothers its dwellers in darkness.

Vicksburg below, and there, with shadows half across its opaque brown waves, the Mississippi. A river barge, a bridge that is probably a toll bridge, and on it automobiles, and among the automobiles a sparkling of headlights coming on. Time to land, and a few miles south is the airport for Vicksburg. But the map says that there are two airports close ahead westward; if I can land at one of these I can be that much farther along my course when the sun begins its launch tomorrow.

Press on, the voice says. If you don't find the airports you can land in a field, and find fuel farther on in the morning. The voice that speaks is the one within that always seeks adventure, and, living only for adventure, doesn't care what happens to aircraft or pilot. Tonight, once again, it wins its case. We leave the Mississippi and Vicksburg behind, and press on. Louisiana rolls onto the map.

The land is all cut into dark squares, in which are probably growing green peppers and peas that have black eyes. And on one square grows a cluster of wooden buildings. A town. There should be an airport here, but I can see no sign of one. It is there, of course, somewhere, but little airports can be impossible to find even in broad daylight. "Airport" is often just a word applied to a pasture, to the side of which a farmer keeps a camouflaged fuel pump. It is a recognized game and point of competition in some parts of the country: Find the Airport. Pick one of the thin blue circles on an aeronautical map, one that no player has ever seen before. Take off at five-minute intervals to find it. The winners, those that find the airport, share a week of superiority over those who may be directly overhead, yet unseeing. "That can never happen to me," I remember saying, when first a friend suggested we play Find the Airport. "What a silly game." But in gracious tolerance I condescended to race him to the airport.

I spent the better part of that afternoon circling above the many-pastured countryside, searching and searching, combing every single pasture, and there were many, before my wife finally saw an airplane parked on the grass and we shakily completed the game. A very official airport, too. Under the trees were not one but two gas pumps waiting, and a row of small hangars, a restaurant, a swimming pool.

So this evening, west of the Mississippi, I do not even bother to circle. I will seek the one next airport, and, failing to find that, will land in a field and wait for the daylight.

The trees are cut far back from the road here, wide farmlands broad to each side, and farmhouses with lights coming on inside. A lonely feeling, watching those lights come on.

Ahead, a town, Rayville, Louisiana. Just to the west should be the airport. And obviously, clearly, there it is. A single narrow strip of asphalt, a short row of open hangars, a lone and tattered wind sock. Crosswind. Hard surface and crosswind. But a gentle one; it couldn't be more than five miles per hour. Surely THAT isn't enough to pose a problem. The crosswind lesson has been a bitter one, one not easily forgotten, but it is going dark on the ground and I must make my decision quickly. If I do not land here, I must pick my field, and a good field will be difficult to choose in the shadows and I will still need the fuel in the morning. It would be good to land at Rayville. So near, only a thousand feet away from me. Yet, with the crosswind, a thousand feet is a long way away. A low pass certainly won't hurt, one of the many voices within has suggested. And truly. Nothing to be lost by a low pass down the runway, except possibly a few minutes.

So into the pattern we go and slide down the invisible ramp of air that leads to the end of every runway ever built. Across the fence, ten feet high. Five feet. It is not good. The biplane has to crab into the wind in order to fly straight down the runway; to land like this would be a very risky thing at best. And look there, pilot. Not thirty feet from the edge of the runway, a long earth embankment paralleling. How high? Two feet? Three feet? High enough; a one-foot embankment would be high enough to shear the landing gear from the biplane were she to run off the narrow runway. And with the crosswind from that direction, that is the way she would turn. If she lost her gear, that would be the end of the story. Propeller and engine would twist and bury themselves into the earth, the lower wing panels rip away and probably take the upper wing with them. There wouldn't be much left. So. Decision?

I must land without hitting the embankment. I'm a good pilot, after all. Haven't I flown almost two thousand hours in many airplanes? I have, and I've flown from zero miles per hour to a shade over twice the speed of sound. Surely, surely I can land an old biplane on a runway with a five-mile crosswind.

Decision made, we're once again down the ramp, this time with intent to stop on the ground. Careful, ease it down, let the mainwheels touch. Good; forward on the stick to hold those mainwheels down and the rudder high in the air. Watch it watch it, she's going to want to swing to the left, into the embankment. Nice touchdown, just a little while longer and we'll be laughing at our fears. Here she comes, tailwheel coming down, now pull hard back on the stick to pin the tail down and hope the tailwheel steering works . . . left rudder, right rudder, full right rudder look OUT BOY SHE'S SWINGING IT'S TOO LATE I CAN'T CONTROL HER WE'RE GOING TO HIT THAT DIRT!

Well, if we're going to hit it, we're going to hit it hard. Full throttle stick forward and maybe we can fly off before the dirt, a chance in a hundred.

WHAT ARE YOU DOING WITH THAT THROTTLE WE'RE GOING TO HIT THE DIRT THERE'S NOTHING YOU CAN DO ABOUT IT LOOK OUT HANG ON HERE WE GO!!

In a second the biplane rolls off the runway, throttle wide open and engine roaring full power, angling sharply toward the dirt wall.

And here, in the space of another second, two people struggling within the pilot. One has given up, is certain that there is to be a big splintering crash in the next instant. The other, thinking still, playing one last card, one very last card, and now, playing, without time even to glance at the airspeed to see if the airplane will fly, slams hard back on the control stick.

The biplane points her nose up, but refuses to fly. The card player is philosophical. We played what we had and we lost. There will be a crashing sound in the next tenth of a second. Pilot, I hope you've learned about crosswinds.

The crash comes, and over the engine roar I can hear it, I can feel it in the controls. A dull thud at first, as though we had hit something that was very heavy but also very soft, with the left main landing gear. And then—nothing.

We're flying!

We are just barely flying, staggering through the air above the grass over the embankment. One tenth of a second for relief, and another for shock; ahead is a barbed-wire fence and a stand of trees. The embankment would have been better. I'm going to hit those trees in full flight, I don't have a chance of clearing them.

Here, let me have it.

It is the gambler again, taking over.

Nose down, we must put the nose down to gain flying speed. The stick inches forward in my hand, and the wheels roll in the grass. They lift again in a moment and the biplane gathers speed. Here comes the fence, and the gambler waits until the last second, gaining every bit of speed he can. Then back on the stick and the fence is cleared and no time to think a full hard right bank and we flash between two poplars, thirty feet above the ground. For a second the world is green leaves and black branches and then suddenly it is darkening blue sky.

OK, the gambler says offhandedly, you can fly it now. That is a weak hand on the control stick, but a hand that would sooner guide the biplane to landing on the highway into the wind than take another try at the crosswind runway. There must be another place to land.

Another circle of the airport and there it is. Like the prayers of the ancients answered in manna all about them, there comes for me the knowledge that the Rayville Airport has two landing strips, and the other strip is grass and it is facing into the wind. Why didn't I notice it before?

Five minutes later the airplane is parked by the hangars and I walk along the embankment to see where the left wheel hit the dirt.

How was it possible? Even the gambler had been sure that we were going to hit the dike, and hit it very hard indeed. But we didn't. We grazed it so softly that there is no sign left in the grass. The biplane had no reason to fly then; only a moment before, she was not even moving fast enough to hold her tail in the air. Being a big inanimate object, some would say, the biplane could not have put forth any special effort to fly. Show me aerodynamically, they could say, one single reason for that airplane to fly before it had reached its proper flying speed. And of course I cannot give one single aerodynamic reason. Then, they say, you must have had proper flying speed at the moment you pulled back on the stick. Case closed. What shall we talk about now?

But I walk away unconvinced. I may not be able to land an old biplane in a crosswind, but the other is true: I have flown airplanes for a long enough time to know what to expect from them. If the biplane, in the space of what was at the very most seventy feet, went from twenty miles per hour to full flight, it is the shortest takeoff I have made in any flying machine, save the helicopters. And I have deliberately and very studiously practiced short-field takeoffs in airplanes heavy and light. The shortest I have ever made took some 290 feet of runway and that was wheels-barely-off-the-ground, not clearing a two-foot dike of earth.

My old impossible beliefs have today been reaffirmed. The last answer to flight is not found in the textbooks of aerodynamics. If it were up to aerodynamics, the biplane would at this moment be a cluttered trail of wheels, fuselage, and wing panels angling off the runway at Rayville, Louisiana. But it is not, and stands whole and complete, without a scratch, waiting for whatever adventures will come our way tomorrow.

The clatter of a pickup truck turning onto the gravel drive of the airport. Painted dimly on its door, ADAMS FLYING SERVICE, and behind the wheel a puzzled smile beneath a wide-brim Stetson turned up in front, as the Old-Timer always turns up his brim in the western movies.

"Couldn't figure out what you were. Came over the house and I haven't heard an engine sound like that for twenty years. Ran out and looked at you and you were too small to be a Stearman, didn't look quite like a Waco and for sure not a Travel-Air. What the heck kind of airplane is that, anyway?"

"Detroit-Parks. Not too many of them made, so don't feel bad you didn't know her. Wright engine. You should have been able to tell the Wright, way it's all covered with oil."

"Adams, the name. Lyle. Yeah. Wright stop throwing oil and you better look out. Mind if I look inside?"

Headlights wash the biplane as the pickup turns and rolls closer. The door squeaks open and there are footsteps on the gravel.

"This is a nice little airplane. Look at that. Booster magneto, isn't it? Boy. Haven't seen an airplane with a booster mag since I was a kid. And a spark advance. Hey. This is a real flying machine!"

"Nice to hear those words, sir. Most people look at her and wonder how such an old pile of sticks and rag ever gets into the air."

"No, no. Fine airplane. Hey, you want to put her in the hangar tonight? I'll roll one of the Ag-Cats out and we can swing you right on in. Never matter if it rain on the Cat. Throw a cockpit cover on her, is all."

"Why, thank y', Lyle. Doesn't look like we'll be getting any rain tonight, though, and I want to be gone before the sun's up tomorrow. Kinda hard to pull out of a hangar for one guy to do. We been sleeping out anyway."

"Suit yourself. But I start dusting about sunup anyway; I'll be out here."

"That's OK. Got a place to get some gas, by the way? Might as well get her all filled up tonight."

"Sure thing. And I'll drive you down to the café to dinner, if you want."

Dinner at the café, with little bits of Louisiana thrown in for flavor. Lyle Adams is a Yankee. Came south to do a little dusting and turned out he liked it and stayed and started his own dusting business. Spraying, nowadays, mostly spraying and seeding. Not a whole lot of dusting still being done. The big modern Ag-Cat is a misty distant offspring of the Parks and her era. A working airplane, with a chemical hopper instead of a front cockpit, all metal and biplane. The Cat looks modern and efficient, and is both. Adams trusts it wholly, loves the machine.

"Great airplane, great airplane. All that wing, she just turns on a dime and gets right back into the field. Course she's not like an old airplane at all. I used to fly a Howard, up in Minnesota. Take hunters and fishermen out to places where no one'd ever been before. Land in the fields . . . I remember one time I took four of these guys way up north . . ."

The hours spin around swiftly, as they always do when new friends meet. At last the café lights go out and we rattle back in the ADAMS FLYING SERVICE pickup truck to the black green grass under the black yellow wing under a shimmering black sky.

"You sure got a lot of stars down here, Lyle."

"Kind of a nice place to live, all right. If you like to farm. If you like to fly airplanes, too. Pretty nice place. You're welcome to sleep at the house, now, like I say. Can't say as I'd make you come, though, night like this. Fact, I should bring my bag out and sleep under that wing with you. Long time since I done any of that. . . ."

The handshake in the dark, the wishes for good sleep, the assurances of meeting when the sun comes up tomorrow, and the pickup is crunching away, dwindling its light, quiet, turning the corner, flickering behind a row of trees, gone.

CHAPTER NINE

MORNING. NO, NOT morning even, just a glow in the direction from which we came last night. The sleeping bag is stowed away in the front cockpit, and with it the last bit of warmth in all the state of Louisiana. The air that I breathe steams about me and the rubber of the tall old tires is brittle and hard. My fingers don't work well at pulling the cowling hold-down clips. The gasoline, as I drain a little of it to check for water, is like liquid hydrogen across my hands. Perhaps I should warm the oil. Drain it out and put it in a big can over the fire, the way the barnstormers used to do with their oil on cold nights. Too late now. Pull the drain plug this morning and the oil wouldn't even pour. It would just lie there in the tank and huddle for warmth.

White lights sweep suddenly across the Parks, and rolling truck wheels crunch again on the gravel.

"*Morn*ing!"

"Oh, morning, Lyle. How are you, beside frozen solid?"

"Cold? Man, this is great weather! Little chill makes you feel like workin', of a morning. You 'bout ready for breakfast?"

"Don't think so, this morning. Want to go as far as we can today, use all the daylight. Thanks the same."

"What daylight you talking about? Sun won't be up enough to fly by for another half hour. And you've got to have some breakfast. Hop in, café's just a minute down the road."

I should explain that I don't like breakfasts. I should tell him that the time till sunup should be spent warming the engine. Perhaps the engine won't even start, in the cold, or it might take half an hour to get it to fire.

But the pickup's door is open in the dark, it is clear that everyone in this state expects a person to eat breakfast, and the task of explaining my hurry is much more difficult than stepping into a truck and closing a door. So I'll lose half an hour, trade it for a doughnut and a quick view of a duster pilot's morning.

A Louisiana duster pilot, I discover, knows everyone in town, and everyone in town is at the café before sunup. As we walk heavy-booted into the bright-lit room, setting the brass doorbells jingling, the sheriff and the farmers look around from their coffee to wish a good morning to the president of the Adams Flying Service. And they mean it, for his good mornings, with smooth air and without wind, are theirs, too. In the calm, his ag-planes can work constantly over their fields, seeding and spraying and killing leaf rollers and lygus bugs and darkling ground beetles, animals that once destroyed both fields and farmers. Lyle Adams is an important and respected man in Rayville.

I collect stares for my strangeness and scarf and heavy flying jacket. Lyle Adams, who lives the same world as I, who worries about engines and flies open-cockpit biplanes every day from the Rayville Airport, collects "Mornin'" and "How're y'?" and "You workin' the rice today, aren't y', Lyle?" My host is not an aviator in this town, he is a businessman and a farmer, and a little bit of a savior, a protecting god.

I learn, over a black Formica tabletop and a cup of hot chocolate, what to expect as I fly west, to the Texas border.

"You want to stay by the road, going out of here. If you go down in the trees a mile off the road, it will be months before they find you. First part of the way, 'round here, is fine . . . you got the fields to land in if you need. But thirty, forty miles out, you better stick by the road.

"Don't know the land much into Texas, but after a while you got fields again, and a little place to come down. Weather's been good the last days, wind picks up toward noon, be a tailwind for you. We might get some thunderstorms the afternoon, but by then you'll be long gone. . . ."

If I ever have need for a detailed knowing of how to fly Louisiana, I can draw on the experience that passed across the tabletop in the café at Rayville. For a moment I am listening to a lonely man, an aviator marooned on an island where no one speaks his language. There is not another person in town who would be happy to know that tailwinds are promised today, or who would be grateful for a warning about trees in the west. My host is practicing a language he doesn't often speak, and it is clear that he enjoys the practice.

"You get a big high-pressure cell sits up over Oklahoma, and the weather's good for days. But with the Gulf down there, we get our share of bad stuff, too. You get so that you know the land pretty well, where the wires are, and that sort of thing, and you can work even when the weather isn't too good. . . ."

By the time the buildings across the street are turning dull red in the dawn, the truck is crunching once again through the gravel, squeaking again to stop by the Parks's bright wingtip.

"Can I give you a hand, here? Help you at all?"

"Sure. You can hop in that cockpit, if you want, Lyle, while I crank the starter. Couple shots of prime, maybe; pump the throttle. She should catch the first time."

The steel handle of the starter handcrank jutting from the cowl is like the steel of an ice-cube tray, cubes installed. I can feel the frost of it through my gloves.

Stiffly, at the very first, t-u-r-n. (Whirring sounds, slowly, within.) And. Turn. And . . . turn; and . . . turn and . . . turn and, turn and turn and turn and turn, turn, turn turn turn turn-turnturnturn . . . pull the crank as the inertia wheel screams and clatters inside, ready to engage and slam its energy into the propeller.

"CLEAR! HIT IT, LYLE!"

One very tiny clink of the *Engage* handle pulled, the falling scream of the starter and one Wright Whirlwind engine blows silence into 10 million tiny pieces. The president of Adams Flying Service is smothered and lost for an instant in a cloud of smoke the color of pure blue fire. Another instant, and the smoke is twisting and shredding in the propeller blast, is tumbling back toward the sun glow, through a fence, and gone.

A tiny voice, shouting from the center of a hurricane:

"STARTS RIGHT UP, DON'T SHE?"

"NICE OLD AIRPLANE! LET HER IDLE ABOUT NINE HUNDRED RPM; TAKE HER A WHILE TO GET WARM."

Ten minutes of warming time for the Whirlwind, of cooling time for its pilot. Ten minutes in shouted promises to stop by if I'm ever in the country again, in assurance that I'll be looked up if Lyle Adams makes it out to the West Coast. No good-byes at all. A fringe benefit of flying, that: a host of friends in odd little places around the world, and the knowing that chances are you'll see them all again, someday.

It was cold enough at ground level; now, at two thousand feet, it is colder than freezing, if that is possible. The highway writhes westward, the trees close back in through Shreveport and across the state line into Texas, almost unseen.

It's like an ice-frozen towel, this wind, pulling and chafing across my face, never stopping. I have to swallow time and again, and it is hard to breathe. The sun crawls up grudgingly, unawake. Even after it is well above the horizon, it refuses to warm the air.

By slipping the leather gloves forward on my fingers, I discover that I can keep them warm for nearly a minute. Stomping up and down on the rudder pedals and turning the big invisible crank does nothing but transform me from cold to cold-and-tired. Below, on the road, no automobiles yet by which to gauge my ground speed, though early smoke shows a tailwind. Good, a tailwind is almost worth freezing for, when one sets out to cover as many miles as he can in a day's race.

Even so, I think of landing soon, so that I can stand still, or curl up in a ball and get warm. I wonder if it would be possible to fly an airplane without getting out of one's sleeping bag. Someone should invent a sleeping bag with legs in it, and arms, so that aviators can keep warm when they cross the South. The invention would come a little late, though. Splash it across every magazine and newspaper in the country, put it in every sporting goods store, and even so one probably couldn't make much money on an Aviator's Form Fitting

Sleeping Bag. Not too many aviators left around that have a great deal of need for them. Those that do will have to take second-best, rely upon an old-fashioned medium-heat G-type star, and hope that it is quick to rise in the mornings.

I look for a ground speed indicator, for any wheeled vehicle to move along the road, against which I can compare my speed. No luck. Hey, drivers! Sun's up! Let's get going down there! One single automobile wheeling down the road toward me. He's no help. Three minutes pass. Five, in the coarse hard wind. At last, turning out of a driveway, a green sedan, heading west. A few moments to allow him to reach his cruising speed; should be about sixty-five this morning with the roads clear. And we pass him handily. It is a good tailwind. I wonder if he knows that he is very important to me, whether he knows that there is an old biplane aloft this morning and watching him. Probably doesn't. Probably doesn't even know what a biplane is.

Even freezing, one learns. Something learned about course and speed from someone who is paying attention only to his own course and speed and who doesn't even know I exist. We owe much to green sedans, and the only way that we can pay our debt to them is just to go our way as best we can and be an indicator ourselves without knowing when, for someone we have never seen.

How many times, I ask, grateful now for the first particle of warmth from the east, have I taken freely and used the example that other men have set in their own lives? My whole life is patterned on examples that others have set. Examples to follow, examples to avoid. More than I can count. The ones that stand out, surely I can single them out, the ones that have greatly formed my own thought. Who am I, after all, but a culmination of my time, one meld of every example that has been set and in turn one single example for another to see and judge? I am a little of Patrick Flanagan, a little of Lou Pisane. There is in my hands a little of the skill of flight instructors named Bob Keech and Jamie Forbes and Lieutenant James Rollins. I am part of the skill, too, of Captain Bob Saffell, one of the few survivors of the air-ground war in Korea; of Lieutenant Jim Touchette, who happily fought the whole Air Force when he thought it was being stupid and who died as he turned a flaming F-86 away from an Arizona schoolyard; of Lieutenant Colonel John Makely, a gruff rock of a squadron commander who cared about nothing but the mission of his squadron and the men who flew its airplanes; of Emmett Weber, of Don Slack, of Ed Carpinello, of Don McGinley, of Lee Morton, of Keith Ulshafer, of Jim Roudabush, of Les Hench, of Dick Travas, of Ed Fitzgerald. So many names, so many pilots, and a little bit of each one of them is in me at the moment I fly an old biplane through a blue-cold Louisiana dawn.

Without bending a bit of effort, I can open my eyes to the great crowd of pilots who are flying this airplane. There's Bo Beaven, looking across at me and nodding coolly. Hank Whipple, who barrel-rolled a cargo transport and taught me how to land in pastures and on beaches and tried so hard to teach me to think far ahead of the airplane and of those who would restrict flight through their own fears and through meaningless regulation. Christy Cagle, who set an example about enjoying old airplanes, who would rather sleep under the wing of his biplane than in any bed.

In the crowd are other teachers, too. Look there, the shining silver Luscombe that first took me away from the jealous ground. A big round-engined T-28 that itself called the crash trucks by trailing a stream of black smoke from its damaged engine, at a time when I was too new to flying to know even that there was something wrong. A Lockheed T-33, the first jet airplane I ever flew, that taught me that an airplane can be flown by holding the control stick in thumb and fore-finger and *thinking* climbs and dives and turns. There's a beauty-queen F-86F to show me how strongly a pilot can become enchanted and in love with his airplane. A little dragonfly of a helicopter, to point the fun of standing still in the air. An ice-blue Schweizer 1-26 sailplane, telling of the invisible things that can keep a pilot drifting on the wind for hours without need of an engine. The good old rock-solid F-84F, covering my mistakes and telling me many things during a night flight over France. A Cessna 310, saying that an airplane can get so luxurious that the pilot is hardly aware it has a personality at all. A Republic Seabee, saying there's no fun quite like turning from a speedboat into an airplane and back, feeling clear water splash and sparkle along the hull. A 1928 Brunner-Winkle Bird biplane, asking me to taste the fun of flying with a pilot who has found a forgotten airplane, spent years rebuilding it and who at last turns it free once again in the air. A Fairchild 24, that in several hundred hours of exploring the sky brought me the sudden revelation that the sky is a real, true, tangible, touchable place. A C-119 troop carrier, much maligned, that taught me not to believe what I hear about "bad airplanes" until I have a chance to see for myself, and that there can be a good feeling in throwing the green-light *Jump* signal and dropping a stick of paratroopers where they want to go. And today, an old biplane, trying to cross the country.

Fast or slow, quiet or deafening, pulling contrails at 40,000 feet or whishing wheels through the grasstops, in barest simplicity or most opulent luxury, they are all there, teaching and having taught. They all are a part of the pilot and he is a part of them. The chipped paint of a control console, the rudder pedals worn smooth during twenty years of turns, the control stick grips from which the little knurl diamonds have been rubbed away: these are the marks of a man upon his airplane. The marks of an airplane upon the man are seen only in his thought, and in the things that he has learned and come to believe.

Most pilots I have known are not what they have seemed. They are two very separate people within the same body. Pick out a name . . . and here's Keith Ulshafer, the perfect example. Here's a man you'd never expect to see in a fighter squadron. When Keith Ulshafer said a word, it was a major occasion. Keith had no need to impress anybody; if you were to step in front of him and say, "You're a crummy pilot, Keith," he'd smile and he'd say, "Probably am." It was impossible to make him angry. He couldn't be hurried. He approached flying as though it were a problem in integral calculus. Although he had calculated his takeoff roll hundreds of times, and when any other pilot would look outside and feel the wind and temperature and guess the takeoff distance within fifty feet, Keith would figure it out with the planning charts before every flight and write it in carefully penciled figures at the bottom of a form that was rarely read. Neat, precise, meticulous. For Keith to hurry or to guess an airspeed or a fuel-consumption figure would have been for a chief accountant to step into the ring with the Masked Phantom. It was almost a joke to sit in a preflight briefing with him and listen to the flight leader outline the details of an air combat mission. Not a word from Keith as the wild vocabulary of the mission to come flew about his ears, as if he were a correspondent for a technical journal that happened to be sitting in the wrong chair when the briefing began. You'd never know that he was listening at all until the end of the briefing, when he might softly say, "You mean two fifty-*six* point four megacycles for channel twelve, don't you?" and the flight leader would stand corrected. More often Keith wouldn't say a word when the briefing was done. He'd amble to his locker, zip his G suit slowly about his legs, shrug into his flight jacket, emblazoned by regulation with lightnings and swords and fierce words that are supposed to typify fighter pilots. Then, carrying his parachute as something a little bit distasteful, he'd stroll to his airplane.

Even the boom of his starter firing wasn't as sudden as those of other airplanes, and his engine wasn't as loud.

Keith flew by the book. In formation, his airplane did not bounce or rock from side to side. It was as solid as if it had been bolted to the wing of the lead airplane. Then the mission, the air combat, would begin. And then, of course, look out.

Flying straight up, flying straight down, rolling streaking twisting flashing through the sky whirled the airplane that you would have sworn had Keith Ulshafer aboard when it left the ground. It was as though Keith had hopped quickly out before takeoff and some wild stranger had gotten in. You felt like pressing the microphone button and asking, "You all right, Keith?"

Keith was all right, and with luck and with attention and with very great skill you might be able to dodge the incredible monster at the controls of his airplane. On other missions of combat, it was always there. Here comes Keith, blazing down on the strafing target, the ground disintegrating in front of him; here he is closing on the Dart, towed for target practice, and blowing the silver thing out of the sky; down he drops on the rocket target and puts four rockets in a fifteen-foot circle. On close air support missions in the war games, Keith comes blasting in just high enough to clear the tanks' whip antennas, pulling up after the last pass in a flawless set of matched aileron rolls, disappearing into the sun. In the landing pattern he flies close and tight to the runway, touching his wheels precisely on the line painted as a touchdown target. Then, while the armorers de-arm the guns, the wild man jumps down from the cockpit, runs into the woods, and the other Keith Ulshafer, the technical-journal correspondent, strolls back in and he takes off his jacket and he unzips his G suit.

There is, I am learning, sleeping within us all, a person who lives only for times of instant decision and quick-blurring action. I saw him a year ago in Keith's wild man, I met him yesterday as a gambler in my biplane. In all of us this person sleeps, in the most unlikely person that logic could pick.

Over Texas, the pine trees are falling back and the plains begin to open ahead. The sun at last is warm in the air and the tailwind holds good; even the fastest automobiles are whisking backward beneath the wings.

I can see the tailwind, when I close my eyes, and I can see the biplane, a tiny dot borne along in it. The tailwind is only one eddy in a huge whirlpool of moving air, a whirlpool turning clockwise about a great center of high pressure somewhere to the north. An airplane flying at this moment in precisely the same direction as I, but north of that center, would be struggling through headwinds. My tailwind cannot hold, of course. I am flying away from the center, and even though I move only a little over one hundred miles per hour I will be able to see the winds begin to change about me before too long. Already, in two hours of flying, the wind has changed from a direct tailwind to a tailwind quartering slightly from the south. In another few hours it will be a crosswind from the south, drifting me to the right of course, and I shall have to fly as low as possible to avoid its ill effects.

Beware the winds that drift you to the right, I have learned. The maxim: "Drift Right into Danger." To drift to the right is to leave the zone of high pressure and good weather and to enter the frowning centers of low pressure and lowering clouds and visibility diminishing down to a mist in the sky. If I turned now just a little to the right, to keep the wind directly on my tail, I could begin a circle that would keep me always in clear weather; I would fly a circle with the whirlpool, about the high. But I would end where I began. To make progress along a course, I must expect a storm or two. But I am grateful for the good already received, the days of pure weather that have attended us. And still it holds; as far as I can see, there is no sign of lowering weather ahead.

Before me on the plain, the first smudge of a city rising. Dallas. Or more properly, Dallas/Fort Worth. Gradually it lifts and looms clearer, a giant sprawled in the sunlight. I shift course to the south, to avoid flying over the city. It should look like any other city from the air, but it does not. I cannot look at Dallas objectively. There has been a furious battle raging over airports in Dallas/Fort Worth. Each claims to have the airport most suited to the needs of both cities, and at last the government had to step in and mediate the case. Much name-calling going on down there, and bad feeling among those who used to fly and are now the operators of Large Steel Desks with "Airport Official" written in nameplates.

Beyond that, the city is a big depressing place, and there is even a sad tone in the sound of the engine, a going-lower sound from the cylinders. This is the city where the president was shot. I am glad that I do not have to land.

The mood of the countryside brightens a bit when the city has fallen out of sight behind, and I find U.S. Highway 80, which will be my primary navigation aid for the next thousand miles. Somewhere soon I should think about landing. Western Hills, it says on the map, and I fly one circle about a little town and its airport. It is eight-thirty in the morning, but there is not a sign of life on the field. The hangars are closed, the parking lot is empty. I will surely have to wait for fuel. I have made good time in the wind and down the road will be another airport at which someone is stirring. Besides, every mile behind is one less mile ahead. Considering this rather basic maxim of the traveler in the open cockpit, I settle down once again with the W of the magnetic compass bobbing under the reference line. By now the wind is a full crosswind and there is nothing to be gained by remaining at altitude. Forward on the stick, then, and down we come into the layer of the sky where the wind is slowed by its contact with the ground. We level fifty feet in the air above the deserted highway and rise and fall with the contour of the low hills.

Here and there an automobile on the road, and I get to know each one well, for I do not pass them so quickly now. A station wagon built sometime way ahead in the years to come, with children who haven't yet been born crowding the rear windows. I wave to them, across time and across five hundred feet of Texas air, and receive in return a little forest of waving hands. It is comforting to see other people moving through this space, and I cannot help but wonder what the others think as they look back into 1929. Does it remind them? Do they remember the days when they crossed this very road (it was a dirt road then) and along about there in the sky was an airplane just like that one that is there now? And it pulled slowly ahead and it vanished gradually to the left of the road, just as that one is vanishing?

I fly the up-sun side of the road from habit, and I wonder if that was a habit in the first days of flight. Probably not. Fly up-sun and they can't read your number. A defensive sort of habit, that. But I think it has saved me trouble now and then. There are not many people who know that it is perfectly permissible for an airplane to fly at less-than-treetop height in uninhabited land. If someone were not feeling happy about old airplanes, they could catch my big registration number and cause me to have to prove my innocence. The regulations say only that I must fly five hundred feet from any person on the ground; whether the five hundred feet is over or to one side of him makes no difference. Now, avoiding the wind and with plenty of smooth places to land, I choose to fly five hundred feet to one side of. The up-sun side.

When the road is clear, I fly over till my wheels straddle the centerline and I sit up tall in the seat and crane over the windscreen and over the long nose and just enjoy flying low. The telephone poles whisk by, and by resting one elbow on the rim of the cockpit I feel again almost as if I am driving an automobile. With the one fine difference of being able to touch back on my steering control and go roaring straight up into the sky.

I have a friend who is a race-car driver and he says racing is the greatest fun in the world. For him; he keeps forgetting to say, for him. For anyone else—well, for me—it is a frightening sort of fun. As in so many pursuits that are pinned to the ground, there is no margin, no time for thinking of other things. He must stay precisely upon that narrow ribbon of asphalt, and if anything looms ahead or even if the ribbon is not properly banked, the driver is in trouble. He has to think hard about driving every second that he holds that accelerator down. The sky, on the other hand, and very happily, is for dreamers, because there is so much margin, so much freedom. In an old airplane the takeoff and the landing are a bit critical, but the flying itself is the simplest, most controllable way to travel since . . . since nothing at all. Something in the way ahead? Climb over it. Turn around it. Fly underneath it. Circle for a while and think about it. None of these can the race driver do. He can only try to stop. With his margin, the airplane pilot can sit back in his cockpit and relax. He can spend long minutes looking behind his airplane, or above it or below it. Looking ahead is a sort of formality that has carried over from habits learned on the ground. He can do anything he wants to do with the ground; tilt it, twist it, put it over his head or directly behind his tail. And he can let it just wander its sleepy way below and look down at it through slitted eyes and make it go all misty and unreal.

The signs and the warnings and the agencies of flight remind solemnly that one should never let his attention shift from the urgent task of flying his airplane, that to let the mind drift for a second is disaster. But, after one has been flying for a very short while, it becomes clear that the agencies take themselves far too seriously. As a student pilot learns early in his first lesson, an airplane will fly itself better than he can fly it. An airplane does not demand the constant concentrated thought to stay in the air that the race car demands to stay on its narrow road. Following only the basic caution of not flying into a tree or the side of a mountain, a pilot finds the sky a perfect place to go and not-think.

Now, driving a foot above Highway 80 in my airplane, I must be a little more cautious than in those hours when there are five hundred or a thousand feet between my wheels and the earth. Now I can be the race driver, but without the penalty that plagues him. If I miss the turn, I can go right on over the guardrail, on over the rocks and boulders and the trees, and not feel the slightest tremor in my machine.

Over the rise of a hill ahead, unexpectedly, a car driving toward me. Back hard on the stick, and a turn into the sun, to gain that five hundred feet. I can't help but smile within myself. What would that feel like for me, to be driving over a little rise of ground along an ordinary road way out in nowhere and suddenly be confronted with an airplane headed directly at my windshield? That's not a very kind thing for an airplane pilot to do to people, despite the legality of it, and I should peek over the hills before I allow the biplane to frighten some poor driver who would rather be alone with his even-chuffing train of thought.

So we go our way, peeking over the hills first, then pressing ourselves tightly to the road, rolling our wheels once or twice on either side of the white line without really meaning to.

A bit of a start as I glance at my watch, for I have been flying for over four hours and am far ahead of my estimate for this hour. Ahead, the town of Ranger, Texas, listed on the map as home to an airport. I climb to see better, and find the water tower, the crossing of another highway, a building being built. And an airport. It is a big airport for such a small town, three dirt runways crossed on the ground and a pair of hangars. Circle once, check the wind sock, and with a silent word of thanks to the man who decided to have more than one runway available for landing, turn into the wind and settle to the dirt.

It is not even lunchtime and I have covered five hundred miles from Louisiana. That seems like so much, and I am proud, but away in the future/past I have flown airplanes that covered that distance in less than an hour, and one that could cover it in twenty minutes. There should be something meaningful in the contrast, in the shifting spectrums of times and airplanes, but now I am tired from four hours of sitting on a stone-hard parachute, and at the moment the meanings come second to the luxury of standing up and taking a step along an unmoving ground. The flight is going like a welcome routine, everything according to plan and as I would have it. And at the moment, at Ranger, Texas, as I wipe the oil from the windscreens and from the cowl, I do not think of the plan or of the future.

CHAPTER TEN

"SORRY, MISTER. I can't swing that prop for you. Can't turn the crank, either. Insurance. My insurance wouldn't cover me if I got hurt."

Strange strange strange, and I'm furious as I storm from the cockpit where I have been ready for engine start. Come all this way having too many willing helpers to tend the biplane and now, in a hurry to be gone, I have to get out here in the ninety-degree sun in a fur-lined jacket and I have to crank the airplane by myself, while the attendant stands back and watches. Anger converts easily into energy, and by the time the inertia flywheel is screaming I am too tired to bother with the fears of the attendant. Pull the starter engage handle, let the engine roar into life and shake a blanket of dry dust behind, taxi to face the wind, run the engine, and let go the brakes. A glance at my watch as the wheels lift from the ground and I begin to tick away another four hours, second by second. I settle down upon my friend the highway and it is as if I had not landed at all, as if I have been sitting constantly behind this propeller from sunrise, and from the night before that and from the day that led into the night. It will be good to get to California and home.

The crosswind has turned now to become a strong breeze, pushing me hard to the right, so that I must fly angled to the highway, fighting the wind with the bright blade of my propeller.

Fighting the wind with the blade. That is sort of poetic. But, when one is pressed shoulder to shoulder with the roiling forces that travel the sky, one needs every weapon he can get. A propeller is one of the pilot's weapons, for as long as it turns he is not really thrown on his own. As long as it turns it is not just a man against the crosswind or the headwinds or the ice over sea, but a man and his airplane, working and fighting together. One doesn't feel quite so lonely. Still, the propeller is not a friend without weakness, and to know the weakness and to supply the need of the weapon in those times is a wise practice. A propeller can be bravely turning full revolutions, as fast as it can turn, and if the airplane flies into a mass of air that is falling faster than the airplane can climb, it is all to no avail and the weapon and the pilot slide toward the earth. But the simple forethought of seeing the weakness and supplying it, of knowing that one can escape downdraft, and turn a mile away to a place where the air is rising, fills the coffers with altitude. So, before the weapon is even unsheathed for battle, before it is needed or the battle has been joined, the man in the airplane can supply the needs of his weapon. Enter this valley on the right side or the left? On one side will be a constant fight, a furious running duel with the wind and the mountain. On the other side, perhaps less than a mile distant, a smooth flight, that needs even less power than normal to maintain altitude. So, as he learns, the pilot begins to think not of left side or right, but upwind side or downwind. At first the student pilot would seek to disregard the wind, to cast it from his thought, for he has too many problems already to concern him, and give him one good reason why he should bother with something he can't even see. The answer, the student learns, is simply to be able to see the wind. The wind is a giant ocean of air surging along the rocky floor of the earth. Where ocean waves would tumble green and rushing down the side of the mountain, look for the wind to do the same. Where ocean would smash against the base of a cliff and shoot straight up, see there, on a day when the wind is strong, a power that will take an airplane by the wings and throw it headlong into the sky. Fly always the upwind side of the mountains and hills and you can fly easily, in the conscious power of one who knows that he needn't even loose his weapon to win a battle or to avoid it.

Where there are no mountains, the pilot who sees the sky sees tall columns of warm blue air rising from heated spots on the ground. Pause for a moment in one of the columns, circling, and the airplane climbs in spite of itself, carried aloft on an elevator denied to those who believe only what they can surely see. The man who flies an airplane, then, to be the best possible pilot, must be a believer in the unseen.

One can get along in the air for a long time without having to believe, for usually the only consequence of unbelieving is a little more strain on the engine, a little more wear on the propeller. But if one flies long enough and far enough there will come the day when the difference between believing and not believing is the difference between winning or losing the whole game of problem solving.

Ahead, the sky goes brown in dust thrown by the wind. Dust that is Texas airborne, and one of the reasons behind the poignant names of Texas towns along my course: Gladewater, Clearwater, Sweetwater, Mineral Wells, Big Spring. A land centered about water, and where the water is scarce in the ground it is made plentiful in thought and in the names of cities.

I look up and see that the dust tops out way over my head . . . 6,000, maybe 8,000 feet. It would be useless to try to climb over it; the winds aloft would be even more on my nose and I would find the cars passing me. As it is, I can stay with the faster autos, just barely hold my own. That is a disconcerting feeling. There is a blue station wagon on the highway, humming along. It falls behind me a little when it has to climb a hill, it catches up and moves on ahead when the hill is in its favor. We have been together for minutes, so long that the passengers no longer bother to look out the window at the biplane flying not far away. The woman is reading a newspaper. I wonder if she knows that I'm looking over her shoulder. Of course not. You wouldn't expect the pilot of an *airplane* to be aware of a car on the road, let alone of the people in the car.

The great wide flat land is all about, as far as I can see. There is room to put ten thousand biplanes into safe harbor. If the dust ahead gets so thick that I cannot see, it will be simple to turn and face the wind and land on any short stretch of clear soil. The stronger the wind, the shorter the space that the biplane will use for a safe landing. If the wind reaches fifty-five miles per hour, I'll be able to land without even rolling the wheels. I could hover for an hour above my landing spot if I wished, and alight as gently as hummingbird upon jasmine branch. Still, the wind across the ground looks vicious, whipping long lashes of sand across the highway, making the dry trees bow and flutter to the force of its will.

We press ahead and I find myself wondering what comes next, from out of the murk, wondering whether the dust and the wind are all that are lying behind the portent of this ominous right drift. Somehow, there is that part of my thought that will be disappointed if there is not something more carnivorous than this waiting to battle.

The little towns of the brown plain slowly appear and slowly vanish behind as the wind shifts to blow more directly against the front of the biplane. Of course, I remind myself, the wind is not blowing on the airplane at all; the only wind that I feel is the wind that the airplane makes in its passage through the air and the blast of the propeller at work. We are like a goldfish in a deep river of air, swimming through the air and at the same time being carried along in its bosom. The classic illustration for the young in flight is, "If you are aloft in a balloon in a hurricane, you could light a candle in the open air and the flame wouldn't even flicker. You're moving just as fast as the wind, my friend, just like a goldfish in a river."

I doubt that the candle/hurricane theory has ever been tested, but it all seems very logical and the goldfish must know that it is true. Still, it is difficult to accept this totally from the windy, gritty cockpit of an airplane over a long and lonely highway. Perhaps if I had a candle . . .

If I had a candle, I would still need the balloon. Settle down, pilot, and think about your flying. If the visibility gets very much worse, you know, you are going to have to land.

One solitary automobile on the highway passes me handily and I must draw my comfort from the fact that it is a new and luxurious machine. He could probably go one hundred miles per hour if he wanted to. In the tiny towns, the people have left the outdoors to the wind, and for the long minutes that the collection of houses drift beneath me they bring rippling reflections of the little villages along the roads of France. Deserted. Utterly deserted. Shutters closed, even in the center of the day. I never did discover where French villagers live, and left Europe as mystified as the other squadron pilots as to what the villages and the houses were for.

Vaguely through the sand comes a longer line of gasoline stations clinging to the highway. There is a city coming, and I look to the map on my knee. City city city, let's see. City should be . . . Big Spring. A strange name, at this moment. North of the city there will be an airport and I should think about landing. No, I won't land. There are two hours left in the tank, and I might fly out of the worst of the dust if I continue. Climb to cross the city, although I'm certain that no one hears the sound of five cylinders over the howl of the wind. Still, in a few things, conforming to regulation becomes a habit. Seven minutes to cross the city. I am certainly not moving very quickly. But if I stick to my task the wind should shift to become a right crosswind, drifting me to the left and portending good things to come.

A long wait. The parachute turns again to stone beneath me, incapable of being the cushion it was designed to be. A gradual Midland floats past below. An equally gradual Odessa, with tall buildings reaching up out of the depths of the ground and making me feel a little giddy to look down the lengths of them. Like many pilots, I would rather fly to 50,000 feet in an airplane than look over the edge of a two-story building. A few people in the streets of Odessa, clothes flapping. And ahead; isn't the sky growing a little brighter? I squint my eyes behind the goggles and maybe, just maybe, the sky is clearer to the west. And the expectant in me goes dead. This is all there will be. A brief dust storm, not even wild in its briefness, and the adversary is defeated. I circle in to land at Monahans and need less than one hundred feet of runway to roll to a stop. What a safe feeling. I can practically fly the airplane after it is on the ground, in the wind alone.

Once facing away from the wind, though, one must be very careful on the ground. An airplane is not built to move slowly along the ground, and unless it moves cautiously and uses its flight controls carefully, a strong wind can pick it up and casually, uncaringly, throw it on its back. It can take many insults from the sun and the weather as it stands on the ground, but one of the two things it cannot take is a very strong wind. The other, of course, is hail.

Easy easy now to the gas pump. Swing into the wind. Let the gritty engine die. It is a shame that there will be no more dragons to attack on this trip. Ahead can only be better weather and later even a tailwind once more. Those first pilots didn't have such a very difficult time of it, after all. Only a little part of Texas to cross, part of New Mexico and Arizona, and we are home. Almost an uneventful flight. If I hurry, I can be home tomorrow night.

So thinking, I put the hose to the gas tank and watch the scarlet fuel pour into the blackness.

CHAPTER ELEVEN

THE SKY IS almost clear when we once again trade land underwheel for sky underwing and turn to follow our faithful navigation highway, which lies like a cracked arrow pointing toward El Paso. Tonight at El Paso, or if I'm lucky, at Deming, New Mexico. We fly low once again with the sky burnt umber in the dust at our back and the sun turning quietly to shine in our eyes. We fly through a tall invisible gate, into the desert. The desert is very suddenly there and looks at us with a perfectly blank expression; no smiles, no frowns. The desert simply is there, and it waits.

Dimly ahead, hazy blue outlines, mountains. They are mountains still of fantasy, faint and softly shimmering. There are three of them, to the left, to the right, and one, with impossibly steep sides, barely to the right of course. The sleeping thirster for adventure wakes, saying, Perhaps a battle? What comes ahead? What do you see out there? A chance to wrestle against great odds? But I put him once again murmuring to sleep with the assurance that there are no windmills ahead, no dragons to slay.

For long minutes as I fly, I relax in the sun and the wind, the biplane needing only a gentle touch to follow its white-line compass down the road to the horizon. The road turns imperceptibly to the left and the airplane turns to follow. The sun and the wind are soft and warm and there is little to do but wait for this flight to reach El Paso, as though I had bought my airline ticket in Monahans and now it is up to the captain to bring me to destination.

I can never help thinking, as I cross the deserts, of those who looked through this air a hundred years ago, when the sun was a fireball in the sky and the wind was a jagged knife along the ground. What brave people. Or did they leave their homes for the West not out of bravery but out of just not knowing what lay ahead along this path? I look for wagon tracks and find none. There is only the highway, the Johnny-come-lately highway, and this white line, angling south of west.

They deserve a lot of respect. Months to cross a continent, that even an old biplane can cross in a mere week. A cliché, that, and easily said mockingly. But it is hard, over this land, not to think of those people. Imagine that, *people* down there on the surface, in the sun, driving oxen! If the sameness and the mile-on-mile exist for a biplane that covers seventy miles in a single hour, how much more it must have existed for them during those months.

Looking up from the gun-barrel road to the horizon, a little shock of ice, and within me the adventurer jerks bolt upright. The three mountains are there ahead, and clearer. But the mountain in the center, with the impossibly steep sides, has moved to stand squarely across my path. From the top of it drifts a short anvil of white. And now beneath it I can see a black column of angled rain. I'm not alone out here after all; the tall white thunderstorm ahead is an absorbing, hypnotic personality in the sky.

Easily avoided. Plenty of room to give it a wide berth; I'll just swing around to the right. . . . FIGHT IT! It is the adventurer, wide-awake now and looking for bright quick things to happen. FIGHT IT, BOY! YOU'RE NOT SOME SHRINKING FEARFUL NAMBY-PAMBY, ARE YOU? YOU GOT ANY COURAGE AT ALL YOU'LL FLY THROUGH THAT THING! THAT'S EXCITEMENT OVER THERE, THAT'S SOMETHING THAT NEEDS TO BE CONQUERED!

Oh, go back to bed. I'd be out of my mind to fly through that storm. At the very least I'd get soaking wet, and at worst the thing would tear the biplane to shreds.

The cloud looms over me now and I can see the anvil of it towering way up high over the top wing of the biplane. I have to tilt my head back to see the end of it in the sky. We begin a turn to the right.

OK. Fine. Turn away. You're afraid of it. That's fine, there's nothing wrong with being afraid of a thunderstorm. Of course the rain beneath it is not a tenth as bad as flying through the center, and I'm not asking you to fly through the center, just the rain. A very mild little adventure. Look, you can almost see through the rain to the other side of the storm, where it's clear again. Go ahead. Turn away. But just you don't talk to me about courage anymore. Mister, if you don't fly through this one little patch of rain, you don't have the faintest idea of what courage is. Nothing wrong with that, nothing wrong with being afraid and being a coward, but, son of a gun, you better not let me catch you thinking about bravery anymore.

It is childish, of course. Not the courageous, but the foolhardy would fly under a storm when avoiding it is a matter only of a shallow turn to the right. Ridiculous. If I believe in caution and prudent action, I will stand up for it and prudently fly around the storm.

The biplane swings to the left and points its nose into the black rain.

It certainly *looks* frightening, close up. But it is just rain, after all, and maybe a tiny bit of turbulence. The top of the cloud is out of sight now, over my head. I tighten the safety belt.

The engine doesn't care. The engine doesn't care if we fly through a tornado. The five cylinders roar on above a wet road, dull under the black base of the cloud.

A light tap of turbulence, just a little thud, and the forward windscreen sprays back the first drops of rain. Here we go. COME ON STORM! YOU THINK YOU'RE BIG ENOUGH TO STOP AN AIRPLANE? THINK YOU'RE BIG ENOUGH TO KEEP ME FROM FLYING RIGHT ON THROUGH?

An instant answer. The world goes grey in a hard sheet of rain, a smashing solid rain much more dense than it had seemed. Even above the roar of the engine and the wind I can hear the rain thundering on the cloth of the wings. Hang on, son.

A thousand feet up in the rain, and abruptly, without warning, the engine stops.

Good God.

Hard turn to the right, looking for a narrow strip to land. You idiot. Wouldn't fly around the thing, would you? Maybe we can land on the highway no the highway is crosswind and we've got to get out of this rain. A few places to land, but they'd be the end of the airplane. Mounds of sand, with tough sage holding them together. What a stupid thing to do. Fly under a thunderstorm.

We float out from under the cloud, and the torrent instantly stops. One beat from the engine, one cylinder firing. Pump the throttle, the primer, if you only would have gone around the rain, throw the magneto switch from *Both* to *Right,* there is the survival kit in the back and the jug of water. Some more cylinders fight into life, but it is an uneven fight; they fire once, miss three times, fire once again. The magnetos. The magnetos must have gotten wet. Of course. Now all they have to do is dry out before we touch the ground. Come along, little magnetos.

Five hundred feet now, and turning toward a clear lane in the sand. If it goes well, I won't hurt the airplane. If everything goes just right. Feel that sun, magnetos. No more storms for you today. A few more cylinders fire, and more often. Switch from right mag to left, and the firing fades completely. Quickly back to right and the propeller blurs faster, and for seconds at a time the engine runs normally. Sounds like those old rotary engines, cutting on and off. And there it is. Still missing every once in a while, but firing enough to keep the biplane in the air. We circle the landing place, three hundred feet above it. Retrieve the map from where it has fallen. Forty miles to the next airport, next airport is Fabens, Texas. Here's a problem for you. Leave a place where I might be able to make a safe landing, or push on across forty miles of desert and hope that the engine will keep running? If I land now and everything goes right, I can let the magnetos dry, take off once again and be sure of reaching El Paso.

And another interesting thing. When the engine stopped, I was not frightened. It was clear that I would have to make a landing; there was no choice. Land. Period. No discussions, no fear.

But now there is time to be concerned. It is not the forced landing that concerns a pilot, but the uncertainty of just when it will come. I can expect the engine to stop at any time; I should not be surprised if it does. I would almost be glad if the engine had not started again; I would be left with no choice but to land, and life would be much simpler. The thing to do now is to get some altitude, staying all the while over the one good strip in the desert. Then I shall set out for Fabens, staying always within gliding distance of a good clear spot. The dumb people who fly under storms.

I discover as the plan turns from thought into action and as the biplane slowly fights for altitude over the desert, engine roaring five seconds, silent for a half second, roaring six seconds more, that ahead are coming the most difficult forty miles of my journey. There is a definite procedure laid down for pilots to follow if the engine stops, and no fear attendant. But if it doesn't quite stop, what then? I'll have to consider this tonight over a bowl of soup and a glass of ice water.

The biplane flies more slowly than normal, despite the full-open throttle. Pull the throttle back and the engine dies. Switch magnetos and it dies. Under a very special set of conditions it will just barely keep running. We'll give her a try. When she stops, we'll be confident and fearless again. I don't care if I smash her to a splinter heap, I know I'll walk away all right. And other soothing statements.

Skirting the right side of the storm, hardly aware that it exists, I help the little biplane through the sky. Any time I want to frighten myself, I have only to switch from the right mag to the left and listen to the silence. The adventurer is wide-awake still, and urges me to overcome the fear in the switch. For his sake, to prove to myself that I am not afraid of listening to the quiet when all about the land below is desert, I switch it. But it is no use. It scares me. Yet if by itself the engine stopped and wouldn't run again, I know that there wouldn't be the slightest fear. Interesting. Lots of little mental relays and shuttle switches working overtime on this leg. From field, to field, to field, to field I travel, engine smoothing for a while, then cutting out again. I have in my mind a picture of the magnetos, the two of them beneath the engine cowling. It is dark in there, with oil mist swirling, but I can see the water in the seams of the magneto housings, and every once in a while another drop splashes down upon them.

I find the road on the other side of the storm and from it gain some measure of comfort. At least now I can land on the road and be near some kind of occasional rolling humanity. I wonder if motorists know how important they are to aviators. They are a source of glee when the tailwinds are there and the airplane passes the automobiles quickly. Glee, too, when the traffic is heavy on the road and a pilot can pass ten cars a second. A reassurance in the desolate lands, bringing their sign of life into view. And a last-ditch help, when glee is gone and one must land on a highway and ask aid.

Over the nose of the biplane, to the right of the road, a search answered. First ahead, then not quite within gliding distance and therefore uncomfortably distant, and at last I have captured Fabens and I don't care if the engine stops or not. I take a sheer cool drink of relief. The wind is heading directly down the dirt strip; blessing on blessing! Throttle back, a gliding turn, steeply, to lose altitude. Imagine that. Too much altitude. I feel like a rich man lighting bonfires with hundred-dollar bills. Level above the dirt, an easing of the stick and we are down again, and stopped. Hurray! Land again beneath me, solid and smooth, and a gas pump! A Coca-Cola machine!

Fabens, Texas, I shall never forget you.

CHAPTER TWELVE

THERE IS A restaurant in Fabens, part of the motel on U.S. Highway 80. Like every other café and restaurant across the country, in the hour before sunrise, it is a very uncomfortable place for criminals. In Rayville it was the sheriff at breakfast, at Fabens it is the highway patrol. Two beaconed squad cars are parked in the gravel outside and four black-uniformed, six-gunned officers take their coffee at the counter, talking about a murderer caught the night before in El Paso.

I feel guilty as they talk, and glad that they aren't still looking for murderers. I am a suspicious-looking character, sitting alone at the far end of the counter, furtively consuming a doughnut. My flight suit is smeared with rocker-box grease, ingrained with Midland-Odessa sand. My boots are white in runway dust, and I am suddenly aware that the survival knife sewn on my right boot could be a very sinister thing, a concealed weapon. I cross my left boot over the right one, feeling more and more the wary fugitive.

"You want a ride out to the airport, mister?"

I hope the sudden startled clatter of my hot-chocolate cup doesn't mark me a murderer.

"You're the fellow with the biplane out there, aren't you?"

"How would you know that?"

"Saw you come in last night. I do a little flying out there myself—Cessna 150."

I forget about my concealed weapon, accept a ride, and the talk changes from murderers to the good old days of flying.

At dawn the magnetos are dry. During the engine run-up before takeoff, they don't miss a beat. That was my problem. There can be no other explanation. The magnetos were wet, and as long as I keep them dry I shall have no more difficulties with engines.

So, before the sun is quite up, a single biplane leaves the ground at Fabens, Texas, and turns to follow a highway leading west. It takes a while to settle down again. It was from this cockpit that I saw the unpleasant difficulties of yesterday, and it will be a minute or two before confidence returns that the difficulties are truly gone. Switch the mag selector from *Right* to *Left* and I cannot hear the slightest change in the sound of the engine. I could not ask for a better ignition system. But it is always good practice to keep a landing place in sight.

El Paso, with its very own mountain, in the first light of the sun. I have watched the sun on this mountain before, but I think now of the times quickly, without searching for meaning. I just know that I have been here before, but now I am in a hurry to leave El Paso, a check-point only, a dwindling crosshatch behind me.

The road is gone, too, and for the next eighty miles the navigation is the traditional kind: railroad track, and is this ever a *desert*! Visibility must be a hundred miles and it's like looking through a microscope at a sheet of grey newsprint: clumps of desert sage on mounds of sand, each clump precisely eight feet from its neighbors on all sides. Any one clump could be the center of the desert and the rest stretch perfect and absolutely constant to the end of the earth. Even the map gives up here and sighs. The black line of the railroad track races inch on inch through the tiny faceless dots that mean there's nothing out here at all.

Stop now, engine, and we'll discover how long we have to wait for a train to cross these tracks. I dare not fly low. First, to give a wider choice of landing places. Second, because I am afraid that I will see rust upon the tracks.

Right magneto. Fine. Left magneto . . . wasn't that the tiniest miss-ing of a beat, there? It couldn't have been; now quick, switch back to *Both*. Oh, it's whistling-up-courage time. There was the smallest choke then, I'm sure. Automatic Rough, boy, just like the missed beats you hear in any engine as soon as it is over water and out of gliding distance from land. Yesyes that's it, good ol' Automatic Rough, the practical joker, and it won't be necessary to check the mags again.

Listening very closely, I can hear the uneven beat of the engine. The only unanswered question is whether the uneven beat is normal or not, for I have never listened so closely to this engine before. I think that I could listen as closely to a sewing machine and hear the stitches missed. As the mechanics say, you can't fix anything till you see something wrong; I'll just have to wait till the missing gets worse.

Uncomfortable miles of desert pass below. Certainly makes a difference when one suddenly has no trust in an engine. I can't help but think that the less I trust the engine, the less worthy of trust it will be, and my little sewing machine will collapse completely.

There you go, engine; I trust the heck out of you. Run on and on, you little devil; bet I couldn't stop you if I tried, you run so well. Remember your brother engines who set the endurance records and pulled the *Spirit of St. Louis* from Roosevelt Field to Le Bourget. They wouldn't be at all happy to hear that you considered stopping over the desert, would they? Now, you've got plenty of fuel and there's plenty of oil for you, warm and clean, it is a fine dry morning. Wonderful for flying, don't you think? Yes, it certainly is a fine dry morning.

I am in a hurry, full in a hurry. I do not care now whether I learn or not, the only thing that matters is that this engine keeps running and that we make it quickly to California. Learning is a misty little will-o'-the-wisp that is gone as soon as one blinks one's eyes and allows thought of something else. When I hurry, the airplane goes dead and quiet beneath me, and I grow tired, and I fly a machine in the air and I learn nothing.

Coming in from the horizon is the first curve in the track and around that curve, Deming, New Mexico. We'll make it to Deming in fine shape, won't we, engine? Of course we will. And after Deming is Lordsburg and my goodness we're not far from home at all, are we? You just keep right on chugging along up there, my friend. Chugging right on along.

Comes Deming, sliding by, and once again a road to follow. And Lordsburg. The engine utters no complaint. After Lordsburg I fly off my map into Arizona. But if I follow the road, it will surely lead to Tucson. I sit in the cockpit and watch the powdered ground reel by. The mountains are surprises now, without a map, as if this were all unexplored territory. The next chart I have is for Tucson.

The road winds for a moment, twisting through the rocky hills. An adobe house to the right, a cluster of mountain buildings to the left, guarding a lake as smooth as engine oil. There is not the faintest ripple of wind.

One certainly becomes impatient when one doesn't know just where one is. Come along, Tucson. Around this curve? This? All right, Tucson . . . let's go, let's go.

We snake down a lonely valley, echoes rebounding from its hills. In Tucson we shall have to look around; big airports and big airplanes there. It will be nice to see another airplane. Why, I haven't seen another airplane since Alabama! Even over Dallas, not a single airplane. Talk about the crowded sky. But perhaps the first thousand feet doesn't count as sky.

And there it is ahead, suddenly, as in the motion pictures of the sailing boats when the lookout shouts land ho and the camera turns to find land only a hundred yards away. There, a silver gleam in the air, an airplane flying. It is a transport making his landing approach to Tucson International. A transport. He looks as foreign in the sky as though he were an oil painting of an airplane, sliding on invisible tracks toward the runway.

To the right is the giant that is Davis-Monthan Air Force Base, with a runway nearly three miles long. I could land on the width of that runway with room to spare, but the mountain-heavy airplanes that fly from the base sometimes need every foot of the length to get off the ground. What a way to fly.

Right there, by the corner where the parking ramp turns, I stood on a weekend alone, with a fighter plane that would not start. Something wrong with the ignition. I could get all kinds of fuel into the burner cans and the tailpipe, but it wouldn't light. . . . I couldn't make it burn. I gravely considered throwing a newspaper afire up that tailpipe, then running around to the cockpit and opening the throttle to spray it with fuel. But a mechanic happened along and fixed the ignition system before I found a newspaper and a match. I can't help but wonder what would have happened.

One other airplane, a little one, in the sky below me, and I rock my wings to him. He doesn't notice. Or he may have noticed, but is one who doesn't believe in wing-rocked greetings between airplanes. That is a custom going out of style, I think, wing-rocking to say hello and don't-worry-I-see-you. Well, I'll give it a chance to live on, anyway. Sort of a comradely thing to do, I think, and I might be able to set the custom going again; have everyone rocking their wings to everyone else. Jet transports, bombers, lightplanes, business planes. Hm. That might be carrying it a little far. Perhaps it's best that only a few keep the custom going.

One mountain north of Tucson and it is time to land once more, at an ex-Army field. Marana Air Park, they call it now. Like planting flowers in a hand grenade. Hard surface here, and straight into the wind. I should be getting used to the biplane by now, but there is that strange wall of hurry between us. We land without incident, and stop. Yet there is a moment in which I know that I could not control the airplane if it veered to left or right, as though we were sliding on buttered glass. Something is gone. My rushing, my placing California before learning has breached the trust between us, and the biplane has not stopped to teach or even to imply a lesson since before the thunderstorm. She has been cold and void of life, she has been a machine only. Watching the familiar fuel pour into the familiar tank, I wish that I could slow down, could take my time. But the closer I come to home, the harder I drive the biplane and myself. I am helpless, I am swept up in a windstorm of hurry and nothing matters except getting home tomorrow.

CHAPTER THIRTEEN

THE MAGNETO AGAIN. Only ten minutes after takeoff, the left mag is misfiring. Clearly it is not Automatic Rough at work, for below is Casa Grande and an airport into the wind. It is just that the engine is misfiring and backfiring whenever the left magneto is called upon to spark the cylinders by itself. The right mag works well, with only an occasional single missing of a single beat. Decision time once again, and more difficult. Land now at a field that has some limited repair facilities and find the trouble, or continue on, using the right mag alone?

No answer from the airplane, as if she is sitting back and watching me dispassionately, not caring whether the decision I make here means safety or destruction. If only I were not in a hurry to be home. It would be prudent to stop. Prudence and I haven't been getting along too well these last days, but after all, one should sometimes follow its leadings.

All the while, Casa Grande drifts slowly behind. I don't have much money, and it would cost money even if the little hangar there would have the parts the engine needs. If I go ahead, I'm gambling that the good magneto will stay good across the next three hundred miles of desert. If I lose, I'll land on the highway and seek the help of my fellow man. That's not too bad a fate, or a very high penalty to pay. What does an airplane engine have two magnetos for, anyway?

So that it can run all day on one magneto, it can run all its life on one magneto. Decision made. We go on.

With the decision, a wind rising out of the west. A time for patience has once again arrived, and at altitude, in the midst of the wind, I am slowed so that a lone automobile, towing a house trailer, keeps in perfect pace with me. The cost of my decision to fly with an ailing ignition system is that I fly at altitude and do not allow myself the trick of flying close to the ground in avoidance of the wind. My only negotiable asset now is altitude and I cannot afford to squander it for a few miles per hour. At least I am moving westward.

I'm not concerned, and engine failure is an academic sort of problem from Casa Grande to Yuma, for this is land that I know well and that I have seen day after day and month after month. Just on the other side of those same Santan Mountains off my right wing lies Williams Air Force Base. Just after I had finally earned the right to wear the wings of an Air Force pilot, I came to this land, and to the magnificent swift airplane that was numbered F-86F and that was coded Sabrejet. From those runways we flew, nervous at first in a single-seat airplane in which the first time we flew, we flew alone. And it was such a simple airplane to fly that we would finish our short before-takeoff checklist there on the concrete and stop and wait and shake our heads and mutter, certain that we had forgotten something. You mean all you do is push this little handle forward and let go of the brakes and then *fly*? That's what they meant, and following that opening routine we came up from those runways to cross this same desert.

To my left are a few hundred square miles marked Restricted Area on my map, and that are indeed restricted, as far as biplanes are concerned. But then Restricted meant Our Very Own, where we flew to find the strafing targets set in cleared squares of desert and the bull's-eye rings of the bomb circles. But best of all for us was the desolate land called the Applied Tactics Range. Applied Tactics gives the student the feel of what close air support really is. There on the desert are convoys of old rusting automobiles and trucks, are tanks waiting in the sage and yucca, are roundhouses and artillery emplacements. Once in a while we would be allowed to practice combat tactics on these, learning such basic tenets as Never Strafe a Convoy Length-wise; Never Attack Twice from the Same Direction; Concentrate Your Fire.

Maybe they're out there today. If I could make it very quiet, maybe I could hear the sound of the engines and the thud of the practice rockets hitting the sand and the popcorn sound of the 50-caliber machine guns firing. This is happy country, from a time of good days, filled with that rare sort of friend that one only finds when adventure is shared, and when one trusts one's life to another.

Where are they in this twist of now? Those other pilots are no longer about me every day, briefing for the first flight before the sun has risen. Some who flew this land with me are still flying, some are not. Some are the same, some have changed. One a purchasing agent now for a giant corporation, one a warehouse manager, one an airline pilot, one in the Air Force, a career man. The friend within them is driven hard in a corner, by trivial things. Talk not to him of rent or taxes or how the home team is doing. The friend within is found in action, in the important things of flying smoothly in the weather, in calling the fuel check, the oxygen check, and in trying to put more bulletholes in the target than any other friend can do.

It is strange to discover this. Here is the same man, that same body whose voice came once on the radio saying, Look at that, and I'd turn and look over my right wing and there would be an isolated mountaintop in spring, with its base all brown and dry, and from its razor top the wind pulling a white tatter of snow, absolutely without sound, and alone. The quiet wind on a quiet mountaintop, and the trial of snow like spray from a mid-ocean stormwave. And in "Look at that" a friend is revealed. There is no triviality in those words. They are to say, Notice our mortal enemy, the mountain. He can at times be so very cruel, yet at times like these he can be very handsome, too, can he not? You've got to have respect for a mountain.

Without mountains over which to be concerned, the friend shrinks away. When the purchase order and the desk become the important things in a life, the friend is difficult to reach. One can break through, of course, with sheer power and anguish and see again for a second or two the friend within. Hey! Bo! Remember the day when I was dialing a radio in my cockpit and you were flying my wing and you touched your microphone and said, Plan on flying into that hill, ace? Don't you remember that?

A stirring within, and an answer from the friend.

I remember; don't worry. I remember. Those days were bright, but we can never live them again, can we? Why must we hurt ourselves in the remembering?

There is a shock of cold when I realize that the desk mind has taken over so much of the thought of a friend and that his brilliant life has become a calm plain. No more the roaring laughing highs of pulling contrails in the sun or rolling down into an attack. No more the furious caged lows of being caught for days on the ground by fog that doesn't show the other side of the flight line. Nothing devastating ever happens to a purchasing agent, and nothing filled with delight.

———

The Restricted Area falls away behind and with it a few lumps of crusted lead, copper-clad, buried in the sand, that once shimmered from my gun barrels. Ahead, another mountain, and a town called Yuma. Almost home country, now, biplane. Almost there. But it is surprising how big even home country can be. And for a reason unknown a fragment of statistic drifts through my mind. The great majority of all aircraft crashes occur within twenty-five miles of an airplane's home base. One of those undoubtedly meaningless things, but of the sort that is so cunningly worded that one remembers it.

Easy to chase that foreboding. I'm not within twenty-five miles of my home base. I'm a lot closer to it than I was a few sunrises ago, but it is still over the horizon ahead.

With the Colorado River below and California air whistling about me, I have the courage to try the other magneto. And now, after two hours running on the right magneto, the left one works perfectly. The last time I tried it, at Casa Grande, backfires and puffs of black smoke from the exhaust. Now, smooth as the youngest of kittens. What a most unusual engine.

Biplane, we are almost home. Hear that? A little more desert to do, one more stop for gasoline, and you'll be in a warm hangar once again. The Salton Sea glimmers ahead and the squares of green-blotter land to the south of it. Anything can happen now and we can say we have made it to California.

Still, it is a California just in name and feels like home only as Saturday feels like Saturday because I've seen a calendar. This desert, and the baked blotter land, doesn't shout *California!* the way the long beaches do, or smooth golden hills or the sudden mass of the Sierra Nevada. One isn't truly in California until one is west of those mountains.

The biplane's wings flick suddenly dull, as if a switch were thrown. Surprised, we have been enveloped in dusk. The switch is the Sierra itself, thrown to block the sun, casting a giant dark knife-shadow across the desert. The familiar first-lights of cautious automobiles sparkle on the road toward Palm Springs, hurrying in for the night. Our night will be Palm Springs, too, nested down in the grey blur at the base of San Jacinto Mountain. There is now the turning greenflash whiteflash of the airport beacon. And there, spilling over the top of a peak marked on my chart as 10,804 feet above sea level, clouds, as black as the mountain itself.

Palm Springs, airplane! Home of motion-picture stars and heads of state and giants of enterprise. Better, Palm Springs is less than a day from your own home, a hangar again, and Sunday-afternoon flights. Like that, airplane?

There is no response from the Parks. As we turn to land, not the faintest hint of reply.

CHAPTER FOURTEEN

THE AIRPORT AT Palm Springs is a rather exclusive place and parked upon it are the most elite and the most expensive airplanes in the world. There is this morning, however, something radically wrong. At the very end of a long row of polished twin-engine aircraft, in fact parked almost in the sagebrush, is a strange oily old biplane. It is tied to the ground by a rope at each wingtip and one at the tail. Underneath the wing, as the grey sun rises, is a dim sleeping bag stretched on the cool concrete.

It is raining. Once a year in Palm Springs it rains, and in the worst years twice. What instrument of coincidence has timed my arrival with the arrival of the Day of Rain? There are no other sleeping bags spread on the concrete of the airport and I must consider this alone.

The rain is light at first, from broken clouds. At first, too, the wetness makes merely the background for a white silhouette in dry of the biplane, and I lie along the dry left wing of the silhouette. The rain goes on, drumming first on the top wing, then slowly falling in big drops from the top wing to boom against the fabric of the lower wing. A pretty sound, and I lie unconcerned and listen. Mount San Jacinto scowls down at me, clouds spraying over its towering peak. I'll cross you today, San Jacinto, and then it is all downhill to home. Two hours' flying from here at most, and I shall discover what it feels like to sleep once again in a bed.

The rain continues, and the wetness takes on a sheen of tiny depth. Lying now with my head on the concrete and with my lowest eye open, I can see a wall of water advancing, fully a sixteenth of an inch high. This is a great deal of rain, and the drumming and booming on my wing should stop any second now.

It doesn't. The wall of water advances slowly into my dry sanctuary. The thirsty concrete drinks, but to no avail. New drops still rush to reinforce the water. By tiny leaps and minuscule bounds, the wall advances. If I were less than a millimeter tall, it would be an awesome spectacle of rampaging nature. Pinpoint twigs and branches are being swept up into that wall, waves thereon are foaming and cresting and the roar of their advance can be heard for inches around. A fearsome, terrifying sight, that water rushing, sweeping over everything in its path. The only reason that I do not run screaming before it is a matter of perspective, an ability to make myself so big that the water is nothing, and of no danger. And I wonder as I watch. Can it be the same with all fearsome things? Can we lift ourselves so far above them that their terror is lost? I wonder, and for the briefest part of a second I can swear that I sense a faint, tired smile. Perhaps my friend is awake once again, briefly returned to lesson teaching.

Phase II of the Lesson of the Advancing Water is that, no matter the perspective, one cannot ignore the problem. Even though it is suddenly only a barely moving film of moisture and not a flash flood of the desert, it can still be annoying and uncomfortable unless I soon solve the problem. My silhouette of dryness grows narrower as the rain continues, and unless I find some way to stop the water's advance or decide that wet sleeping bags aren't so bad after all, I'll be forced to flee.

Unshaven, oil-covered, disheveled with the worst of the barnstormers, I gather my sleeping bag and race for shelter in the luxurious office and waiting room of the general-aviation terminal. Would a good barnstormer have gotten wet? I wonder as I run through the rain. No. A good barnstormer would have climbed into the cockpit, under the waterproof cover, and have been asleep again in an instant. Ah, well. It takes time to learn.

Against one wall of the deserted room is a telephone, a direct line to the weather bureau. It is a strange feeling to hold a telephone in my hand again. A voice comes from the thing, with an offer of general aid.

"I'm at Palm Springs. Want to get across into Long Beach/Los Angeles. How does it look through the pass?" I should have said The Pass. Almost every pilot who flies to Southern California has flown through the gigantic slot cut between the mountains San Jacinto and San Gorgonio. On a windy day, one can count on being tossed about in the pass, but so many new pilots have exaggerated its rigors that even old pilots are beginning to believe that it is a dangerous place.

"The pass is closed."

Why is it that weathermen are so smug when the weather is bad? At last they can put the pilots in their places? The arrogant devils need to be set back a notch, now and then? "Banning has a two-hundred-foot overcast with one-mile visibility in rain; probably won't get much better all day long."

The devil it won't. The chances of that weather staying so bad all day are about the same as the chances of Palm Springs being flooded in the next half hour.

"How about the pass at Borrego or Julian, or San Diego?"

"We don't have any weather for the passes themselves. San Diego is calling three thousand overcast and light rain."

I'll just have to try them and see.

"How's the Los Angeles weather?"

"Los Angeles . . . let's see . . . Los Angeles is calling fifteen hundred broken to overcast, light rain. Forecast to remain the same all day. A pilot report has the pass closed, by the way, and severe turbulence."

"Thanks."

He catches me before I hang up, with a request for my airplane number. Always the entries to make in his logs, and no doubt for a very good reason.

Once I get on the other side of the mountains, there will be no problem. The weather is not quite clear, but it is good enough for finding one's way about. Banning is in the middle of the pass, and the weather it is reporting is not good. But the report may be hours old. I can't expect much so early in the morning, but I might as well give Banning a try before I run down along the mountain chain, poking my nose into every pass for a hundred miles. One of them is sure to be open.

Twenty minutes later the biplane and I round the corner of San Jacinto and head into the pass. It certainly does not look good. As if someone has made a temporary bedroom out of Southern California, and has hung a dirty grey blanket between it and the desert, for privacy. If I can make it to Banning, I can stop and wait for the weather to lift.

Below, the highway traffic goes unconcernedly ahead, although the road is slick and shiny in rain. A few drops of rain smear the front windscreen of the biplane, a few more. I have my spot all picked to land if the engine stops in the rain, but it doesn't falter. Perhaps the biplane, too, is in a hurry. The rain pours down and I discover that one doesn't get wet flying rainstorms in an open-cockpit airplane. The last rainstorm I flew into, I hadn't noticed. The rain doesn't really fall, but blows at me head-on, and the windscreen kicks it up and over my head. If I want to get wet, I have to stick my head around to one side of the glass panels.

Funny. It doesn't feel as if I'm getting wet at all. The rain feels like rice, good and dry, thrown a hundred miles an hour into my face. It is only when my head is back in the cockpit and when I feel my helmet with an ungloved hand that I find it wet. The rain gets goggles sparkling clean.

After a few minutes of rain, the first turbulence hits. Often I have heard turbulence described as a giant fist smashing down upon an airplane. I have never really felt it that way in a small airplane until this second. The fist is just the size of a biplane, and it is swinging down at the end of a very long arm. It strikes the airplane so hard that I am thrown against the safety belt and have to hold tightly to the control stick to keep my hand from being jerked away. Strange air, this. Not the constant slamming of the twisted roiled air that one expects from winds across rocky places, but smooth . . . smooth, and BAM! Then smooth . . . smooth . . . BAM! The rain grows heavier, in great weeping veils sorrowing down to the ground. The sky is solid water ahead. We can't get through.

We turn away, not really discouraged, for we hadn't expected to get through the first thing in the morning.

Whenever I turn away from bad weather in an airplane not equipped to fly by instruments, I feel very self-righteous. The proper thing to do. The number one cause of fatal accidents in light aircraft, the statistics say, is the pilot who tries to push the weather, to slip through without going on instruments. I'll push the weather with the best of 'em, I say sanctimoniously, but I'll always do it with a path open behind me. The biplane, with its instruments that give only a rough approximation of altitude and a misty vague idea of heading, on a wobbly compass, is not built to fly through any weather. Any weather at all. If I absolutely had to, I might be able to get it down through an overcast, flying with my hands off the stick and holding perhaps the *W* in the compass by rudder alone. But that's a last-ditch effort, taken only where the land below is flat and I know for sure that the ceiling is at least one thousand feet.

There are those who say that you can spin down through an over-cast, and I'd agree with them; a good procedure. But I have heard that with a few of the old airplanes the spin turns into a flat spin after three or four revolutions, and from a flat spin there is no recourse save the parachute. This may be one of the rumors, and untrue. But the danger therein is my thought, I do not *know.* Not the flat spin, but the fear of the flat spin keeps me from an otherwise practical and effective emer-gency procedure. It is much easier to stay away from the weather.

The first round goes to San Jacinto, and taking its strange knock-ing about, we fly, filled with righteousness, back out of the pass. What a fine example we are setting for all the younger pilots. Here is a pilot who has flown instruments before and often, for hours and in thick cloud, turning back from a bit of mist that obscures the ground. What a fine example am I. How much the prudent pilot. I shall live to be very old. Unfortunately, no one is watching.

We turn south along the eastern edge of the mountains, over the bright green squares in the sand that irrigation has wrought. And we climb. It takes a long time to gain altitude. Playing the thermals and the upslope winds as hard as I can, I rise only to the level of the lower peaks; a little more than 8,000 feet, where it is freezing once again. At least here, when I can no longer stand the cold, I have only to come down a little to be warm once again.

We won't even try Borrego Pass. A long narrow gorge running diagonally through the mountains, it is walled only a short way down its length by the same blanket of grey that covers the pass at San Jacinto.

South some more and third time must be the charm. More rough, high country, but at least the cloud is not so bad. I turn at Julian toward a narrow gap in the mountains, and follow a winding road.

The wind through the gap is a direct headwind as I fly west. It flattens the grass along the roadside and the road's white line creeps reluctantly past my wing. It must be blowing fifty miles an hour at this altitude. There is an awesomeness about it, an uneasy feeling that I am not wanted here, as if I am being lured into the gap in order that some hungry dragon within can have his fill of warm engine and crushed wingspars. We fly and fly and struggle and fly against the wind, and finally the gap is ours. We are through, to a land of high valleys and peaceful green farms in mountain meadows. But look down there. The grass, even the short grass, is being flattened silver by the wind, it is being ironed onto the ground by it. That wind must be fifty miles per hour now at the *surface*!

This is work, and not fun at all. If the wind would only be on my tail, it would be fun. Ahead, the clouds, watching me and grinning maliciously. The only way out of the valley ahead is to follow the road, and the cloud turns into fog that lies on the road like a big fuzzy barbell that can never be lifted. It is sad. We have fought so hard to get here. Perhaps we can land. If we land here, surely we can outwait the clouds and continue westward this afternoon. The meadows look very good for landing. Light rain in the air, but much sun too. Suddenly they combine off the right wing into a brilliant full-circle rainbow, a really bright one, almost opaque in its radiance. Normally the rainbow would be a beautiful sight, worthy of awe, but I still must fight to move an inch against the wind and I can only take snapshots with my eyes and hope that later, when I am not fighting, I'll be able to remember the rainbow for what it is, and as fresh and as bright as it is.

I shall land, and save the advance I've made. So, decision made, down comes the little biplane from its rainbow, toward the wet green grass of the meadow. A good landing place ahead, worth inspecting closely. Grass is taller than it looked. And wet. Probably a lot of mud under that grass, and these are hard narrow high-pressure tires, perfect for bogging up to axles in. Look there: a cow. I've heard of cows eating the fabric right off old airplanes. Something in the dope that they like.

So much for that meadow.

Near a farmhouse, another field to check. Except for the trees, it looks soft and smooth. Should be able to hover right in over the top of them. But what would happen if the wind stops? I'd never be able to get out again. Remember, this valley is four thousand feet high, and that's some pretty thin air. Only way I'd ever get off again would be in this hurricane wind. Hot day, or no wind, and I'd need four times as much room to get into the air at all. Two fields, two vetos. One more chance, anyway; maybe the pass to San Diego is open, down by the Mexican border.

Landing forgotten, we turn the headwind into tailwind and shoot from the high valleys of Julian like a wheat puff from a cereal gun.

Being cuffed about like a toy glider has a wearing effect on one's nerves. Last chance, coming up. San Diego. South again across more miles of desert, thinking of nothing but how lonely it would be to have to land here, and how much land we really have in this country that we do not use. Think of all the houses that could be put on this one little stretch of desert. Now all we have to do is coax somebody to come out and live here.

One last highway, the one that leads to San Diego. I have only to fly along this road, as though I were an automobile, and I shall get to San Diego; from there an easy matter to fly up the beach to home. I am an automobile. I am an automobile.

We bank and follow the road. The wind is a living thing, and it doesn't like the biplane at all. It punches at us constantly, it jabs and batters as if there is an urgent need for it to perfect its style and its rhythm. I hold to the stick very tightly. We must be making progress, but the hilltop to our left is certainly not moving very quickly. It has been there for two minutes. I check the road.

Oh, merciful heavens. We're moving backward! It is a dizzying feeling, and the first time I have ever seen it from the cockpit of an airplane. I have to steady myself and hold even more tightly to the stick. An airplane must move through the air in order to fly, and almost always that means that it moves over the ground, too. But now white lines in the road are passing me, and I have the strange feeling that I had over Odessa, that I have when I stand at the top of a ladder or a tall building and look down. As if there is a tremendous fall coming in the next few seconds. The airspeed needle is firm on eighty miles per hour. The wind must be at least 85 mph on my nose. The biplane simply cannot move to the west. Nothing I can do will make her move in the direction of the Pacific Ocean.

This is getting ridiculous. We bank hard to the right, dive away from the wind, and I can pluck one single straw of consolation from seeing the highway scream past as I turn east. With the tailwind, my ground speed must be 180 miles per hour. If I could only hold it, I could set a new biplane speed record to North Carolina. But I am wiser than to really believe that the wind will hold, and I know that just before I cross the South Carolina border into North Carolina the wind would shift to become an eighty-mile headwind, and I would hang suspended in the air one hundred yards from the finish line, unable to reach it. This is a wonderful day for playing all kinds of improbable games with an airplane. I can land the biplane backward today and take off straight up. I can fly sideways across the ground, in fact be more maneuverable than a helicopter could be. But I do not feel like playing games. I only want to accomplish what should be the simple task of reaching the other side of these mountains. Possibly I could tack back and forth, a sailboat in the sky, and eventually reach San Diego. No. Tacking is a meek and subservient thing to do, not befitting the character of an airplane. One must draw the line somewhere.

The only fitting technique is to fight the mountains for every inch I gain, and if the mountains for a moment prove the stronger, to retire, and rest and turn and fight again. For, when the fight belongs to the mountain, it is not proper to seek sly and devious means of sneaking around its might.

There is no mistaking the rebuff of the lesser mountain passes. They are making it clear that my adversary shall be the giant San Jacinto, ruling the pass into Banning.

I have burned a full tank of fuel in the fight to get across the mountains, and have gotten nowhere. Or, more precisely, I have gotten to Borrego Springs Airport, one hard runway standing alone in the sagebrush and clouds of dust. Circling overhead, I see that the wind sock is standing straight out, across the runway. In a moment it gusts around to point down the asphalt strip, and in another second it is cross again. To land on that runway in the gusting changing high-velocity wind will be to murder one biplane. Yet I must land, and haven't the fuel to reach for Palm Springs again. I shall land in the desert near the Borrego Airport.

An inspection of the dry land rules that out. The surface is just too rough. Catch the wheels in a steep sand dune and we'll be on our back in less than a second, and only with incredible luck could we escape with less than forty broken wingribs, a bent propeller and an engine full of sand and sagebrush. So much for landing in the desert.

The infield of the airport itself is dirt and sand, dotted with huge sage. I turn the biplane down through the shuddering wind and fly over the wind sock, watching the infield. It was level, once. The bulldozers must have leveled it when they scraped a bed for the runway. The brush is three feet high over it, four feet, some places. I could land in the brush, dead slow in the wind, and hope there aren't any pipes or ditches in the ground. If there are, it will be worse than the open desert. We fly two more passes, inspecting the brush, trying to see the ground beneath it.

At the gas pump, a man stands and watches, a small figure in blue coveralls. What a gulf lies between us! He is as safe and content as he can be, he can even go to sleep leaning against the gas pump, if he wants. But a thousand feet, a hundred feet away, the Parks and I are in trouble. My cork-and-wire fuel gauge shows that the tank is empty. We got ourselves into this affair and we've got to get ourselves out. The wind gusts at a wide angle to the runway, and a brush landing is the least of our evils. With luck, we will emerge with a few minor scratches.

One last climb for a few hundred feet of working altitude, throttle back, turn into the wind and drop toward the brush. Should the wind shift now, we shall need more than luck.

The Parks settles like a snail in a bright-colored parachute, barely moving across the ground. The brush is tall and brown beneath us, and I fight to keep from pushing the throttle and bolting safely back into the sky. As we scrape the tops of the sage, it is clear that we are not moving slowly at all. Hard back on the stick, hold tight to the throttle and in a crash and rumbling clatter we plow into a waist-high sea of blurred and brittle twigs. There is a snapping all about us, like a forest fire running wild, and twigs erupt in a whirling fountain from the propeller, spraying in a high arc to spin over the top wing and rain into the cockpit. The lower wing cuts like a scythe through the stuff, shredding it, tumbling it in a wide straight swath behind. And we are stopped, after breaking our way almost to the edge of the asphalt, all in one dusty piece, trembling in the wind, still throwing fresh-snapped twigs from the propeller. Throttle forward, we grimly crush ahead to the runway, turn to slowly follow a taxiway leading toward the gas pump.

"That was quite a landing you made, there." The man hands up the hose, and searches for the sixty-weight oil.

"Make 'em that way all the time."

"Wasn't quite sure just what you were doing. Can't remember anybody ever landing out in the brush like that. That's kind of hard on the airplane, isn't it?"

"She's built for it."

"Guess you'll be staying the night, in this wind?"

"No. You got a candy machine around, peanuts or something?"

"Yeah, we got a candy machine. You say you won't be staying?"

"No."

"Where you headed?"

"Los Angeles."

"Kind of a long way, isn't it? A hundred miles? I mean for an old biplane like this?"

"You are right, there. One hundred miles is a long, long way."

But I am not dismayed, and as I pull the *Peanuts* selector handle, the oily image in the mirror is smiling.

CHAPTER FIFTEEN

IN FIFTEEN MINUTES we are airborne again, slamming through the whitecaps in the air, beating north across the wind. The safety belt is strained down tight, and the silver nose is pointed toward the shrouded peak of San Jacinto.

All right, mountain, this is it. I can do without my self-righteousness now. I'll fight you all day long if I have to, to reach that runway at Banning. Today there will be no waiting for the weather to clear. I will fight you until the fuel tank is empty again, then fill the tank and come back and fight you for another five hours. But I tell you, mountain, I am going to make it through that pass today.

San Jacinto does not appear to be awed by my words. I feel like a knight, lance leveled, plumes flying, galloping at The Pass. It is a long gallop, and by the time I arrive at the tournament grounds we have used an hour of fuel. Plenty of fuel left to fly to Banning, and to spare. Come along, my little steed. First the lance, then the mace, then the broadsword.

The mountain's mace hits us first, and it slams us down so hard that the fuel is jerked from the carburetor, the engine stops for a full second and my hand is ripped from the control stick. Then calm again.

San Jacinto is inscrutable, covered in its Olympian mist. Quite some mace it swings. Lance broken, it is time for my broadsword.

Another impossibly hard crash of air upon us, the engine stops for the count of two and I clutch the control stick with both hands. We are sheathed again in rainwater and raindrops whip back over my head like buckshot. We don't scare, mountain. We'll make Banning if we have to taxi there on the highway.

In reply, another smash of the mace, as if the mountain needs the time between blows to swing the spinning iron thing high over its head, to get the more power. In the force of it, I am fired against my safety belt, my boots are thrown from the rudder pedals, the world blurs as my head snaps back. And still Banning is not in sight. Airplane, can you take any more of this? I am asking much of you today, and I have not inspected your spars and fittings.

I can take it if you can, pilot.

The words smash into my mind as though the mace had driven them there. My airplane is back! It is a strange and wonder-filled time. A glorious time. I am no longer fighting alone, but fighting with my airplane. And in the middle of a fight, a lesson. As long as the pilot can believe in his fight, and battle on, his airplane will battle with him. When he believes his airplane has failed him, or will soon fail, he opens the door to disaster. If you don't trust an airplane, you can never be a pilot.

Another mace, and I can hear it hit the biplane. Above the wind, above the engine and the rain, the hard WHAM of an incredible blow.

But ahead, now, ahead! Lying low in the rain, a shiny slick runway. In white letters across the end of it, BANNING. Come on, my little friend, we have almost won. Two strikes of the mace in quick succession, loud strikes that pitch us almost inverted, and I would not be surprised to hear spars snapping with the next blow. But I must trust the airplane. I lost my broadsword long ago, and we fight now with our bare hands. Only another minute . . .

And Banning is ours. We can turn now and land and rest.

But again, look ahead. The clouds have lifted, ever so slightly. I can see light between a foothill of the mountain and the cloud. Fly through that crack and the fight is over, I'm sure the fight will be over.

Banning fades slowly into the rain behind us.

This is a foolhardy thing to do. We could have stayed at the airport until this all lifted clear. You won your fight, you could have gloated over that piece of ill judgment without adding another to it. If that crack closes now ahead of you, where would you go, with Banning lost behind? Ninety percent of the crashes, they say, within twenty-five miles of home base.

Quiet, caution. I'll land in the fields down there and in this wind I won't roll very far. Now be quiet.

It is quiet from the dissenter's gallery for the moment, the quiet of someone phrasing in his mind the most vengeful way of saying I told you so.

The mace is not hitting us squarely anymore and the engine no longer stops in the force of it. We are one mile from the opening between cloud and ground over the hill. If it stays open for another minute and a half, we'll be through. There will be perhaps a thirty-foot clearance. A mace blow glancing, smashing the biplane into a wild right bank.

Recovering, wheels swishing the top of the hill, we squeak through the crack, and instantly fly out of the dark rain. Instantly, in the blink of an eye. Whoever has been directing the action for this flight has been doing a magnificent job, so good that no one save a pilot will believe the land spread out before us as we cross the hill.

The clouds ahead are broken, and through them the golden shafts of sunlight pierce down like bright javelins thrown into the earth. A bit of an old hymn is tossed into my thought: ". . . from mist and shadow into Truth's clear day."

The day has color again. Sunlight. I have not known what sunlight means until this moment. It brings life and brilliant things to the air and to the ground under the air. It is bright. It is warm. It turns the dirt into emerald and lakes into the deep clear blue of a washed sky. It makes clouds so white that you have to squint even behind your dark goggles.

If the people working in the green fields below could have listened very carefully, they would have heard, high in the eucalyptus-wind, mixed with engine noise from that little red-and-yellow biplane, a tiny voice singing. I no longer have to hurry.

The first buildings of Los Angeles and its thousand suburbs slide beneath us, and from habit we climb. No chance of being lonely if we must land now. Stop the engine this moment and we shall land on the city golf course. This, and it's the parking lot at Disneyland, big enough to land transports on. This, and we have the engineered concrete bed of the Los Angeles River.

But in no moment does the engine stop, as if the biplane is eager to see her new home and hangar, and has no patience for failures. "You can't go wrong with a Wright," the barnstormers used to say, and so it has proved. After playing its few harmless practical jokes, the Whirlwind engine has laughed at us and shows now the truth of the saying. We haven't gone wrong.

We turn one last time, to enter a busy traffic pattern. One last runway tilting beneath us, rising out of the city. Compton Airport. Home. We have come twenty-seven hundred miles across a country, and now, oil trailing back from our silver cowl, wet dust spraying from beneath our tall wheels, past fitting smoothly into present, our journey is done. We have been splintered across runways; frozen in midair; blasted in flying sand; soaked in rain; beaten in mountain winds; scourged in brittle sage; we have flickered back and forth through the years, a brightwinged bird in time, and we have arrived home. Has the arriving been worth the travail of the journey? A good question. I rather doubt that a biplane cross-country craze will soon be sweeping the nation.

We wheel slowly into a hangar and rumble its giant heavy door closed against the busy modern sounds of a busy modern time.

In the miles and sand and rain and years, we have learned only a little about ourselves, picked up just a tiny fraction of knowing about one man and one old biplane, and about what they mean to each other. At the last, in the sudden quiet of a dark hangar, man and biplane alone together, we find our answer to the question of the journey. Four words.

It was worth it.

NOTHING BY CHANCE

CHAPTER ONE

THE RIVER WAS wine beneath our wings—dark royal June Wisconsin wine. It poured deep purple from one side of the valley to the other, and back again. The highway leaped across it once, twice, twice more, a daring shuttlecock weaving a thread of hard concrete.

Along the thread, as we flew, came villages the color of new grass here in the end of spring, washing their trees in a clean wind. It was all the tapestry of summer beginning, and for us, of adventure.

Two thousand feet above the ground, the air was silver about us, sharp and cold, rising on up over our two old airplanes so deep that a stone dropped up into it would have been lost forever. Way high up in there I could just barely see the dark iron blue of space itself.

Both of these guys trusting me, I thought, and I don't have the faintest idea what's going to happen to us. It doesn't matter how many times I tell them, they still think since the whole thing is my idea I must know what I'm doing. I should have told them to stay home.

We swam the silver air like a pair of ocean minnows, Paul Hansen's sleek little sportplane darting ahead at a hundred miles an hour once in a while, then circling back to stay in sight of my fire-red, flower-yellow, slow-chugging open-cockpit wind-and-wire flying machine. Like giving the horses their rein, this turning our airplanes loose over the land and letting them fly back into their own time, with us hanging on for the ride and waiting to see the golden world of gypsy pilots forty years gone. We agreed on one thing—the grand old days of the barnstormer must still be around, somewhere.

Silent and trusting, Stuart Sandy MacPherson, age nineteen, peered over the edge of the cockpit in front of my own, looking down through his amber jumping-goggles to the bottom of an ocean of crystal air. Barnstormers always had parachute jumpers, didn't they? he had said, and parachute jumpers were always kids who worked their way and earned their keep selling tickets and putting up signs, weren't they? I had to admit that they were, and that I wasn't going to stand between him and his dream.

Once in a while now, looking down through the wind, he smiled to himself, ever so faintly.

We flew in a sheet of solid thunder. The clatter and roar of my Wright Whirlwind engine burst out just as loud and uncaring as it did in 1929, brand-new, seven years before I was born, and it soaked us in the smell of exhaust fires and hot rocker-box grease; it shook us in the blast of propeller-torn air. Young Stu had once tried to shout a word across the space between our cockpits, but his voice was swept away in the wind and he hadn't tried again. Those gypsy pilots, we were learning, didn't do much talking when they flew.

The river turned sharply north, and left us. We pressed on over-land into soft low meadowed hills, sun-glittering lakes, and farms everywhere.

Here it was . . . adventure again. The three of us and our two airplanes were the remnant of what had opened in spring as The Great American Flying Circus, Specialists in Death-Defying Displays of Aerial Acrobatics, Authentic Great War Dogfighting, Thrilling and Dangerous Aeroplane Stunts, and the Incredible Free-Fall Parachute Leap. (Also, Safe Government-Licensed Pilots Take You Aloft to See Your Town From the Air. Three Dollars the Ride. Thousands of Flights Without a Mishap.)

But the other Great American aviators and airplanes had commitments in modern times; they had flown their planes back into the future from Prairie du Chien, Wisconsin, and had left Paul and Stu and I flying alone in 1929.

If we were to live in this time, we had to find grass fields and cow-pastures to land in, close to town. We had to fly our own aerobatics, take our own chances, find our own paying passengers. We knew that five airplanes, a full circus, could bring out crowds of weekend customers; but would anyone move on a weekday to watch just two airplanes, and those unadvertised? Our fuel and oil, our food, our search for yesterday and our way of life depended upon it. We weren't ready to admit that adventure and the self-reliant individual had had their day.

We had thrown away our aeronautical charts, along with the time they came from, and now we were lost. There in the middle of the high cold silver roaring air, I thought we might be somewhere over Wisconsin or northern Illinois, but that was as far as I could pin it down. There was no north, no south, no east, no west. Only the wind from somewhere, and we scudded along before it, destination unknown, circling here over a town, over a meadow, over a lakeside, looking down. It was a strange afternoon without time, without distance, without direction. America spread from horizon to horizon before us, wide and big and free.

But at last, low on fuel, we circled a town with a little grass runway near at hand, and a gas pump and a hangar, and we got set to land. I had hoped for a hayfield, because old barnstormers always landed in hayfields, but the village sparkled with a certain magic lostness. RIO, it said, black letters on a silver water tower.

Rio was a hill of trees rising out of the low hills of earth, with rooftops down beneath the green and church spires like holy missiles poised pure white in the sun.

Main Street stretched two blocks long, then fell back into trees and houses and farmland.

A baseball game raged at the school field.

Hansen's trim Luscombe monoplane was already circling the airstrip, down to its last few gallons of gas. He waited for us, though, to make sure that we didn't change our mind and fly off somewhere else—for had we separated in that unknown land, we never would have seen each other again.

The strip was built on the edge of a sudden hill, and the first quarter of it lay at a fierce angle that must have made fine skiing, in winter.

I turned and landed, watching the green grass cartwheel up in slow motion to touch our wheels. We taxied to the deserted gas pump and shut down as Paul swished in overhead to land. His plane disappeared over the hillcrest as he touched down, but in a minute it reappeared, engine chugging softly, and rolled down the slope to us. With both engines silent at last, there was not a sound in the air.

"I thought you were never going to see this place," Paul said, unfolding from the Luscombe. "What took you so long? Some barnstormer you are. Why didn't you find a field two hours ago?"

He was a wide powerful man, a professional photographer, concerned because the world's image wasn't quite as beautiful as it should be. Under a carefully combed shock of black hair he had the look of a gangster trying hard to go straight.

"If it was me only, be no problem," I said, taking the bags that Stu handed down from the biplane. "But pickin' a place where your ground-hog airplane could fly from . . . yes sir, *that* was the problem."

"What do you think," Paul said, letting the slur about his airplane go by, "should we try a jump today, late as it is? If we want to eat, we'd better find some paying passengers."

"I don't know. Up to Stu. Up to you. You're supposed to be leader today."

"No, I'm not. You know I'm not the leader. You're the leader."

"OK, then. If I'm the leader, I say let's go up and do some aerobatics first and see what happens before we push poor Stu overboard."

"That means I have to unload my airplane."

"Yes, Paul, that means you have to unload your airplane."

As he turned to his task, a red pickup truck rolled from the highway and onto the dirt road leading to the airport gas pump. There were red letters on the side: AL'S SINCLAIR SERVICE. And according to the name stitched on his pocket, it was Al himself aboard.

"Quite some airplanes there," Al called, slamming the hollow steel door with a hollow steel slam.

"Sure are," I said. "Kind of old."

"I'll bet. You want some gas, I guess?"

"In a little while, maybe. Just flyin' through, barnstormin' a bit. Think it might be OK to try and hop a few passengers out of here? Folks see the town from the air?" A fifty-fifty chance. He could accept us or he could throw us off the field.

"Sure, it'd be OK! Glad to have you! Do a lot of good for the airport if we could get people to come out here, in fact. They've just about forgotten we *have* an airport, in town." Al looked over the leather rim into the old cockpit. "Barnstorming, you say. Rio's a big enough town for you?" He pronounced it Rye-O. "Population 776?"

"Seven hundred seventy-six is just right," I said. "We'll go up for some aerobatics for a while, then come get gas. Stu, why don't you get the signs up now, out on the road?"

Without a word, the boy nodded, picked up the signs (red letters on white linen, FLY $3 FLY), and strode silently off toward the highway, earning his keep.

The only way for a barnstormer to survive, we knew, is for him to fly passengers. Many passengers. And the only way to get passengers is first to attract their attention.

We had to make it quite clear that there was suddenly something strange and wild and wonderful going on at the airstrip, something that hadn't happened in forty years and might never happen again. If we could fire a spark of adventure within the hearts of townsfolk we hadn't even seen, we could afford another tank of gasoline, and perhaps a hamburger.

Our engines burst alive again, bouncing hard echoes off the tin-hangar walls, flattening the grass back in two loud mechanical windstorms.

Helmets buckled, goggles down, throttles ahead to wide-open power, the two old airplanes rolled, thumped, and lifted from green into deep clear blue, hunting passengers as hungrily as wolves hunt deer.

I looked down as we climbed over the edge of town, watching the crowd at the baseball game.

A couple of years ago, I wouldn't have cared. A couple of years ago my cockpit was all steel and glass and electronic controls and a sweptwing Air Force fighter that burned five hundred gallons of fuel per hour, that could outrun sound. No need for passengers then, and if there were, three dollars wouldn't cover the cost of a flight, or a takeoff, or an engine start. It wouldn't even cover the Auxiliary Power Unit cost, to feed the electricity for the start. To use a fighter-bomber for barnstorming, we'd need two-mile concrete runways, a corps of mechanics and a sign to say, "FLY $12,000 FLY." But now, that three-dollar passenger was our entire livelihood: gas, oil, food, maintenance, salary. And at this moment we flew without any passengers at all.

At 3,000 feet over the cornfields we began our Death-Defying Display of Aerial Acrobatics. Paul's white wing snapped up, I had a quick rolling glance at the bottom of his airplane, streaked in oil and dust, and then he was diving right straight down. A second later the smooth-cowled nose pulled up again, and up, until his airplane was flying out toward the afternoon sun, roaring up past my biplane, then over on his back until he was upside down, wheels in the sky, then nose back down again to finish the stunt. If he had a smoke flare on board, he would have traced a full vertical loop in the sky.

Way down in the crowd, I imagined I saw a face or two upturned. If we could fly just half the people watching that game, I thought, at three dollars each . . .

The biplane and I rolled into a great diving turn to the left, pushing down until the wind screamed in the wires. The black-green earth lay full in front of our nose, the wind pounded my leather helmet and set the goggles vibrating in front of my eyes. Then quickly back on the control stick and the ground fell away and blue sky filled the way ahead. Straight up, looking out at the wingtips, I saw the earth sweeping slowly around behind me, and I leaned my helmet back on the headrest and watched the fields and tiny houses and cars moving up from behind until they all stood directly overhead.

Houses, cars, the church spires, the sea of green leaves, all there in tiny full-color detail while I watched it above the biplane. The wind went quiet while we were upside down and moving slowly through the air. Say we flew a hundred people. That would be three hundred dollars, or one hundred dollars for each of us. Less gas and oil, of course. But maybe we wouldn't fly that many. That would be one out of every eight people in town.

The world pivoted slowly to come back in front of the biplane's nose, and then beneath it again, with the wind screaming in the wires.

Across the air, Paul's airplane was standing still in the sky, its nose pointing straight up, his whole machine a blue-white plumb-bob on a long string down from heaven. Then, abruptly, it broke its string, pivoted left, and pointed down just as straightly.

It wasn't all quite as death-defying as our handbills had said; in fact, there's nothing an airplane can do to be death-defying, as long as it stays in its own place, the sky. The only bad times come when an airplane tangles with the ground.

From loop to roll to snap roll, the airplanes tumbled over the edge of town, gradually losing altitude, every minute a few hundred feet closer to that multicolored earth.

At last the monoplane came whistling toward me like some fast smooth rocket and we fell into the Authentic Great War Dogfighting, snarling around in rolls and hard-turning spirals and dives and zooms and slowflight and stalls. All the while, as we flew, a white smoke flare waited, tied to my left wing strut. We blurred the world about for a few minutes, juggling it all green and black and roaring wind from one hand to the other, the houses of the village now standing on this edge, now on that.

Say we made two hundred dollars clear, I thought. What would that be for each of us? What's three into two hundred? I slid under the monoplane, turned to the left, watched as Paul fell into place behind the biplane's tail. What the devil is three into two hundred? I watched him over my shoulder, rising and falling as he followed, turning hard to stay with the steep spiral of the biplane. Well, if it was $210, that would be $70 each. Seventy dollars each, not counting gas and oil. Say $60 each.

In that wild screaming hurricane of a power dive, I touched the button taped to my throttle. Thick white smoke burst from the left wing and I traced a death-spiral down to the airport, leveling just above the trees. As far as they could tell at the baseball game, that old two-winger had just been shot down in flames.

If it had worked with five planes, even for such a short while, it should work all summer with two. We don't really need the $60 each, all we really need is the gas and oil, and a dollar a day left for food. We can survive all summer if we just make that.

I slipped in to land as the smoke stopped, and rolled free downhill to the gas pump. One advantage of being shot down every time, I thought, is that you always get to the gas pump first.

Cold red fuel poured into the biplane's tank as Paul landed. He shut down his engine as he came down the hill, and coasted the last hundred feet with the propeller still and silver in front of him. Above the sound of the gasoline pouring from the nozzle under my glove, I could hear his tires crunching on the gravel that edged pump and office.

He waited for a moment in his cockpit, then slowly climbed out. "Boy, you sure take it out of me with all those turns. Don't turn so tight, will you? I don't have all that wing out there that you have."

"Only trying to make it look real, Paul. Wouldn't want to make it look too easy, would you? Any time you want, we can tie the flare to *your* airplane."

A bicycle turned in from the highway—two bicycles, going full speed. They slid to a stop that smashed grass into the rubber of their rear tires. The boys were eleven or twelve years old and after all that pell-mell arrival they didn't say a word. They just stood and stared at the airplanes, and at us, and back to the airplanes.

"Feel like flying?" Stu asked them, working his first day as Seller of Rides. With the five-plane circus, we had had a barker, complete with straw hat and bamboo cane and a roll of golden tickets. But that was behind us, and now it was up to Stu, who was more given to a quiet intellectual kind of persuasion.

"No, thanks," the boys said, and they were silent again, watching.

A car rolled onto the grass and stopped.

"Go get 'em, Stu-babe," I said, and made ready to start the biplane again.

By the time the Wright was chugging around, soft and gentle as a huge Model T engine, Stu was back with a young man and his woman, each laughing at the other for being so mad as to want a ride in this strange old flying machine.

Stu helped them up into the wide front cockpit, where he fastened them side-by-side under one seat belt. He called over the sound of the Model T for them to hold on to their sunglasses if they wanted to look out over the windscreen, and with that warning, stepped down and clear.

If they had fears about riding in this clattering old machine, it was too late now for mind-changing. Goggles down, throttle forward. The three of us were engulfed in the sound of a Model T gone wild, blasting hundred-mile winds back over us, sweeping the world into a grassy blur, jouncing at first, a sort of long muffled crash as the tall old wheels sped along the ground. Then the crash fell away with the earth and it was pure engine sound and wind beating us, and the trees and the houses shrank smaller and smaller.

In all that wind and engineblast and earth tilting and going small below us, I watched my Wisconsin lad and his girl, to see them change. Despite their laughter, they had been afraid of the airplane. Their only knowledge of flight came from newspaper headlines, a knowledge of collisions and crashes and fatalities. They had never read a single report of a little airplane taking off, flying through the air and landing again safely. They could only believe that this must be possible, in spite of all the newspapers, and on that belief they staked their three dollars and their lives. And now they smiled and shouted to each other, looking down, pointing.

Why should that be so pretty to see? Because fear is ugly and joy is beautiful, simple as that? Maybe so. Nothing so pretty as vanished fear.

The air smelled like a million grassblades crushed, and the sun lowered to turn it from silver air into gold. It was a pretty day and we were all three glad to be flying through the sky as if this were all some bright loud dream, yet detailed and clear as no dream had ever been.

Five minutes above the ground, turning into the second circle of town, my passengers were relaxed and at home in flight, unconscious of themselves, eyes bright as birds' for looking down. The girl touched her companion's shoulder, one time, to point out the church, and I was surprised to see that she wore a wedding ring. It couldn't have been too long ago that they had walked out the door of that church into a rice-storm, and now it was all a little toy place, a thousand feet below. That tiny place? Why, it had been so big then, with the flowers and the music. Maybe it was big only because it was a special time.

We circled down lower, took one last long look at the town, and slid in over the trees, air going soft in the struts and wires, to land. As soon as the tires touched, the dream was broken in the clatter and rumble of hard ground holding us as we moved, instead of soft air. Slower, slower and stopped at last where we began, the Model T ticking quietly to itself. Stu opened the little door and cast loose the seat belt.

"Thanks a lot," the young man said, "that was fun."

"That was *wonderful*!" his wife said, radiant, forgetting to adjust the mask of convention about her words and her eyes.

"Glad to fly with you," I said, my own mask firm in place, my own delight well down within myself and under tight control. There was so much more I wanted to say, to ask: Tell me how that all felt, first time . . . was the sky as blue, the air as golden for you as it is for me? Did you see that deep deep green of the meadow, like we were floating in emerald, there after takeoff? Thirty years, fifty years from now, will you remember? I honestly wanted to know.

But I nodded my head and smiled and said, "Glad to fly with you," and that was the end of the story. They walked away arm in arm, still smiling, toward their car.

"That's it," Stu said, approaching my cockpit. "Nobody else wants to fly."

I came back from my far thoughts. "Nobody to fly? Stu, there's five cars out there! They can't all be just lookin'."

"They're going to fly tomorrow, they say."

If we had five airplanes, and more action going on, I thought, they'd be ready to fly today. With five airplanes, we'd look like a real circus. With two airplanes, maybe we're just a curiosity.

The old-timers, I thought, suddenly. How many of them ever survived, leading a gypsy pilot's life?

CHAPTER TWO

IT WAS ALL simple and free and a very good life. The barnstorming pilots, back in the twenties, just cranked their Jennies into the air and they flew to any little town and they landed. And then they took passengers up for joyrides and they earned great bales of money. What free men, the barnstormers! What a pure life that must have been.

These same sky gypsies, full of years, had closed their eyes and told me of a sun fresh and cool and yellow like I had never seen, with grass so green it sparkled under the wheels; a sky blue and pure like skies never come, anymore, and clouds whiter than Christmas in the air. A land there was, in the old days, where a man could go in freedom, flying where he wanted to fly, and when; answering to no authority but his own.

I had asked questions and I had listened carefully to the old pilots, and way in the back of my mind I wondered if a man might be able to do the same thing today, out in the great calm Midwest America.

"On our own, kid," I heard. "Aw, it used to be great. Weekdays we'd sleep late, and work on the airplanes till suppertime, then we'd carry folks up to sunset and beyond. Special times, pshaw, a thousand-dollar day was nothin'. Weekends we'd start flyin' at sunup and we wouldn't stop till midnight. Lines of people waitin' to fly, lines of 'em. Great life, kid. Used to get up in the morning . . . we'd sew a couple blankets together, sleep under the wing . . . get up and say, 'Freddie, where we goin' today?' And Freddie . . . he's dead now; a fine pilot, but he never came back from the war . . . and Freddie'd say, 'Where's the wind?'

"Comin' out of the west,' I'd say. 'Then we go east,' Freddie'd say, and we'd crank up the old Hisso Standard and throw in all our junk and off we'd go, headin' with the wind and savin' gas.

"Course the times got rough, after a while. There was the Crash in '29, and the folks didn't have much money to fly. We were down to fifty cents a ride where we had been five dollars and ten dollars. Couldn't even buy gas. Sometimes, two fellas workin', we'd drain gas out of one plane to keep the other flyin'. Then the Air-Mail came along and after that the airlines started up, needin' pilots. But for a while there, while it lasted, it was a good life. Oh, '21 to '29 . . . it was pretty good. First thing out, when you'd land, you'd get two boys out, and a dog. First thing, before anybody . . ." Eyes were closed again, remembering.

And I had wondered. Maybe those good old days aren't gone. Maybe they're still waiting now, out over the horizon. If I could find a few other pilots, a few other old planes. Maybe we could find those days, that clear clear air, that freedom. If I could prove that a man does have a choice, that he can choose his own world and his own time to live in, I could show that highspeed steel and blind computers and city riots are only one side of a picture of living . . . a side we don't have to choose unless we want to. I could prove that America isn't all really so changed and different, at heart. That beneath the surface of the headline, Americans are still a calm and brave and beautiful people.

When my vague little dream was known, a few folk of differing opinion rushed to stamp it to death. Time and again I heard that this was not just a chancy impractical quest, but impossible, without hope of success. The good old days are gone . . . why, everybody knows that! Oh, maybe it used to be a slow and friendly place, this country, but nowadays people will sue a stranger—and like as not a friend—at the drop of a hat. It's just the way people are, now. You go landing in a farmer's hayfield and he'll throw you in jail for trespassing, take your airplane for damages to his land and testify that you threatened the lives of his family when you flew over the barn.

People today, they said, demand the best in comfort and safety. You can't *pay* them to go up in a forty-year-old biplane all open-cockpit with wind and oil lashing back all over them . . . and you expect them to pay *you* for the pain of all that? There wouldn't be an insurance company—Lloyd's of London wouldn't cover a thing like that, for a cent less than a thousand dollars a week. Barnstorming, indeed! Keep your feet on the ground, friend, these are the 1960's!

"What do you think about a jump?" Stu asked, and snapped me back to afternoon Rio.

"Getting a bit late," I said, and the gypsy pilot and doom voices faded. "But, heck, a good calm day for it. Let's give it a try."

Stu was ready in a minute, tall and serious, shrugging into his main chute harness, snapping the reserve parachute across his chest, tossing his helmet into the front seat, making ready for his part of the quest. A bulky clumsy deep-sea diver, all buckles and nylon web over a bright yellow one-piece jumpsuit, he pulled himself into the forward cockpit and closed the little door.

"Alrighty," he said, "let's go."

I had a hard time believing that this lad, filled with inner fires, had chosen to study dentistry. Dentistry! Somehow we had to convince him that there was more to life than the makeshift security of a dentist's office.

In a moment, as we blasted off the ground and into the air, I was all of a sudden singing "Rio Rita," making it "Rye-o Rita." I knew only a part of the first line of the song, and it went over and over as we climbed to altitude.

Stu looked overboard with a strange faint smile, thinking about something way off in the distance.

Rita . . . Rye-o Ritah . . . noth . . . thing . . . sweetah . . . Rita . . . Oh-Rita. I had to imagine all the saxophones and cymbal-clashes over the thunder of the engine.

If I were Stu, I wouldn't be smiling. I'd be thinking about that ground down there, waiting for me.

At 2,500 feet, we swung around into the wind, and flew directly above the airport. Rye-o Ritah . . . la . . . dee . . . deedah . . . deedah . . . oh Ritah . . . My-baby-an'-me-o, Ritah . . .

Stu came back from whatever far land it was he saw, and peered down over the side of his cockpit. Then, looking, he sat straight up and carefully dropped a bright roll of crepe paper overboard. It just missed the tail, unfurled into a long yellow-red-yellow streak of color and snaked straight down. I circled, climbing, and Stu was intent, watching the color. When it hit the ground, he nodded and smiled briefly back at me. We turned back on course for the airport, level at 4,500 feet. I shuddered at the thought of actually jumping out of an airplane. It was a very long way down.

Stu opened his cockpit door while I slowed the biplane to ease the windblast for him. It was an odd feeling, to watch my front-seat passenger climb out onto the wing and make ready to get off while we were a mile in the air. He was going to go through with it, and I was afraid for him. There is a gigantic difference between standing on the ground talking glibly about parachute jumping, and the fact itself, when one is standing on the wing, fighting the wind, looking down through empty empty air at the tiny little trees and houses and filaments of roads laid flat on the ground.

But Stu was all business now. He stood on the rubber mat of the wing root, facing the tail of the airplane, watching for his target to slide into view. He held on to a wing strut with one hand, the edge of my cockpit with the other. If anything, he was enjoying the moment.

Then he saw what he wanted to see; the center of the grass runway, and the wind sock, barely visible in smallness. He leaned toward me. "GOIN' DOWN!" he said. And then, as simply as that, he vanished.

On the wing root, where he had been standing, was nothing. One instant there, talking, next instant gone. I wondered for a second whether he had ever been in the airplane at all.

I looked down over the side and saw him, a tiny figure, arms outstretched, falling straight down toward the ground. But it was more than falling. It was much faster than falling. He blurred down, fired from a cannon, right at the ground.

I waited for a long time as he changed from a tiny cross into a round speck. No parachute opened. It was not a good feeling, to wait for that chute. After an agonizing long while I knew that it was not going to open at all.

The very first jump of our two-plane circus and his parachute failed. I felt a little bit cold. His body might be that leaf-shaped dot there by the grove of trees that bordered the airport, or the one by the hangars. Darn. We had lost our jumper.

I didn't feel sad for Stu; he knew what he was gambling when he began parachute jumping. But just a second ago he had been standing right there on the wing, and now there was nothing.

His main chute must have failed and he didn't get the reserve open in time. I pulled back the throttle and spiraled down, watching the place where he had disappeared. I was surprised not to be shocked or remorseful. It was just a shame that it had happened this way, so early in the summer. So much for the dentistry.

In that instant, a parachute snapped open, way down below me. It came as quickly as Stu had gone from the wing, a sudden orange-white mushroom floating softly in the air, drifting very gently with the wind.

He was alive! Something had happened. At the last instant he had finally wrenched the reserve chute into the wind, with one second left he had untangled from death, had pulled the rip cord, had lived. Any moment now he would be touching down with a wild terrible story to tell, and a word that he would never jump again.

But the fragile colored mushroom stayed long in the air, drifting.

We dived down toward it, the biplane and I, wires singing loud, and the closer we came to the parachute, the higher it was from the ground. We eased out of the dive at 1,500 feet and circled a little man dangling by strings under a great pulsing dome of nylon.

He had altitude to spare. There never had been any trouble, there had never been any danger at all!

The figure swinging beneath the nylon waved across to me, and I rocked my wings in reply, grateful, puzzled that he should be alive.

And as we circled him, it wasn't we that turned, but his parachute, spinning around and around the horizon. A strange dizzy feeling.

The angle, of course! That's how he could be so high in the air now, when I was so sure he had hit the ground . . . the angle that I had watched him from. I had been looking right down on top of him, and his only background was the wide earth all around. His death was an illusion.

He pulled one of the suspension lines and the canopy twisted swiftly around, one turn left, one turn right. He controlled the direction of the parachute at will; he was at home in his element.

It was hard to believe that this courageous parachute artist was the same soft-spoken boy that had shyly joined The Great American a week ago when it had opened in Prairie du Chien. I thought of a maxim learned in twelve years' flying: Not what a man says, that matters, or how he says it, but what he does and how he does it.

On the ground, children popped like munchkins from the grass, and they converged on Stu's target.

I circled the chute until it was two hundred feet above the ground, then held my altitude while the mushroom went on down. Stu swung his feet up and down a few times, last-minute calisthenics before his landing.

He was one moment drifting peacefully on the gentle air, and the next instant the ground rose up and hit him hard. He fell, rolled, and at once was on his feet again as the wide soft dome lost its perfect shape and flapped down around him, a great wounded monster of the air.

The monster-picture deflated with the parachute and became just a big colored rag on the ground, unmoving, and Stu was Stu in a yellow jumpsuit, waving OK. The children closed in on him.

When the biplane and I circled to land, I found that we had problems. The Whirlwind wasn't responding to its throttle. Throttle forward, nothing happened. A little farther forward and it cut back in with a sudden roar of power. Throttle back and it roared on; full back, and it died away unnaturally. Something wrong with the throttle linkage probably. Not a major problem, but there could be no passenger flying till it was fixed.

We came down rather unevenly to land, coasted over the hill and shut down the engine. Al, of AL'S SINCLAIR SERVICE, walked over.

"Hey, that was nice! There's quite a few folks here want to fly the two-winger. You can take 'em up this afternoon, can't you?"

"Don't think so," I said. "We like to end the day with the parachute jump . . . leave 'em with something nice to watch. We'll sure be here tomorrow, though, and love to have 'em come back."

What a strange thing to find myself saying. If that was our policy, I had just made it up. I would have been glad to fly passengers till sunset, but I couldn't do it with the throttle linkage as it was and it would not do to have them see that their airplane had to be repaired after every little flight around the airport.

Stu came in from the target, and the biplane captured quite a number of his young admirers. I stood near the airplane and tried to keep them from stepping through the fabric of the lower wings whenever they climbed up to look in the cockpits.

Most of the grown-ups stayed in their cars, watching, but a few came closer to look at the aircraft, to talk with Paul, polishing the Luscombe, and with me, shepherding children.

"I was at the Little League game when you guys flew over," a man said. "My boy was going crazy; he didn't know whether to look down at the game or up at the planes, so finally he sat on the roof of the car, where he could see both."

"Your jumper . . . he's a pretty young guy, isn't he? Couldn't make me jump out of an airplane for all the money in the world."

"This all you do for a living, fly around places? You got a wife or anything?"

Of course we had wives, of course we had families just as involved in this adventure as we, but that wasn't something we thought people would want to hear. Barnstormers can only be carefree, footloose, fun-loving bright colorful people from another time. Who ever heard of a *married* sky gypsy? Who could imagine a barnstormer settled in a *house*? Our image demanded that we shrug the question aside and become the picture of gay and happy comrades, without a thought for the morrow. If we were to be shackled at all that summer, it would be by the image of freedom, and we tried desperately to live up to it.

So we answered with a question: "Wife? Can you imagine any woman let her husband go flyin' around the country in planes like these?" And we had lived a little more closely to our image.

Rio was changed by our arrival. Population 776, with a tenth of the town on the airport the evening after we arrived. And the biplane was grounded.

The sun was down, the crowd slowly disappeared into the dark and at last we were left alone with Al.

"You guys are the best thing that happened to this airport," he said quietly, looking toward his airplane in its hangar. He didn't have to speak loudly to be heard in the Wisconsin evening. "Lots of people think about us flying our Cessnas, they're not sure we're safe. Then they come out here and see you throw those airplanes around like crazymen and jump off the wings and all of a sudden they think we're *really* safe!"

"We're glad we can help you out," Paul said dryly.

The tree frogs set in to chirping.

"If you want, you guys can stay in the office here. Give you a key. Not the best, maybe, but it beats sleepin' out in the rain, if it rains."

We agreed, and dragged our mountain of belongings in to carpet the office floor in a jagged layer of parachutes, boots, bedrolls, survival kits, ropes, and toolbags.

"Still don't see how we get all this stuff into the airplanes," Paul said, as he set down the last of his camera boxes.

"If you guys want a ride in town," Al said, "I'm goin' in; be glad to take you."

We accepted the offer at once, and when the airplanes were covered and tied, we leaped into the back of the Sinclair pickup truck. On the way, wind beating down over us, we divided up our income for the day. Two passengers at $3 each.

"It's kind of good," Stu said, "that all the airplanes from Prairie didn't stay. By the time you cut six dollars ten ways, there wouldn't be much left."

"They could have flown those other passengers, though," I said.

"I'm not worried," Paul offered. "I have a feeling that we're going to do pretty well, just by ourselves. And we made enough money for dinner tonight . . . that's all that matters."

The truck rolled to a stop at the Sinclair station, and Al pointed down the block to the A & W root-beer stand. "They're the last ones

open and I think they close at ten. See you tomorrow out at the airport, OK?"

Al disappeared into his dark service station and we walked to the
root-beer stand. I wished for once that I could turn off the barnstormer image, for we were watched as closely as slow-motion tennis
balls by the drive-in customers of the Rio A & W.

"You're the fellows with the airplanes, aren't you?" The waitress
who set our wooden picnic table was awed, and I wanted to tell her to
forget it, to settle down and pretend that we were just customers. I
ordered a bunch of hot dogs and root beer, following the lead of Paul
and Stu.

"It's going to work," Paul said. "We could have carried twenty
passengers tonight, if you weren't so afraid of working on your airplane for a few minutes. We could have done well. And we just got
here! Five hours ago we didn't even know there *was* such a place as
Rio, Wisconsin! We're going to make a fortune."

"Maybe so, Paul." As Leader for the day, I wasn't so sure.

Half an hour later we walked into the office and snapped on the light,
blinding ourselves, destroying the night.

There were two couches in the office, which Paul and I claimed at
once for our beds, pulling rank as the senior members of The Great
American. We gave Stu the pillows from the couches.

"How many passengers are we going to carry tomorrow?" Stu
asked, undisturbed by his low status. "Shall we have a little bet?"

Paul figured we would carry 86. Stu guessed 101. I laughed them
both to scorn and said that the proper number was 54. We were all
wrong, but at that moment, it didn't matter.

We snapped out the lights and went to sleep.

CHAPTER THREE

I WOKE UP humming "Rio Rita" again; I couldn't get it out of my head.

"What's the song?" Stu asked.

"C'mon. You don't know 'Rio Rita'?" I said.

"No. Never heard it."

"Ah . . . Paul? You ever stop to think that Stu, young Stu, probably doesn't know any songs from the war? What were you . . . born about . . . nineteen *forty-seven*! Good grief! Can you imagine anybody born in NINETEEN FORTY-SEVEN?"

"We're three caballeros . . . ," Paul sang tentatively, looking at Stu.

". . . three gay caballeros . . . ," I went on for him.

". . . three happy chappies, with snappy serappies . . ."

Stu was mystified at the odd song, and we were mystified that he wouldn't know it. One generation trying to communicate with another just halfway down, in that office-bunkhouse on a morning in Wisconsin, and getting nowhere, finding nothing but an uncomprehending smile from our parachute jumper as he belted his white denim trousers.

We tried a whole variety of songs on him, and all with the same effect. ". . . Shines the name . . . Rodger Young . . . fought and died for the men he marched among . . ."

"Don't you remember that song, Stu? My gosh where WERE you?" We didn't give him a chance to answer.

". . . Oh, they've got no time for glory in the infantry . . . oh, they've got no time for praises loudly sung . . ."

"What's next?" Paul was hazy on the lyrics, and I looked at him scornfully.

". . . BUT TO THE EVERLASTING GLORY OF THE INFANTRY . . . ,"

His face brightened. "SHINES THE NAME OF RODGER YOUNG! Shines the name . . . ta-ta-tata . . . Rodger Young . . ."

"Stu, what's the matter with you? Sing along, boy!"

We sang "Wing and a Prayer," and "Praise the Lord and Pass the Ammunition," just to make him miserable for not being born sooner. It didn't work. He looked happy.

We began the hike to town for breakfast.

"Can't get over that," Paul said at last.

"What."

"Stu's starting so young."

"Nothing wrong with that," I responded. "It's not when you start that makes your success in the world, but when you quit." Things come to you like that, barnstorming.

The card in the café window said *Welcome Travelers—Come In,* and above it was a neon sign with the paint gone from its tubes, and so saying E̸A̸T .

It was a small place, and inside was a short counter and five booths. The waitress was named Mary Lou, and she was a girl from a distant and beautiful dream. The world went grey, she was so pretty, and I leaned on the table for support, before I sat down. The others were not affected.

"How's the French toast?" I remember saying.

"It's very good," she said. What a magnificent woman.

"Guarantee that? Hard to make a good French toast." What a beautiful girl.

"Guarantee. I make it myself. It's good toast."

"Sold. And two glasses of milk." She could only have been Miss America, briefly playing the part of waitress in a little Midwest village. I had been enchanted by the girl, and as Paul and Stu ordered breakfast, I fell to wondering why. Because she was so pretty, of course. That's enough right there. But that can't be—that's bad! From her, and from our crowded opening at Prairie du Chien, I was beginning to suspect that there might be tens of thousands of magnificent beautiful women in the small towns across the country, and what was I going to do about it? Be entranced by them all? Give myself up to bewitchment by ten thousand different women?

The bad thing about barnstorming, I thought, is that one sees only the swift surface, the sparkle in the dark eye, the brief glorious smile. Whether it's all emptiness or an utterly alien mind behind those eyes and that smile, is something that takes time to discover, and without the time, one gives the benefit of the doubt to the being inside.

Mary Lou was a symbol, then. Without knowing it, knowing only that one of the men at Table Four has ordered French toast and two milks, she has become a siren upon a murderous shore. And the barnstormer, to survive, must lash himself to his machine and force himself to be spectator only as he drifts by.

I went all through breakfast in silence.

There is Wisconsin so deeply in her words, I thought, it's almost Scottish. "Toast" was *toahst*, "two" was a gentle *too*, and my compadres' hash browns were *poataytoahs*. Wisconsin is Scottish-Swedish American with long long vowels, and Mary Lou, speaking that language as her native tongue, was as beautiful to listen to as she was to look upon.

"I think it's about time for me to wash some clothes," Paul said over his coffee.

I was shocked from my girl-thoughts.

"Paul! The Barnstormer's Code! It breaks the Code to get all washed clean. A barnstormer is a greasy oily guy . . . you ever heard of a *clean* barnstormer? Man! What you tryin' to do?"

"Look. I don't know about you, but I'm going down to the Laundromat . . ."

"THE LAUNDROMAT! What are you, man, a big-city photographer or somethin'? We can at least go down to the river and beat our clothes out on some flat rocks! Laundromat!"

But I couldn't move him from the heresy and he talked about it with Mary Lou as we left.

". . . and on the dryer, it works better on Medium than Hot," she said in her language and with a dazzling smile. "It doesn't shrink your cloathes. As much."

"The Great American Flying Laundry," Stu said to himself as he pushed our clothes into the machine.

While they thrashed around, we sauntered lazily through the market. Stu paused reflectively by the frozen-food locker at the rear of the wooden-pillared room.

"If we took a TV dinner," he mused, "and wired it on the back of the exhaust manifold, and ran the engine up for fifteen minutes . . ."

"There would be gravy all over the engine," Paul said.

We walked the blocks of Main Street under the wide leaves and deep shadow of daytime Rio. The Methodist church, white and lap-strake, pushed its antique needle-spire up out of sight in the foliage to anchor the building in the sky. It was a quiet day, and calm, and the only thing that moved was an occasional high branch to shift some dark shadow across the lawn. Here, a house with window-halves of stained glass. There, one with an oval-glass door all rose and straw-berry. Now and then a window framed a fringed cut-glass lamp. Man, I thought, there is no such thing as time. This is no dusty jerking Movietone, but here and now, slow and soft and full fragrant color softly swirling down the streets of Rio, Wisconsin, United States of America.

Another church, as we walked, and here children were tended on the lawn, singing. Singing in earnest, "London Bridge Is Falling Down." And holding hands and making the bridge and ducking under. All there on the lawn, not giving us a glance, as though we were people traveled back from another century and they could see right through us.

Those children had been playing London Bridge forever on that lawn, and would go on playing it forever. We were no more visible to them than air. One of the women tending the game looked up ner-vously, as a deer looks up, not quite scenting danger, not quite ready to disappear into the forest. She didn't see us stopped and watching except in a sixth-sense way; no word was said, and London Bridge fell and claimed two more children, who in turn became another Bridge. The song went on and on, and we finally walked away.

At the airport, our airplanes waited just as we had left them. While Paul neatly folded his clothes in his very neat way, I stuffed mine into a bag and walked out to fix the throttle linkage on the biplane. It took less than five minutes of silent work in the slow quiet daytime hours that are a barnstormer's weekday.

Paul, who had been a sky diver himself, once, helped Stu lay his main parachute canopy in the calm air of the hangar. By the time I wandered over to them, they were kneeling at the end of the long loom of nylon, deep in thought. Nobody moved. They just sat and thought, and paid me no mind.

"I'll bet you got problems," I said.

"Inversion," Paul said absently.

"Oh. What's an inversion?"

Paul just looked at the nylon lines and thought.

"I let the canopy come down on top of me yesterday," Stu said at last, "and when I got out from under I got the suspension lines mixed a little."

"Ah." I could see it. The smooth bundle of cords that ran from Stu's harness to the edge of the canopy was marred by one pair, twisted.

"OK. Unhook your Capewell there," Paul said suddenly, "and run it right through here." He spread a set of cords apart hopefully.

Stu clicked the harness quick-release and did as Paul asked, but the lines were still twisted. It fell quiet again in the hangar, and the quiet was weighted down at the corners with very heavy thinking.

I couldn't stand the atmosphere, and left. It was as good a time as any to grease the Whirlwind's rocker boxes. Outside, there was no sound but sun and growing grass.

Around noontime, engine greased and parachute untangled, we walked the familiar road to the EAT Café, sat down in Booth Four for lunch and were charmed again by the enchantress Mary Lou.

"You get used to it all pretty quickly; you get known, don't you?" Paul said, over his roast beef. "We've been here a day and we know

Mary Lou and Al and most everybody knows who we are. I can see where we could feel pretty secure, and not want to go on."

He was right; security is a net of knowns. We knew our way around town, we knew the main industry was the glove factory, which shut down for the day at four-thirty and released potential customers for us.

We were safe here, and the fear of the unknown beyond Rio had begun to creep in upon us. It was a strange feeling, to begin to know this little town. I felt it, and rather moodily tasted my chocolate milkshake.

It had been the same way at Prairie du Chien, a week ago, when we opened. We were secure there, too, with $300 guaranteed just to appear for the Historical Days weekend, plus all the money we could make carrying passengers.

In fact, by Saturday afternoon, in great crowds of people emerging from winter, we had earned nearly $650. There was no denying it was a good start.

Part of the guarantee, though, was the Daring Display of Low-Altitude Stunt Flying, and in an hour quieter than the others, I thought I might as well run my Handkerchief Pickup.

Snagging the white square of silk from the ground with a steel hook on my lower left wingtip wasn't all that difficult, but it looked very daring and so made a good air-circus stunt.

The biplane had climbed like a shot into the wind, which had freshened to a brisk twenty miles per hour. The stunt felt right, in all the noise and engine-thunder, the wing was coming down at just the right instant; but each time I looked out to see an empty hook, and back over my shoulder I could see the handkerchief untouched on the grass.

By the third try, I was annoyed at my bumbling, and concentrated wholly on the task, tracking the white silken spot directly down the line it should go, seeing nothing else but the green blur of ground a few feet below, moving a hundred miles per hour. Then a full second ahead of time, I tilted the wing down, waited until the white had blurred into the hook and pulled up in what was planned to be a victorious climb.

But I had missed it again. I sat tall in the seat and looked out at the wingtip, to make sure that the hook was still there. It was, and it was empty.

Those people waiting on the ground must think this is a poor kind of flying circus, I thought grimly, that can't even pick up a plain old handkerchief in three tries.

The next time I turned hard down in a steep diving pass and leveled off just at the grasstops, a long way from that mocking handkerchief, and on a line directly into it. I will get it this time, I thought, if I have to take it ground and all. I glanced at the airspeed dial, which showed 110 miles per hour, and eased a tiny bit forward on the control stick. The grass flicked harsh beneath the big tires, and bits of wild wheat spattered against them. A tiny turn left, and just a little lower.

At that instant, the wheels hit the ground, and they hit it hard enough to jerk my head down and blur my sight. The biplane bounced high into the air and I eased forward again on the stick and made ready to drop the wing for the pickup.

Then in that second there was a great snapping explosion, the world went black and the engine wailed up in a shriek of metal running wild.

The prop is hitting the ground I am crashing what happened the wheels must have torn off I have no wheels and now the propeller is hitting the ground hitting dirt we're going over on our back way too fast dirt flying pull up pull up full power flying again but nothing I'm getting nothing out of the engine prop's gone where land wires trees field wind . . . All at once that concussion of thought burst across me. And behind it, the dead knowing that I had crashed.

CHAPTER FOUR

I FELT THE tremendous power of the airplane smashing into the ground, clenched down tight in the cockpit, jammed full throttle and jerked the machine back into the air. The only thing I got from the throttle was a loud noise forward. There was no power at all. The biplane staggered back up on sheer momentum.

We were not going to make it over the telephone wires ahead. It was strange. They had been close, at 110 mph, but now they were not close. We turned into the wind by reflex and at full throttle, engine screaming a hundred feet in the air, everything slowed down. I felt the airplane trembling on a stall and I was keen and aware of it, knowing that to slow any more would be to pitch nose-down into the ground. But I knew the biplane, and I knew that we would just hang there and come down slowly slowly into the wind. I wondered if the people on the ground were frightened, since it must all look pretty bad; a big burst of dirt and wheels flying off and the strange howling of the engine and the shuddering high in the air before it falls. Yet the only fear I felt was their fear of how this all must look from the ground.

We came down in slow motion, facing the wind, into the tall grass. Not a single obstacle to clear. The earth came leisurely up to meet us and at last it brushed us lightly with its green. In that moment the engine was of no further use, and I flicked the magneto switch off. We slid slowly through the weeds, less than twenty miles per hour, and with nothing else to do, I moved the mixture lever to *Idle-Cutoff* and the fuel selector to *Off*. There was no shock of touchdown, no lurching forward in the seat. All in very slow motion.

I was impatient to get out and see what had happened, and had my safety belt off and was standing up in the cockpit before we had slid to a stop.

The biplane tilted wildly down, right wing low, grass and dust settling through the air. My beautiful darn airplane.

It did not look good. The right lower wing was a mass of wrinkles, which could only mean a broken spar beneath the fabric. How sad, I thought, standing there in the cockpit, to end this barnstorming all so quickly after it had started.

I watched myself very carefully, to see when I would begin to be afraid. After this sort of thing happens, one is supposed to be afraid. The fear was taking its time, though, and more than anything, I was disappointed. There would be work ahead, and I would much rather fly than work.

I stepped out of the airplane, all alone in the field before the crowd arrived, pushed my goggles up and looked at the machine. It was not easy to be optimistic.

Besides the spar, the propeller was bent. Both blades, bent hard back from the tips. The right landing gear had broken loose, but not off, and had smashed back into the wing when we landed. That was the extent of the damage. It was not nearly so bad as it had felt.

Off across the field, the men walking, the boys running, the crowd came to see what was left of the old airplane. Well, I thought, I guess it had to be, guess I'd want to come over and look, if I were in their place. But what had happened was now old news to me, and the thought of saying it over and over again was not one that I relished. Since my fear still hadn't arrived, I would spend the time thinking of some good understatements to fit the occasion.

A big official truck rolled out across the grass. GO NAVY, it said in big white letters, and on top of it was mounted a pair of loudspeakers to reinforce the words. At this point going Navy was a much sounder bet than going Air Force.

Paul Hansen had been first to arrive, cameras around his neck, out of breath.

"Man . . . I thought . . . you . . . had bought it . . ."

"What do you mean?" I said. "We just touched down a little hard there. Felt like we ran into something."

"You don't . . . know. You hit the ground, and then . . . went way over . . . on your nose. I thought you . . . were going to nose over for sure . . . on your back. It was a bad . . . scene. I really thought . . . you had it."

He should have had his breath back by now. Was the sight of the crash so bad that it could affect him so? If anybody had a right to be concerned, it was me, because it was my airplane all bent up there in the grass.

"Oh, no, Paul. Not a chance of going over. Did it really look that way?"

"Yeah. I thought . . . my God . . . Dick's bought it!"

I didn't believe him. It couldn't have been that bad. But thinking back, I remembered that the first impact had been very hard, though, and the sound of that explosion. And we did nose forward then, too. But nothing like we were going over.

"Well," I said, after a minute, "you got to admit that's a pretty hard act to follow." I felt springs loosening inside me, springs that had been tight in the air, to let me feel every tiny motion of the airplane. Now they were loosening, and I felt relaxed, except that I didn't know how long it would take to fix the airplane. That was the only tense thought. I wanted to fix the plane as soon as possible.

Thirty hours later, the biplane had been repaired, tested and was flying passengers again.

It is kind of a miracle, I thought, and I wondered at it.

When we left Prairie du Chien, Rio was the Unknown. And now, with Rio become Known, we felt the tug of security, and were uneasy.

The wind came up that afternoon and it changed Stu MacPherson at once from parachute jumper to a groundling ticket-seller.

"It's about fifteen miles an hour now," he said, worried. "That's a bit too much for me to feel good about jumping."

"Aw, c'mon," I said, wondering how powerful a wind could be on the big silken dome. "Fifteen crummy miles an hour? That can't hurt you." It would be fun to know, too, whether Stu could be bullied out of his better judgment.

"That's getting pretty windy. I'd rather not jump."

"We got all these people coming out to see you. Crowd's gonna be unhappy. Somebody said yesterday that your jump was the first ever made on this field. Now everybody's all set to see the second. You better jump." If he gave in, I had a lecture all prepared on how only weaklings give in to what they know isn't right.

"Fifteen miles is a lot of wind, Dick," Paul said from the hangar. "Tell you what. We have to test the canopy out, make sure that the inversion's gone. Why don't you strap on the harness for us and we'll throw the canopy up into the wind and see that it opens out all right."

"I'll strap on your parachute," I said. "I'm not afraid of your parachute."

Paul brought the harness over and helped me strap into it, and as he did, I remembered the stories I had heard in the Air Force of pilots dragged about helplessly by parachutes in the wind. I began, in short, to have second thoughts.

But by that time I was strapped in, my back to the wind, which seemed to be blowing much harder now, and Paul and Stu were down by the canopy laid on the grass, ready to throw it up into the quick-moving air.

"Ready to go?" Paul shouted.

"Just a minute!" I didn't like his word about "going," for I meant to stay right where I was. I dug my heels into the ground, unsnapped the safety catch on the quick release that would spill the canopy if anything went wrong.

"Don't punch the Capewell," Paul said. "It will get the canopy all tangled up again. If you want to spill the chute, pull on the bottom risers. You ready?"

Directly downwind was a low fence of timbers and steel cables. If I dragged, I'd drag right into it. But then again I'm two hundred pounds all dug in here, and no little breeze could drag that much all the way to the fence. "Ready!"

I braced against the wind and Paul and Stu tossed the skirt of the canopy into the air, with what seemed like altogether too much enthusiasm. The wind caught the chute at once, it popped out like a racing-boat spinnaker, and every ounce of that force snapped down the risers and into my shoulders. It was like a tractor lurching into gear, and all hooked to me.

"HEY!" I flew out of my special braced place, and out of the second place I dug my boots into, and out of the third. I thought of losing my balance behind this big thing, and being whipped across that fence. The monster jellyfish pulled me in jerks, wham-wham-wham across the ground while Paul and Stu just stood and laughed. It was the first time I had heard Stu laugh.

"Hold on there, boy!"

"This is just a little breeze! This is nothing! Hey, hang on!" I got the idea about wind and parachutes and grabbed for the lower risers to collapse the thing while I skidded for the fence. I pulled, but nothing happened. If anything, I skidded faster, and nearly lost my balance.

At that point I ceased to care about the delicacy of Stu's canopy, and pulled hard on all the bottom lines I could get hold of. Very suddenly the chute collapsed and I was standing in the mild wind of afternoon.

"What's the matter?" Paul called. "Couldn't you hold the thing?"

"Well, I thought I'd just as soon not cut your lines all up on the fence, there. Save you some repair work."

I unsnapped the harness, quickly. "Stu, I don't think you'd better jump today. This wind's up a little too high. Of course you want to jump anyway, but it's wiser for you just to stay down this afternoon. I think it's a lot wiser."

We rounded up the giant canopy and bundled it into the calm of the hangar.

"You really ought to jump sometime, Richard," Paul said. "There's nothing like it. That's real flying. Man, you get up there, no engine or nothing. Just . . . you. Dig? You really ought to do it."

I have never had any intention of jumping out of an airplane and Paul's pitch did not make me eager to start now.

"Sometime," I said. "I'll give it a whirl, when the wings fall off my airplane. I want to start right out with a free-fall, and not go through all those static-line things they make you do in the jump schools. At the moment, let us say that I'm not quite ready to begin my jumping career."

Al's Sinclair pickup truck arrived, and with him in the cab was a tall distinguished fellow we met as Lauren Gilbert, who owned the airport. Lauren couldn't do enough to make us welcome. He had learned to fly when he was fifty years old, was completely caught up in the fun of flying, and had just yesterday passed the tests to earn his instrument-flight license.

Our policy insisted that he have a free ride, since he owned the field, and the biplane was airborne ten minutes later on its first flight of the afternoon. This was our advertising flight; the first one up, to tell the town that we were in business and already flying happy passengers and why weren't they up in the sky with us, looking down at the city?

We had to work a flight pattern over each town, and the pattern over Rio was takeoff west, climb south and east in a shallow left turn, level at 1,000 feet, turn back and circle the town in a right turn all the way to the airstrip, steep turns north, slip down over the telephone wires, land. This came to a twelve-minute ride, gave our passengers a view of their home, the feeling of the freedom of flying, and an adventure to talk about and paste into scrapbooks.

"That's pretty nice," Lauren said as Stu opened the door for him. "You know that's the first time I've ever been up in an open-cockpit airplane? That's really flying. That's wonderful. The wind, you know, and that big old engine up there . . ."

A pair of boys appeared, Holly and Blackie by name, wheeling their bicycles, and we all walked together to the office after Lauren's ride.

"Boys, you want to go for a ride?" he asked down at them.

"We don't have any money," Holly said. He was perhaps thirteen years old, of bright and inquisitive eye.

"Tell you what. You come out here and wash down my Cessna, polish it all up, and I'll pay for your rides. How's that sound?"

There was an uncomfortable silence from the boys.

"Ah . . . no thanks, Mr. Gilbert."

"What do you mean? Boys, this is probably the last of these old biplanes you'll ever see! You'll be able to say that you've flown in a biplane! And there's not many people left, even grown-ups, anymore, that can say that they've flown in a real biplane."

Silence again, and I was surprised. I would have worked on that Cessna for a year, when I was thirteen, to get a ride in an airplane. Any airplane.

"Blackie, how about you? You help get my airplane all clean and there's a ride for you in the old biplane."

"No . . . thanks . . ."

Lauren was selling them hard. I was astonished at their fears. But the boys looked down at the floor and said nothing.

At last, very reluctantly, Holly agreed to the deal, and all of Lauren's firepower turned on Blackie.

"Blackie, why don't you go on up with Holly, you boys can fly together."

"I don't think so . . ."

"What? Why, if little Holly here flies and you don't, you're a sissy!"

"Yeah," Blackie said quietly. "But it doesn't matter, 'cause I'm bigger than him."

At last, however, all resistance fell to Lauren's enthusiasm and the boys climbed aboard the biplane, expecting the worst. The engine burst into life, fanning their sober faces with exhaust wind; a moment later we were lifting up into the sky. A thousand feet higher, they were peering down over the leather edge of the front cockpit, pointing down once in a while and occasionally shouting to one another above the noise. By the end of the flight, they were veterans of the air, laughing through the steep turns, looking fearlessly straight down the wing to the ground.

When they stepped down out of the cockpit, back safely on the earth, they maintained a dignified calm.

"That was fine, Mr. Gilbert. It was fun. We'll come work this Saturday, if you want."

It was hard to tell. Would they remember the flight? Would it ever be a meaningful thing to them? I'll have to come back in twenty years, I thought, and ask if they remember.

The first of the automobiles arrived, but they arrived to watch, not to fly.

"When's the parachute jump?" The man got out of his car to ask. "Pretty soon now?"

"It's too windy today," Stu told him. "I don't think we're going to do the jump today."

"What do you mean? I came all the way out here to see the parachute jump and here I am and you say it's too windy. Look, the wind isn't hardly blowing at all! What's the matter? You scared to jump, you going to chicken out?"

His voice had just enough fire to burn.

"Boy, I am glad you came out!" I turned on him in genuine heartiness, protecting young MacPherson. "Am I glad to see you! Gee, we were afraid that we'd have to scrub the jump today because of the wind, but heck, here you are. Wonderful! You can make the jump for Stu, here. I always thought the boy was a little chicken anyway, aren't you, Stu?" The more I talked, the more annoyed I got with the guy. "Hey, Paul! We got a jumper! Bring the chute over and we'll get him all suited up!"

"Well, just a minute . . . ," the man said.

"Do you want to go out at three thousand, or four? Whatever you say is OK with us. Stu's been using the wind sock for a target, but if you want to come in a little closer to the wires . . ."

"Hey, friend, I'm sorry. I didn't mean that I . . ."

"No, that's fine. We're really glad to find you. We wouldn't have had the jump at all today without you. We sure appreciate your coming up and making it for us . . ."

Paul caught the idea and hurried our way, carrying Stu's parachute and helmet.

"I don't think I better. I understand about the wind," the man said, and waved and walked quickly to his car. The whole scene could have been from a screenplay, it worked so well, and I put the method down on my list to use again with unhappy jump-expecters.

"What would you have done if he didn't back out?" Stu said. "What if he said he wanted to jump?"

"I woulda said fine, and popped him into that chute like nothin' flat. I was darn ready to take him up and throw him over the side."

For a while the people sat in their cars and watched, and wouldn't budge when Stu walked to their windows.

"Come on up and fly!" he said at one window. "Rio from the air!"

The figure inside shook its head. "I like to see it from the ground."

If this was typical modern barnstorming, I thought, we were dead; the good old days were truly gone.

At last, about five-thirty in the afternoon, a fearless old farmer drove in. "I got a place about two miles down the road. Fly me over and see it?"

"Sure thing," I said.

"What'll it cost me?"

"Three dollars cash, American money."

"Well, what are we waitin' for, young fella?"

He couldn't have been less than seventy, but he lived the flight. Snowy hair streaming back in the wind, he pointed the way to fly, and then down to his house and barn. It was as neat and pretty as a Wisconsin travel poster: bright green grass, bright white house, bright red barn, bright yellow hay in the loft. We circled twice, to bring a woman out on the grass, waving. He waved back wildly to her and kept waving as we flew away.

"A good ride, young fella," he said when Stu guided him down from the cockpit. "Best three dollars I ever spent. First time I been up in one of these machines. Now you made me sorry I didn't do it a long time ago."

That ride started our day, and from then till sunset I stayed in the cockpit, waiting only long enough on the ground for new riders to step aboard.

Stu caught on to a nice bit of passenger psychology, and took to saying, "How'd you like it?" when the fliers deplaned. Their clear fun and wild enthusiasm convinced the doubtful waiting to go ahead and invest in flight.

A few passengers came back near my cockpit after their flight and asked where they might learn to fly, and how much it might cost. Al and Lauren had been right, thinking we could do something for Rio aviation. One more airplane hangared at the airstrip would increase the flying by 25 percent, three more airplanes would double it. But the nature of the barnstormer is to come and be gone again all in a day, and we never heard what happened at Rio after we flew away.

The sun dropped down around us. Paul and I went up for one last formation flight for fun and watched the lights slowly sparkle on, down in the dark streets. When we landed, we could hardly see to taxi, and we felt as if we had been working much longer than one afternoon.

We covered the airplanes, paid the gas bill, and just as we were all cocooned in our sleeping bags, and as Stu had uncocooned at the request of his seniors to turn out the light, I saw a pair of beady black eyes watching me from under the tool kit, near the door.

"Hey, you guys," I said. "We got a mouse in here."

"Where do you see a mouse?" Paul said.

"Tool kit. Underneath it."

"Kill him. Get him with your boot, Stu."

"PAUL, YOU BLOODTHIRSTY MURDERER!" I shouted. "There will be no killing in this house! Pick up that boot and you got that mouse and me both to face, Stu."

"Well, sweep him out, then," Paul said, "if you're going to be that way."

"No!" I said. "The little guy deserves a roof over his head. How would you like somebody to sweep you out in the cold?"

"It's not cold outside," Paul said peevishly.

"Well, the principle of the thing. He was here before we came. This is his place more than ours."

"All right, all right," he said. "Leave the mouse there! Let the mouse walk all over us. But if he steps on me, I'm gonna pound him!"

Stu obediently snapped out the lights and groped back to his couch pillows on the floor.

We talked in the dark for a while about how kind our hosts had been, and the whole town, for that matter.

"But you notice we carried no women here, or almost none?" Paul said. "There was hardly one female passenger. We had all kinds of them at Prairie."

"We made all kinds of money, and we didn't quite do that here," I said.

"How'd we do in all, by the way, Stu?"

He reeled off statistics, "Seventeen passengers. Fifty-one dollars. "Course we spent nineteen for gas. That's what"—he paused for figuring—"ten bucks each, today, about."

"Not bad," Paul said. "Ten bucks for three hours' work. On a weekday. That works out to fifty dollars a week with all expenses paid except food, and not counting Saturday and Sunday. Hey! A guy can make a living at this!"

I wanted very much to believe him.

CHAPTER FIVE

FIRST THING NEXT morning, Paul Hansen was on fire. He was all crushed up in his sleeping bag, and from the end of it, from just by his hat brim, a veil of smoke curled up.

"PAUL! YOU'RE ON FIRE!"

He didn't move. After a short aggravated pause, he said, "I am smoking a cigarette."

"First thing in the morning? Before you even get up? Man, I thought you were on fire!"

"Look," he said. "Don't bug me about my cigarettes."

"Sorry."

I surveyed the room, and from my low position it looked more like some neglected trash-bin than ever. In the center of the room was a cast-iron wood-burning stove. It said *Warm Morning* on it, in raised iron, and its draft holes looked at me with slitted eyes. The stove did not make me feel very welcome.

Lapping all around its iron feet were our supplies and equipment. On the one table were several old aviation magazines, a tool-company calendar with some very old Peter Gowland girl-shots, Stu's reserve parachute, with its altimeter and stopwatch strapped on. Directly beneath was my red plastic clothes bag, zippered shut, with a hole chewed about the size of a quarter in the side . . . THERE WAS A HOLE IN MY CLOTHES BAG! From one crisis to another.

I sprang out of bed, grabbed the bag and zipped it open. There beneath shaving kit and Levi's and a packet of bamboo pens were my emergency rations: a box of bittersweet chocolate and several packs of cheese and crackers. One square of chocolate had been half-eaten and one cheese section of a cheese-and-crackers box had been consumed. The crackers were untouched.

The mouse. That mouse from last night, under the tool kit. My little buddy, the one whose life I saved from Hansen's savagery. That mouse had eaten my emergency rations!

"You little devil!" I said fiercely, through gritted teeth.

"What's the matter?" Hansen smoked his cigarette, and didn't turn over.

"Nothing. Mouse ate my cheese."

There was a great burst of smoke from the far couch. "THE MOUSE? That mouse from last night that I said we'd better throw outside? And you felt sorry for him? That mouse ate your food?"

"Some cheese, and a little chocolate, yeah."

"How'd he get at it?"

"He ate a hole through my clothes bag."

Hansen didn't stop laughing until quite a while later.

I drew on heavy wool socks and my boots with the survival knife sewn to the side. "Next time I see that mouse around my clothes bag," I said, "he gets six inches of cold steel, I guarantee ya, no questions asked. Last time I stick up for any mouse. You think at least he'd eat your crazy hat, Hansen, or Stu's toothpaste or somethin', but *my cheese*! Man! Next time, baby, cold steel!"

At breakfast, we dined on Mary Lou's French toahst for the last time.

"We're on our way today, Mary Lou," Paul said, "and you didn't come out and fly with us. You sure missed a good chance. It's pretty up there, and now you'll never know what the sky is like, firsthand."

She smiled a dazzling smile. "It's pretty up there," she said, "but it's a silly bunch that lives in it." So that is what our enchantress thought of us. I was, in a way, hurt.

We paid our bill and said good-bye to Mary Lou and rode out to the airport in Al's pickup.

"Think you guys could get back around this way July sixteen-seventeen?" he asked. "Firemen's Picnic, then. Be lots of people here love to have an airplane ride. Sure like to have you back up here."

We began packing our mountain of gear back into the airplanes. The wings of the Luscombe rocked as Paul tied his camera boxes firmly to the framework of the cabin.

"Never can tell, Al. We got no idea where we're gonna be, then. If we're anywhere around here, though, we'll sure be back."

"Glad to have you, anytime."

It was Wednesday morning, then, when we lifted off, circling one last time over Al's place and the café. Al waved and we rocked our wings farewell, but Mary Lou was busy, or had no time for the silly bunch that lived in the sky. I was still sad about that.

And Rio was gone.

And spring changed to summer.

CHAPTER SIX

IT CAME TO us as all Midwest towns did, a clump of green trees way out in the middle of the countryside. At first it seemed trees only, and then the church steeples came in sight, and then the fringe houses and then at last it was clear that under those trees were solid houses and potential airplane passengers.

The town lapped around two lakes and a huge grass runway. I was tempted to fly right on over it, because there were at least fifteen small hangars down there, and lights along the sides of the strip. This was getting pretty far away from the traditional hayfield of the true barnstormer.

But The Great American Flying Circus was low on funds, the strip was less than a block from town, and the cool lakes lay there and sparkled clear in the sun, inviting us. So we dropped down in, touching one-two on the grass.

The place was deserted. We taxied to the gas pit, which was a set of steel trapdoors in the grass, and shut the engines down into silence.

"What do you think?" I called to Paul as he slid out of his airplane.

"Looks good."

"Think it's a bit too big to work?"

"Looks fine."

There was a small square office near the gas pit, but it was locked. "This is not my idea of a barnstormer's hayfield."

"Might as well be, for all the people around here."

"They'll be comin' out about suppertime, like always."

An old Buick sedan rolled out toward us from town, lurching heavily over the grass driveway to the office. It stopped, and a spare, lined man eased out, smiling.

"You want some gas, I guess."

"Could use some, yeah."

He stepped up on the wooden porch and unlocked the office.

"Nice field, you got here," I said.

"Not bad, for bein' sod."

Bad news, I thought. When the owner doesn't like sod, he's looking for a concrete runway, and when he's looking for a concrete runway, he's looking to make money on business planes, not barnstormers.

"What were you boys doin', tryin' to see how close you could come without hitting?" He touched a switch that set the gas pump to humming.

I looked at Paul and thought I-told-you-so; we don't want to have anything to do with this place.

"Just a bit of loose formation flying," Paul said. "We do it every day."

"Every day? What are you boys doing? You part of an air show?"

"Sort of. We're just barnstormin' around," I said. "Thought we might stay here a few days, hop a few passengers, get people out to look at the airport."

He thought about this for a while, considering implications.

"This is not my field, of course," he said while we gassed the airplanes and added some quarts of oil to the engines. "Owned by the city and run by the club. I couldn't make the decision by myself. I'd have to call a meeting of the directors. Could do that tonight and maybe you could come on down and talk to them."

I couldn't remember anything about barnstormers meeting with directors to decide whether or not to work a town. "It's nothin' that big," I said. "Just us two airplanes. We do formation and a few aerobatics, and then Stu here does a little parachute jumpin'. That's about it, and carrying passengers."

"Still have to have the meeting, I'd think. How much do you charge?"

"Charge nothin'. It's all free," I said, reeling the gas hose into the pit. "All we're tryin' to do is make gas and oil and hamburgers on the passenger rides, three dollars a throw."

Somehow I got the idea that the town had been hurt in the past by a troupe of roving sky gypsies. It was a completely different meeting than the normal cheer we had come to expect at smaller towns.

"Joe Wright's the name."

We introduced ourselves around, and Joe got on the phone and called a few of the directors of the Palmyra Flying Club. When he was done, he said, "We'll be getting together tonight; like to have you come on down and talk. Meanwhile, I guess you'd like to get something to eat. Place is just down the way. Give you a ride, if you want, or there's a courtesy car."

I would rather have walked, but Joe insisted and we piled into his Buick and drove. He knew the town well, and gave us a pretty little tour of it on the way to the café. Palmyra was blessed with beautiful grass places; a millpond that was still as a lily pad and green-reflecting quiet like millponds should be; dirt roads through the country, arched overhead by tall curving trees, and quiet back streets with timeless lapstrake and stained glass and oval strawberry-glass front doors.

Every day's barnstorming made the fact a little clearer . . . the only place where time moves is in the cities.

By the time we arrived at the D&M Truck Stop Café, we were well appraised of the town, whose primary industry was a foundry sheltered back in the trees; and of Joe Wright, who was a kind-thinking volunteer airport-operator. He dropped us at the door and left to do some more calling and meeting-arranging.

"I don't like it, Paul," I said when we had ordered. "Why should we bother with a place if it's gonna be no fun? We're free agents, remember . . . go anywhere we want to. There's eight thousand other places than here."

"Don't be so quick to judge," he said. "What's the matter with going to their little meeting? We just go there and act nice and they'll say fine. Then we don't have any problems and everybody knows we're good guys."

"But if we go to the meeting we hurt ourselves, don't you see? We came out here to get away from committees and meetings, and to see if we could find real people, you know, in the little towns. Just being greasy old barnstormers, free in the air, goin' where we please and when we please."

"Now look," Paul said. "This is a good place, right?"

"Wrong. Too many airplanes here."

"It's close in to town, it has lakes, it has people, OK?"

"Well . . ."

We left it at that, though I still wanted to leave and Paul still wanted to stay. Stu didn't want to take sides, but I thought he leaned to the staying side.

When we walked back to the airplanes, we found a few cars parked, and a few Palmyrans looking into the cockpits. Stu unrolled the FLY $3 FLY signs and we went to work.

"PALMYRA FROM THE AIR, FOLKS! PRETTIEST LITTLE TOWN IN THE WORLD! WHO'S THE FIRST TO FLY?" I walked toward the parked cars when the cockpit-watchers said they were just browsing. "Are you ready for an airplane ride, sir?"

"Heh-heh-heh-heh." That was the only answer I got, and it very clearly said you poor con man, do you really think I'm stupid enough to go up in that old crate?

The quality of that laugh stopped me cold, and I turned abruptly away.

What a crushing difference between this place and the other little places where we had been so welcome. If our search is for the real people and the true people of America, then we should get out of here now.

"Can you take me for a ride?" A man walking boldly from another car changed my attitude at once.

"Love to," I said. "*Stu!* Passenger! Let's go!"

Stu trotted over and helped the man into the front cockpit while I strapped into the rear one. I was very much at home in this little office, with the board of familiar dials and levers around me, and I was happy there. Stu began cranking the inertia-starter handcrank, the device recognized time and again by farm folk as a "cream separator." Straining at the handle, turning it slowly at first, throwing heavy effort into the steel mass of the geared flywheel inside the cowl, Stu drained pure energy from his heart into the starter. At last, starter flywheel screaming, Stu fell away and called, "CLEAR!" I pulled the starter-engage handle and the propeller jerked around. But it turned for only ten seconds. The propeller slowed, and stopped. The engine didn't fire one single time.

What's wrong, I thought. This thing starts every time; it has never missed starting! Stu looked at me in a glazed sort of shock, that all his torture on the crank had gone for nothing.

I was just shaking my head, to tell him I couldn't understand why the engine didn't fire, when I found the trouble. I hadn't turned the switch on. I was so familiar with the cockpit that I had expected the switches and levers to work by themselves.

"Stu . . . ah . . . hate to say this . . . but . . . I forgot to turn the switch on sorry that sure was a silly thing to do let's crank her one more time OK?"

He closed his eyes, imploring heaven to destroy me, and when that didn't work, he made to throw the crank at my head. But he caught himself in time and with the air of a church martyr, inserted the handcrank once again and began to wind it.

"Gee, I'm sorry, Stu," I said, sitting back in my comfortable cockpit. "I owe you fifty cents for forgetting."

He didn't answer, as he had not the strength to talk. The second time I pulled the engage handle the engine roared awake at once, and the jumper looked at me as one looks at a poor dumb beast in a cage. I taxied quickly away and was airborne a moment later with my passenger. The biplane fell into a pattern for Palmyra at once, with a circling detour to look at one of the lakes and to climb a little higher, for there was no emergency landing field anywhere east of town.

The pattern took ten minutes exactly. Touching down, the biplane swerved for a second as I was thinking about what a pretty grass runway this was. Wake up! she was telling me. Every landing, every take-off is different, every one! And don't you forget it!

I did quick penance by stomping on a rudder pedal to stop the swerve.

As we taxied in, Paul was taxiing out in the Luscombe with a passenger of his own. My spirits brightened a little. Maybe there was hope for Palmyra, after all.

But that was the end of it for the afternoon. We had watchers, but no more passengers.

Stu collected my rider's money, and walked to the cockpit. "I can't do anything with 'em," he said over the engine roar. "If they stop and get out of their cars, we get passengers. But if they stay in the cars, they're watchers, and they just aren't interested in flying."

It was hard to believe that we could have all those cars and no more riders, but there it was. The watchers all knew each other, and soon a lively conversation was going on. And the Directors arrived to size us up on their own.

Paul landed, taxied in, and lacking more passengers, shut his engine down into silence. A fragment of talk drifted to us. "... he was right over my house!"

"He was right over everybody's house. Palmyra isn't that big."

"... who told you we were having a meeting tonight?"

"M'wife. Somebody called her and got her all shook up ..."

Joe Wright came over and introduced us to some of the directors, and we told our story again. I was getting tired of this becoming such a big thing. Why couldn't they tell us right out that we were welcome or not? Just a simple thing like a couple of barnstormers.

"You have any schedule for your shows?" one man asked.

"No schedule. We fly when we please."

"Your airplanes are insured, of course; how much would that be?"

"The insurance on these airplanes is what we know about flying," I said, and I wanted to add, *"fella!"* sarcastically. "There is not one cent of any other kind of insurance; no property damage, no liability." Insurance, I wanted to say, is not a signed scrap of paper. Insurance is knowing within us about the sky and the wind, and the touch of the machines that we fly. If we didn't believe in ourselves, or know our airplanes, then there was no signature, no amount of money in the world that could make us secure, or make our passengers safe. But I simply said, again, ". . . not one penny of insurance."

"Well," he paused, startled. "We wouldn't want to say that you're not *welcome* . . . this is a public field . . ."

I smiled, and hoped that Paul had learned his lesson. "Where's the map?" I asked him fiercely.

He had a there-there tone as I stalked to the biplane. "Now look. It's dark almost, and they're going to have their meeting, and we can't go anywhere now so we might as well stay the night and move on tomorrow morning."

"We no more belong here than we belong barnstorming at Kennedy International, man. We . . ."

"No, just listen," he said. "They have a flight breakfast coming up here Sunday. They promised to have a Cessna 180 in here, carrying passengers. Little while ago I heard somebody say that the 180 canceled out, so they have no one to carry passengers. And here we come. I think after this meeting they're having now, they're going to want us to stay. They're in a bind, and we can help them."

"Shame *on* ya, Paul. By Sunday we'll be in Indiana. Sunday is four days away! And the last thing I want to do is help them out at their flight breakfast. I tell you, we don't belong here! All they want around here is the little tricycle-gear modern airplanes that you drive like a car. Man, I want to be an *airplane* pilot! What the heck's the matter with you, anyway?"

I took a grease rag and began wiping down the engine cowl in the dark. If the biplane had lights I would have flown away that minute.

After a while, the meeting in the office broke up and everyone was hearty and kind to us. I was immediately suspicious.

"Think you boys could stay over till Sunday?" a voice said, out of a crowd of directors. "We're having a little flight breakfast then, be hundreds of airplanes here, thousands of people. You stand to make a lot of money."

I had to laugh. So this is what it felt like to be judged by our vagabond appearance. For just a moment, I was sorry for these people.

"Why don't you stay in the office tonight, boys?" another voice said, and then in a lower tone to someone close by, "We'll take inventory of the oil in there."

I didn't catch the implication of the last sotto voce, but Paul did, at once. "Did you hear that?" he said, stunned. "Did you hear that?"

"I think so. What?"

"They're going to count the oil cans before they trust us in the office. They're going to count the oil cans!"

I replied to whoever had offered the office. "No thanks. We'll sleep out."

"Love to have you stay in the office, really," came the voice again.

"No," Paul said. "We wouldn't be safe there with all your oil cans. You wouldn't want to trust us around all that expensive oil."

I laughed again, in the dark. Hansen, our champion of Palmyra and its people, was furious now at their slur to his honesty.

"I leave fifteen hundred dollars' worth of cameras unlocked in my plane while we go and eat, trusting these guys, and they think we're going to steal a can of *oil*!"

Stu stood quietly by, listening, and said not a word. It was full dark over supper at the D&M before Paul was cool again.

"We're trying to find an ideal world," he said to Joe Wright, who was brave enough to join us. "All of us have lived in the other world, the cutthroat, cheap world, where the only thing that matters is the almighty buck. Where people don't even know what money means. And we've had enough of that, so we're out here living in our ideal world, where it's all simple. For three bucks we sell something priceless, and with that we get our food and gas so we can go on." Paul forgot his fried chicken, he was talking so hard to the Palmyran.

Why are we working on Joe, why are we justifying ourselves to him? I thought. Aren't we sure, ourselves? Maybe we're just so sure that we want to turn a few converts our way.

Our missionary effort, however, was wasted on Joe, who gave little sign that there was anything new or meaningful in what we said.

Stu did nothing but eat his supper. I wondered about the person within the boy, what he thought, what he cared about. I would like to have met him, but for now, he was listening . . . listening . . . not saying a word, not offering a single thought to the roar of ideas going on about him. Well, I thought, he's a good jumper and he's thinking. There's not much more we could ask.

"I'll drive you back out to the office, if you want," Joe said.

"Thanks, Joe," Paul said. "We'll take you up on that, but we're not going to stay in that office. We'll sleep under the wing. If somebody counted the oil wrong, and then counted it right, after we were gone, you see, we'd automatically be thieves. It's better for us to have that place all locked up and us sleeping out under the wing."

In half an hour, the biplane was a huge silent arrangement of black over our sleeping bags and above the black was the bright mist of the Milky Way.

"Center of the galaxy," I said.

"What's that?"

"Milky Way. That's the center of the galaxy."

"It makes you feel kind of small, doesn't it," Paul said.

"Used to. Not so much anymore. Guess I'm bigger now." I chewed a grass stem. "What do you think now? We gonna make money here or not?"

"We'll just have to wait it out."

"I think it's going to work all right," I said, an optimist under the stars. "Can't imagine anybody not coming out to see old airplanes, even in this town."

I watched the galaxy, with its Northern Cross like a big kite in a wind of stars, sparkling on and off. The grass was soft beneath me, my boots made a firm leathery pillow.

"We'll find out tomorrow." It fell silent under the wing, and the cool wind moaned low in the wires above us, between the biplane's wings.

Tomorrow dawned in fog, and I woke to the slow cannon-boom of fog-drops falling from the top wing down onto the drum-fabric of the bottom one. Stu was awake, quietly rolling a new drift-streamer out of twenty yards of crepe paper. Paul was asleep, his hat pulled down over his eyes.

"Hey, Paul. You awake?"

No answer.

"HEY PAUL! YOU STILL ASLEEP?"

"Mmm." He moved an inch.

"I guess you're still asleep."

"Mm."

"Well, you go ahead and sleep, we won't be flyin' for a while."

"What do you mean?" he said.

"Fog."

The hat was raised by a hand snaking out of the green sleeping bag. "Mm. Fog. Up off the lakes."

"Yeah. Burn off by ten o'clock. Betcha nickel." There was no answer. I tried licking fog from some larger grassblades, but it wasn't much of a thirst quencher. I rearranged my boot pillows and tried for a bit more sleep.

Paul came suddenly awake. "Ar! My shirt's all wet! It's soaking wet!"

"Man. City pilots. If I wanted to get my shirt just as wet as I could, I'd lay it out on the wing like you did. You're supposed to put your shirt under your sleepin' bag."

I slid out of my bag and into the dry warm shirt that I had slept on and mashed all kinds of wrinkles into. "Nothing like a nice dry shirt, of a mornin'."

"Ha, ha."

I pulled the cover from the cockpits and unloaded the tool kit and oil cans and FLY $3 FLY sign from the front cockpit. I ragged down the windshields, pulled the propeller through a few times, and in general made ready hopefully for a busy day of barnstorming. The fog was lifting already.

As he finished breakfast, Stu sat back in his chair and stretched his legs. "Shall we try a day jump, see what happens?"

"If you want," Paul said. "Better check with the Leader first." He nodded at me.

"What do you mean? I am always winding up Leader! I'm no leader! No leader! I quit! As Leader, I resign!"

We decided together, then, that it would be good to try a midday jump, to see if anyone was about with time to come and fly.

"Let's not waste any time with free-fall stuff," Paul said, "nobody will see you. How about a clear-and-pull from three thousand?"

Stu did not buy this idea. "Rather have time to stabilize a bit. Thirty-five hundred's OK."

"Sounds fine," said Paul.

"If you don't pull, Stu, or your chute doesn't open," I said, "we'll just fly right on to the next town."

"I'm sure it won't make any difference to me," he answered, with a rare smile.

By noon we were airborne, climbing in formation toward the top of the sky. Stu sat in the open door on the right side of Paul's airplane, looking downward, his drift streamer in his hand. As we came near the jump altitude, I broke away and flew some loops and rolls and then clawed my way back up to altitude. There wasn't a person moving anywhere in the streets below. The Luscombe was level on course over the airport, and the long crepe streamer plummeted overboard, slowed to the speed of an open parachute, and twisted down toward the grass. It landed several hundred yards west of the target, in the wind.

Way up in Paul's airplane, high over my head, Stu was picking his jump point to correct for the wind, to miss the trees and wires. I stopped cavorting and circled beneath the little sportplane, which by now had nearly reached jump altitude. Paul turned his airplane onto the jump run, into the wind, and we all waited. The Luscombe droned along at a walk; only if I watched carefully could I tell that it was moving at all. And then Stu MacPherson jumped.

A tiny black speck, moving instantly at high speed and straight down, his body turned left, stabilized, turned right, tumbled end over end. I blinked again at the speed of it. In seconds he was no longer a black speck, but a man streaking down through the air, a falcon striking.

Time stopped. Our airplanes were frozen in the air, the sound and the wind were still. The only motion was that sizzling speed of the man whom I last saw crushing himself into the tiny right seat of the

Luscombe, and he was moving at least 150 miles per hour toward the flat unmoving earth. In the silence, I could hear him fall.

Stu was still above me when he brought both arms in close to his body, flung them out again, and the long bright rocket of a parachute streamed from his back. It didn't slow him a bit. The narrow line of the chute simply stopped in the air as the man went streaking on down. Then it caught him. All in an instant the chute burst wide open, closed again, and opened to a soft thistle-fluff under which the man floated, still above me.

Time fell back into gear at once, and Paul and I were airplanes flashing again through the sky, the earth was round and warm, and the only sound was the roar of wind and engine. The slowest thing in sight was the orange-and-white canopy drifting down.

Paul arrived in the Luscombe, at high speed, and we circled the open chute, one of us on each side of our jumper. He waved, spun his canopy around, slipped heavily into the wind, which was stronger than he had bargained for. He slipped again, pulling down hard on the risers and almost collapsing one side of his canopy.

All to no avail. We held our altitude at five hundred feet while Stu went on down to smash into a tall field of rye that bordered the runway. It looked soft until the instant he crashed into the ground, and then it looked very hard indeed.

I circled and dived to make one low pass over his head, then followed Paul in to land. I taxied to the edge of the rye and got out of the cockpit, expecting to see the jumper at any moment. He didn't appear. I got out of the airplane and walked into the shoulder-high grass, the sound of the engine fading away behind me. "STU?"

No answer. I tried to remember if I had seen him standing up and waving OK after he landed. I couldn't remember.

"STU!"

There was no answer.

CHAPTER SEVEN

THE RYE FIELD was set on rolling ground and the tops of the stalks made a waving unbroken carpet, hiding everything but the trees on the quarter-mile horizon. Darn me. I should have marked the place better where he went down. He could be anywhere in here. "Hey! *STU!*"

"Over here . . ." It was a very weak voice.

I thrashed through the tall grain in the direction the voice had come and suddenly broke through to an unconcerned jumper, field-packing his chute. "Man, I thought we lost you there. You OK?"

"Oh, sure. Hit kind of hard. This stuff is deeper than it looks from the air."

Our words were strange and oddly quiet; the grass was a sponge for sound. I couldn't hear the airplane engine at all, and had it not been for the trail I had left, walking in, I would have had no idea where it was.

I took Stu's reserve chute and his helmet and we beat our way through the Wisconsin Pampas.

"Jumper in the Rye," Stu mused.

At last the engine-sound filtered in to us, and a minute later we broke out into the clear short grass of the strip. I threw his gear into the front cockpit and he stood on the wingwalk while we taxied back.

There were four passengers waiting, and a small crowd of spectators wondering what we were going to do next. I flew the passengers, two couples, and that was the end of the midday jump experiment. Not bad, for the middle of a weekday.

We tired of the airstrip after a while and ambled through the silent day to Main Street, three blocks long. We were tourists on the sidewalk, looking in the shop windows. There was a poster in the dime store:

AMERICAN LEGION & FIREMEN'S PICNIC
SULLIVAN, WISC.

Saturday–Sunday, June 25–26
COLORFUL PARADE
Drum and Bugle Corps   Kiltie Kadets
Home made pies!   Sandwiches at all times!
WRESTLING Both Nights
2 out of 3 falls

THE MASK	JOHNNY GILBERT
from parts unknown	Michigan City, Ind.

The Firemen's Picnic would be an exciting time. The wrestlers were shown, in their fighting togs. The Mask was a great mound of flesh, scowling through a black stocking mask. Gilbert was handsome, rugged. There was no question that the conflict between good and evil would be a colossal one, and I wondered if Sullivan, Wisconsin, had a good hayfield, in close to the ring.

The dime store itself was a long narrow room with board-wood floors, and the smell of popcorn and hot paper hung in the air. There were elements of forever: a glass-front counter with its chutes and trays of candy, a worn sheet-metal candy scoop half-buried in Red-Hots, a square glass machine filled with multicolored jawbreakers, and way down at the end of the room, at the point where the long counters converged in the distance, a tiny voice sifted to us: "Can I help you boys?"

We felt almost apologetic for being there, travelers from another century, not knowing that folks don't walk into dime stores in the middle of the day.

"I need some crepe paper," Stu said. "Do you have any wide crepe paper?"

The little tiny lady way off down the rows walked toward us, and walking, she grew. She was a full-size person by the time she reached the paper goods section, and there, surrounded by marble-paper composition folders and nickel Big Gun notebooks, was the material for Stu's wind-drift indicator. The lady looked at us strangely, but said nothing more until she said thank you and we walked bell-jangling through the doorway and out into the sun again.

I needed heavy oil for the biplane, and Stu and I walked out a side street to the implement dealer's. Paul went exploring down another street.

The implement dealer's place was a rough-floored wooden cave, with stacks of tires, bits of machinery and old advertising scattered about. The place smelled like new rubber, and it was very cool inside.

The dealer was a busy man and it was twenty minutes before I could ask if he had any heavy oil.

"Sixty weight, you say? Might have some fifty, but sixty I don't think. What you usin' it for?"

"Got an old airplane here, takes the heavy stuff. Fifty's OK if you don't have sixty."

"Oh, you're the guys with the airplanes. Saw you flyin' around last night. Don't they have any oil at the airport?"

"Nope. This is an old airplane; they don't carry the oil for it."

He said he'd check, and disappeared down a flight of wooden stairs to the cellar.

I noticed, while we waited, a dusty poster stapled high on the planks of the wall: "'We Can . . . We Will . . . We Must . . .' *Franklin D. Roosevelt.* Buy US War Savings Bonds & Stamps NOW!" There was a picture in stark colored silhouette of an American flag and an aircraft carrier sailing over some precise scalloped water-ripples. It had been nailed to that wall longer than our parachute jumper had existed on the earth.

We browsed among the pulleys, the grease, the lawn mowers for sale, and at last our man returned with a gallon can of oil.

"This is fifty, best I could do you. That OK?"

"Fine. Sure do thank you."

Then for $1.25 I bought a can of Essentialube, since there was none of the barnstormer's traditional Marvel Mystery Oil available. *The Modern Motor Conditioner—It Powerizes,* the label said. I wasn't sure that I wanted the Wright to be powerized, but I had to have something for top-cylinder lubrication, and this promised that, as well.

Our rule said that all gas and oil was paid from Great American money, taken off the top before we split the profits, so I made a note that the Great American owed me $2.25, and I paid it out of pocket.

By the time we got back to the airport, there were two cars of spectators on the field.

Stu laid out his chute for packing, and I wanted to learn something about it, so Paul took the time to fly two young passengers in the Luscombe. It was a good feeling, to see Paul flying and making money for us while we worked with the thin nylon.

For once Stu talked and I listened.

"Pull out the line guide, will you . . . yeah, the thing with the angle iron on it. Now we take all the lines from these risers . . ."

The packing of a parachute was a mystery to me. Stu took great care to show how it all was done, the laying of the suspension lines (". . . we don't call them shroud lines anymore. I guess that's too scary . . ."), the flaking of the panels into one long neat skinny pyramid, the sheathing of the pyramid into the sleeve, the folding of corners that somehow is supposed to prevent friction burns during opening, and the smashing of the whole thing down into the pack.

"Then we just slip the rip cord pins in like . . . so. And we're ready to jump." He patted the pack and tucked in some loose flaps of material with the packing paddle. Then he was the laconic Stu once again, asking tersely if we might be running another jump again this afternoon.

"I don't see why not," Paul said, walking into earshot and casting an appraising eye at the finished pack. I wondered if he was tempted to jump again. It had been years since he had quit, a battered skydiver after some 230 jumps, grounded with injuries that kept him in a hospital for months.

"Might as well go up right now," he said, "if you promise to come a little closer to the target."

"I'll try."

Five minutes later they were off in the Luscombe, and I was watching from the ground, holding Paul's movie camera and charged with the job of getting some good shots of the jump.

In the zoom-lens viewfinder, Stu was a tumbling black dot, stabilizing in a cross, turning a huge diving spiral one way, pausing, turning the other way. He was in complete control of his body in flight; he could go any direction, I thought, but up. He fell for nearly twenty seconds, then his arms jerked in, and out, pulling the rip cord, and the chute snapped open. The sound of the nylon firing open was a single shot from a 50-caliber pistol. As loud and sharp as that.

Like every jumper, Stu lived for the free-fall part of the jump, that bare twenty seconds in a twenty-four-hour day. He was now "under canopy," which term must be spoken in a very bored tone, for the *real* jump is over, although there is two thousand feet yet to fall, and some delicate handling still to do of a cloth flying machine that is twenty-eight feet wide and forty feet tall.

He was tracking well, coming right down toward me as I stood by the wind sock. I filmed the last hundred feet of the jump and his touchdown, moving back to keep his boots out of Paul's expensive lens.

A jumper, I saw in the viewfinder, is moving at a pretty good clip at that moment he crashes into the ground. I felt the world shudder as Stu hit, twenty feet away. The canopy drifted down to catch me, but I dodged north. I was proud of Stu, suddenly. He was part of our little team, he had courage and skill that I didn't have, and he worked like a professional, a seasoned jumper, though there were only twenty-five jumps in his log.

"Pretty nice, kid."

"At least I didn't get off in the rye patch." He slipped out of the harness and began gathering the suspension lines into a long braided chain. A moment later Paul landed and walked over to us.

"Man, I really burned off the altitude," he said. "What did you think of that slip? I really had her stood up on the wing, didn't I? Coming down like a ROCK! What did you think of that?"

"I didn't see your slip, Paul. I was taking pictures of Stu."

At precisely that moment a girl of six or seven walked into our group, offered a small blank book, and shyly asked Stu for his autograph.

"Me?" Stu said, stunned to be onstage and in the center of the spotlight.

She nodded. He wrote his name boldly on the paper and the girl ran off with her prize.

"The STAR!" Hansen said. "Everybody wants to watch the STAR! Nobody watches my great slip, because the old glory-hound is ONSTAGE!"

"Sorry about that, Paul," said Stu.

I made a note to get a box of gold stars at the dime store and stick them all over everything Stu owned.

The Star laid out his chute at once, and soon was lost in the task of repacking for tomorrow. I walked toward the biplane, and Paul followed.

"No more passengers, this time," he said.

"Quiet before the storm." I patted the biplane. "Want to fly her?"

It was a loaded question. The old Detroit-Parks biplane, as I had told Paul over and over, was the most difficult airplane I had ever learned to fly.

"There's a bit of a crosswind," he said cautiously, giving me a way to withdraw my invitation.

"No problem, if you stay awake on landing," I said. "She's a pussycat in the air, but you got to stay pretty sharp on the landing. She wants to swerve, once in a while, and you have to be right there with the throttle and the rudder to catch her. You'll do a great job."

He didn't say another word, but climbed quickly into the cockpit and pulled on helmet and goggles. I cranked the inertia starter, called "CLEAR!" and fell back while the engine roared into life. It was a strange light feeling to see my airplane start engine with someone else in the cockpit.

I walked around and leaned on the fuselage, by his shoulder.

"'Member to go around and try again if you don't like any landing. You got an hour and a half fuel, so no problem there. If she wants to swerve on you, just give her throttle and rudder."

Paul nodded, and in a burst of power swung the plane about and taxied to the grass strip. I went back and picked up his movie camera, focused down on him with the zoom lens, and watched his takeoff through the viewfinder. I felt as though it was my first solo in the biplane, not Paul's. But there he was, smoothly off the ground and climbing, and I was struck with what a pretty sight the biplane made in the air, and the sweet soft chugging that the Whirlwind made in the distance.

They climbed, turned, swooped gently through the sky as I walked with the camera to the far end of the strip, ready to film the landing. I was still nervous, and felt lonely without my airplane. That was my whole world this summer, circling around up there, and now it was all under the control of someone else. I had just four friends that I would allow to fly that airplane, and Hansen was one of them. So what? I thought. So he breaks the thing up to nothing. His friendship is more important to me than the airplane. The airplane is just a bunch of sticks and wires and cloth, a tool for learning about the sky and about what kind of person I am, when I fly. An airplane stands for freedom, for joy, for the power to understand, and to demonstrate that understanding. Those things aren't destructible.

Paul now had the chance he had been awaiting for two years. He was a good pilot and he was measuring himself against the hardest machine he had ever heard of.

The sound of the biplane went silent, high overhead, and as I watched, she flew through a series of stalls while Paul taught himself how she handled at low speeds. I knew what he would be feeling. The aileron control went to nothing, the elevator was very poor, the control stick was loose and dead now in his hand. The rudder was the best control he had left, but when he would need it most, rolling over the ground after landing, it was useless. It took a good firm rudder pedal and power, rudder and a great blast of wind over it, to make the biplane respond, to keep her from tearing herself to pieces in a twisting smashing groundloop across the grass.

The engine roared back as he tested just how much wind he would need over that rudder. Good boy, I thought, take your time with her.

The last of my nervousness vanished when I realized that what mattered was that my friend met his own special challenge, and found courage and confidence within himself.

He swung around some wide soaring turns and came down low over the grass at high speed. I filmed the pass with his movie camera and wished I could remind him that when he was ready to land, that big huge silver nose would be higher in front of him, so that he wouldn't be able to see ahead. It was like trying to land blindfolded, and he had to do it right, first time out.

How would I feel, in his place? I couldn't tell. Somewhere, a long time ago as I flew airplanes, something clicked in me and I had won a confidence with them. I knew within myself that I could fly any airplane ever built, from glider to jetliner. Whether it was true or not was something that only trying would prove, but the confidence was there, and I wouldn't be afraid to try anything with wings. A good feeling, that confidence, and now Paul was working out there for that same little click within himself.

The biplane swept into the landing pattern, close enough to land on the strip no matter where the engine might fail. It turned toward the grass, slowing, settling gently, evenly, across the trees, across the highway, wires whistling softly with the engine throttled back, across the fence at the end of the strip, eased its glide, settled all smooth, under control. As long as he's under control, he's safe, I thought, and I watched him through the viewfinder, finger down on trigger, driving battery-power to turn the film sprockets.

The touchdown was smooth as summer ice melting, the wheels slid on the grass before they began to roll. The man made me jealous. He was doing a beautiful job with my airplane, handling it as though it were built of paper-thin eggshells.

They rolled smoothly along, the tail came down into the critical time of landing, when the passengers were wont to wave and turn and smile, and the plane tracked straight through the grass. He had made it. My sigh of satisfaction would no doubt show on the movie screen.

At that moment the bright machine, huge in the zoom lens, began to swerve.

The left wing dipped slightly, the airplane curved to the right. The rudder flashed as Paul slammed the left pedal down. "Power, boy, hit the power!" I said. Nothing. The wing dipped farther down, and in a second it touched the ground in a little shower of flying grass. The biplane was out of control.

I looked away from the viewfinder, knowing that the film would show only a rocking picture of some close blurred grass, but uncaring. Maybe he could still survive, maybe the biplane would come out of the groundloop in one piece.

There was a very dull *whump*—the left wheel collapsing. The biplane slid sideways for a moment, bending first, then breaking. It pitched forward, and at last it stopped. The propeller swung through one last quick time and buried the tip of one blade in the dirt.

I pointed the camera, still clicking, back onto the scene. Oh, Paul. How long would it be now, to win your confidence? I tried to think of how I would feel, breaking Paul's Luscombe, when he had trusted it to me. It was a horrible feeling, and I stopped imagining at once. I was glad I was me, and not Paul.

I walked slowly over to the airplane. It was worse than the crash at Prairie had been. The long trailing edge of the top wing rippled in wild anguished waves. The fabric of the lower left wing was deeply wrinkled, the tip down in the dirt. Three struts were torn into angles of agony, screaming that a giant twisting force had grabbed and bent. The left wheel was gone, under the airplane.

Paul hopped out of the cockpit and threw the helmet and goggles down into the seat. I searched for some telling understatement but could come up with nothing that told how sorry for him I was, that he should have to hurt the biplane.

"Win a few, lose a few" was all I could say.

"You don't know," Paul said, "you don't know how sorry . . ."

"Forget it. Not worth worrying about. Airplane's a tool for learning, Paul, and sometimes a tool gets a little bent." I was proud to be able to say that in a calm voice. "All you do is straighten it out again and go back flying."

"Yeah."

"Nothing happens by chance, my friend." I was trying to convince myself more than Paul. "No such thing as luck. A meaning behind every little thing, and a meaning behind this. Part for you, part for me. May not see it all real clear right now, but we will, before long."

"Wish I could say that, Dick. All I can say now is I'm sorry."

The biplane looked like a total wreck.

CHAPTER EIGHT

WE DRAGGED THE airplane, all limp-winged, into the lee of a corrugated tin hangar, and barnstorming came to a sudden halt. The Great American Flying Circus was out of business again.

Not counting the bent struts and broken landing gear fitting, two other gear fittings had begun to tear away, a brake arm had been ripped off, the top of the cowl was bent, the right shock absorbers were broken, the left aileron fittings were twisted so that the control stick was jammed hard.

But the hangar next to us was owned by one Stan Gerlach, and this was a very special kind of miracle. Stan Gerlach had been owning and flying airplanes since 1932, and he kept spare bits and pieces of every plane he'd owned since then.

"Look, you guys," he said that afternoon, "I got three hangars here, and in this one I think I got some old struts off a Travelair I used to have. You're free to take anything you find in here can get you flying again."

He lifted a wide tin door. "Over here are the struts, and some wheels and junk . . ." He banged and screeched his way into a waist-high stack of metal, pulling out old welded airplane parts. "This might do for something . . . and this . . ."

Struts were our biggest problem, since it would take weeks to send out for streamlined steel tubing and make up new pieces for the biplane. And the blue-painted steel that he piled on the floor looked almost like what we were looking for. On impulse I took one and measured it against the good interplane strut at the right wing of the Parks. It was a sixteenth of an inch longer.

"Stan! This thing's a perfect fit! Perfect! She'll drop right in there!"

"Will it? That's fine. Why don't you just take that, then, and look-see if there's anything else here you can use."

My hope came flooding back. This was beyond any coincidence. The odds against our breaking the biplane in a random little town that just happened to be home to a man with the forty-year-old parts to repair it; the odds that he would be on the scene when the breaking happened; the odds that we'd push the airplane right next to his hangar, within ten feet of the parts we needed—the odds were so high that "coincidence" was a foolish answer. I waited eagerly to see how the rest of the problem would be solved.

"You're gonna need to pick this airplane up, somehow," Stan said, "get the weight off the wheels while you weld those fittings. I got a big A-frame here, we can set up." He clanked around some more in the back of his hangar and came out dragging a 15-foot length of steel pipe. "It's all back in there; might as well bring it out now. It all fits together."

In ten minutes we had assembled the pipe into a high overhead beam, from which we could hang a winch to lift the whole front half of the airplane. All we lacked was the winch.

"Think I got a block and tackle down at the barn . . . sure I do. You want to go down and pick it up?"

I rode along with Stan to his barn, two miles out of Palmyra. "I live for my airplanes," he said as he drove. "I don't know . . . I really get a kick out of airplanes. Don't know what I'll do when I flunk my physical . . . go on flying anyway, I guess."

"Stan, you don't know . . . you don't *know* how much I thank you."

"Heck. Those struts might as well help you as set out in the hangar. I advertise a lot of this stuff, and sell a lot to guys who need it. Any struts there you can have, but they'd be fifty bucks to a jockey that would just turn around and resell 'em. I got some welding tanks, too, and a torch, and a lot of other stuff there in the hangar that you might be able to use."

We turned off the highway and parked by the side of an old flake-painted red barn. From one rafter hung a block and tackle.

"Thought it might be here," he said.

We took it down, put it in the back of the truck and drove back to the airstrip. We stopped at the airplane, and in the last of the day's sunlight fastened the block to the A-frame.

"Hey, you guys," Stan said, "I got to get goin'. There's a trouble light here in the hangar and an extension cord somewhere, and a table and whatever else you can use. Just lock the place up when you leave, OK?"

"OK, Stan. Thanks."

"Glad to help."

We went to work removing the bent struts. When they came away, the wings sagged more than ever and we propped the lower wingtips with sawhorses. By dark, we had the aileron fittings straightened again and the cowl hammered smooth.

After a while we knocked off work and went to supper, locking Stan's hangar behind us.

"Well, Paul, I have to say you sure beat Magnaflux. 'If there's a weak place anywhere in your airplane, folks, Hansen's Testing Service will find it and break it up for you.'"

"No," Paul said. "I just touched down, you know, and I said, 'Oh, boy, I got it down!' and ka-*pow!* You know the first thing I thought? Your wife. 'What will Bette think?' First thing."

"I'll call her. Tell her you were thinking of her. 'Bette, Paul was thinking about you today while he was tearing the airplane all up.'"

We ate in silence for a while, then Paul brightened. "We made some money today. Hey, treasurer. How much money did we make today?"

Stu put down his fork and pulled out his wallet. "Six dollars."

"But there's some Great American money comes off the top," Paul said. "I paid out the quarter to the boys who found the drift marker."

"And I bought the crepe paper," Stu said. "That was sixty cents."

"And I got the oil," I said. "This is gonna be interesting."

Stu paid us our two dollars each, then I put in a claim for their share of the oil money, seventy-five cents each. But I owed Paul eight and a third cents for my share of the wind-drift recovery fee and I owed Stu twenty cents for the crepe paper. So Stu paid eight cents to Paul, deducted the twenty cents I owed him from his bill to me, and handed me fifty-five cents. Paul took my eight cents off his bill and owed me sixty-seven cents. But he didn't have the change, so he gave me fifty cents and two dimes and I gave him two pennies. Tossed 'em into his coffee saucer, is what I did, clinking.

We sat at the table with our little piles of coins, and I said, "We all square? Speak now or forever hold . . ."

"You owe me fifty cents," Stu said.

"Fifty cents! Where do I owe you fifty cents?" I said. "I owe you nothin'!"

"You forgot to turn on the switch. After I cranked myself to death on the crank, you forgot to turn on the switch. Fifty cents."

Was that just this morning? It was, and I paid.

Joe Wright had stopped by to insist that we sleep in the office. There would be no oil-can count.

There were two couches, but we piled all our equipment inside the building, and our sleeping place again looked more like an airplane factory than an office bedroom.

"You know what?" Paul said, lying in the dark, smoking a cigarette.

"What?"

"You know, I wasn't ever scared that I was going to get hurt? The only thing I was scared of was that I might hurt the airplane. I sort of knew the airplane wouldn't let me get hurt. Isn't that funny?"

The future of the Great American depended upon a pilot, jumper, mechanic, and friend, all of them named Johnny Colin, who had flown with us at Prairie du Chien and worked the miracle of repairing the biplane after its crash there.

That next afternoon at three, Paul fired up the Luscombe and took off west, toward Apple River, where Johnny had his own airstrip. If everything worked to plan, he would be back before dark.

Stu and I tinkered around the airplane, finishing everything we could before the welding had to be done, and at last there was nothing more to do. Everything turned on whether Paul would return with Johnny in the Luscombe.

Stan came out after a time and wheeled out his Piper Pacer for an afternoon flight. A tricycle-gear Cherokee landed, turned around, took off again. It was a quiet afternoon at a little airport.

A car stopped by the wingtip and some Palmyrans stepped out that we recognized from the day before.

"How's it going?"

"Going OK. A little welding and she'll be all ready to put back together again."

"Looks kind of bent, to me, still." The woman who spoke smiled wryly, to say that she meant no hurtful thing, but her friends didn't notice.

"Don't be so hard on 'em, Duke. They've been working out here all day long on this poor old airplane."

"And they'll be flying it again, too," said Duke.

She was a strange woman, and my first impression was that she was a thousand miles away and that this part of her that was living in Palmyra, Wisconsin, was just about ready to speak some mystic word and disappear.

When Duke talked, everyone listened. There was an aura of faintest sadness about her, as though she was of some lost race, captured as a child and taught in our ways, but always remembering her home on another planet.

"This all you fellows do for a living, fly around and give airplane rides?" she said. She looked at me with a level gaze, wanting to know the truth.

"That's pretty well it."

"What do you think of the towns you see?"

"Every one's different. Towns have personalities, like people."

"What's our personality?" she said.

"You're kind of cautious, steady, sure. Kind of careful with strangers."

"Wrong there. This town's a Peyton Place," she said.

Stan came flying down in a low pass over the field and we all watched him whisk by, engine purring.

By now Paul was an hour overdue and the sun was just a little way above the horizon. If he was going to make it, he'd have to be nearly here.

"Where's your friend?" Duke said.

"He's out getting a guy who's a pretty good welder."

She moved to sit on the front fender of the car, a slim alien woman, not unpretty, looking at the sky. I went back to retouching an old patch on the wingtip.

"Here he comes," someone said, and pointed.

They were wrong. The airplane flew right on over, heading toward Lake Michigan, out to the east.

Another airplane appeared after a while and it was the Luscombe. It glided down, touched its wheels to the grass and rolled swiftly by us. Paul was alone; there was no one else in the Luscombe. I turned around and looked at the welding torch. So much for the barnstorming.

"We have lots of airplanes, today," Duke said.

It was an Aeronca Champion, following Paul, and in the cockpit was Johnny Colin. He had brought his own airplane. Johnny taxied right in close to us and shut his engine down. He stepped out of the airplane, unfolding, dwarfing it in his size. He wore his green beret, and he smiled.

"Johnny! Kinda nice to see you."

He picked a box of tools from the back of the Aeronca. "Hi. Paul says he's been workin' on your airplane, keepin' it all bent up for you." He set the tools down and looked at the struts that waited for the torch. "I got to get out pretty early tomorrow, go down to Muscatine, pick up a new airplane. Hi, Stu."

"Hi, Johnny."

"So what's wrong here? This wheel?" He looked down at a broken heavy-steel fitting, and the other work waiting. "That won't be much."

He slipped on a set of black goggles at once and popped his welding torch into life. The sound of that pop was a sound of sheer confidence, and I relaxed. All day long, till that second, I had been carrying myself tense, and now I relaxed. Praise God for such a thing as a friend.

Johnny finished the brake arm in three minutes, touching it with the long welding rod and the razor flame. Then he kneeled by the heavy wheel fitting and in fifteen minutes it was strong again, ready to hold the weight of the airplane. He set Paul to sawing the strut reinforcing pieces to size, while Stu walked through the dusk for food.

One strut was finished by the time Stu came back with hamburgers, hot chocolate and a half gallon of milk. We all ate quickly, in the shadows of the trouble light.

Then the torch popped into life again, hissing, the black goggles went down and the second strut was underway.

"You know what he said when I got to his house?" Paul said quietly. "It was right after work, he had just come in, his wife had dinner on the stove. He grabbed that box of tools and he said, 'I'll be back in the morning, I got a broke airplane to fix.' How's that, huh?"

Glowing white, the strut was laid aside, finished, in the dark. Two more jobs to go, and the most difficult of all. Here the torn metal was within inches of the fabric of the airplane, and the fabric, painted heavily with butyrate dope, would burn like warm dynamite.

"Why don't you get some rags, and a bucket of water," Johnny said. "Build us a dam around here. We're workin' pretty close."

The dam was built of dripping rags, and I held it in place while the torch did its job. Squinting my eyes, I watched the brilliant heat touch the metal, turning it all into a bright molten pool, fusing it back together along what had been the break. The water sputtered on the rag dam, and I was tense again.

After a long time, one hard job had been done, and the last one was the worst. It was a heavy bolt carry-through, surrounded by doped fabric and oily wood. Ten inches above the six thousand degrees of the welding torch, cradled in old dry wood, was the fuel tank. It held 41 gallons of aviation gasoline, just enough to blow the whole airplane about a thousand feet high.

Johnny put out the torch and looked at the situation for a long time, under the light.

"We better be careful on this one," he said. "We'll need the dam again, lots of water, and if you see a fire starting, yell, and throw some water on it."

Johnny and I settled down underneath the airplane, between the big wheels. All the work and fire would be overhead, as we crouched on the grass.

"Stu," I said, "why don't you get up in the front cockpit there, and watch for anything like a fire, under the gas tank. Take Stan's fire bottle. If you see something, don't be afraid to sing out, and shoot it with the bottle. If it looks like the whole thing is gonna go up, just yell and get the heck out of there. We can lose the airplane, but let's not us get hurt."

It was nearly midnight when Johnny popped the torch on again and brought it overhead, near my dripping dam. The steel was thick, and the work was slow. I worried about the heat going through the metal and firing the fabric beyond the dam.

"Paul, kind of watch over it all, will you, for any smoke or fires?"

The torch, close up, had a tremendous roar, and it sprayed flame like a rocket at launch. Looking straight up, I could see through a narrow slit into the little place beneath the fuel tank. If there was a fire there, we'd be in trouble. And it was hard to see, in the glare and the sound of the torch.

Every once in a while the flame popped back, a rifle shot, spraying white sparks over us all. The torchfire was buried in smoke where it touched the airplane. It was our own private hell, there under the belly of the biplane.

There was a sudden crackling over my head and I heard Stu say something, faintly.

"PAUL!" I shouted. "WHAT'S STU SAYING? GET WHAT HE'S SAYING!"

There was a flicker of fire overhead. "HOLD IT, JOHNNY! FIRE!" I slammed a dripping rag hard up into the narrow crack overhead. It hissed, in a rolling cloud of steam.

"STU! DARN IT! SPEAK UP! YOU GOT A FIRE UP THERE?"

"OK, now," came the faint voice.

The distance, I thought. The roar of the torch. I can't hear him. Don't be hard on him. But I had no patience with that. We'd all be blown to bits if he didn't make us hear him when there was a fire.

"LISTEN TO 'IM, WILL YA, PAUL? I CAN'T HEAR A WORD HE SAYS!"

Johnny came back in with the torch, and the crackling began overhead, and the smoke.

"That's just grease cookin' off there," he said, next to me.

We lived through three fires in our little hell, and stopped every one of them short of the fuel tank. None of us were sorry, at 2 A.M., when the torch snapped out for the last time and the gear was finished, glowing in the dark.

"That ought to do it," Johnny said. "You want me to stick around and help you put it back together?"

"No. No problem, here on out. You saved us, John. Let's get some sleep, OK? Man, I don't want to live through that again."

Johnny wasn't noticeably tired, but I felt like an empty balloon.

At five-thirty Johnny and I got up and walked out to his dew-covered Aeronca. He fired the engine coldly awake and put his tools in the backseat.

"Johnny, thanks," I said.

"Yeah. Nothin'. Glad I could help. Now take it easy, please, with that airplane?" He rubbed a clear space in the dew beads on his windshield, then climbed aboard.

I didn't know what else to say. Without him, the dream would have been twice vanished. "Hope we fly together again soon."

"We'll do it, sometime." He pushed the throttle forward and taxied out into the dim morning. A moment later he was a dwindling speck on the horizon west, our problem was solved, and The Great American Flying Circus was alive again.

CHAPTER NINE

By FIVE O'CLOCK in the afternoon, two days after her second crash of the season, the biplane was a flying machine right out of an old barnstormer's scrapbook: silver patches on her fabric, welded plates on her cabane struts, scorched places and painted-over places.

We went around all the attach points, checking that safety wires and cotter keys were in place, double-checking jam nuts tight, and then I was back again in the familiar cockpit, the engine ticking over, warming from the quick fires in the cylinders. This would be a test flight for the rigging and for the landing gear welds—if the wheels collapsed on the takeoff roll, or if the wings fell off in flight, we had failed.

I pushed the throttle forward, we rolled, we hopped up into the air. The gear was good, the rigging was good. She flew like a beautiful airplane.

"YA-HOO!" I shouted into the high wind, where no one could hear. "GREAT! LOVE YA, YA OL' BEAST!" The beast roared back, happy.

We climbed on up to 2,000 feet over the lake and flew some aerobatics. If the wings wouldn't fall off with the airplane pulling high G and flying upside down, they never would. That first loop required a bit of courage, and I double-checked my parachute buckles. The wind sang in the wires like always, and up and over we went, as gently as possible the first time, looking up at the ground over our head, and

336

smoothly back. Then a tighter loop, watching for the wires to start beating in the wind, or struts to bend, or fabric to tear away. She was the same old airplane she had always been. The tightest loop I could put on her, the quickest snap roll, she didn't make a single cry.

We dived back down to the ground, and bounced the wheels hard on the grass during a high-speed run. This was not easy to do, but I had to make it harder on the wheels now than it would ever be with passengers aboard.

She passed her tests, and the last thing left was to see if the rewelding of the gear made any difference in her ground-handling. A tiny misalignment of the wheels could mean an airplane harder than ever to control.

We sailed down final approach, crossed the fence, and clunked down on the grass. I waited with glove ready on the throttle, boots ready on the rudder pedals. She made a little swerve, but responded at once to the touch of throttle. She seemed the faintest bit more skittish on the ground than she had been. We taxied back to Stan's hangar, triumphant, and the propeller windmilled down into silence.

"How is she?" Paul said, the second the engine stopped.

"GREAT! Maybe just a shade on the dicey side, landing, but otherwise, just great." I jumped down from the cockpit and said what I knew I had to say, because some things are more important than airplanes. "You ready to give her another try, Paul?"

"Do you mean that?"

"I wouldn't say it if I didn't mean it. If she's bent again, we'll fix her again. You ready to go?"

He thought for a long moment. "I don't think so. We wouldn't be getting much barnstorming done, if I hurt her again. And we're supposed to be out here to barnstorm, not to fix airplanes."

It was still light, in the afternoon of a Saturday.

"Remember how you said if it was right for us to be here Sunday, nothing could keep us away?" Paul said. "Looks like it was right for us to be here Sunday, unless you want to bug out tonight."

"Nope," I replied. "Sunday here is fine. The only way I could have been forced to be here was just the way it happened. So I figure that something interesting is waiting for us tomorrow."

* * *

Sunday morning was the Annual Palmyra Flight Breakfast, and the first airplanes began arriving at 7 A.M. By seven-thirty we had carried our first passengers, by nine we had both airplanes flying constantly and a crowd of fifty people waiting to fly. A helicopter was carrying passengers at the other side of the field. Our crowd was twice as large as his, and we were proud.

The air cluttered up with little airplanes of every modern kind, coming for the giant breakfast that was a tradition at the airport. The biplane and the Luscombe surged in and out of the traffic pattern, passing each other, working hard, snarling at the other airplanes, which were in no hurry to get back on the ground again.

We had learned that it is not wise to fly a landing pattern so far from the field that we could not glide to the runway if the engine stopped, but at Palmyra we were alone in our learning. There were long lines of aircraft all over the sky, and if all the engines stopped at once, there would be airplanes down everywhere except on the airport.

We flew constantly, drinking an occasional Pepsi-Cola in the cockpit while Stu strapped in more riders. We were making money by the basket, and we were working hard for it. Around and around and around. Palmyrans were out in force; most of our passengers were women and most of them were flying for the first time.

I watched the high wind of flight buffet and blow forward over graceful sculptured faces and was astonished again that there could be so many attractive women in one small town.

The flights fell into a solid pattern, not only in the air, but in our thought.

Buckle the belt down tight on them, Stu, and don't forget to tell them to hold their sunglasses when they look over the side. Taxi out here, careful of other airplanes, recheck the final-approach path for anyone else coming in. Swing onto the grass runway, stay sharp on the rudder here and see if you can lift off right in front of our crowd, so they can see the bright crosses on the wheels spin around, after the biplane is in the air. If we lose the engine now, we can still land on the runway. Now, and we shoot for the meadow beyond. Up over the farm, a little turn so they can look down on the cows and the tractor, if we lose the engine now there's a fine little field across the road. Level at eight hundred feet, swing out to circle Blue Spring Lake. We sure are making a lot of money today. I have lost track of the passengers . . . at least $200 today, for sure. But you really work for it. Watch for other airplanes, keep looking around, lose the engine now and we land right across from the lake; nice flat place there to come down. Turn now so the folks can see the sailboats out in the breeze, and motorboats and skiers pulling white trails across the lake. A place to land over there on the left, one more circle here, throw that in for free to give them one last long look at the blueness of that lake, then down across the green meadow into the landing pattern and over town look out now there are all kinds of airplanes around. Fall into place behind the Cessna . . . poor guy doesn't know what he's missing not having an open-cockpit airplane to fly; has to drive around in that milk stool. Of course he can get places twice as fast as we can and that's what he wants, so fine, I guess. Wish he would keep his pattern closer, though, someday his engine will stop in the pattern and he's gonna feel pretty dumb, not able to glide to the runway. There he's in, turn here, slip off some altitude, look at the wind again, crosswind, but no problem. Aim for the right side of the runway and plan to cut in toward the center so we'll be slow enough by our crowd and ready to pick up more passengers boy the old barnstormers worked for their keep, forget it, it's time to land now and every landing's different remember stay sharp and awake you sure would look dumb groundlooping in front of a crowd like this, even if you didn't hurt the airplane. Wheels are stronger than ever, good ol' Johnny can really weld, that guy, and a better friend you aren't gonna find anywhere. Ease her down, now, across the fence, those cars better look out for airplanes, driving by there, and we're down and this is the hardest part of the whole thing keep her straight, straight, wait on the throttle, on the rudder they're glad they're down but they liked the ride, too. Slow and swing around in toward Stu let 'em out careful boy and keep them from stepping on the fabric and two more ready to fly, the brave people overcoming their fears and trusting me just because they want to see what it looks like from the air. A mother and her daughter this time, they don't know it yet, but they're going to like flying, too. Buckle the belt down tight on them, Stu, and don't forget to tell them to hold their sunglasses when they look over the side . . .

Over and over and over again.

But once, the pattern changed, and while Stu was loading passengers, an angry man came to stand beside my cockpit. "I know you're a hot pilot and all that," he said venomously, "but you might be careful in the landing pattern for a change. I was coming down final in the twin there, the Apache, and you cut me right out, you turned right in front of me!"

My first thought was to say how sorry I was to do such a thing, but then his attitude struck me. Would I act like that to a fellow pilot on a crowded day? For some distant reason I remembered a pilot named Ed Fitzgerald, back with the 141st Tactical Fighter Squadron, USAF. Fitz was one of the finest pilots I knew, and a staunch friend, but he was the fiercest man in the Air Force. He always frowned, and we said that he was spring-loaded to the *explode* position. If a man made the mistake of crossing Fitz in any tiny way, he had to be ready for hand-to-hand combat with a wild leopard. Even if he was wrong, Ed Fitzgerald wouldn't wait a second to slap down a stranger that dared antagonize him.

So I thought of Fitz then, and smiled within myself. I stood up in the cockpit, which made me a yard taller than this Apache pilot, and frowned down at him, furiously, as Fitz would have done.

"Look here, buddy," I said. "I don't know who you are, but you're flying the pattern in a way's gonna kill somebody. You drag all over the country and then turn toward the airport and expect everybody to get out of your way 'cause you got two engines on your crummy airplane. Look, buddy, you fly like that and I'll cut you out of the pattern every time; you go up there now and I'll cut you out again, you hear me? When you learn to fly an airplane and fly the pattern, then you come back and talk to me, huh?"

Stu had finished strapping the passengers in and I pushed the throttle forward, to press the man off balance with the propeller blast. He stood back, mad, and I pulled my goggles down and taxied off in a windstorm impossible to answer. I laughed all the way out to take-off. Good ol' Fitz, come back to help me.

By three o'clock the field was just as empty and quiet as it had been all the rest of the year. There was not another airplane in sight, save the Luscombe and the biplane. We walked across the cornfield to lunch, and collapsed at our table.

"Three hamburgers and three Barnstormer Specials, Millie." Another aspect of security. You not only know the waitress, you have your own table and add things to the menu. Our table was for three, against the side wall, and the Barnstormer Special was strawberry sherbet with Seven-Up, whipped on the malt machine. Stu had even written it down, and it might still be there on a menu in Palmyra.

After a long time, Paul spoke, rubbing his eyes. "What a day."

"Mm," I agreed, unwilling to make the effort to open my mouth.

"What's with Duke?" Stu said, after a moment, and when it was clear that nobody was going to do much talking, he went on. "She was out there all day watching you guys fly, but she never bought a ticket. Says she's scared."

"That's her problem," I said.

"Anyway, we are invited over with her and some of her friends for dinner tonight. Right across from the lake. Do we want to go?"

"Sure we want to go," Paul said.

"Said they'd be back at five, pick us up."

A silence again, which I finally broke. "Does it work? Can a barn-stormer survive?"

"If your bird could survive that groundloop and get flying again two days later," Paul said, "disaster has been ruled out. And I don't know how much money we made, but we made a pile of money. If a guy sat down and scheduled himself so he could make all the fly-in breakfasts, and all the county fairs and all the homecomings at little towns, he could buy out Rockefeller in about a week and a half."

"Long as you keep the airplanes flying, carrying passengers, you're in business," Stu said. He paused a moment. "Duke said today when I was selling tickets that they had a pool going in town, said the biplane would never fly again, after the crash."

"She was serious?" I asked.

"Seemed to be."

"Shows to go ya. You see how the helicopter finally gave up. The old Great American was really rackin' 'em up, and I guess he finally just couldn't stand the competition."

It was silent for a while, then Paul spoke again. "You know, that girl flew with me three times."

"What girl was that?"

"I don't know. She never said a word, she never smiled, even. But she rode three times. Nine bucks. Where does a girl get nine bucks to throw away on airplane rides?"

"Throw away?" I said. "Throw away? Man, the girl's *flyin'*! Nine bucks is *nothin'*!"

"Yeah. But you don't find too many like that, who think that way. And hey, you know what? Two autographs today. I signed two autographs!"

"Nice," I said. "Knocked me over, too. I had one little fella came up and wanted me to sign his book. How about that, Stu? You are no longer the Star."

"Poor Stu," Paul said loftily. "Did you sign any autographs today . . . Star?"

Stu answered softly. "Twelve," he said, and looked away.

By five o'clock we had the airplanes covered for the evening. We could have carried more passengers, but we were not in the mood for it, and closed our airplane-ride stand.

Duke and her friends arrived and drove us out to a house just across from Palmyra's other lake. There was time for a swim, but Paul chose to stay on shore; the water was looking cold.

"Borrow your comb, Stu?" I said after an hour in the lake, when we were back at the house.

"Sure." He handed me a fractured stick of plastic that had five teeth on one end, a long space, a brief forest of eighteen teeth, and all the rest empty.

"Jumper's comb, I guess," Stu apologized. "A few hard landings kinda wiped it out."

The comb was not too effective.

We returned to the gathering, a crowd of people in the living room, and munched on sandwiches and potato chips. They were quizzing Paul on what we were up to, barnstorming.

There was a certain wistfulness in the room, as though we had something that these people wanted, that they might have had a distant wish to say good-bye to everything in Palmyra and fly away into the sunset with The Great American Flying Circus. I saw it most of all in the girl Duke. And I thought: If they want to do something like this, why do they wait? Why don't they just do it, and be happy?

Paul, talking with hard logic, had brought Duke around to the idea of a flight in the Luscombe.

"But it's got to be at night," she said.

"Why at night? You can't see nearly so . . ."

"That's just it. I don't want to see. I get this urge to jump. Maybe I won't get it at night."

Paul stood up. "Let's go."

They went. It was solid black outside; an engine failure on takeoff would give him a busy few moments. We listened, and some time later we heard the Luscombe taking off, and then saw its navigation lights moving among the stars. They stayed over town and circled higher. Good for Paul. He wouldn't be caught out of gliding distance to the field.

We talked for a while longer, back in the house, about what a strange girl Duke was; how long she had been afraid to go up in an airplane, and how there she was up there in the middle of the night where no one else would think of flying, first time.

Stu took his licks for not being very talkative, and I found an old ornamental guitar and began tuning it. The E string broke at once, and I was sorry I ever saw the thing. A piece of fishline as an emergency string tuned way too high.

After a while the fliers came back.

"It's beautiful," Duke told us all. "The lights and the stars. But after five minutes I said, 'Take me down, take me down!' I could feel myself wanting to jump."

"She couldn't have jumped out of that airplane if she tried," Paul said. "She couldn't even open the door."

Duke talked for a bit about what it felt like, but in cautious, withdrawn words. I wondered what she really thought.

In an hour we thanked our hosts, bid them good-bye, and walked through the night back to the airstrip.

"I would have been in trouble if the engine quit on takeoff." Paul said. "I knew the meadow was out there, but I sure couldn't see it. Man, I was on instruments as soon as we broke ground . . . it was BLACK! I couldn't even tell where the horizon was. That spooky feeling, you know, whether the stars are the town or the town is stars."

"Least you stayed in gliding distance, once you got up," I said.

"Oh, once we were up it was no problem at all. Just that one little time right at liftoff."

We tramped into the office, and snapped on the light.

"What a day."

"Hey, treasurer, how much money did we make today?"

"I don't know," said Stu, and he smiled. "We'll count it up tomorrow, boys." Stu was older now than when he'd joined the circus. He knew us, was the difference, I thought, and I wished we could say the same of him.

"The devil we count it up tomorrow," I said. "Tomorrow we wake up and find our treasurer is on his way to Acapulco."

"Count 'er out, Stu," Paul said.

Stu began emptying his pockets onto the couch from the biggest day's work we'd had all summer. There were great crushed wads of money in all pockets, and his wallet was stuffed with bills. The final pile on the couch was wrinkled and impressive.

Stu counted it into $50 piles, while we watched. There were seven piles and some bills left over; $373. "Not bad, for a day's flyin'," I said.

"Just a minute," Paul said, calculating. "That can't be right. It is three dollars a ride, so how can we come out with a number like three hundred and seventy-three?"

Stu patted his pockets. "Ah, here's a whole wad I missed," he said, and to a chorus of suspicious mutterings, he counted another seventeen dollars onto the last pile. "Don't know how that could have happened."

"There's our warning, Paul," I said. "We gots to be careful of the treasurer."

There was $390 laid out now, a mirror of 130 passengers, most of whom had never flown before in their lives. You can destroy that pile of bills, I thought, or spend it right up, but you can never destroy the flights that those 130 people had today. The money is just a symbol of their wish to fly, to see far out over the land. And for a moment I, oily barnstormer, felt as if I might have done something worthwhile in the world.

"What about gas and oil? What do we owe on that?"

I checked the tally sheet on the desk and added the figures.

"Comes out to $42.78. We used 129.4 gallons of gas and twelve quarts of oil. We should pay Stan for the stuff of his, too, that we used. Acetylene and oxygen and welding rod and stuff. What do you think? Twenty bucks sound right?" They agreed it did.

Stu was figuring how to split the money four ways, keeping one pile for Johnny Colin. "OK. That makes $81.80 apiece with two cents left over. Anybody want to check my figures?" We all did, and he was right. We put the odd two cents on Johnny's pile, for mailing the next day.

"You know," I said, when we were all rolled up for the night, "maybe it's a good thing we didn't wind up with ten airplanes, or whatever, on this show. The only time we could keep ten airplanes busy flying passengers is a day like this. We'd have starved, ten of us; we couldn't even pay our gas."

"You're right," Paul said. "Two airplanes be about it, maybe three, unless you want to get all organized and follow the county fairs and fly-in breakfasts."

"Can you imagine us organized?" I said. "*Today, men, we will all fly one eight zero degrees for eighty-eight miles to Richland, where we will all carry passengers from noon to two-thirty. Then we will proceed west for forty-two miles, where we will fly passengers from four o'clock to six-fifteen . . .*' Bad news. Glad it's just us."

"You probably say we're being 'guided,' that the other airplanes just couldn't make it?" Paul said. "And that all these crashes don't stop us?"

"You better believe it, we're being guided," I said. I was growing more confident of this, in the light of our miracles. Yet while Midwest America appeared both beautiful and kind, I still wondered what sudden adventures might next be guided across the path of The Great American Flying Circus. I wasn't quite so eager for adventure, and hoped for a time of calm.

I forgot that calm, for a gypsy pilot, is disaster.

CHAPTER TEN

WE SENT JOHNNY'S money off to him the next morning, all cash in a bulky envelope, and a note saying thanks.

Over a late breakfast at the D&M, Paul looked at the list of clients he had promised to photograph.

"I have a company down in Chicago, on the outskirts there. I really should go down and shoot that. Then there's one in Ohio, and Indiana . . . are we going to get to Indiana?"

"You're leader today," I said.

"No, come on. You think we'll ever hit Indiana?"

"Got me. Depends on how the wind is blowing, you know."

"Thanks. I do have to get this Chicago guy, then as long as I'm there I might as well hop over to Indiana. I could join up with you guys again later on, wherever you are."

"OK. I'll leave word with Bette, tell her where we are. You call her, fly in and meet us when you can." I was sorry to have Paul think more of his shooting than of barnstorming, but he was free to do whatever he wanted to do.

We said good-bye to Millie, leaving monster tips on the table, and walked back to the planes. We took off together, stayed in formation up to eight hundred feet, and then Paul waved and banked sharply away toward the distance of Lake Michigan and the 1960's.

We were alone. The Great American Flying Circus was now one

biplane and one pilot and one parachute jumper; destination, as always, unknown.

The land below went flat. It began to look like Illinois, and after an hour's flying we saw a river in the distance. There was no other airplane in the sky, and on the ground everyone was working at some kind of reasonable, respectable job. It was a lonely feeling.

We followed the river south and west, the biplane trailing a little stream of roiled air behind it, above the stream of water.

There were few places to land. The fields close to the towns were hemmed in by telephone wires or planted in corn and beans. We flew for several hours in random directions, staying close to the water, and at last, just as I was about to give up in disgust, we found a field at Erie, Illinois. It was short, it had trees across one end, it was half a mile from town. All of these things were bad, but down on the field the hay was being raked and baled and a wide strip had been left clear. We whistled down over a cornfield and landed in the adjoining hay, rolling to a stop not far from where a farmer was working over a huge rotary rake. He was having some trouble with it, and I shut down the engine.

"Hi, there," I said.

"Howdy."

Stu and I walked to the rake. "Can we help you out at all?"

"Maybe. I'm tryin' to get this thing hooked up to the tractor, but it's too heavy."

"Can't be. We can lift that little thing up there." Stu and I lifted the tongue of the rake, which was solid steel, set it in the tractor hitch, and dropped the locking pin down through.

"Thank you kindly, boys," the farmer said. He wore a denim jacket over his coveralls, a railroad engineer's cap and a manner of unruffled calm at an airplane dropping down into his field.

"You've got a nice hayfield here," I said. "Mind if we fly out of here a bit, carry some passengers?"

"Just one time?"

"Lots of times, we hope."

"Well . . ." He was not sold on the idea, but at last he said it would be all right.

I unloaded the airplane for some trial flights, to see how much clearance we'd have, over the trees. It didn't feel good. We cleared the top branches with much less margin than I had hoped for, and with the weight of passengers aboard, it would not be comfortable. But there was no other field in sight, all the way around town. Everything was corn.

It was no use trying. Our field was just not good enough and we had to move on. By now the sun was low, and so was our fuel. We chose to stay overnight and move out early in the morning. The plan was firmed when the farmer stopped by just at dusk.

"Just as soon you not fly much out of here, boys. Your motor exhaust might hurt m'hay."

"OK. Mind if we stay the night, here?"

"Go right ahead. Just don't want that exhaust to get to the hay, is all."

"Thank y', sir." We began to walk into town for our hamburgers, keeping to the right of the road, scuffing through the weeds.

"What about his tractor?" Stu said. "Doesn't his tractor have an exhaust?"

"Yeah, but it doesn't make any difference. He wants us out of here, we get out. No questions. It's his land."

At sundown we went back to the plane and the sleeping bags. There were 10 billion river mosquitoes waiting for us. They cruised, humming gently, at low power, and all of them were quite eager to meet us.

Stu, not quite so silent since Paul had left, had suggestions. "We could put out a quart of blood for them, on the wing," he said. "Or tether a couple hundred frogs around here. Or we could start the engine and fan them away . . ."

"You're very creative, my lad, but all that's needed is that we come to an understanding with the mosquitoes. They have their place to live in the world, you see, and we have ours . . ."

"We could go back into town and get some repellent stuff . . ."

". . . and as soon as we understand that they don't have to conflict with our peace, why, they'll just . . . go."

At ten o'clock we were walking to town. Every seven minutes, as we walked, a shiny new automobile, without muffler, came blazing out from town at something over seventy miles an hour, stopped, turned around and went blazing back in. "What the devil are these nuts doing?" I said, mystified.

"Dragging Main."

"What?"

"It's called Dragging Main," Stu explained. "In little towns, the kids have nothing to do, so they just go back and forth, back and forth, in their cars, all night long." He had no comment whether he thought it good or evil. He just told me it was.

"This is entertainment? This is what they do for fun?"

"Yeah."

"Wow."

Another car went shrieking by. No. It was the same car that we had seen seven minutes ago.

Good grief, I thought. Would we have had an Abraham Lincoln, a Thomas Edison, a Walt Disney, if everyone spent their nonschool hours Dragging Main? I watched the split-second faces at the wheel, and saw that the young men passing by were not so much driving as being driven, by sheer and desperate boredom.

"I eagerly await the contributions these guys are gonna make to the world."

It was a warm night. Stu knocked on a market door just as it was closing, explained about the mosquitoes, and paid fifty cents for a bottle of promises to keep them away. I bought a pint of orange sherbet, and we walked back to the airplane.

"You want some of this stuff?" Stu asked.

"Nope. All you need is an understanding . . ."

"Darn. I was going to sell you a squirt of it for fifty cents."

Neither one of us reached a peace with the little creatures.

At five-thirty in the morning we were airborne, ghosting southeast over calm rivermist, toward a black mark on a road map that was supposed to be an airport. We had one hour's fuel on board, and the flight would take thirty minutes.

The air was still as the sun, pushing light up over the cool horizon, and we were the only moving thing in a thousand miles of sky. I could see how an old barnstormer might remember his days in gladness.

We flew on through a difficult week, surprised at how few were the Illinois towns that could be good homes for gypsy pilots. Our Palmyran profits were gone.

We landed in desperation once, at a grass airport near Sandwich. It was a soft green runway, many thousand feet long, and fairly close to town. We were tired from so much nonprofit flying, and even though it wasn't a hayfield, we thought this would be a good place to spend the evening.

The airport office had just been remodeled, was paneled in deep-stained satin wood, and I began to wonder if we belonged here from the first moment that I saw the owner, by the window. He had watched this grease-spattered biplane land, he had worried about its oil dripping on his grass, and now its filthy occupants were going to *step inside his new office!*

He tried to be polite, that much can be set down for him. But he welcomed The Great American Flying Circus about as warmly as he would have welcomed the Loch Ness monster to his doorstep.

I told him brightly what we were doing, how we had never carried a dissatisfied passenger, how we could bring many new customers to his field and increase his own passenger-flying business.

"I'm a little on the conservative side," he said when I was through. And then, cagily, "You do your own maintenance?"

To do one's maintenance, without a license, is illegal, and he waited like a vulture for our answer, thinking of the price on our heads. He was disappointed, almost, to hear that the biplane was properly signed and provided for. Then he brightened. "I'm having the opening of the new building next month. I could use you then . . ."

Being used did not sound like much fun. Stu and I looked at each other and moved to leave. At that instant, as in a motion-picture script, a customer walked in the door.

"I want to have an airplane ride," he said.

The owner began a long apologetic explanation about how his flying license was not up-to-date and it wouldn't be worth it to call out a pilot from town to give just one ride and his airplanes were all down for maintenance anyway. We didn't say a word. We just stood there, and so did the customer. He wanted a ride.

"Of course these fellows could ride you. But I don't know anything about them . . ."

Ah, I thought, the fraternity of the air.

The customer was almost as frightened of the biplane as the airport manager had been, although in a more straightforward way. "I don't want any dadoes, now, no flip-flops. Just take it kind of easy, around town and back down again."

"Gentle as a cloud, sir," I said, with a flourish. "STU, LET'S GET THIS THING FIRED UP!"

The flight was gentle as a cloud, and the man even said that he liked it. A few seconds after we landed, he was gone, leaving me puzzled over why he wanted to go up in the first place.

We were airborne again in fifteen minutes, glad to leave Sandwich and its gleaming new office behind. Droning on north again, aimless, looking down, some of the old doubts about surviving came back to mind.

We landed at last at Antioch, a resort town a few miles south of the Wisconsin border. The grass field lay on the edge of a lake and we found that the owner sold rides on weekends in his Waco biplane. He charged $5 the ride, and he was not interested in any competition, anytime, and he would be happiest if we would leave. But before we could go, a modern Piper Cherokee landed and taxied to our side. A businesslike fellow in white shirt and tie walked purposefully toward us and smiled in the way of a man whose job forces him to meet many people.

"I'm Dan Smith," he said over the engine noise, "Illinois Aeronautics Commission."

I nodded, and wondered why he had made such a big thing of his title. Then I saw that he was looking for an Illinois State Registration tag on the biplane. He hadn't found one. The tag is a mandatory thing in that state. It costs a dollar or so, which apparently pays the field worker's salary.

"Where are you from?" he asked.

From anyone else, a normal, harmless question. From this man, it was sinister. If I'm from Illinois, I'm fined on the spot.

"Iowa," I said.

"Oh."

Without another word, he walked to the hangar across the way and disappeared within it, checking for hidden airplanes, without registration tags.

What a way to make a living, I thought.

Airborne again, we were getting desperate. In all this lake country, we could find no place to land near a lake. Simple criteria, we had: near town, near lake. But there was no such thing. We circled for more than an hour over a score of lakes, and found nothing. Thirst had a sharp edge, there in the high hot cockpits, and we flew north again, looking for any place to land.

We crossed Lake Geneva and looked down thirstily at all that water. Water-skiers, sailboats, swimmers . . . drinking as much of the lake as they wanted.

The first airstrip we saw, we landed. It was the wrong place. *Lake Lawn,* a bright sign said. The grass was immaculately trimmed, and we discovered that this was the private airstrip of the Lake Lawn Country Club.

Parking the greasy biplane out of sight, we snuck out of the cockpits and walked down the road toward the club after the manner of working gardeners. The guards at the gate caught us, but had compassion and showed us the way to water.

"I'm beginning to doubt your method of finding fields," Stu said.

Then we were up again, grimly heading south in the third giant circle of the week. There is no such thing as chance, I thought, gritting my teeth, there is no such thing as luck. We were being led where it is best for us to go. There is a good place waiting, this minute. Just ahead.

A long open summer field slanted beneath us, far from any town, but a fine place for airplanes to land.

I thought about landing there and giving rides to the cows grazing about. For a half-second I was serious, wondering if it could work. It always came back to this. We had to prove it all over again, every day . . . we had to find human, paying passengers.

CHAPTER ELEVEN

THE TOWN OF Walworth, Wisconsin, is a fine and friendly place. It showed that friendliness by spreading before us a smooth soft hayfield, all mowed and raked. The field was three blocks from the center of town, it was long and wide, and the approaches were good save for one set of low telephone wires. We landed, on our last reserves of money and morale.

The owner of the field was kind, mildly amused at the old airplane and the strange people who came down from it. "Sure you can fly out of the field, and thanks for the offer of a ride. Take you up on it." Hope stirred. Somebody had said we were welcome!

The signs were out in a flash, and we flew two free rides for the owner and his family. By sundown, we had flown three paying rides, as well. That evening, the treasurer informed me that on this day we had paid $30 for gasoline, but that we had taken in $12 from passengers. Clearly, our fortunes were changing.

Gazing back at me in the morning from the gas station mirror was a horrible image, a scraggly rough-bearded Mr. Hyde so terrible that I drew back in alarm. Was that me? Was that what the farmers had seen whenever we landed? I would have run this monster off with a pitchfork! But the bearded image disappeared at last to my electric shaver, and I felt almost human when I walked again into the sunshine.

We had to make money at Walworth, or quit. We reviewed the ways we had to bring customers: Method A, flying aerobatics at the edge of town. Method B, the parachute jump. Then we began experimenting with Method C. There is a principle that says if you lay out a lonely solitaire game in the center of the wilderness, someone will soon come along to look over your shoulder and tell you how to play your cards. This was the principle of Method C. We unrolled our sleeping bags and stretched out under the wing, completely uncaring.

It worked at once.

"Hi, there."

I lifted my head at the voice and looked out from beneath the wing. "Hi."

"You fly this airplane?"

"Sure do." I got to my feet. "You lookin' to fly?" For a fleeting moment, the man looked familiar, and he looked at me with the air of one who was trying to remember. "It's a nice flight," I said. "Walworth's a pretty little town, from the air. Three dollars American, is all."

The man read my name from the cockpit rim. "Hey! You're not . . . Dick! Remember me?"

I looked at him again, carefully. I had seen him before, I knew him from . . . "Your name is . . ." I said. What was his name? He rebuilt an airplane. He and . . . Carl Lind had rebuilt an airplane a couple of years ago . . . "Your name is . . . Everett . . . Feltham. The Bird biplane! You and Carl Lind!"

"Yessir! Dick! How the heck you been?"

Everett Feltham was a flight engineer for some giant airline. He had been brought up on Piper Cubs and Aeronca Champs, was an airplane mechanic, pilot, restorer. If it flew through the air, Everett Feltham knew about it; how to fly it and how to keep it flying.

"Ev! What are you doin' here?"

"I live here! This is my hometown! Man, you never can tell what kind of riffraff gonna fall down on you from the sky! How's Bette? The children?"

It was a good reunion. Ev lived only two miles north of the field we had landed in, and our friend Carl Lind kept a country house on Lake Geneva, ten miles east. Carl had flown airplanes in the late twenties, barnstorming around this very countryside. He quit flying when he married and raised his family, and he was now the president of Lind Plastic Products.

"A gypsy pilot," Ev said. "Might have known it was you, doing a crazy thing like this, landing in a hayfield. You know there's an airport just down the road."

"Is there? Well, it's too far out. You got to be close to town. We're a bit in the hole after flyin' around all week for nothin'. We got to get some passengers up in the air this afternoon or we'll be starvin' again."

"I'll call Carl. If he's home, he's gonna want to come out and see you, probably want you over to the house. You need anything? Anything I can bring you?"

"No. Rags, maybe—we're runnin' out of rags. If you got some around."

Ev waved and drove away, and I smiled. "Funny thing about flying, Stu. You can never tell when you're gonna run into some old buddy somewhere. Isn't that somethin'? Go land in a hayfield, and there's ol' Ev." Nothing by chance, nothing by luck, the voice, almost forgotten, reminded.

After suppertime, the passengers started coming. One woman said the last time she had flown was when she was six years old, with a barnstormer in a two-winger airplane, just like this one. "My boss told me you were here and I better not miss it."

A young fellow with a fantastic mop of a haircut stopped and looked at the airplane for a long time before he decided to fly. As Stu fastened him into the front seat he said, "Will I see tomorrow?"

This was pretty strange sentence structure, coming from a fellow who proclaimed himself illiterate. (For shame, I thought, judging the man by his haircut!) In flight, he braced hard against the turns, fearful, and after we landed he said, *Wow!* He stayed for a long time after his ride, looking at the airplane almost in awe. I put him down as a real person, in spite of the haircut. Something about being above the ground had reached through to him.

A pair of pretty young ladies in kerchiefs put our account book in the black for the day, and they laughed happy in the sky, turning over their hometown.

I checked the fuel, and with ten gallons left I was at the end of my margin, and it was time to fill the tank even though passengers had to wait.

I took off at once for the airport that Ev had mentioned, and in five minutes was rolling to a stop by the gas pump. I was just topping the tank when a burly, bright-eyed businessman in a snap-brim straw hat brisked out to the airplane.

"Hey, Dick!"

"CARL LIND!" He was just as I remembered him, one of the happiest people in the world. He had survived a heart attack, and now enjoyed the very air he breathed.

He looked the airplane over with an appraising eye. "Is it good, Carl?" I said. "Is it the way you remember?"

"We didn't have all that flashy gold paint, in my day, I can tell you. But the skid's pretty nice, and the patches in the wings. That's how I remember it."

"Hop in, Carl, get in the front here, if you trust me. You got no controls in front. I'm goin' back over to the field."

"Are you going to let me go along? Are you sure I can go?"

"Get in or you make us late. We got passengers waiting!"

"Never let 'em wait," he said, and stepped up into the front seat. We were airborne in less than a minute and it was good to see the man again in the sky he loved. He took off his hat, his gray hair blew in the wind, and he smiled hugely, remembering.

The biplane gave him a gentle landing in the hay, and I left the engine running while Carl stepped down.

"You go ahead and fly your passengers," he said. "Then we'll cover the airplane up and you come on over to the house."

We flew riders steadily till the sun was below the horizon, and all the time Carl Lind watched the biplane fly, waiting with his wife, and with Ev. It was the best weekday yet; twenty passengers by sundown.

* * *

"I don't know if this is in the Barnstormer's Code," I said to Carl as we drove around the edge of Lake Geneva and wound among the estates there. "We're supposed to get all dirty and always stay under the wing when we're not flying."

"Oh, no. They used to do this. Someone who liked airplanes would take you home for dinner."

But not, I thought as we turned into his drive, in quite this manner. It was a scene clipped from a Fine House magazine, all in full color and with deep carpets and full-length glass facing the water.

"This is our little place . . . ," Carl began, apologetically.

Stu and I laughed at the same time. "Just a little shack you keep out in the woods, Carl?"

"Well . . . you like to have a place you can come and relax, you know?"

We got a brief tour of the elegant house, and it was a strange feeling. We felt close to something civilized. Carl enjoyed his house immensely, and it was a glad place, because of this.

"You fellows can change in here. We'll go down for a swim. You will. I'll catch two fish in the first five casts. Betcha, I will."

It was nearly full dark when we walked barefoot down the velvet sloping lawn to his dock. At one side of the white-painted wood was a boathouse, and an inboard speedboat hung there on winches.

"The battery's probably dead. But if we get it started, we'll go for a ride."

He lowered the boat into the water on its electric winch and pressed the starter. There was only a hollow clank and silence.

"I've got to remember to keep that battery up," he said, and hoisted the boat back into the air.

Carl had brought a little fishing pole with him and he began working for his Two Fish in the First Five Casts just at the moment that Stu and I hit the water in running dives off the dock. The lake was clear dark black, like pure oil that had been aged twenty years in ice. We swam furiously out to the light-float a hundred feet offshore and from there we watched the last sun fade from the sky. As it disappeared, so did every single sound in the Midwest, and a whisper from our float carried easily to shore.

"Carl, you've got a pretty rugged life," I said, from way out in the water.

"Two more years and then I'm going to retire. Quicker than that, if I get all this business done on my flying medical. Why, if I could fly alone, I'd retire this year! But if I can't fly, and just had to stay around here, it would get pretty bad." He caught a fish on his second cast, and let it fall back into the dark water.

We cast off from the buoy and swam slowly to the dock. The wooden ladder-rungs were smooth and soft in moss, and when we stood again on the white planks, the air was warm as summer night.

"I lose my bet," Carl said. "All your splashing scared my fish away. Five casts and only one fish."

By the time we had returned to the house and changed into our least-greasy clothes, Everett had gone and come again, setting a huge steaming bag on the table. "I got twelve hamburgers," he said. "That ought to be enough, don't you think? And a gallon of root beer."

We sat that evening around a table by the fireplace in Carl's glass-walled den, eating hamburgers.

"I had to sell the Bird, you know," Carl said.

"What? Why? That was your *airplane*!"

"Yes, sir. But I couldn't stand it. Going out there and washing her down and waxing her, and not being able to fly by myself; this medical thing, you know. It wasn't right for the airplane, it wasn't right for me. So I sold her. Thelma still has her Cessna, and we go places now and then." He finished his hamburger. "Hey, I have something I want you to see." He left the table and went into the living room.

"I do hope that medical paper comes through," Thelma Lind said. "It means a lot to Carl."

I nodded, thinking it unjust that a man's life be so much affected by what to all the rest of the world was only a scrap of paper. If I were Carl, I'd burn all the paper in the fireplace and go out and fly my airplane.

"Here's something you'll love to see," Carl said, returning.

He unrolled a long photograph on the table and we looked down at a row of ten biplanes parked in front of a hangar. White-ink letters at the lower right corner said *June 9, 1929.*

"These are the boys I used to fly with. Look at those guys. What do you think of that?"

He named each one of the pilots, and they looked out at us proud and unfaded, arms folded, standing by their airplanes. There at one side stood a young Carl Lind, in white collar and tie and knickers, not yet president of Lind Plastic Products, not yet concerned about a medical certificate. He wouldn't be thinking about that for another thirty-five years.

"Look here, huh? Long-Wing Eaglerock, Waco Ten, Canuck, Pheasant . . . now there's some real airplanes, don't you think? We used to go out to the Firemen's Picnic . . ."

It was a good evening, and I was glad that my years had overlapped Carl's. He had been flying and smiling up out of that photograph seven years before I was born.

"Be glad for your friends," Carl said. "We know people, don't we, Thelma, with millions of dollars, but without one friend in the world. Boys, be glad for your friends." He was deadly sincere, and to break the gravity of the moment he smiled at Stu. "You having fun out here in the cow pastures, flying around?"

"I'm having more continuous fun than I've ever had in my life," the kid said, and just about startled me off my chair. He hadn't said such a revealing thing all summer long.

It was midnight when we zipped ourselves into our hot sleeping bags and settled down under the wing of the biplane.

"It's a tough life, isn't it, Stu?"

"Yep. Mansions, chocolate cake, swimming in Lake Geneva . . . this barnstorming is rough!"

A farmer was out by the huge Gothic cow-barn across the way at 6 A.M. He was a tiny dot by the base of the barn, dwarfed by the tremendous double-sloped roof with its four giant ventilators lined along the rooftrees seventy feet in the air. He was a quarter mile away, but his voice came clear across the calm morning hay.

"BIDE BIDE BIDE BIDE BIDE! HURRY IT UP, BOSSY! C'MON C'MON C'MON!"

I woke and lay under the wing in the early light, trying to figure out what *Bide* meant. And *Bossy*. Do farmers still call their cows Bossy? But there was the call again, coming across the fragrance of the hay, making me feel guilty to be lying abed when there were cows to be gotten out.

A dog barked, and day began in America.

I reached for pen and paper, to remind me to ask about *Bide*, and as I wrote, a tiny six-legged creature, smaller than my pen point, came hiking across the blue-lined page. I added, "A very small pointy-nosed bug just walked across this page—purposefully, definitely going somewhere ⌐→. He stopped here."

Were we, also, hiking along some cosmic journal-page? Were the events about us all part of a message we could understand, if only we found the right perspective from which to read them? Somehow, with our long series of miracles, of which this field at Walworth was the latest, I thought so.

Our morning check of the biplane showed that we had come up against our first problem of maintenance. The tail skid was wearing thin. At one time it had a steel roller and metal plate to guard it, but the constant takeoffs and landings had worn those away. If we had to, we could whittle another skid from a tree branch, but this was the time for preventive work. We talked about it on the way in for breakfast, and decided to look around the hardware store.

Close as it was to the resort lands of Lake Geneva, Walworth was becoming a very modern small town, and we found Hardware in the shopping center.

"May I help you?" the clerk said.

"Well, yes," I said, slowly and carefully. "We are looking for a tail skid shoe. Would you have anything in that line?"

How strange it was. If one doesn't stay well within the bounds of what one is expected to say, his words might as well be Swahili.

"Beg pardon?"

"A tail . . . skid . . . shoe. Our tail skid is wearing out."

"I don't think . . . a what?"

"We'll browse around, thanks."

We walked the rows of hardware, looking for a long narrow strip of metal, with holes for screws to mount it on the wooden skid. There were some big hinges that might work, a mason's trowel, a big heavy end wrench.

"Here we go," Stu said, from across the room. He held a tail skid shoe. The label on it said *Vaughn Spring Steel Super Bar.* It was a small flat crowbar that had clearly been made by a tail-skid-shoe company.

"Oh, you mean a pry-bar!" the clerk said. "I wasn't sure what you were looking for."

The room where we had breakfast had been in town somewhat longer than the shopping center. The only thing that had changed since saloon days was they had replaced the batwing doors, turned the furniture into museum pieces, and mounted lifelike detail drawings of *"Hamburger," "Cheeseburger,"* and *"French Fries"* in wide glowing plastic cases over the mirror, and over at least a thousand glasses stacked upside down.

Hanging on the wall was a rough old triangle of oak, notched like a great blunt saw along one edge, and bolted to some other moving sections of wood. *"Wagon Jack"* was printed on a board a few inches beneath it.

"Stu."

"Yeah?"

"The tail of the Parks weighs more than all the rest of the airplane put together. We've got to lift it to put on our new skid shoe."

"We'll lift it."

"Do you figure we could maybe borrow that wagon jack over there, somehow, and use it?"

"That's an antique wagon jack," he said. "They'd never loan it out to pick up an airplane."

"Won't hurt to ask. But how do we make it work?"

We looked at the jack, and it was dead quiet in our booth. There was no possible way that the jack could have lifted anything. We couldn't imagine how it might have picked up any wagon ever built. We sketched all over the backs of napkins and place mats, drawing little wagons and the way that the oaken triangle might have done its work. At last Stu thought he understood, and tried to explain it to me, but it didn't make any sense. We didn't bother to ask about borrowing the wagon jack, and paid our bill mystified by that thing hanging on the wall.

"We could start the engine," I said, "and pick up the tail with the prop blast. Course it might get a little windy while you sit back under the tail and put the thing on. About a hundred miles an hour, the wind."

"While *I* sit back there?"

We'd find some way to do it, I was sure.

Stu's thought wandered from the immediate problem. "How about flour?" he said. "Should I try flour? Take a bag of flour and cut it open just before I jump, and leave a trail coming down?"

"Give it a try."

So The Great American invested in fifty-nine cents' worth of King's Ransom Pre-Sifted Flour. It was five cents cheaper than any other brand, is why we bought it.

The answer to the problem of holding the tail in the air was solved as soon as we returned to the biplane. It was simple.

"Just take a couple of those oil cans, Stu, that we haven't opened yet. I'll pick up the tail good as I can and you set those cans under the rudder post to hold it up. OK?"

"Are you putting me on? That big heavy tail on these cans of OIL? There'll be oil all over the place!"

"A college man, and he says a thing like that. Have you never learned the Incompressibility of Fluids? I shall lecture upon that subject, if you wish. Or if you would rather, Mister MacPherson, you can just get down under the tail and stick those cans under the rudder post."

"OK, professor. Ready when you are."

With agonizing tremendous great effort, I lifted the tail a foot in the air for three full seconds, and Stu set the cans in place. They held, and I was as surprised as he was that they did.

"Now if you would like the mathematical details, Mister MacPherson, we can discuss them at length . . ."

The skid shoe was in place in ten minutes.

We stretched out under the wing to put Method C to the test, and sure enough, two cars stopped at the roadside before we were half-asleep. Our passengers were girls on vacation from college, and they were goggle-eyed at the biplane.

"You mean it *flies*? Up in the *air*?"

"Yes, ma'am. Guaranteed to fly. Look down on all the world. Three dollars a ride and a prettier day we couldn't ask, could we?"

Jouncing out to the far end of the hayfield, and as we turned into the wind to begin the flight, my riders were overcome by second thoughts. They shouted quickly to each other, over the noise of the engine and the rattling of the hollow-drum flying machine. About the time they had decided that they had been out of their *minds* to even *think* of going up in this *old dirty machine*, the throttle came forward, they were engulfed in the great twisting roar of the engine, and we were clatterbanging over the hard ground, hurtling toward the highway and the cars and the telephone wires. They clutched the soft leather rim of the front cockpit and at the moment we left the ground they gasped and looked and held even tighter. Someone screamed. The wires flashed below and we climbed easily up into the sky.

They turned to look back at the ground and at me, quizzically. The realization swept over them that this madman sitting in the cockpit behind them now held the key to their entire future. He looked unshaven. He looked as if he didn't have much money. Could he be trusted?

I smiled in what I hoped was a disarming way, and pointed to the lake. They turned to look at the table-napkin sailboats and the cutglass sparkle of sun on the water, and I went back to picking my forced-landing fields, turning ever so slightly so that we would never be out of gliding range from them.

It was fun to see what a different pilot I became for my different passengers. I had flown a few folk who had left mink jackets in their Cadillac convertibles, and for these few I was a two-dimensional creature, a blank-faced chauffeur, taking this flying all as a very boring job and unaware that the lake from the air was even mildly attractive. A hired man cannot be expected to appreciate the finer things. These people got a straight conventional ride, a ride that they would get from an uninspired workhouse chauffeur. Take off.

Circle town. Circle lakeshore. Circle town. Land. Everything by the book.

The college girls, all windblown ahead of me now, had taken the biplane for something of a gay novelty, and for them I was a gay novelty of a pilot, with a bright disarming smile. For them, I could know that flying can be pretty, I could even point a good place to look. One of the girls looked back at me with a how-pretty-it-is glance, and I smiled again, to say that I understood.

Most of the passengers flew just for the fun and adventure of the flight, and with them I made experiments. I found that I could make most people look where I wanted them to look; it was just a matter of banking the airplane in that direction.

I could test their aptitude for flying, too, by banking. When a person sits up straight in the seat, riding with the airplane through the turns, when he looks fearless down to the ground during a steep bank, when he doesn't bother to grip the cockpit rim, he is a natural-born airplane pilot. About one passenger in sixty met the tests, and I always made it a point to tell them of the fact . . . that if they ever wanted to fly an airplane, they would be very good pilots. Most just shrugged and said it was fun. I felt sad, knowing that I couldn't have passed those tests myself, before I began to fly.

For the girls, now, as I steepened the bank, the biplane was a noisy high carnival ride. At forty degrees of bank, the girl on the right screamed and hid her eyes. When we leveled, she looked out again, and again we would gradually increase the bank. Every time, when we tilted to precisely forty degrees, she would make some kind of cry and bury her face in her hands. At thirty-nine degrees she looked down happy; at forty, she screamed. Her friend looked back at me and shook her head, smiling.

On the last turn before landing, the turn closest to the ground and with the most sense of speed and blurred action, we banked up to seventy degrees and fell like a cannonball toward the ground. The girl on the right didn't uncover her eyes until we were stopped again next to her car.

I shut the engine down while Stu helped them from the cockpit.

"Oh it's *WONDERFUL*! It's just *WONDERFUL*!" she said.

Her companion thanked us quietly, but the other girl couldn't get over how wonderful it was. I shrugged. The wonderfullest parts to me were the parts that she had closed her eyes upon.

They left, waving, and in a few minutes Method C brought Everett Feltham back to us, with a box of rags.

"Hey, you sack rats! Why don't you come on out to the house and eat up some strawberries, huh?"

It took us three minutes to tie the covers on the airplane and find a place in his car. We spent the next hours with Ev, fetching a case of oil for the biplane and sitting in the shade of his elms, consuming great bowls of strawberries and vanilla ice cream.

"Man, this barnstorming is rugged, Ev," I said, leaning back in my lawn chair. "You don't ever want to try it."

"I'll bet. You guys sure look overworked, lyin' down under that wing out there. I wish I had a biplane. Be with you in a flash."

"OK. Get a biplane. Join The Great American. Any other problems?"

Ev had a schedule to fly out of O'Hare International that afternoon, so dropped us off on his way toward Chicago. We said those good-byes that fliers say, a confident sort of "See you 'round," certain that they actually will, as long as they don't make any very dumb mistakes while handling their airplanes.

Stu dragged out his parachute, still field-packed from his last jump, and stretched it out on the ground for final packing. A pair of boys arrived to watch and ask questions about what it feels like to fall all alone through the air, and what the parts of the chute were called and where you learn to jump.

"Gonna jump today?" one said. "Pretty soon, maybe?"

"Not if the wind comes up much more."

"Gee, it isn't windy."

"It is if you're coming down in this thing." He worked on in silence.

An airplane flew up from the south, circled town, then swung down low over our field. It was Paul Hansen in the Luscombe, flashing overhead at 120 miles per hour, pulling up steep into the blue, swinging back down for another pass. We waved to him.

The Luscombe flew across the field three times, measuring it. I put myself in his cockpit, looking down at the hayfield, flying the heavy-laden sportplane. I squinted my eyes and finally shook my head. I wouldn't do it; I wouldn't land. The field was right for the biplane, but the biplane had more than twice the wing area of the Luscombe. The field was too short for Paul's airplane; he could make it, but just barely, with no margin over the telephone wires. If he landed here, I would make a big thing of how unwise he was.

On the fourth pass, he kicked the rudder back and forth to signal "No," and flew out to the airport down the road.

The problems of working with a single-wing airplane, I thought. He needs just too much runway. And this is a good field, right in close to town, that saved us when we were broke, and that has lots of passengers yet to fly.

I pulled the covers off the Parks and made her ready to go. Darn. A good hayfield . . .

When I landed at the airport, Paul was tying down his airplane. He was still wearing his white shirt and tie.

"Halloo," I said. "'D you get your pictures all took?"

"Yeah. Made it in here nonstop from Ohio, that's why I didn't stay any longer over the field there. Just about out of gas. And that field is too short for me." He was apologetic, as if it were his fault that the field wasn't right.

"No prob. Throw your stuff in the front seat and we'll hop on over. If you trust me. No controls up front . . ."

It took a while for the 1960's to fade from Paul, and as he helped Stu finish packing the chute, he told us about the shootings he had done. It was depressing to hear that the other world still existed, out there, with people still running around in business suits and discussing abstracts that had nothing to do with engines or tail skids or good fields to land in.

That evening, even without a parachute jump, the biplane had fifteen passengers to carry, and when she was covered for the night, we were sure again that an unorganized barnstormer could get along in spite of a few lean days.

There was the usual lively conversation over the restaurant table, but all the while, in the back of my mind, I was thinking about the Luscombe unable to work the short fields. If it had been hard to find this place where the biplane could land, it was going to be twice as hard to find a hayfield long enough for both airplanes to work well.

A barnstormer can survive, but is he stacking the cards against himself by working with an airplane that wasn't built for short-field flying? Would the Luscombe be the downfall of The Great American and its dreams? I couldn't get the questions out of my mind.

CHAPTER TWELVE

I CHECKED THE tail skid shoe first thing in the morning. It needed some extra wire to hold it in place and this meant lifting the tail back onto the oil cans.

Paul stood glumly by.

"Think you could give me a hand with lifting the tail?" I said. "Stu, you ready for us to lift?"

"Lift away," said Stu from his oil cans underneath the tail.

Paul apparently hadn't heard me, for he didn't move to help. "Hey, Paul! Why don't you stop sucking that cigarette for a minute and give us a hand here?"

Paul looked at me as though I were some kind of repugnant beetle, and moved to help. "All right, all right I'll help you! Take it easy."

We picked up the tail and set the skid on its oil-can jack. Later, we walked to town for breakfast and Paul trailed behind, saying nothing, the picture of depression. Whatever his problem is, I thought, it is none of my business. If he wants to be depressed, that's his option. It was the quietest, most uncomfortable breakfast we ever had. Stu and I traded comments about the weather and the tail skid and the wagon jack, how it couldn't possibly work, and all the time Paul said not a word, made no sound at all.

We all had separate places to go after breakfast, and for the first time since we began the summer, we did not walk together, but went three separate ways. It was an interesting sort of thing, but puzzling, for the same wave of depression hit us all.

Well, heck, I thought, walking alone back to the airplane, I don't care. If the other guys want to do something else and feel bad, I can't stop 'em. The only guy I can control is me, and I'm out here to barnstorm, not to waste time feeling bad.

I resolved to fly to the airport and change the biplane's oil, and then I was pushing on. If the other guys wanted to come along, that was fine with me.

When I walked onto the hayfield again, Paul was sitting alone on his sleeping bag, writing a note. He said nothing.

"OK, buddy," I said at last. "What you do is none of my business except when it starts to affect me. And it's starting. What is bugging you?"

Paul stopped writing, and folded the paper. "You," he said. "Your attitude has changed. You've been acting different ever since I got back. I'm leaving today. I'm on my way home."

So that was the problem. "You're free to go. You mind telling me just how my attitude has changed? I no longer want to fly with you, is that it, you guess?"

"I don't know. But you're just not there. I might as well be some brand-new guy you never met before. You can treat other people like outsiders, but you can't treat me that way."

I scanned back over everything I had done or said since Paul returned. I had been a trifle stiff and formal, but I had been that way a thousand times since I had known Paul. I am stiff and formal with my airplane when we haven't flown for a few days. It must have been my comment about the cigarette this morning. Even as I had said it, it sounded a bit harsher than it was meant to be.

"OK," I said. "I apologize. I'm sorry for my crack about the cigarette. I keep forgetting you're so darn sensitive . . ."

Heck of an apology, I thought.

"No, it's not that only. It's your whole attitude. It's like you can't wait to get rid of me. So don't worry. I'm getting out. I was writing a note to leave for you, but you came back too quick to finish it."

I stood there. Had I been so wrong for so long? Would this man, whom I considered among the very best friends I had in the world, judge me without listening for my defense, find me guilty and then leave without a word?

"The only thing I can think of . . . ," I started slowly, trying to speak as truly as I could, ". . . is that I wish to goodness you would have been able to land in this field. I was mad at you when you didn't land, because this is such a good field. But I wouldn't land the Lus-combe here myself, and I think you'd be dumb to try it. You did the right thing, but I just wished that the Lusk could be a little better barnstorming airplane, is all." I began to roll my sleeping bag. "If you want to bug out, fine. But if you leave because you think I want to get rid of you, you're wrong, and that's your problem to overcome."

We talked the trouble back and forth, and gradually we were talking like ourselves again, bridging a chasm that had been hidden under ice.

"Are you going to settle down now," Paul said, "and treat your troops like they were human beings?"

"All this time I thought we had forgot about who was the leader," I said, "and you've been thinking I was the honcho. I resign, I tell you, I resign!"

Airborne, flying again as barnstormers in formation, we searched to the north first, without results. The land close to the towns was everywhere too rough and too short for both airplanes. I looked down again at the broad grass strip at Lake Lawn and thought that we could be an interesting diversion for the golfers, and probably make much money. But golfers were urban people, living way out ahead of us in time, concerned about unreal things . . . profit margins and credit ratings and the life of giant cities. We were looking to fly with the people of the world to which our airplanes belonged.

We followed the road west and south, and again crossed down into the heat of summer Illinois. We circled eight or ten little towns, left the road for a river, and finally rolled our wheels in the grass of an airstrip by the river. It was a good long strip. There was plenty of room for the Luscombe to work fully loaded, and we were one mile from a town. A little far out, but worth trying.

The field was surrounded by oats and corn, set low in the wide long valley of the river. There was a farmhouse at the end of the strip, and a small hangar.

Two minutes after we landed, a light twin-engine airplane touched down and taxied near the hangar.

"Sure," the owner said. "You boys can work out of here if you want. Be nice to get some folks out to the airport."

We were working again. Our first acquaintance with Pecatonica, Illinois, was a friendly one.

In long sheds near the farmhouse were a great number of pigs, snarkling and gorkling as we found that pigs are wont to do. A man and his wife came from the house to wonder who we were, shyly followed by a little girl who peeked around her mother's skirts. The girl was stricken silent in awe. She was convinced that we were Martians landing in some strange sort of saucers, and goggled at us, set to dash screaming into the house at the first monster-word we said. Stu walked down the lane to post our signs, and the girl kept an eye on him, lest he creep up behind and devour her in one toothy gnash.

There were two hundred pigs in the shed, we learned, and wandering around somewhere were nine cats and a horse. The horse, at the moment, was kept in a grassy lot, and trotted over to talk with us when we walked near his gate.

"This is Skeeter," the woman said. "Raised him from a colt. Skeeter is a wonderful horse . . . aren't you, Skeeter?" She rubbed his velvet nose.

Skeeter made some comment, a low polite whinny, and nodded his head. He left us then, trotted once around the perimeter of his grass and came back to lift his head sociably over the gate. Skeeter had a very outgoing personality.

"Goin' toward town . . . you boys want a lift?" the owner said. We did, and jumped into the back of a red pickup. As we turned down the lane and onto the highway, it was Paul who asked the question.

"How do you think it's going to go?"

"Looks OK," Stu said.

"Little far out, maybe," I said, "but we'll do all right."

Pecatonica's main street was high-curbed and lined with glass storefronts and wood facades. The center of town was one block long: hardware, cafés, the Wayne Feed Dealer, service station, dime store. We hopped down from the truck at the beginning of the block, called our thanks and walked to a café for lemonade.

It was full hot summer, with the round plastic advertising thermometers pointing ninety-five degrees. We ordered giant lemonades and looked at the ceiling and walls. It was the same long narrow room we had come to expect, with booths down one wall, and the counter and mirror and stacked glasses down the other, kitchen way at the back with a round order-wheel hanging from its pivot in the pass-through window. The ceiling was at least fifteen feet high, tiled in green floral-stamped tin. It was all a clever electrical museum out of 1929, with animated people who could move and talk and blink their eyes.

Our waitress was a startlingly pretty girl who smiled as she brought our lemonade. She didn't seem at all electrical.

"Are you going to come out and fly with us?" Paul asked.

"Oh! You're the boys with the airplanes! I saw you fly over a little while ago. Two of you?"

"And a jumper," I added.

It was beyond understanding. We had made only a half-circle of town, but surely half the people in Pecatonica knew about the two airplanes waiting at the airport.

We piled our lemonade money on the table.

"You'll be out to fly with us?" Paul said.

"I don't know. I might."

"She won't," Paul said. "Why is it that waitresses never come out and fly with us?"

"Waitresses are the best judges of character in the world," I told him. "They know never to fly with people who wear nutty green hats."

Taking our lemonade with us, we set out for the airport. It was a fifteen-minute walk, and by the time we reached the strip we were thirsty again. In the shed next to the pigs' home there were several tractors and some bales of hay for Skeeter. The children were out in the yard, and no sooner had Stu laid himself down on the hay than they ran over and began burying him in kittens. There was a mother cat with them, and while Paul and I chatted with Skeeter, Stu was flat on his back in the hay, being trampled by a child-directed stampede of kittens. He was enjoying it greatly, and I was surprised. Stu was stepping out of character; this was not the sort of thing I had come to expect from our thoughtful, taciturn jumper.

Paul and I soon had the airplanes fired up and we flew one brief dogfight over the edge of town. There were four cars waiting when we landed, and a few passengers. We went to work flying.

At last I got a thumbs-down signal from Stu that there were no passengers waiting, and shut down the Whirlwind.

Paul had just come down, and his passenger, an attractive young lady of nineteen or twenty, in a rather low-cut summer dress, walked directly to me.

"Hello," she said, "my name is Emily."

"Hi, Emily."

"I just got down from my very first airplane ride and it's just wonderful! Everything's so pretty! But Paul said that if I *really* wanted to have fun, I should ride with you!"

Paul thought I was off-balance whenever confronted by a pretty woman, and Emily could only be a part of his experimenting to prove it. I glanced at the Luscombe, and there was Paul, all right, polishing spots from his spotless engine cowl, all of a sudden looking very intently at his work.

I'd show him. "Why, Emily, ol' Paul was 'zackly right. You want to know what flying really is, you just pop right over to that young fella there in the yellow jumpsuit and get yourself a ticket, and we'll go flying."

She looked downcast for a moment, and moved to stand very close to me. "I'm all out of money, Dick," she said softly.

"I don't believe it! Three dollars is nothin' for a ride in a biplane! Not many left, nowadays, you know."

"I'd sure love to fly with you," she cooed.

"Be worth it, too, ma'm. A beautiful day to fly. Well—as you know, if you were just up with Paul."

She was in no hurry to rush off and pay Stu her $3 and was happy just to stand and talk and let the sun reflect bright colors from her low summer dress.

Just then an earlier passenger was back, wanting another "wild ride." I said a careful good-bye to the girl, started the Wright and taxied out. As I passed the Luscombe, I shook my head slowly at Paul, who was now quite vigorously polishing the propeller. We never saw Emily again.

The morning roadside on the walk back from breakfast was deep in purple flower.

"Hey, you guys," I said, "honey clover!"

"Pretty."

"No, it's not pretty, it's good to eat. Like when you were a kid, remember?" I picked a boll and tasted the hollow petals. There was a tenth of a drop of nectar in each one, a delicate sweet flavor of morning. Paul and Stu tried one each, as we walked.

"Tastes like eating a flower," Stu said.

"Can't figure you guys out." I picked another handful of purple, and crunched on the tender petals. "This great stuff growin' all over, and you walk right by."

There was a concrete bridge between town and the airport, crossing the one straightest mile on the length of the Pecatonica River. We heard the sound of outboard motors, and a pair of tiny racing hydroplanes came buzzing full throttle down the river, battling for the lead. They roared echoing under the bridge and through in an instant. The drivers wore helmets and heavy life jackets, and they were completely absorbed in their race. At the end of the straight they slowed, turned and came back again, tall arcs of spray leaping behind them. It was a sort of aquatic Dragging Main, but somehow it seemed a much cleaner sport.

We walked on across the bridge, and past a lawn where a boy was beating a rug with a twisted wire hoop.

"What's the plan?" Paul said as we walked by Skeeter, who whinnied, and out to the airplanes. "You want to try for something during the day again? Might get somebody."

"Anything you say."

"I'm running out of time," Paul said. "I should head back pretty soon. Take me three days to get home from here, about."

"Well, let's give it a try; go up and fly a bit," I said. "Might get a couple people out to fly. Be cool, anyway."

We took off and climbed to 3,000 feet in formation over the summer town. The hydroplanes hadn't stopped; their twin white wakes still ran neck and neck along the dark river. The boy was still beating the rug half a mile beneath us and I shook my head. It had been twenty minutes since we walked by. What a devoted young fellow that must be, beating a rug for twenty minutes. Three minutes of rug-beating used to be my outside limit. The world is an earnest place, in 1929.

Paul broke away in a wide sweeping turn and swung around toward me to begin the old familiar aerial battle. I pulled the biplane's nose straight up in the air, hoping for the Luscombe to swish right on by beneath me and give me the chance of dropping down on her tail. The first part of our dogfights were never staged; we were trying our best to work into a firing position behind each other. It was only at the end that I had to let Paul win, because I had the smoke flare and was still the only one eligible to go down in flames.

The earth twisted around us in green, sky in blue, and for a while I didn't care whether potential passengers were watching or not. It would not do, in this first part of our game, to let Paul get behind the biplane. I had Air Force training in this business long before he learned to fly; I had practiced air combat in frontline military fighters while Paul was still taking fashion pictures in his elegant studio.

Everyone else I knew began to fly in slow airplanes, little airplanes, old airplanes, and then went with the times. In a few years they were flying faster, bigger, more modern machines. It had been just the other way around for me.

First had come the seamless military trainers and fighters and air combat at transsonic speed, then the transports, then modern business planes, then an aging lightplane, now this biplane locked firmly into the day before yesterday. From airborne weapons radar to modern electronics to a simple panel of radio to nothing at all—the biplane was not only without radio, she was entirely without electricity. She was back in the days when a pilot was his own man, with no links to ground-people to aid him or to annoy him. Nineteen twenty-nine is a happy year, but sometimes, watching a contrail pulling along way up in the stratosphere, I had to admit to myself that I missed the power and speed and the high lonesome joy of the fighter pilot. Sometimes.

The Luscombe was beside me now, trying desperately to slow down, to fall behind the biplane's tail. I pushed full throttle, held the nose up, looked across the air at Paul, and laughed. The little sport-plane could stand it no longer; all at once it shuddered and fell away toward the ground, stalled out. I pressed full rudder as the Parks stalled a second later and dropped down on the Luscombe's tail. My reputation was secure. No matter what happened now, I could tell Paul that I deliberately gave him the advantage, after once having been on his tail. He pulled up again, rolling inverted, dropped away, spinning the sky around us both as I rolled to follow.

Stu was already at work convincing the customers it was a great day for flying, and by noon we had flown five passengers. We spent the afternoon in the shade of the wings, trying to stay cool. It wasn't an easy job.

A few minutes after I had finally made it into sleep, Paul came over and woke me up. "What do you say to some watermelon? Wouldn't that be great? Nice cold watermelon?"

"Sounds keen. You go in and get it and I'll help eat."

"No, c'mon. Let's go get a watermelon."

"You're out of your mind. It's a mile to town!"

"Stu! How about going in and us getting a watermelon?" Paul said. "Then we could bring it out here and eat it and not give Bach any."

"You go in and get it," Stu said. "I'll wait here for you."

"Aw. I just can't wait around here doing nothing. I'm going to go up and do some flip-flops."

"Fine," I said. Stu was already asleep.

Paul took off a few minutes later and I watched some of his flying. Then I turned over and found a cooler place under the wing.

I didn't hear him taxi in and stop, but he woke us again. "Hey, we have to get some watermelon. Nobody's coming out to fly."

"Tell you what, Paul," I said. "You go in and get the watermelon, and I'll let you use my knife to cut it. How's that sound?"

A few minutes later a truck pulled out from the hangar, headed for town, and Paul was aboard. He had a fixation about that watermelon. Well, I thought as I went back to sleep, if he wants a watermelon that much, he should get his watermelon.

Half an hour later we heard Skeeter whinny hello and Paul was back, a watermelon under his arm. It was one hundred degrees in the sun and he had lugged the thing all the way from town.

"Hey, you guys," he called. "Watermelon!"

It was hard to understand, I thought, munching on the cool goodness. If I were Paul, I would have let the lazy louts starve out there under the wing. At most, I might have thrown them a bit of rind. But share the first part of my watermelon with them? Never!

"I guess I better bug on out," Paul said. "We're not going to have many passengers, at least till late. It's a long way back to California, and I might as well get started on it today." He began separating his belongings from the pile of equipment, and set them neatly into his airplane. Cameras, film cases, bedroll, clothes bag, maps. "I'll leave you guys the watermelon," he said.

A car drove into the lane, and another.

"We have discovered a delayed-action Method C," I said as a third car parked across the grass.

We started the Parks and Stu went over to talk to the people. First passengers were a man and his boy, and the man wore a set of goggles he had last worn in the tank corps in Africa. They said a few wind-blasted words and we were airborne, climbing toward the river up to the cool high air.

"Hey, that's really nice," the man said, eleven minutes later, as Stu helped him out. "Really nice. You can really see a long way from up there, can't you?"

Stu closed the door after the next passengers and stopped by my cockpit. "You've got two first-timers and one's a little scared."

"OK." I wondered why he had said that. Most of our passengers were up for the first time, and most were a bit apprehensive, though they didn't often show it. These must be more worried than usual about flying in the rackety old biplane. But as soon as we were halfway through the first circle of town, they had relaxed and were asking for steep banks. It is the unknown that worries our passengers, I thought. As soon as they see what flying is like, and that it is even a little bit pretty, then it becomes known and nice, and there's no cause for fear. Fear is just a way of thinking, a feeling. Get rid of that feeling by knowing what is true in the world, and you aren't afraid.

Business was suddenly going strong. There were eight cars parked on the grass, and Stu was ready with two more passengers when I rolled to a stop.

Paul walked to my cockpit. "Looks like a thunderstorm west. I'll be doing good to make Dubuque by dark," he said. "I'm pushing it, aren't I?"

"You're never pushing it as long as you can control your airplane, remember," I said. "If you don't like the looks of things, just go down and land in a field and wait it out. You might as well stay one more night here, don't you think, anyway?"

"Nope. Better be on my way, get back home. You've got four passengers waiting for you, no need me waiting around to say good-bye. I'll get right on out."

"OK, Paul. It's been fun."

Stu closed the door on the new passengers and waved that they were ready to go.

"Yeah. Been fun," Paul said. "We should run it again next year, huh? Maybe a little longer."

"OK. Take it easy. Fly good, and set down if the weather gives you a hard time."

"Yeah. Put me on your postcard list."

I nodded and pulled my goggles down, pushed the throttle forward. What a brusque good-bye, after flying together for so long.

We took off over the corn, and climbed up through the warm evening air, turning toward town, over the river. I saw the Luscombe airborne, turning my way. Paul fell into formation for a minute or so, to the delight of the passengers, each of whom aimed a camera and jotted the moment down on film.

What did it mean, that this man who had flown with us, who was part of the risks and joys and work and trials, of the understanding and misunderstanding of barnstorming, was now leaving?

Paul waved good-bye, kicked the Luscombe up into a sudden sharp breakaway and accelerated out into the west, where the sun was blocked by a giant thundercloud.

It meant, strangely enough, not that he was leaving at all, but that he was there. That if the time ever came for another test of freedom, another plan to prove that we don't have to live any way but the way we wish, it might not have to be a lonely time. How many others like him are left in the country? I couldn't tell if there were ten or a thousand. But I did know there was one.

"See you around, buddy," I said. No one heard but the wind.

CHAPTER THIRTEEN

THE THUNDERSTORM hit us at five in the morning, and we woke to raindrops clattering on the wing.

"We are going to get wet," Stu observed calmly.

"Well, sir, yes. We can either stay under this wing or we can chicken out and run for the tractor shed."

We decided to chicken out, grabbed our sleeping bags and ran for the shed, pelted all the way by heavy drops. I settled down by a doorway in the shed, where I could watch both the storm and the wind sock. The rain didn't worry me, but it would have been nice to know whether or not there would be any hail. It would have to be large and sharp hail, and coming straight down, before it could hurt the airplane. I took some comfort in the thought that hail that bad would also hurt the corn and oats, and that corn and oats were rarely damaged by hail.

The biplane didn't seem at all concerned by the storm, and after a while I moved my sleeping bag over into the steel bucket of a Case 300 skip-loader. The heavy steel ridges of that bucket, covered by two layers of sleeping bag, made a comfortable bed. The only shortcoming was the rather noisy nearness of the pigs, with their ork-orking and clanging their metal feed-lids every few seconds. If I were a manufacturer of feed bins for hogs, I thought, I would glue big rubber strips on those lids to deaden the sound. Every twenty seconds . . . *clang!* I didn't know how Skeeter could stand it.

The rain stopped in an hour and Stu walked over to look at the animals eating. In a few minutes he walked back and began gathering his equipment from the shed. "Now I know where they get the expression 'pushy pig,'" he said.

We had our breakfast at the other café, and looked over our Texaco road map for Eastern United States.

"I'm getting tired of all this north stuff," I said. "Let's swing down into southern Illinois or Iowa or Missouri. Not Illinois. I'm tired of Illinois."

"Whatever you want," said Stu. "We could try a jump here, see what happens. Yesterday was a good day. Haven't had a chance to try out that flour, yet."

Later, Stu stood bulky on the wingwalk, holding to the strut and looking down. His target was the center of the field, but the wind was blowing hard at altitude, and carried the drift indicator a half mile east of the strip. I thought he might cancel the jump, but he stood on the wing and motioned corrections that would take him to his jump point. The first jump run was not where he wanted it, and to make it worse, a patch of clouds hid the runway. We swung around to try again.

With Stu on the wing, the airflow over the tail of the biplane was broken all out of smoothness . . . the horizontal stabilizer bucked and jumped painfully, and the control stick shuddered in the force of the roiled wind. It was always a tense time, with him there, but this was even worse, swinging slowly around to try another pass in high winds aloft and with the stabilizer blurred under the strain of that shattered airflow.

The cloud crept slowly from over the field and the pass looked better to Stu. He waved me two degrees right, two more degrees right, and then slit the bag of King's Ransom flour. It trailed over-board in a great tunnel of white, our own contrail there at 4,000 feet. Then he jumped, still trailing flour.

I cut the throttle, banked hard to keep him in sight, and followed him down. It would never be routine; I was already wishing that he would hurry up and pull the rip cord.

Stu was a missile, launched in reverse. He had been still and waiting on the wing, he had fired down, and now he was going through his own sonic barriers and high-Q pressures.

At last he stopped his turns and deltas, pulled the rip cord, and the canopy snapped out into the sky. It was a piece of cake. He tracked into the wind, centered over his grassy target, and came down dead center, falling and leaping up again at once to spill the canopy.

By the time I landed he was ready to hop aboard for the short ride in.

"Nice jump, Stu!"

"Best one yet. Went just like I wanted it to go."

There was a crowd waiting, and I settled down for a long run of flying. It didn't work out that way. Only five people felt like flying, although one man handed Stu a $10 bill and said, "Can you give me this much a ride?" We spent thirty minutes out over the countryside, and he still didn't tire of looking down.

A farmer was last to ride that morning, and we flew over his house and lands, green and bright after the rain. He didn't look at his land as much as he reflected upon it; I could see the thought in his face. So this is my land, so that is where I've spent my life. Sure, there's fifty other places like it all around, but this is my land and it's every acre good.

We broke for lunch when there were no passengers left to fly, and caught a ride to town with one young man who had flown and stayed to watch.

"I sure envy you guys," he said as we turned onto the highway. "Bet you see a lot of girls, flying around."

"Yep, we see a lot of girls, all right," I said.

"Boy. I'd like to join you. But I got a job that ties me down."

"Well, quit your job," I said, testing him. "Come on and join us!"

"I couldn't do that. Couldn't quit my job . . ." He had failed his test. Not even girls could lure him away from a job that tied him down.

When we returned from lunch, I saw that the biplane was getting a little greasy. I selected a rag and began wiping the silver cowl.

"Why don't you get the windscreens, Stu? There's so much grease on 'em the poor people can hardly see out."

"Sure thing."

We talked as we worked, and decided to stay in Pecatonica the rest of the day, and leave early next morning.

I backed off and looked at the airplane, and I was pleased. She was much prettier. Stu wiped the top of the cowl, which wasn't necessary. But there was something about the rag that he was using . . .

"Stu? That rag IS MY T-SHIRT! THAT'S MY T-SHIRT YOU'RE USING!"

He opened his mouth in terror, and froze solid.

"It was with all the other rags," he choked. "And it looked so . . . raggy." He unfolded it, helplessly. It was no longer cloth, but a mass of gooey rocker-grease. "God knows I'm sorry," he said.

"Aw, heck. Go ahead and use it for a rag. It was only my T-shirt."

He debated for a moment, looked at the shirt, and went back to wiping grease with it. "I thought something was funny," he said. "It was an awful clean rag."

Method C picked up some passengers that afternoon, and the first was the man and his wife who lived at the airstrip. "We've been watching you, and you look pretty safe, so we decided to take the plunge."

They enjoyed the plunge. We circled over their house on the strip before landing, and as we did a car drew up and a man got out and knocked on the door.

The woman smiled and pointed down at him, so her husband could see. Their caller waited patiently for the door to be answered, not thinking to look up in the sky for his friends, a thousand feet overhead.

We landed and the woman ran laughing to keep him from driving away from an empty house.

Then business died away, though there were still some people standing to look at the biplane. One lean gentleman walked up and looked in the cockpit after I shut the engine down. "You ever heard of Bert Snyder?" he said.

"Can't say as I have . . . who's Bert Snyder?"

"Used to be Bert Snyder Circus, in 1923. Used to come into this town for the county fair. He had a whole lot of airplanes, a whole lot of them. And I used to be the most envied kid in town. I'd go up in the front of one of them airplanes and throw handbills out, advertising, all over the place. He had quite a circus. This town would be so full of people come to see him and come to the fair you couldn't turn around . . . old Bert Snyder."

"Sounds like quite a guy."

"Sure was . . . quite a guy. And you know, these kids you fly, they'll remember this ride for the rest of their lives. Oh, they'll fly jets all over the world, but they'll tell their kids, 'I remember when I went up, summer of '66, it was, in an old open-cockpit . . .'"

Of course he was right; sure he was right. We weren't here just for ourselves, after all. In how many albums and scrapbooks had The Great American already found immortality? In how many thoughts and memories did our images sleep this moment? I suddenly felt the weight of history and eternity upon us all.

At that moment another car arrived; our friend the tank driver. He had brought his wife out to fly, and as soon as she stepped from the car, she began laughing.

"Is this . . . the *airplane* . . . you wanted me to fly?"

I did not see what was so funny about it all, but she was laughing so hard that I was forced to smile. Maybe it *would* look funny, to some people.

The woman could not control herself. She laughed until there were tears in her eyes; she leaned against the side of the fuselage, buried her face in her hands and laughed. It wasn't long before everyone was laughing; she made us a very happy group.

"I admire your courage," she said, choking on her words. After a long while she settled down and even said that she was ready to fly.

We flew around town, made our turns and came back in to land, and she was still smiling when she got out of the airplane. I could only hope that the reason for the smile had changed.

The sun dropped into low gold on the horizon, and there was a faint mist through the valley that caught the color and sprayed it across the countryside. We had a crowd of twenty people around us, but all had either flown or had no wish to fly.

They had no idea what they were missing; this would be a magnificent sunset from the air.

"Come along, folks," I said. "Sunsets for sale this evening! The Great American Flying Circus guarantees a minimum of two sunsets this evening, but only if you act now! Watch the sun go down here, then up in the sky to watch her go down once more! A sight you will never see again, as long as you live! Prettiest sunset all summer! It's a burnt-copper afternoon—right out of Beethoven's heart! Who's ready to step up there into the air with me?"

One lady, sitting in a car nearby, thought I was speaking all to her. Her words came clear in the soft air, louder than she meant. "I don't fly unless I have to."

I was angry, sad. The poor people had no idea; with their caution, they were passing up paradise! How do you convince them of good? I made one last appeal, then, meeting no response, started the engine and took off alone, just to fly and to see the land from the air.

It was more beautiful than I had promised. The haze topped out at less than a thousand feet, and from 2,000 feet the earth was a silent lake of gold, with a few brilliant emerald hilltops rising to be islands in the crystal air. The land was all a golden dream, where only good and beautiful lived, and it was spread out below us like a tale from Marco Polo, with the sky going deep-velvet black overhead. It was another planet, that Earth, one never seen by man, and the biplane and I held the splendor of it all to ourselves.

We started our first roll a mile in the air, and the biplane did not stop rolling and soaring and diving and singing strong in her wires until the ground was dark and the mist was gone and the gold had disappeared from the sky.

We whispered down into the grass and swung to park, shutting the engine into hot-ticking silence. I sat alone for a full minute, not wanting to talk to people or to hear them or to see them. I knew I'd never forget that flight, and I wanted a quiet moment to lay it carefully away in my thought, for I would be coming back here many times again, in the years ahead.

Someone said low, in the crowd, "He has the courage of ten men, to fly that old crate."

I felt like crying. They didn't understand . . . I . . . could . . . not make . . . them . . . understand.

Gradually the cars drove away and the ground went very dark indeed. The hills on the horizon were powder-black against the last light of the sun; they stood with their trees and windmills and rolling fields in razor silhouette, like the skyline in a planetarium, just as the stars are being flashed upon the dome. Sharp and black and clear.

The old-timer was the last one left, and as he slid into his car to leave, he said, "Young fella, how much would you say that airplane's worth, about?"

"Mister, if Henry Ford were to walk up here and want this machine, I'd tell him, 'Hank, you ain't got enough money to buy that airplane.'"

"I believe you'd say that," the man said, "I really believe you'd say that."

We counted our money over breakfast. We had flown twenty-eight passengers, and we showed a handsome profit.

"You know, Stu, with the little fields like this, the little airstrips around the country, barnstorming can be a lot better business now than it was back then."

"Makes you feel sort of powerful, doesn't it?" he said.

We walked out of Pecatonica for the last time, past a dog sitting chained to his doghouse. He had barked at us before. "How many times is the dog going to bark, Stu?"

"The dog is going to bark two times."

"I say the dog is going to bark four times. At least four times."

We walked by him and he didn't make a sound. He just sat there and watched our every move.

"Why, Stu, I believe the dog has come to know us!" I stopped in the road and looked the dog in the eye. "He is now our friend!"

At that, the dog burst into barking, and by the time we were over the bridge, we had counted twelve full, rapid barks.

Stu found a half-size comic book lying by the road and picked it up. It was an advertising thing for Wrangler jeans, and it was all about Tex Marshall, rodeo star. Stu read aloud as we walked, acting out the part of young Tex, starting his career as a bulldogger on the rodeo circuit. The theme of the story was Stay in School, Kids, documented by Tex's fierce will to get his college degree before turning full-time to rodeo and earning a pile of money.

We wondered how that degree helped Tex hog-tie Hereford calves in six seconds flat, but that was apparently something that all the guys take for granted. You get that degree, and you'll make more money in any job.

Again I urged Stu to get out of school until he decided what he wanted to do in the world, that he was just postponing living until he found that out, that it was doom to ever become a dentist if he was an adventurer at heart. He remained unconvinced.

We said good-bye to Skeeter, telling him that he was a good horse and we would remember him, and loaded the airplane. The engine warmed for the next adventure, beating back the tall grass in fifth-second impulses. It looked like a 1910 movie of a biplane running in tall grass, jerky and flickering.

By ten o'clock we were on a long run crosswind, dragging our shadow like a giant salmon fighting and thrashing at the end of a thousand-foot line. We didn't settle down to our next sight of Midwest America until the wheels touched and rolled on the grass of Kahoka, Missouri.

CHAPTER FOURTEEN

THERE WERE TWO boys and a dog, waiting.

"You in trouble, mister?"

"Nope, no trouble," I said.

"D'ja see me wavin' at you?"

"Didn't you see us wavin' back? You don't think we'd fly over and not wave, do you? Geemanee, what do you think we are, anyway?"

We unloaded our supply mountain and carried it across the deep green grass into the shade of a crumbling hangar. By the time we had the signs up and were open for business, there were eleven boys and seven bicycles scattered across the airplane and the grass.

It was an uncomfortable time. We didn't want to scare them all away, but neither did we want them walking through the fabric of the wings.

"Sure you can sit in the front seat, fellas, just stay on the black part of the wing, there, don't walk on the yellow. Careful, there." I turned to one boy looking soberly on. "How many people live in Kahoka, my friend?"

"Two thousand one hundred and sixty." He knew the exact figure.

There was a sharp explosion near the tail of the airplane and a little spray of grass jerked into the air. "Hey, fellas, let's keep the firecrackers away from the airplane, OK?"

There was some giggling and laughing from one knot of boys, and another explosion burst beneath the wingtip. More than anything at that moment, I felt like a junior-high teacher with a problem in discipline.

"NEXT GUY THROWS A FIRECRACKER BY THIS AIR-PLANE I'M GONNA PICK UP AND THROW ACROSS THAT ROAD! YOU WANTA PLAY WITH THAT STUFF, YOU GET IT OUTA HERE!"

Violence worked at once. There were no more explosions in a hundred yards of the biplane.

Boys surged around us like pilot fish around sharks. When we walked clear of the airplane, everybody walked clear. When we leaned on the wing, everybody leaned on the wing. They were busy daring each other to fly . . . a giant challenge.

"I'd fly, if I had the money. I just don't have the money."

"If I loaned you three dollars, Jimmy, would you fly?"

"Nope," Jimmy said. "I wouldn't pay you back."

Their fear of the airplane was staggering. Every boy spoke of crashing; what do you do when the wings fall off . . . what if you jump and the chute doesn't open? There was going to be great disappoint-ment in Kahoka if we didn't dive into the ground with at least one fatality.

"I thought you were all brave guys," Stu said. "And here nobody's got the courage to go up one time."

They gathered together, found that they could raise three dollars, and sent a spokesman. "If we paid you three dollars, mister, would you do some stunts for us?"

"You mean nobody goin' for a ride?" I said. "You all just watchin' from the ground?"

"Yeah. We'll pay you three dollars."

It was human society at work. If individual daring is ruled out, we can band together as spectators.

The boys all massed at the end of the strip, sitting down in the grass by the road. I taxied to the far end of the strip, so that we'd be taking off over their heads and toward town, all good advertising.

They were just little dots when the biplane's wheels lifted off the grass, but instead of climbing, we stayed low, skimming the grasstops, picking up speed and pointing straight into the young crowd.

If the engine quits here, I thought, we pull up, turn right and land in the bean field. But the boys didn't know this. All they could see was the biplane growing into a huge thing, roaring right straight at them, not turning, not climbing, coming bigger and louder than a five-ton firecracker.

They had just begun to scatter and dive for cover when we pulled steeply up and banked hard right, to keep the bean field in gliding range.

We circled the town once for advertising, and then back over the strip we dropped down through loops and rolls and cloverleafs and a one-turn spin. The air show lasted ten minutes, including the climb, and I waited to hear some general disappointment that $3 could be shot up so fast.

"That was nice, mister!"

"Yeah! Gee, that part right at first, where you went zzzZZZZOOOOOOMM! right at us! That was scary!"

In a minute the first automobiles arrived, and we were glad to see them. Stu went into action, telling the joys of flying on a hot day like this, selling the idea of Kahoka from the cool, cool sky.

As Stu strapped him in, the first passenger said, "I want a thrill." A man walked to the cockpit just as we began to taxi out, and said in a low voice, "This fella is sort of the town cutup. Take 'im up and turn 'im upside down a few times, OK?"

In every town we worked, all summer long, the one dominating personality was the water tower. In fact, the water tower became as much the symbol *Town* to us as it had become for the people who lived in its shadow. But now, up in the sun and the wind and the leather and the wires of the biplane, our passengers were for the first time looking down on that tower and its great black town-name painted.

I watched my riders carefully, at Kahoka, and every one of them looked long and thoughtfully at the top of the water tower, and then out to the road that led off over the horizon. It was part of the flight, when I saw this, to fly a separate little conquering circle over the shining four-pillared thing and its eight-foot letters KAHOKA. To rise above that tower was an event unforgotten.

By sundown we had flown nineteen passengers.

"What do I keep telling us, Stu," I said as we walked through the dark toward town. "We get right close in and we can't lose!"

We finished our hamburgers at the Orbit Inn and walked into the town square in the dark. The stores were closed, and silence drifted like slow fog in the branches of the elm trees.

There was a bandstand in the park, slope-roofed and faced about by rows of quiet wooden benches, all peaceful and silent in the warm summer night. The Seyb Emporium was across the way, and the sundries store, the hotel, with its wooden fans turning in the high lobby air. If I gave a dollar for every change in this square since 1919, I would still have been rich from the day's earnings.

We walked down the quiet sidewalks, back toward our field, listening to the faint strains of radio music rippling out from the yellow light of the houses.

The peace of Kahoka, however, did not extend to its mosquitoes. It was Erie all over again, and worse. At last I devised a Method D of Mosquito-Avoiding, which requires one to lie down fully clothed on a sleeping bag, throw a silken hammock over his head, and leave only a tiny hole for air. This worked fairly well, though it didn't spare me the hypersonic hum of a thousand tiny wings.

We were awake at the first cock-crow, about the time that the mosquitoes retired for the day.

I got up and poured a couple quarts of oil into the engine and looked it over well; we might have a busy day, close in. I had just closed the cowl when a car stopped by the field, sifting a cloud of fine flour-dust up from the dirt road.

"Are you flying yet, this morning?"

"Yes, ma'am. All ready to start engines for you."

"I missed you yesterday and I was afraid you might leave . . ." She was a schoolteacher, there was no question about it. She had that kind of confidence and control over the world that comes only from forty years of channeling American history into ten thousand high-school pupils.

The go-mile wind over the morning town destroyed the set of her silver-blue hair, but she gave no heed. She looked down on Kahoka and out toward the horizon farms exactly as children did, without any consciousness of herself at all.

Ten minutes later she gave Stu three one-dollar bills, thanked us both, and left in a slow trail of summer dust.

There is America, I thought. There is real frontier America, reflected in daughters a hundred years removed from her pioneers.

"What do you think of that?" Stu said. "I think we're in for a good day when they start coming out this early to fly."

"What's the estimate?" I began the walk toward town and breakfast. "How many passengers today?"

"I'll say . . . twenty-five. We'll fly twenty-five people today," Stu said, falling into step.

"Aren't we optimistic, this morning. Oh, it'll be a good day, for sure, but not that good. We'll fly eighteen people."

We were joined at the restaurant by one of our passengers of the day before, one Paul, by name, who owned a drag strip on the road out of town.

"Have a cup of coffee with you, for just a minute here," he said.

I was reflecting at the moment that there is nothing so horrible in the world as a stale glazed doughnut for breakfast.

"Always wanted to fly," Paul said. "Always wanted to, but never got around to it. At first, my folks were against me flyin', then my wife was thumbs-down. But last night I kind of got the go-ahead to go again."

The doughnut was modifying my thinking. What would the world be like if we all had to have permission from wives and family before we did anything that we wanted to do; if we were all required to committee-think our desires? Would it be a different world, or are we living in one that is pretty much that way right now? I refused to believe that we were, and put the doughnut into the ashtray.

"You should get old Kenny up. Man, he would just go wild in that thing! I'm gonna bring him out. Bring 'im out tonight! I'm gonna see you guys get a good crowd . . . it's a fine thing, your comin' here. That little old airport just sits out there and nobody cares about it. Used to have a flying club with a couple airplanes, but they all lost interest and now there's just one plane left. You might get it goin' again."

Paul left in a few minutes, and we walked out into the sun-heat of July Missouri. A farm tractor drove swiftly by the square, its huge rear wheels singing on the pavement.

By ten-thirty business was going strong. One young man flew four times, firing rolls of color film through his Polaroid camera. He was leaving to join the Army in two weeks, and he spent his money as though he had to get rid of it all before the two weeks were up. I was reminded of the gay and happy lives of the young kamikaze pilots a few years back . . . this poor fellow was going to be heartbroken if he somehow managed to survive his first week in the Army.

Next to fly was a giant of a man, and he was clutching a plastic bag full of candy bars. "Hey, Dick," he said, reading my name on the cockpit rim. "How much you charge me to fly out over my farm, so I can toss these down to my kids? About nine miles north on State 81."

"Gee. That's eighteen miles round-trip . . . 'd cost you . . . fifteen dollars. Awful steep price, but you see, whenever we go out of the local area . . ."

"Nothin' wrong with that price. That's fine. Kids'll go crazy, see their ol' dad comin' over in an airplane . . ."

In five minutes we had left Kahoka behind and were chugging over the softly rolling hills and gentle farmland south of the Des Moines River. He pointed the way, and at last down to a white farmhouse set a half mile back from the road.

We dropped lower and circled the house, and the chugging roar of the Whirlwind brought his wife and children running out to see. He waved hard at them, and they all waved back, two-handedly. "GO RIGHT OVER 'EM!" he shouted, holding up the candy bag so I'd get the idea.

The biplane settled fifty feet above the cornfield, and came streaking in over the little crowd on the ground. His arm moved, the candy bag hurtled down. Children were on it like mongeese, lightning fast, and sprang up to wave again to their dad. We circled twice and he signaled to return.

I had never flown with a more satisfied customer. He had the smile of Santa himself, aloft in a red and yellow sleigh in the middle of summertime. He had come and gone as he had promised, the good little children were all happy, and now the story could come to a close.

But there was plenty of work waiting for the sleigh when we returned.

An elderly skeptic finally agreed to fly, but reminded me, "None of them dadoes, now, 'member. Keep 'er nice and smooth."

It was a nice and smooth flight, until we were gliding down final approach to land. My passenger picked that time to suddenly begin waving his arms and shouting wildly.

I nodded and smiled, intent on landing, and didn't hear him until we had rolled to a stop once again by the road. "What was the matter?" I said. "Something go wrong up there? What were you tryin' to say?"

"HOO-EE!" he said, with the astonished smile of one who has cheated death. "Way we was comin' down, there, all turnin' and angled up . . . hoo-*ee!* I saw we was gonna land right in the pond, so I hollered, 'STRAIGHTEN 'ER OUT, BOY, STRAIGHTEN 'ER OUT!' And you pulled 'er out just in time."

The day was full hot, and as long as the engine was running, there was a flock of boys standing in the cool hurricane behind the tail of the biplane. They were all young trout in the river of air, flopping around happily whenever I pushed the throttle forward to taxi out. Between passengers, I put my goggles up and relaxed, myself, in the breeze over the cockpit.

Once, when I landed, Stu was talking with a pair of news reporters. They were interested in the airplane and in us; they asked questions, took pictures. "Thanks a lot," they said as they left. "You'll be on the ten-twenty local news."

We flew passengers on and off all afternoon, but this was our second day at Kahoka, and it was time to think about moving on.

"I'm torn between staying here and making money," Stu said, "and moving on and making more."

"Then let's stay on tonight and push off tomorrow, early."

"Hate to leave a good spot. But we can always come back, can't we?"

We lay in the heated afternoon shade of the wing, trying to escape into the cool of sleep. There was a small sound in the sky.

"Airplane," Stu said. "Hey, look. Doesn't that look familiar?"

I looked. Way up overhead there was a yellow Cub circling, looking down. It turned, dropped swiftly down, pulled up in a loop and around in a roll. It was the same Cub that had flown with the five-plane Great American, at Prairie du Chien.

"That's Dick Willetts!" I said. "That's . . . now how did he know . . . sure, that's him!"

A few minutes later the Cub was down on the grass, rolling to a stop beside us. A good sight. Dick was a tall, calm and very skillful pilot, a reminder of how lonely it was to barnstorm with one single airplane.

"Hi! Thought I might find you down this way, somewhere."

"How'd you know where we were? You call Bette or something? How'd you find us?"

"I don't know. Just thought you might be around here," Dick said, sitting relaxed in the Cub's cockpit, puffing slowly on his pipe. "This was the last place I was going to try, really."

"Hm. That's fantastic."

"Yeah. How's it goin', barnstormin'?"

Dick stayed and flew through the afternoon with us, and carried five passengers. I had a chance to stay on the ground and listen to the people after they had flown, and discovered that there is a great driving force toward believing that the pilot that one flies with is the best pilot in the world.

"Could you feel it when he landed?" one man said. "I couldn't feel when he landed. I could hear it, but I couldn't feel it, it was so smooth."

"Y'know, I have a lot of faith in him . . ."

"What do you think of your pilot, Ida Lee?" a coveralled farmer asked his wife, after she had flown with Dick.

"Everything was so pretty, and fun," she said. "I'd say he's *good*."

Just before 5 P.M. I saw that my fuel was getting too low to last through the heavy flying till sunset, and at the same time we found that the man who had the key to the gas pump was out of town.

"I'll hop over to Keokuk, Richard," I said, "and you keep the folks happy, flyin'."

"Take your time," he said.

In twenty minutes I was looking down in dismay at the Keokuk airport. It was all concrete runway, with new construction everywhere. To land on the hard surface would be to grind the tail skid to nothing, and I didn't have enough fuel to find another airport. But there was one short section of grass left on the west side of the field, and we landed there.

We had to cross a new runway to reach the pumps; all along the edge of the runway was a muddy deep ditch, with a five-inch lip of concrete to jump. We taxied back and forth along the edge of the runway, picked the least muddy section for crossing, and charged at it straight on.

It didn't work. The mud slowed the biplane to a walk, and by the time we reached the concrete lip, full power on the engine wasn't enough to drag it across.

I shut down the Wright, holding unkind thoughts about aeronautical progress and the wholesale destruction of the grass runway, vowed never again to land at Keokuk or any modern airport, and went for a towing machine.

A tractor, mowing grass, was the answer.

"Hi!" I said to the driver. "Got a little problem here, trying to cross your new runway. Think that machine of yours could tow me out?"

"Oh, sure. She can tow airplanes ten times that size."

He left his grass-mowing at once and we rode together back to the airplane. When we got there, there was a line service man from the flight school across the field, looking in the cockpit.

"Looks like you got stuck," he said.

"Yes, sir," I said. "But we'll have 'er out in a minute here and I'll come over get some gas from you." I took a coil of stout rope from the tractor and tied it from the iron hitch to the landing gear of the biplane. "That oughta do 'er. We'll kinda help the wingtips here and you see if that tractor can do the job."

"Aw, she'll do the job. Don't you worry."

The tractor made it look easy. In a few seconds the biplane was standing free on the concrete, ready to start engine and taxi for gas.

"Thanks. You really saved me, sir."

"Think nothin' of it. She can pull airplanes ten times that big."

The line service man was looking nervously at the big steel propeller, hoping that I wouldn't ask him to swing that by hand to start the engine. It is a frightening thing to one who has never hand-propped a Wright, but we had no choice; the starting crank was in Kahoka.

"Why don't you hop in the cockpit, here," I said, "and I'll swing the prop." I walked back as he climbed aboard and showed him the throttle and ignition switch and brakes. "Just pull the throttle back a bit after she starts," I said. "She should start right off."

I pulled the propeller through a few times, and said, "OK, give me contact and brakes, and we'll start her goin'."

I pulled the big blade down and the engine fired at once. Good old reliable Wright.

I was walking casually toward the cockpit when I saw that the man in the pilot's seat was frozen in horror, and that the engine was much louder than it should have been. The throttle was nearly full open, and in all the wind and sudden noise, my helper had forgotten what to do. He sat there, staring straight ahead, as the biplane, all by herself, began to move.

"THE THROTTLE!" I screamed. "CUT THE THROTTLE!" Quick visions flashed of the Parks leaping into the air with a man at the controls who had no faintest idea how to fly. I ran toward the cockpit, but already the airplane was rolling swiftly across the concrete, engine roaring wildly. It was a dream, like running from a railroad train. I threw myself desperately at the cockpit, grabbed the leather rim with one hand, but could not move any farther. The immense propellerblast kept me from moving; it was all I could do to race alongside the biplane.

The vision of my airplane a total wreck gave me one burst of strength to claw my way against the hurricane, up onto the wing. We were moving twenty miles an hour, accelerating quickly. I clung to the edge of the cockpit with every ounce of strength I could squeeze from my body. The man was cold wax in the seat, his eyes glazed, his mouth open.

The biplane was moving far too fast, and turning, now. We were going to ground-loop. In one desperate motion I reached over the cockpit rim, grabbed the throttle and slammed it back. It was too late, and all I could do was hold on as we went around. The tires cried out, dragging sideways, one wing lifted, the other went hard down, scraping concrete. I clung there and waited for a wheel to collapse, or the gear to break away.

After five seconds tense as shredding steel, the wings leveled and we coasted to a stop, all in one piece.

"That," I said, panting, "was a ground loop."

The man climbed like a robot from the cockpit, and not one word did he say. He set his feet on the ground and began walking woodenly toward the office. It was the last I saw of him.

The engine was still running. I set myself down into the seat and talked to the biplane for a while. This had been her way of telling me not to leave her to unknowing people, and I promised that I would never let that happen again.

It was nearing sundown by the time we landed at Kahoka, and Dick was ready to leave.

"I gotta get goin'," he said. "I told my wife I'd be home at seven, and it's seven right now. I shall do some violent aerobatics over the field and be on my way. Let me know when you're back around here."

"Thanks, Richard. We'll do 'er."

I propped the Cub for him and he was off. He flew a pretty set of aerobatics overhead, as he promised, plus a few strange things of his own—flying sideways through the air, flat turns, steep climbs and pushovers.

The crowd was on us before Dick had disappeared in the west, and we flew the last hour steadily, till dark. By the time we covered the airplane and walked to the Orbit Inn, we felt as if we had been working for a living. We had flown twenty-six passengers by the end of the day, and Dick had flown another five. He had made his gas-and-oil money, and Stu and I split $98.

"Almost made it, Stu. Almost broke a hundred-dollar day." We felt affluent, and ordered double milkshakes.

Stu was worried that we would miss the ten-twenty local news, so we walked into the hotel lobby and found the antique television set going unwatched.

It was an interesting lobby. The fans washed mild vertical air down over us, in reminder of times that hadn't quite gone by. There was a bell on the counter, the kind that dings when you tap the button on the top. Against the wall was a monster Firestone Air Chief radio console, four feet high and three feet wide, with stick-on paper squares over the pushbuttons: WGN, WTAD, WCAZ. If I pressed those buttons, I wondered, would I find Fred Allen, strolling in gentle static down Allen's Alley; or Jack Armstrong, the All-American Boy; or Edgar Bergen and Charlie McCarthy? I was afraid to try.

The ten-twenty news came and went without any mention of those delightful barnstormers out by the edge of Kahoka, and Stu was crushed. "My one chance to get on television! One chance! And I ended up on the newsroom floor!"

That night Stu tried using cheesecloth for a mosquito net, taping a peak of it to the bottom of the wing. From what I could see in the dark it looked good, but it didn't work. The mosquitoes learned at once that the trick was to land, to walk under the edge of the net, then take to the air once they were inside. It was another hard night.

As we settled sleepily into the breakfast booth, I said, "Well, Stu, is it moving-on time?"

"Oi thonk so," he said, yawning. "'Scuse me. Darn mosquitoes."

We were blessed with a charming waitress, who had somehow missed her Warner Brothers screen test. "What are we having for breakfast this morning?" she asked sweetly.

"Cherry pancakes, please," I said, "bunch of 'em, with honey."

She wrote the order, and stopped. "We don't have cherry pancakes. Is that on the menu?"

"No. Awful good, though."

She smiled. "We'll give you cherry pancakes if you get the cherries," she said.

I was out the door in a flash, into the market two doors down, and laying out twenty-nine cents for a can of cherries. The waitress was still at the table when I returned, and I set the can down triumphantly. "You just take these and dump 'em right in the batter."

"The whole can?"

"Yes, ma'am. Zonk. Right in the batter. Great pancakes."

"Well . . . I'll ask the cook . . ."

A moment after she left, I noticed that we had company. "Stu, there is an ant on our table."

"Ask him where we're going to go today." He unfolded the road map.

"Here you go, little fella," I said, and helped the ant onto the map. "This is known as the Ant Method of Navigation, Mister MacPherson. You just follow after him with a pen, now. Wherever he goes, we go."

The ant was frightened, and traveled east across Missouri at a great rate. He stopped, wandered nervously south, turned west, stopped, turned northeast. The line under Stu's pen passed some promising towns, as he followed, but then the ant struck out due east, toward the sugar bowl. He stepped across a fold in the map, and in that one step covered three hundred miles, all the way across southern Illinois. Then he leaped off the map and ran for the sugar.

We consumed our magnificent cherry pancakes and looked at the line. Up to the fold, the ant had a pretty good plan. Push east and south, swing around in a big circle to end at Hannibal, Missouri. We'd get a taste of southern Illinois, and the county fair season was upon us as summer burned on. There might be some good places to work, at the fairs.

Decision made, water jug filled, we said good-bye to our waitress, tipping her for being pretty, and walked to the plane.

In half an hour we were off again, pushing into a headwind. The ant had not told us about headwinds. The longer we flew, the more annoyed I got at that dumb ant. There was nothing down there. A few little towns with no place to land, an isolated Army outpost, a million acres of farmland. If there was sugar to the east, we certainly weren't finding it.

There was a fair in progress at Griggsville, Illinois, but no place to land, except in a wheatfield adjacent. The gold of that wheat was no illusion. At the going wheat prices, it would cost us $75 to roll down a landing swath of the tall grain.

We flew on, and days passed, and our affluence dwindled.

There was a fair at Rushville, with horses and sulkies trotting stiffly around the quarter mile, and crowds of potential passengers. But there was no place to land. We circled dismally overhead, and finally pushed on, cursing the ant.

At last we staggered into Hannibal, and talked with Vic Kirby, an old barnstormer who ran the airport there. We stayed awhile with him, bought some gas at discount because all antique planes get discounts at Hannibal, and then at his suggestion, flew north to Palmyra, Missouri.

There was no comparison to Palmyra, Wisconsin, which was centuries away now, in the distant past. This strip was short and narrow, lined by farm equipment and tall corn. We stopped long enough to fly one passenger, and then were off again, aimlessly south, weaving back and forth across the Mississippi, then east again into Illinois.

Landing in a grass field at Hull, I figured we had set a record for biplane crossings of the Mississippi in one day.

We sold three quick rides in the town of five hundred souls, and found that the hayfield we had landed upon had only the day before been approved by the State of Illinois as a landing area. The flying club was going strong, volunteer-building a cement-block office.

"You're the first airplane to land here since this field became an airport!" We heard it over and over again, and we were told it was an honor. But it was ironic. We wanted to have nothing to do with airports, we were just looking for little grassy places to land on, and here our hayfield had been declared an airport beneath our very wheels.

Flying all that day long, using two full tanks of gas, we had earned a total of $12 cash.

"I don't know, Stu. 'Cept for Pecatonica, Illinois just don't seem to be our piece of cake, huh? Next thing you know, ol' what's-his-name is gonna be down here askin' about our Illinois registration tag."

Stu mumbled something, rigged his useless mosquito net and flopped down on his sleeping bag. "You were born in this state, weren't you?" he said, and was asleep at once. I never did figure out what that remark was supposed to mean.

CHAPTER FIFTEEN

I WOKE UP at six-thirty in the morning, to the click of a Polaroid camera-shutter. A man was taking pictures of us sleeping under the wing.

"Mornin'," I said. "Feel like flyin' this mornin'?" It was more reflex than a hunger for $3.

"Maybe in a little while. Takin' some pictures now. You don't mind, do you?"

"No." I dropped my head down on my hammock-pillow and went back to sleep.

We woke up again at nine, and there was a crowd standing a discreet distance away, looking at the airplane.

One fellow looked at me strangely, and studied the name painted by the cockpit rim.

"Say," he said at last. "You wouldn't be the Dick Bach that writes for the flying magazines, would you?"

I sighed. Good-bye, Hull, Illinois. "Yeah. I do a little story, once in a while."

"How do you like that. Why don't you stand over by the cockpit, there, and I'll get your picture."

I stood, glad that he liked my stories, but no longer the anonymous barnstormer.

"Let's pack up, Stu."

*   *   *

Illinois in midsummer was a scenic green hazy oven, and we droned through the broiled air like a worried bee. We wandered north on the Illinois River for days, finding no profit. And then one afternoon a city flowed in from the horizon. Monmouth, Illinois. Population ten thousand. Airport north.

Stu looked back at me as we circled the city and I shrugged. It was a sod field, anyway, we could say that much for it. The question was whether a city this size would be interested in barnstormers.

We'd find out, I thought. We'd work it just as if it were a little town. We landed, taxied to the gas pump and stopped the engine.

There was a row of nine airplanes parked, and a large brick hangar with an antique steam locomotive inside.

The man who drove out to unlock the pump was an old-timer who had worked at Monmouth Airport for thirty years. "I seen it when there was six, eight instructors here," he said. "Thirty people here at one time, a whole big line of airplanes. Had another runway, then, too, out into where that cornfield is now. This is the oldest continuous-used airport in Illinois, you know. Since 1921."

By the time he unloaded us at the restaurant, a half mile from the airport, we had learned something about the way things were in Monmouth aviation. A glory that was past; once the stopping place for the glittering names of flight, now the quiet resort of a few weekend pilots.

In the frosted air of the restaurant, the name "Beth" began our list of Monmouth Knowns. She was interested in the airplane, but she brought us little hope with our hamburgers.

"Summer's the wrong time for you. All the kids from the college are gone home." There was a long silence, and she smiled sadly for us and left us alone.

"So," said Stu, tired. "No kiddies. Where do we go from here?"

I named some places, none of which was much more promising than Monmouth. ". . . and as a very last resort, we could try Muscatine."

"Sounds too much like Mosquito." That spiked Muscatine.

"Well, heck. Let's just work Monmouth and see what happens. Give it a chance, you know. Might do a jump, maybe, see if we can get the people out."

The jump was first priority. By the time we had the airplane unpacked and ready to work, it was five o'clock, the best time for crowd-attracting.

Stu jumped from 3,500 feet, down into horizonless haze, moving at meteor speed toward the runway grass. His canopy snapped open in a great poof of white, the last of the King's Ransom packed into the folded nylon, and now he drifted downward like a small tired cumulus cloud.

While we dived to circle him, I saw a few cars gathering, but not nearly so many as I expected from a town that size. We flew some mild aerobatics over the cornfields and landed. Stu had logged another good jump, and I taxied to find him working the cars, saying over and again how cool was the air at 3,500 feet.

The people didn't want to fly. "That thing state-inspected?" I heard one man ask, looking at the biplane.

We're a long way from small-town flying, I thought. It sounds as if city people live in the present day, as if they live at modern speeds and expect modern guarantees for their safety. We carried two passengers by sundown.

The local pilots were very kind, and promised bigger crowds the next day. "We had a parachute meet here a month ago, and there were cars backed all the way up to the main highway," they said. "Just takes a little while for the word to get around."

By the time we walked into the restaurant for supper, I was having doubts all over again about Monmouth.

"Stu, what do you think about pressing on, tomorrow? This place feel right to you?"

"Two rides. That's normal first-day, you know."

"Yeah, but the place just doesn't seem with it, you know? In the little towns, we're a big thing, and people at least come out to look. Here we're just another airplane. Nobody cares." We ordered from Beth, who gave us a happy smile and said that she was glad to see us back.

"Might as well give the place a try," Stu said. "We hunted a long time, remember. Some other places looked bad, too, at first."

"OK. We'll stay." Another day, at least, would confirm my fears about big-city barnstorming. It just did not feel comfortable; we were out of our element, out of our time.

Stu and I slept in the airport office that night. There were no mosquitoes.

It plagued me all through the next day. We carried passengers well, until by seven o'clock we had flown eighteen rides, but the spirit of barnstorming was gone. We were just a couple of crazy guys selling airplane rides.

At seven, a man came to us as we sat under the wing.

"Hey, fellas, I wonder if you could do something a little special for me."

"Speak special speak," I said in archaic Air Force slang. Stu and I had been talking about Air Force life.

"I'm having a party over at my house . . . wonder if I could hire you to give us a little air show. We're just on the edge of town, right over there."

"Doubt if you'd see much," I said. "My minimum altitude is fifteen hundred feet above the ground, and I'd start at three thousand. Be just a little speck to you, is all."

"That doesn't make any difference. Could you give us a show for say . . . twenty-five dollars?"

"Sure thing, if you want it. But I'm not coming down less than fifteen hundred feet."

"Fine." He took two tens and a five-dollar bill from his wallet. "Could you be up at seven-thirty?"

"No problem. You keep your money, though. If you think it was worth it, you can stop by and give us the money later. If you don't like it, don't bother."

At seven-thirty we were over the cornfields at the edge of town, and starting our first loop. By seven-forty the show was over, and we circled down over the park to watch the baseball game.

When we landed, Stu had two passengers ready to go.

"Give us a wild ride!" they said.

They got the Standard Wild Ride; steep turns, sideslips, with the wind smashing over them, dives and zooms. They were as gay and excited in the air as though the biplane were the biggest fastest roller-coaster in the world, and all of a sudden I was surprised at it. During the minutes we had been flying, I was thinking about moving out of Monmouth, and wondered where we might go next. I wasn't seeing the ride as wild or the Parks as a roller-coaster. Fun, perhaps, in a mild sort of way, and interesting, but hardly exciting.

A revelation, that, and a warning of evil. The summer was beginning to go stale, I was taking even the strange and adventurous life of a gypsy pilot for granted, and as just another job.

I pulled the airplane up into a half-roll, which set them to clutching the leather cockpit-rim in fearful delight, and talked out loud to myself. "Hey, listen, Richard! That's the wind! Hear it through the wires, feel it on your face, beating these goggles! Wake up! This is here and now, and time for you to be alive! Snap out of it! See! Taste! Wake up!"

All at once I could hear again . . . the blast and concussion of the Whirlwind went from an unheard Niagara to the roar of a wild old engine again, a high-speed metronome firing dynamite with each beat of its blade.

That magnificent perfect sound . . . how long had it been since I had ceased to listen to it? Weeks. That sun, bright as incandescent steel in a blue-fire sky . . . how long since I had leaned back my head and held the taste of that sun in my mouth? I opened my eyes and looked right up into it and drank the heat of it. I took off one glove and grabbed a handful of wind, never breathed by anybody in 10 billion years, and I grabbed it and snuffed it deep within me.

The people ahead of you, Richard, open your eyes! Who are they? Look at them! See! They changed at once from passengers into living people, a young man, a young woman, bright and happy and beautiful in the way that we are all beautiful when we are for a moment completely unconscious of ourselves, when we are looking out toward something that absorbs us completely.

We banked again, steeply, and they looked together down fifteen feet of brilliant lemon wings and nine hundred feet of hard transparent air and five feet of corn-plant sea and a tenth-inch of black loam, stuffed with minerals. Wings, air, corn, loam, minerals and birds and lakes and roads and fences and cows and trees and grass and flowers— every bit of it moved in a great sweeping stroke of colors, and the colors went in through the wide-open eyes of these fellow-people of mine, and deep into their hearts, to surface in a smile or a laugh and the brave beautiful look of those who have not yet chosen to die.

Never stop being a kid, Richard. Never stop tasting and feeling and seeing and being excited with great things like air and engines and the sounds of sunlight within you. Wear your little mask, if you must, to protect the kid from the world, but if you let that kid disappear, buddy, you are grown up and you are dead.

The tall old wheels rumbled and thumped on earth soft as a giant petrified pillow, and the flight, the first ride for my passengers and the thousandth for me, was over. They became conscious of themselves again and said thank you that was great and paid Stu $6 and got into their automobile and drove away. I said thank you, it's been nice flying with you, and I was absolutely dead certain that we would all remember our flight together for a very long time.

That night, Stu and I laid out the couch cushions into islands of soft on the office floor, cast mild and pleasant wrath upon the man who never returned to pay us for our $25 air show, and settled down with strawberry soda pop in mosquitoless air. The only light in the room came from the sun, reflected off the moon bright enough to show the colors of the biplane outside.

"Stuart Sandy MacPherson," I said. "Who the devil are you?"

The boy's mask of solemn quiet was more and more clearly a pure fake, for quiet solemn people do not jump from the wings of airplanes a mile in the air, or travel halfway across the country to become a barnstormer. Even Stu realized that the question was in order, and didn't dodge it.

"Sometimes I'm not too sure who I am," he said. "I was on the varsity tennis team, in high school, if that helps you very much. I did some mountain climbing . . ."

I blinked. "You mean regular mountain climbing? With the ropes and pitons and crampons and rock walls and all that? Or do you mean just hills that you can walk up?"

"The whole works. It was fun. Until I got hit on the head with a rock. Knocked me out for a while. I was lucky I was roped to the guy ahead of me."

"You were just dangling there in space, at the end of a rope?"

"Yeah."

"Boy."

"Yeah. Well, then I quit mountain climbing and took up flying. Got my private license. Flying Piper Cubs."

"Stu! Why didn't you say you had your license? You know, my gosh! You're supposed to tell us things like that!"

I thought, in the darkness, that he shrugged.

"I did a lot of motorcycle riding. It's fun, to try to be good with a machine . . ."

"Fantastic, kid!" The nice thing about not talking very much is that when you do talk, you can startle people so much that they listen. "Now. Look," I said. "I've heard of some pretty dumb things, some people who really sold themselves down the river, but you take the cake, about. You have all these great things going for you, like a real live person, and yet there you are in Salt Lake at dentist school. Please tell me . . . *why?*"

He set his pop bottle down with a heavy clink on the floor. "I owe it to my folks," he said. "They've paid my way . . ."

"You owe it to your folks to be happy. Don't you? They've got no right to force you into something where you aren't happy."

"Maybe." He thought for a moment. "Maybe that's the trouble . . . it's too easy to stay in the system, the way things are. If I did drop out, I'd get sucked up in the draft, and then where would I be?"

"Ah—Stu?" I said. I wanted to talk about his school, but the last words frightened me. "What's patriotism, do you imagine? What do you think it means?"

There was the longest silence then, that I had heard all summer.

The boy was trying, he was turning it over and over in his mind. And he was coming up with nothing. I lay there and listened to him think, wondering if the same emptiness was in the minds of all the other college youth around the country. If it was, the United States of America was facing some more difficult times.

"I don't know," he said at last. "I don't know . . . what . . . patriotism . . . is."

"No wonder you're scared of the draft, then, fella," I snapped. "This patriotism stuff is three words: Gratitude. For. Country. You go out, climb your mountains, you drive your motorcycles; I can fly wherever I want, write what I want to write, and I can jump all over the government whenever it's being stupid. How many guys do you think have been shot all to bits so you and I can run our lives the way we want? Hundred thousand guys? Million guys?"

Stu sat on the pillows, his hands clasped behind his head, looking across the dark room.

"So we take a year or two or five out of this fantastic freedom," I said, "and we say, 'Hey, country, thanks!'"

At that moment I wasn't talking to Stu MacPherson, but to all my poor vacant young countrymen who couldn't understand, whining about the draft in the midst of sacred rare beautiful liberty.

I wanted to box them all up and ship them to some slave nation, and make them stay there until they were ready to fight their way back home. But if I nailed the crates down on them, I'd be destroying the very freedom I wished them to see. I had to let them whine, and pray they'd see the picture before they broke the country into jelly blobs of self-pity.

Stu was silent. I didn't want him to talk. I prayed, very deeply, that in the silence, he was listening.

CHAPTER SIXTEEN

By TEN O'CLOCK in the morning the oven Illinois was a kiln. The grass scorched beneath our feet. There was a very light hot breeze, a low oriental woodwind through the flying wires as we sat in the shade under the wing.

"OK, Stu-babe, here is a map. I shall take my knife and hurl it into the map. Wherever the knife hits, we go."

I tossed the knife down end over end, and to my surprise, the blade struck hard and firm through the map. A good omen. We checked the slit eagerly.

"Great," I said. "We are supposed to go land in the Mississippi River. Thanks a lot, knife."

We tried again and again, and the only result was a map full of holes. There was a reason not to fly to any place the knife suggested.

A car stopped, and a man and two boys walked toward us.

"When they get out of the car, they are already sold," Stu said. "Do we want to fly anybody today, or just get going?"

"Might as well fly 'em."

Stu went to work. "Hi, folks."

"You with the airplane?"

"Yes, sir!"

"We want to fly."

"Glad to have you aboard. Why don't you just step right over here . . ." He broke off in midsentence. "Hey, look, Dick. A biplane."

It came small and quiet, whispering in from the west, easing down toward us through the sky.

"Stu, that's a Travelair! That's Spencer Nelson! He made it!"

It was a bomb set off in our midst. I leaped into the cockpit and tossed the starting crank to Stu.

"You don't mind waiting a minute, folks, do you?" I said to the man and his sons. "This other airplane is all the way from California. I'll go up and welcome him in, and then we'll fly."

They didn't have a chance to protest. The engine, screaming from the inertia starter, burst into life and we were taxiing at once, gathering speed, lifting off the ground, turning toward the newcomer. He was swinging into the landing pattern when we caught him, and closed into formation alongside.

The pilot waved.

"HEY, SPENCE!" I shouted, knowing he couldn't hear a word over the wind.

His airplane was beautiful. It was just out of the shop, finished by this airline captain who couldn't get enough of flying. The machine shined and sparkled and flashed in the sunlight. There wasn't a single patch, not one oil streak or spot of grease down its whole length, and I blinked at its perfection. The big air-balanced rudder touched over and we turned for a low pass along the grass runway.

Travelair Aircraft Co. went the smooth professional letters on the tail, *Wichita, Kansas.* The airplane was a sleek eager dolphin in the sky, a much larger machine than the Parks, and much more elegant. We felt like a seamy tar-stained little tugboat nosing the *United States* into harbor. I wondered if Spence knew what he was getting into, if his glossy blue airplane was going to look as pretty going home as it looked this minute.

We whistled once more through the pattern and landed, that queen of a biplane leading the way, taxiing to the passengers, shutting down into a stately silence.

I had never met the pilot, and knew him only through letters and telephone calls as he had struggled to get his airplane ready for the summer. When he took off his helmet and climbed down from the high cockpit, I saw that Spencer Nelson was a short quick man with the hawkish look of an old-time pilot: firm angled face, intense blue eyes.

"Mr. Nelson!" I said.

"Mr. Bach, I presume?"

"Spence, you nutty guy. You made it! Where you in from this morning?"

"In from Kearney, Nebraska. Five hours' flying. I called your house, Bette said you had called from here." He stretched, glad to be out of the cockpit. "That old parachute gets kind of hard to sit on after a while, don't it?"

"Well, from here on out, you are in the land of happy barnstorming, Spence. But you come out here to stand 'round and talk, or you wanta do some work? We got passengers waitin'."

"Let's go," he said.

He piled a mass of equipment from the front cockpit onto the ground, and Stu led two of the passengers to the big airplane. I helped the other one into the Parks, which was looking rattier every moment she stood alongside the Travelair.

"I'll follow you," Spence called, as Stu cranked his engine into blue smoke and roar.

We took off and fell into the Monmouth Barnstorming Pattern, one long turn around the city, a circle over a little lake west with sun-sparkles on the water, and gliding turns to landing . . . ten minutes exactly. The Travelair was much faster than the Parks, and zoomed by her in the first turn after takeoff. Spence took far too long, making double turns and side excursions all over the place.

He landed five minutes after the Parks.

"Hey, what are you tryin' to do?" I said. "The people are not paying to ride along while you break the biplane endurance record, you know. They're paying to get a taste of the wind in the wires, and to see how it all looks from the air. I'd hate to have you for competition."

"Was that too long? I'll watch that. Just breakin' in here, you know."

We walked to the restaurant and heard his story of trials and frustration with officials and paperwork while he had put the finishing touches on the Travelair and raced across the country to catch us.

"I've only got five days left on my vacation, with all that delay at first. I'll have to be gettin' on home here in a couple days."

"Spence! You come all the heck way out here for *two days'* barnstorming? That is bad news! You are some kind of a nut, I hope to tell ya!"

He shrugged his shoulders. "Never been barnstorming before."

"Well, we sure got to get out of here, give you something a little more typical, and make you some money to get home on, anyway."

"How about Kahoka?" Stu said. "Remember they said they had drag races or some big thing coming up. Lots of people. Close to town."

"That's an airstrip, though. We want a good hayfield."

We thought it over for a while, and at last Stu prevailed. With just two days left for our new pilot, we couldn't afford to wander aimlessly.

By three o'clock we were airborne, heading south and west into Missouri. Stu rode the Travelair front seat, and I had a cockpit full of baggage and parachutes.

We had a problem at once. The Travelair was too fast; Spence had to keep his power way back to fly slow enough for me to stay with him. Every once in a while he would forget, and think about something else, and then turn around to find a tiny speck of a Parks trailing a mile behind. But by the time we crossed the Mississippi, we were working together and our shadows flicked over the brown water in good formation. It was a fine feeling, not to be alone, to have another biplane out there going the same way through the old sky. We felt happy, my airplane and I, and we did a little swooping and turning just for fun.

A barnstormer, I found, gets to know the country well. It wasn't necessary to look once at the map. Head toward the sun till you hit the Mississippi. Fly down the river till you can see the Des Moines River coming in from the west. Cut north of Keokuk and angle a little south for ten minutes and there's Kahoka.

The drag strip was overflowing with people. We flew one circle to let the world know that we had arrived, and turned to land.

"Hey, this looks nice," Spence said as soon as we had landed. "Nice grass, town's right here, this looks real nice."

The passengers came at once and it was luxury to let the Travelair carry the first ones, just to sit on the ground and let Spence bring in the money.

We were big-time now, with a Ship Number One and a Ship Number Two to work for us. Unfortunately I couldn't enjoy the luxury long, for greasy old Ship Number One had customers walking toward her, ready to fly. I climbed into my familiar seat and we were on our way through the afternoon. There were just a few hours left till sundown, but we worked straight through, and carried twenty-three riders before the day was over.

I heard bits and pieces of passenger talk, between takeoffs.

"I been twenty-five years trying to get my wife off the ground, and today she finally goes up in that blue plane."

"This is real flying. The modern stuff is transportation, but this is real flying."

"Sure glad you guys showed up—it'll do a lot for this town."

It was like coming home, Kahoka. The Orbit Inn was still there and going strong, with its jukebox music; and the young people sitting on the fenders of their cars in the warm night air.

"This is fun," Spence said. "Not just the money, but talking to the people. You're really doing something for 'em."

Stu and I saw it all again for the first time, through the other pilot's eyes as he talked. It was good to see Spencer Nelson there in night Kahoka, carried away with the fresh new joys of barnstorming.

CHAPTER SEVENTEEN

―――――

"I GOT AN oil leak!" Spence was concerned, and pointed to a tiny line of clean oil from the engine cowl.

"You want to trade oil leaks, Mr. Nelson?" I said. "Now I've got a few nice leaks that you might find interesting . . ."

"Your engine's supposed to leak," he said. "But a Continental's supposed to be tight as a drum." He was worried and loosened the Travelair's bottom cowl in the first rays of cool morning sunlight.

Oh, well, I thought, if we have early passengers, I'll do the flying. I dragged out my tool kit and we began checking over his big engine.

"Everything's so new," he said. "Probably just some fittings working in, and they're loose now."

Which was part of the trouble. Some of the oil-hose connections were loose enough to turn a full time around before snugging tight again.

"That ought to do her up," he said after half an hour's work. "Let's give her a try."

"I'll crank it for you." I set the starter crank into the side of the cowl and thought that it was a pretty light little fitting for the heavy crank.

"It's a bit flimsy there, that crank thing," Nelson said, from the cockpit. "When I get back I'm gonna beef that up."

I turned the crank three turns, and the shaft snapped off under my hand.

"What's the matter?" he called.

"Spence, kiddo, I think you're gonna have to beef this thing up before you get back."

"It didn't break, did it?"

"Yessir."

"Well, I'll find a place in town and get it all welded up. Just as soon get it out of the way now, huh?"

He took the shaft loose and set off for town. If this was to be his only maintenance problem in two days, he would be doing well indeed as a gypsy pilot.

A man drove up and looked at the airplanes. "You fly those?"

"Sure do," I said, walking over to the window of the Chevrolet. "You lookin' to ride today?"

"I don't know," he said, thoughtfully. Sitting next to him in the car was a completely beautiful young woman, with long black hair and very wide dark eyes.

"Town's awful pretty in the morning . . . air's nice and still and smooth," I said. "Cooler up there, too."

The man was interested, teetering on the brink of adventure, but the girl looked at me as a frightened doe would, and didn't make a sound.

"Think I should go up?" the man asked her.

There was no reply, not a single word. She shook her head the tiniest bit no.

"Never had a passenger who didn't think the ride was great—your money back if you don't like it." I surprised myself with that. I really didn't care if the man flew or not; there would be plenty of passengers later on. The money-back guarantee was a good stunt, but I hadn't even considered it until that second. It was a clash of my world against the world of that girl, and the man was our battleground.

"I think I'll go. Take long?"

"Ten minutes." I had won, that quickly.

"Be right back," he said to the girl. She looked at him with her deep dark eyes, afraid, but still she didn't say a word.

We flew ten minutes, and because I was curious, I kept looking back and down, as we flew, at the Chevrolet. The car door did not open, there was no face looking up through the window. Something strange about that woman, and the bright summer day went eerie and uncomfortable.

The landing was normal, every bit normal, like every landing we made those days. We were down and rolling along the grass, moving perhaps forty miles per hour. Suddenly a voice spoke within me: "Move it over to the right, swing out to the right." There was no reason to do it, but I did, wondering that I would.

In that instant, as the biplane moved right, an airplane flashed past on our left, landing in the opposite direction on the grass, moving perhaps fifty miles per hour.

For a second I was stunned, a sheet of cold went through me. I hadn't seen the other plane, he clearly hadn't seen me. If we hadn't moved to the right, the biplane's barnstorming days would have come to a very quick, spectacular end. The other plane turned, lifted again into the air, and disappeared. I thanked that voice, that angel-thought, and since the incident was all over I would best be very casual about it, or better, not speak of it at all.

The man handed Stu three dollar bills and got back into his car. The girl had not moved, she had not spoken.

"Thanks a lot," my passenger said, happy, and with his strange strange person, drove away. We didn't see them again.

Spence came back with a welded starter shaft of solid iron, strong enough to hang his whole airplane from.

"This ought to do the job," he said. "Let's try her again."

The engine fired at once and he was off for a test flight. When he returned ten minutes later, there was still a faint spray of oil from the crankcase breather.

"Well, gee," he said. "I'd sure like to get rid of that oil."

"Spence, that's the *breather*! That is oil *mist*, you're talking about. I don't know too many barnstormers who worry about oil mist on their airplanes. All we care about here is that the wings are on good and tight, you know?"

"OK. But still, I don't like it on my pretty new Travelair."

Spence got the next two passengers, a man and his boy. When they were strapped aboard, he lowered his goggles, pushed the throttle forward and started his takeoff across the grass. I turned to Stu. "Sure is nice to have somebody else to do the work, so we . . ." I stopped in midsentence, stricken. The Travelair engine had quit on takeoff.

"Oh, no." This, I thought, in a tenth of a second, is not our day.

The big airplane glided down again to the grass, rolling soundlessly toward the far end of the strip; the engine had stopped soon enough to allow a quick safe landing.

In a second it cut in again, purring smoothly, but Spence didn't try another takeoff. He taxied straight back toward us.

"Wonder what the passengers think of that," Stu said, with a faint smile.

I opened the cockpit door for them when the biplane arrived. "Kind of a short ride, wasn't it?" I said, sounding cool. It would have terrified me, if I were in the front seat when everything stopped.

"Oh, it was long enough, but we didn't get very high," the man said, helping his son down to the grass. It was a remarkable thing to say, and I was proud of him.

"You want to ride in Ship Number One?"

"No, thanks. We'll give you a chance to fix this one . . . be back tonight and fly."

I accepted this as a brave excuse, and crossed them off the list of passengers who would ever trust a biplane. When they had left, we got to work.

"Clearly, the thing isn't getting any gas, to stop like that," I said.

"Dirt in the gas?" Spence said.

"Sounds good. Let's give it a try."

The engine had been stored in Arizona, and there was a teaspoonful of sand in the fuel strainer.

"That's part of the problem, anyway," Spence said. "Let's try it again."

We tried again, but the engine would sputter and cough at full throttle, then cut out completely.

"How's your fuel?"

"Oh, I got half a tank." He thought of something and ran the engine up again. It worked perfectly. "Center-section tank," he said. "It works fine if it's running on gas out of the high tank."

He experimented with it and found that there was nothing he could do to make the engine quit as long as it was taking fuel out of the big overhead tank buried in the middle of the top wing.

"That's it," he said at last. "Float level or something in the carburetor isn't quite right. She wants that extra pressure when she's going full throttle."

The problem was solved and we celebrated with a parachute jump. Stu was anxious to enter a "Travelair Jump" in his sky diver's logbook, and we were airborne in midafternoon, flying formation on the way up to jump altitude.

I broke away at 2,500 feet and circled to wait for Stu to come down.

We could expect heavy business if the parachute jump went as planned; the drag-strip crowd was out in force. But it didn't go quite as planned. Stu missed his target. I followed him down, knowing that from my angle I couldn't tell where he was going to land. But the lower he got, the clearer it was that he wouldn't make the runway, and that he might end up in the telephone wires across the weedlot to the south.

He missed the wires by a few feet and was down in the weeds, then up again, waving that he was OK. Spence and I flew a formation advertising flight, broke apart and landed. There was a crowd waiting to fly, and Stu was just panting onto the field, carrying his parachute.

"Man! I thought I got those wires! I waited around too long before I did anything about the wind. Bad jump!" But that was it. We avoid disaster and we go on working.

He dumped the chute on his sleeping bag and was selling rides at once. I nodded here-we-go to Spence and we got into the airplanes. Again we didn't stop flying till sundown. To my great surprise, Spence's engine-failure passengers, the man and his boy, came back to fly again. This time the Continental kept on running for them, and they saw Kahoka from the air, a town sailing serenely across the flat green sea of Missouri.

I flew one clod who turned out to be drunk; after we were airborne he made as though to climb out of the front cockpit, and generally proved himself a fool. I gave him a few hard turns to smash him down in the seat, all the time wishing that it would be legal to let the blockhead throw himself out of the airplane.

"You give me another passenger like that, Stu," I said after landing, "and I will part your hair with a Crescent wrench."

"Sorry. Didn't know he was so bad."

The sun went down, but Spence kept hopping passengers. To each his own, I thought. The Parks and I quit as soon as we lost ground detail in the darkness.

It was full dark when at last he shut down his engine. In fourteen years with Pacific Southwest Airlines he was conditioned to haul every person he could possibly fly.

We collapsed on our sleeping bags and broke out the flashlight. "How'd we do, Stu?"

Stu heaped up the money. "We've got quite a bit. Twenty, thirty, thirty-five, forty-five . . ." It did look like it had been a good day. ". . . one fifty-three, fifty-four, fifty-five . . . one hundred and fifty-six dollars. That is . . . fifty-two passengers today."

"We broke it!" I said. "We broke our hundred-dollar day!"

"I tell you guys," Spence said. "This is not a bad way to make a living! Man, I wish I didn't have to get back so soon."

"We've got to get you some hayfield somewhere, Spence. Some little field for real barnstorming-type flying."

"There's not much time," he said. "Might have to wait till next year."

Stu's time was running out, too, and he talked with Spence about hitching a ride home.

I flew two leftover passengers the next morning, and we loaded our airplanes. Spence had one day left.

We took off west, and idled down the road, looking for a field-bordered town. It was as bad as ever. The fields were beautiful between the little villages. The hay was mowed and raked and baled away, and the land stretched long and clear into the wind.

But as soon as we approached a town, the telephone poles shot up like giant bamboo and the fields went short and rough and crosswind. We drifted down to look at a few borderline places, but nothing good came. We were not starving, and there was no need to work a difficult place.

Finally, over Lancaster, Missouri, we saw a field. It would be none too good—ridgetop land with steep hillsides to go tumbling down if we didn't roll straight out after landing—but it was long enough, and close to town.

Just after I pointed it out to Spence and Stu, I saw that the darn thing was an airport. No hangars, no gas pump, but the wheel-marks were there to give it away.

We were getting tired of wandering, so we landed. During the roll-out I had doubts about carrying passengers out of there, even if it was an airport.

I watched the Travelair land. Smooth as a river, it flowed down the strip; the sight of an old pro at work, no matter how much Nelson protested his amateur status at barnstorming.

A low sign by a log in the grass said, "William E. Hall Memorial Airport."

"What do you think, Spence?" I said when he had shut down his engine.

"Looks OK. Fun comin' in. I went over town and revved the engine. I could see people down there, and they stopped, you know, and they were lookin' up."

"Well, we're close enough to town, but I don't quite dig the airport. It's a bit squirrelly for me, and if you lose the engine on takeoff you got no place to go without bending the airplane."

A car drove up and a man got out, carrying a movie camera. "Hi," he said, "mind if I take some pictures?"

"Go right ahead." The rest of our meeting was recorded in living color, to the whir of a spring-wound camera.

"I don't like it," I said. "We're not far south of Ottumwa, and that's home base for me. We need fuel anyway. Why don't we hop up there and get gas and oil and you can check the weather going west. Make a decision then."

"Let's do it."

We were airborne a few minutes later, heading north, and in half an hour we landed at Ottumwa, Iowa.

The weather growing in the west was not encouraging, and Spence was worried. "They've got some pretty strong stuff coming down our way," he said. "High winds and low ceilings. I think I better hold the barnstorming till next year, Dick. If I get caught out by the weather I won't make my airline schedule. That wouldn't be too good. I better get out today and try to beat this stuff."

"Stu, you make up your mind?" I asked. "Last chance for a free ride home, probably."

"I guess I'd better go back with Spence," he said. "It's been a pretty good time . . . I'd be stretching it a little if I stayed. School starting before too long."

They packed up the Travelair at once; parachutes and oil and clothes bags and shaving kits. I cranked the engine alive and handed one of the FLY $3 FLY signs to Stu. "Souvenir, Mister MacPherson."

"You gonna autograph it for me?"

"If you want." I laid it out on the wing and wrote, SEE YOUR TOWN FROM THE AIR!, then signed it and handed it up to him as he made his place in the front cockpit.

I shook hands with Spence. "Glad you could make it. You're pretty nutty to come all the way across the country for two days' barnstorming."

"It was fun! We'll do it again next year, huh?"

I stepped up on the wingwalk and nodded once to the young jumper, wondering how to say good-bye. "Good times, Stu," I said at last. "Do what you want to do, remember."

"Bye." Way down in his eyes, the glimmer of a signal that he was learning, and for me not to worry.

The big biplane taxied out to the runway, pointed into the increasing wind and swept along up into the air. There were two quick waves from the cockpits and I waved back, thinking of myself through their eyes, a lone figure down on the ground, getting smaller and smaller and finally lost in distance. I stood there and watched the Travelair until the sound of it was gone, then until the sight of it disappeared in the west. And then there was nothing left in the sky. Stu, and Spence, too, had joined Paul. Gone, but not gone. Dead, but not dead at all.

I was surrounded by modern airplanes on the parking ramp, but for some reason as I walked back among them, I felt that it was they that were out of their time, and not I.

CHAPTER EIGHTEEN

THE AFTERNOON SKY was low gray, light rain whipped across the windscreen, and The Great American Flying Circus was down to one man, one biplane, alone in the air.

I had one tank of gasoline, and eleven cents cash in my pocket. If I wanted to eat again, I had to find somebody down there with $3 and a burning wish to fly in the rain.

Prospects did not look good. Kirksville, Missouri, canceled itself in rows on rows of alfalfa bales in the hayfields and flocks of sullen cows in the pastures. And in Kirksville the rain poured solid down, intent on turning the city into a major inland sea; the windscreen changed into a sheet of water bolted to the airplane. It was not comfortable flying.

As we turned from Kirksville, spraying rain, I remembered a town on the way north that was worth a try. But again it was the wrong moment to strike. One good field, a block from town, was covered in hay bales. Another was surrounded by a fence. A third lay at the bottom of a square maelstrom of high-tension lines.

We circled and thought, the biplane and I, ignoring the grass airstrip and hangars a mile south. It would be a good town to work, but a mile away was too far. Nobody walks a mile in the rain to fly any airplane. At last, with the heavy Kirksville rains almost caught up with us again, we landed in the field with the fence, hoping there would be a gate. As the wheels touched, a fox leaped for cover in a neighboring stand of corn.

There was no break in the fence, but the two boys appeared, playing the part assigned them by destiny, rain or sun.

"Hey, where's the gate?"

"Isn't any gate. We climbed over. There's an airport just down the way, mister."

It was raining harder. "You boys know of any way a body could get in here, if I was to take 'em for an airplane ride?"

"Sure don't know. Climb the fence, I guess."

Another field crossed off the list. The airport, then. They might know there of some other place. Another two hours and it would be too dark to fly, with the rain and cloud hiding the sun. I chose the airport, because I didn't know where else to go.

Even that was a struggle. Along one side of the strip was a fence, along the other side a sea of corn. It was harder to land on that airport than on any hayfield we had worked, and I thought that even if this place was swarming with passengers I wouldn't fly one of them. It was all I could do to keep the biplane rolling straight between the solid obstacles, steering only by the high blur at each side of the cockpit and hoping that the path ahead was clear.

Waiting in the rain at the end of the strip were five metal hangars, a dripping wind sock, and a pickup truck with an interested family within, watching. The man stepped shirtless from the driver's seat as I climbed from the cockpit, leaving the engine running.

"Want some gas?"

"No, thanks. Pretty good on gas. Looking for a place to fly." I opened my road map and pointed to a town twenty miles southwest. "What do you know about Green City? Any place to land, there? Hayfield or pasture or somethin' like that?"

"Sure. They got a airport there. South of town, by the water reservoir. Whatcha doin'? Crop dustin'?"

"Carryin' passengers."

"Oh. Yeah, Green City might be nice. Probably a lot of people right here'd like to fly with you, though. You could stay right here, if you wanted."

"Bit too far from town," I said. "You have to be close to town. Nobody comes out if you're too far."

The rain slackened for a moment, and off to the southwest the sky didn't look quite as dark as it had an hour before. To fly again was to use gasoline that couldn't be replaced until we earned some money, yet if we stayed at the airport we would be jobless and hungry, both.

"Well, I'd better get goin'. Might as well push on off while there's light."

In a minute we were blurring between corn and fence, and then lifted above them and swung down into the south.

The hills in this part of Missouri roll on like green sea-billows, cresting in a fine spray of trees, sheltering roads and tiny villages in their troughs. It is not the easiest kind of country for navigators. There are none of the precise north-south section lines that lattice the states to the north. I sighted the nose a bit to the south of the lighter grey spot in the sky that was the setting sun.

Green City. What a name, what a poetic piece of imagery. I thought of tall wind-swayed elms, and streets of bright lawns, close-cut, and sidewalks in summer shade. I peered over the windscreen, looking for it. After a long moment, the town drifted in under the biplane's nose. There the reservoir, there the tall elms, there the water tower, all silver with the black letters GREEN CITY.

And there, good grief, the airport. A long strip along the crest of a ridge, narrower than the one I had just left. For a moment I wondered if the biplane would even fit in the width of it. At each edge, the ground dropped sharp and roughly away into tangled earth. The end was a row of barrels at the top of a cliff. Halfway down the strip was a metal building, almost overlapping the landing area. Green City was the most difficult airport to land upon that I had ever seen. I would not have picked that spot for a forced landing, even, if the engine stopped.

But there was a wind sock, and a hangar. On the approach was a set of telephone wires, and as I flew a low pass down the field I saw that the last half of the strip was rolling, and tilted first to the left, then to the right. The narrow twisting runway was edged every fifty feet with tall white wooden markers. The owner must have figured that if you ran off the path you were going to hurt your airplane anyway, and a few wooden posts smashing into your wings wouldn't make that much difference. I saw that we'd have about eight feet clearance on each wingtip, and I swallowed.

We made one last pass over the field, and as we did, two motorcycles sped out the dirt road and braked hard at the edge of the grass to watch. As our wheels touched, I lost sight of the strip ahead, held my breath, and watched the white markers blur past the wingtips. I held the airplane as straight as I had ever held it and pressed down hard on the brake pedals. After an agonizing fifteen seconds, we had rolled to walking speed, and with much power and brake, the biplane turned very carefully in her tracks and taxied back to the road and the motorcyclists.

As I stepped out of the cockpit I wondered how much food and gasoline I could buy for eleven cents.

"You fellas feel like flyin'? Green City from the air; a real pretty place. Give you an extralong ride, since you came out to meet me so nice. Three dollars each, is all." I was aghast, listening to my own words. Carry passengers from this field? I am out of my mind!

But I had landed here once, and I could do it again. What was this airplane built for, but to fly passengers?

"Let's go, Billy!" one of the boys said. "I've never been up in one of these open jobs, and that's the kind Dad learned on. Can you carry us both?"

"Sure can," I said.

"Well, wait. I don't think we have the money."

They were leafing through their billfolds, picking sparse green bills. "Five-fifty is all we got between us. You fly us for that?"

"Well, since you came on out so quick . . . OK." I took the five dollar-bills and two pieces of silver and suddenly felt solvent again. Food! I would have steak tonight!

I emptied the cargo from the front seat and strapped my two passengers aboard, unconsciously pulling their safety belt a bit tighter than usual.

Settled down into my cockpit, I lined carefully on the bent strip of grass, and pushed the throttle forward. In spite of all the signs that I was going too far out on a shaky limb, I was glad to be aloft with my passengers. I had this moment gained title to that cash in my pocket, and after a few minutes buzzing around, I would have only to land and eat. I searched again for other places to come down, but there was none. Hills, money-crops, too short, too far from town. The motorcycles were still at the airport, anyway; we had to make one more landing on the high trapeze.

In ten minutes we circled the strip again, and in the dimming light it did not look any easier to land upon. The passengers were curious to see over the nose as we landed, and they blocked what little view I had in the moment I cut the throttle.

We hit the ground and bounced, and it felt as if we moved to the right. I thought of the embankment on the right side of the strip, and pushed left rudder. Too much. The biplane swerved left, and her left wheel went off the runway. By the time I hit right rudder, the left wing was flashing a foot above jumbled grassy hillocks and harsh earth there, streaking toward a wooden marker and that metal building. I slammed full right rudder and hit the throttle, rolling thirty miles per hour. The airplane jumped back onto the runway an instant before the building flashed by, and we swung hard to the right. I came back with full left rudder and full brakes. We stopped just at the edge of the embankment, and I went limp. So this is what barnstormers did when they were desperate for cash.

"Hey, that was great! Did you see 'em come runnin' out when we went over the house?"

My passengers couldn't have been nearly as happy as I was to be down again, and I gratefully took a ride to town on the back of a motorcycle.

The town square was a small Kahoka. There were picnic tables in the park, a Liberty Bell on a stand, a home plate and pitcher's mound, and a telephone booth with the glass broken out on the home-plate side. Square storefronts looked at the park from all four sides, and one of the squares was Lloyd's Café. Lloyd was sweeping out, and the place was empty.

"I could fix somethin' for you," he said, "but you probably wouldn't care much for my cookin'. Wife's out shoppin'."

The Town House Grill (Stop-N-Eat) was closed. Only Martha's was left, across the corner from Lloyd's. Martha's was not only open, but had two customers inside. I took a table and ordered my hamburgers and chocolate shakes, feeling rich. How money can change! On a good day, $6 was nothing, a tiny droplet in the great bucket of prosperity. Today, my $5.50 was wealth, because it was more than I needed. Even after supper and corn chips and candy bars, I had $4 clear.

Walking back to the biplane, I was an intruder in the town. Lights were coming on in the houses and voices drifted to the sidewalk. Now and then someone puttered in a dark flower garden, and looked up to watch me pass. The roof crests of the houses carried strange ornaments, dragonlike, silhouettes of Viking ships, all cut from metal.

The reservoir was only a short walk from the biplane, and I turned aside. The ground was soft and hidden in deep grass. Flowers were tiny pure palettes strewn carelessly about. Reeds shuddered along the shore, more like arrows down from the sky than plants up from the water. Across the way a frog clacked like a Spanish castanet, and an invisible cow said, "mmMMMm," loud, out in the distance. The reservoir was a tiny Walden, with only the smallest ripples across its dark-mirror face.

I crunched back through the grass to the biplane and unrolled the sleeping bag. The moon went in and out of the clouds while the evening melted into night. I ate a lemon drop, and listened to the sound of the engine still roaring in my ears. Solitude, I decided, is barnstorming all by yourself.

At 9 A.M. on a day I didn't know, we circled Milan, Missouri, trailing sound and color, and landed in a hayfield a half mile away. Before I had the sign on the gatepost, the first townsfolk arrived. Two pickup trucks clattered down onto the furrows and the drivers stepped out looking.

"Have a little motor trouble, did y'?" He was an old fellow, in coveralls.

"Aw, no," I said. "Flyin' around, givin' airplane rides."

"What d'y know. She's an old one, all right, too."

"Feel like a ride today? Nice and cool up there."

"Oh, no. Not me," he said. "I'm scared."

"Scared! This airplane been flyin' since 1929! Don't you think she might make one more flight without crashin' all to flinders? I don't believe you're scared."

"She'd go down sure enough if I got in there."

I pulled my sleeping bag from the front cockpit and turned to the other watcher.

"Ready to fly today? Three dollars, and Milan from the air. Pretty town it is."

"I'd go, if I could keep one foot on the ground."

"Can't see much from that height." It was clear that I wasn't going to be deluged with customers. My only hope had been that the biplane would be a strange enough thing in an airportless town to bring out the curious. Something had to happen soon. The fuel stick showed that we were down to twenty-four gallons of fuel. We'd need more gasoline before long, and we'd need passengers first, to pay for it. We had come from poor to rich to poor again.

A bright red late-model Ford sedan drove through the gate, purring in its mufflers. Instead of a license plate on its front bumper, it said CHEVY EATER. From the little crossed flags in chrome on the fender, I thought it might have some kind of huge engine under the hood.

The driver was an open-faced young man, a sort of enlightened hot-rodder, and he walked over to look in the cockpit.

"Feel like flyin' today?" I said.

"Me? Oh, no. I'm a coward."

"Hey, what is with all this coward stuff? Everybody in Milan scared of airplanes? I just better pack up and move out."

"No . . . there'll be lots of folks out to fly with y'. They just don't know you're here yet. You want to ride in town, get somethin' to eat?"

"No thanks. Might ride over to that place over there, though. What is it, a Buick place? Think they'd have a Coke machine?"

"Sure, they got one there," he said. "Come on, I'll give you a ride over. I'm not doin' anythin' anyway."

The pickup trucks had left and no one else appeared on the road. It seemed as good a time as any for breakfast.

The big engine was there in the Ford, and tires screeched all the way down the road.

"You flyin' that airplane came in a while ago?" the Buick dealer asked when I walked into his shop.

"Sure am."

"Not havin' any trouble, are you?"

"Nope. Just flyin' around givin' rides."

"Rides? How much do you get for a ride?"

"Three dollars. Trip over town. About ten minutes. You got a Coke machine?"

"Right over 'gainst the corner. Hey, Elmer! Stan! Go take an airplane ride with this guy. I'll pay your way."

I dropped a dime in the machine while the owner insisted that he was serious, and that his boys were to go out and fly.

Elmer put down his socket wrench at once. "Let's go." Stan wouldn't budge. "No, thanks," he said. "Don't quite feel like it today."

"You're scared, Stan," my Ford driver said. "You're scared to go up with him."

"I don't see *you* flyin', Ray Scott."

"I told him. I'm scared. Maybe I'll go up later."

"Well, I'm not scared of any old airplane," Elmer said.

I finished my Coke and we piled into the red Ford. "I was a special jumper in Korea," Elmer said as we drove. "Used to go up in a Gooney Bird and jump out from three thousand feet, with a ten-foot chute. Ten foot eight inches. I'm not scared of no airplane ride."

"A *ten-foot* chute?" I said. Elmer would have been hitting the ground at about forty miles an hour.

"Yeah. Ten foot eight inches. You know that I'm not afraid of no airplane ride."

The Ford stopped at the wing of the biplane and my passenger climbed aboard. In a minute we were airborne, engine and air thundering about us, the land piled in hills of crushed emerald below. We turned over town, trying to herd some passengers out to the hayfield.

People on the ground stopped and looked up at us, and some boys on bicycles began wheeling out, and I had hope.

Elmer was not enjoying the flight. He braced himself hard against the side of the cockpit, and he didn't look down. Why, the man was frightened! There must be quite a story behind the guy, I thought. We glided down to land and he got out before the engine had windmilled to a stop. "See? Nothing about an airplane ride can scare me!"

Wow, I thought, and wondered about that story.

"Ready to go for a ride now, Ray?" he said.

"Maybe this afternoon. I'm scared."

"Ray, darn it," I said, "why is everybody in this town so scared of airplanes?"

"I don't know. Well, we had a couple pretty bad airplane crashes here this year, right around here. Guy got lost around Green City and went into a cloud and then crashed onto a hill. Then a little ways north a two-engine plane, brand-new one, had the motors stop and hit a lot of trees and rocks. Killed everybody. People still worried, I guess. But you'll get some out after work, today."

So that was it. With airplanes falling like silly moths out of the air, no wonder the people were frightened.

When they left, in a screech of blue tire smoke, it was time for decision. I had $6.91 in my pocket, and twenty-two gallons of gasoline. If I waited there with no passengers, I'd be wasting time and getting hungrier. I couldn't spend money for lunch, or there would be nothing for gas. Later on, there might be passengers. And there might not. I wished Paul were there, or Stu or Dick or Spence, to be Leader for the Day, but I was stuck with Leader, and at last I decided to spend my money on gas, now. Maybe there would be a good town on the way north.

Centerville was forty miles away, and there was an airport there. I loaded the front cockpit, started the engine with the crank, running back to the starter engage handle before the big whining wheel ground down, and took off north. It wasn't until we had been in the air for ten minutes that I thought $6.91 wasn't going to buy much aviation gasoline. Thirteen, fourteen gallons, maybe. I should have stayed to fly more passengers. But there was nothing to be done about it then, midway between Milan and Centerville. The best plan was just to pull the throttle back and use as little fuel as possible.

Car gas, I thought. The old engines were built for low-octane fuel. I knew antique-airplane pilots who used nothing but Regular auto gas in their engines. Someday I'll try car gas, when I don't have passengers to fly—see how it works.

Centerville swept serenely under the wing, and five minutes later we rolled to the 80-octane pump.

"What'll it be?" the attendant said. "Want some gas?"

"Take some eighty-octane from you."

He pushed a lever that started the pump humming, and handed up the nozzle to where I stood in struts and wires over the gas tank. I rechecked my cash supply and said, "Tell me when I've got . . . six dollars and eighty-one cents' worth." I held back a dime for emergencies.

"Kind of a funny way to buy gas," he said.

"Yep." The nozzle poured fuel down into the black emptiness of the 50-gallon tank, and I was thankful for every second that it did. I had worked hard for that $6.81, and the fuel that it bought was precious stuff. Every drop of it. When the pump stopped, I held the nozzle there so that the last thin droplets fell down into the blackness. There was still a distressing amount of emptiness down the filler hole.

"Comes to sixteen gallons."

I handed down the hose and with it the money. Well, sixteen gallons was more than I thought I was going to get . . . now if I could go back to Milan at the lowest possible throttle setting, I might have a little more gas in the tank than I did when I left.

We chugged south with the engine turning 1,575 revolutions per minute, nearly 200 rpm slower than low-cruise power. We crawled through the air, but the time that it took to get back to Milan was not so important as the amount of fuel we used. In thirty minutes we had covered thirty miles, and glided once again to land on the hay. No one waited.

Since I couldn't afford fuel for aerobatics, since Stu and his parachute were 1,500 miles away, I was left with Method C. I unrolled the sleeping bag under the right wing, and resolved to employ C for one hour. If there were no passengers by then, I'd move on.

I studied the hay stubble a few inches away. It was a huge jungle, with all kinds of beasts roaming it. Here was a great crack in the earth, wide enough to keep an ant from crossing. Here was a young tree of a hay stem growing new, a half inch tall. I pulled it up and ate it for lunch. It was tender and tasty, and I looked for others. But that was it, the other hay was all old and tough.

A spider climbed a tall grassblade and threatened to jump down onto my sleeping bag and torment me. Easily met, that challenge. I uprooted the blade and moved the spider two feet south. I rolled over and looked up at the bottom of the wing for a while, and drummed my fingers on its tightness.

One-thirty. In half an hour I'd be on my way . . . the people here were just too frightened. That little town of Lemons, on the way to Centerville, might have some chances.

A pickup truck clattered down toward me. Like every pickup in every town, it had its owner's name painted on the door. *William Cowgill, Milan, Mo.* I read upside down, under the wing. A black pickup truck.

I got up and rolled my sleeping bag; it was time to leave.

An interested sharp mind peered at me from under a shock of white hair, through quick blue eyes.

"Howdy," I said. "Lookin' to fly at all today? Nice and cool up there."

"No thanks. How y' doin'?" Next to him sat a boy of twelve or so.

"Not too good. Not too many people feel like flyin', 'round here, I guess."

"Oh, I don't know. Think you'd probably get quite a few this evening."

"This is too far out," I said. "You got to be close to town, or nobody even sees you."

"You might have better luck over at my place," he said. "It's not too far out."

"Sure didn't see it from the air. Where is it?"

The man opened the door of the truck, took a wide board from the back and drew a map. "You know where the cheese factory is?"

"No."

"Lu-Juan's?"

"No. I know where the school is, with the racetrack."

"Well, you know the lake. The big lake, south of town?"

"Yeah. I know that."

"We're just across the street from that lake, on the south. Ridge land. There's some cows in the place now, but we want 'em out anyway and you can land there. Fact, I've been thinking of making an airport out of it. Milan needs an airport."

"Guess I could find that. Just across from the lake." I was sure that the pasture wouldn't work, but I had to be on my way anyway, and I might as well have a look at it.

"Right. I'm driving the truck, and Cully here's got the jeep at the corner. We'll go on over and meet you."

"OK. I'll look at it, anyway," I said, "'f it don't work out, I'll be on my way."

"All right. Cully, come on." The boy was standing by the cockpit, looking at the instruments.

In five minutes, we were circling a strip of ridged pasture. A flock of cows clustered around the center, apparently eating the grass. We dropped down for a low pass, and the land looked smooth. The pasture was on the side of a long hill, and rose like a gentle roller-coaster to the crest. Just beyond the crest was a barbed-wire fence and a row of telephone poles and wires. If we rolled off the ridgeline, we'd be in trouble, but then if we did that it would be our own fault. Carefully used, this would be a good strip to work from. We could take off downhill and land uphill.

Best of all, there was a hamburger stand a hundred yards down the road. If I carried only one passenger, I could eat!

The cows galloped away after the first pass over their horns. There was one scrap of paper on the whole strip, a crushed newspaper just by a place where the ridge turned right. As soon as I saw that paper go by, I'd touch right rudder, just a little.

It was more difficult than it looked, and our first landing was not as smooth as I wanted it to be. But cars were already parking by the fence to watch the biplane fly, and passengers came out at once.

"How much do you want for a ride?"

"Three dollars. Nice and cool up there, too." Passengers before the sign went up, I thought. A good omen.

"OK. I'll fly with you."

Ha-ha, I thought, lunch. I emptied the front cockpit again, feeling that I had spent the whole day loading and unloading that front seat, and strapped my passenger aboard. The view from the ridgetop was a pretty one, rolling hills away off to the horizon, the trees and houses of the town they called "*My*-l'n" resting easy on a soft rise of ground. Taking off downhill, the biplane leaped ahead, was airborne in seconds, and climbed quickly over the fields.

We circled town, the passenger looking down at the square and the county courthouse centered there, the pilot thinking that he just might have found a good place to barnstorm. A circle to the left, one to the right, a turn over a private lake and boat dock, a gliding spiral down over the pasture, with a gathering row of automobiles waiting, and our second landing on the ridgetop. It went smoothly. The place would work. Finding this field was finding a diamond hidden in a secret green jewel-box.

It was a different town, here. The people were much more interested in the airplane, and they wanted to fly.

"You might go out east, over the golf course," Bill Cowgill said as he arrived in the pickup, "get some folks out there, maybe." He was more interested in making the flying a success than anyone we had worked with. Probably because he wanted to see how the land worked as an airport.

"How are you fixed for gas, Bill?" I said. "There a filling station around, have a five-gallon can of gas, regular car gas?"

"Got some down at the house, if you want. Got plenty."

"Well, I might take you up on ten gallons, maybe."

Two more men stepped from the cars. "You giving rides?" they said.

"Sure thing."

"Well, let's go." We went.

Circling to land, I saw that the cars had parked exactly across the end of my strip. If we touched down too long, and rolled straight along the ridgeline, we'd run right into the middle of them all. I cut the throttle back and decided that if we were rolling too fast, I'd turn left, down the side of the ridge, up the side of the crest and then deliberately ground-loop right. If everything went well, I wouldn't even damage the airplane. Still, I didn't want to land long.

As a result of all this thinking, we dropped in to a hard landing, bounced up into the air again, and staggered along the ridge to a stop. It was a reminder that we didn't want to land too short, either.

From these first passengers I now had $9 in my pocket, and I left the airplane to her spectators for a while and walked across the street to the hamburger stand, Lu-Juan's. Ah, food! As the gasoline was precious to the biplane, so those two hot dogs and two milkshakes were precious to the pilot. I was happy just to sit there quietly and eat something more filling than hay.

The airplane now had a good crowd of spectators standing around her, and I began to worry about her fabric. I ordered an orange drink to go and then walked back to the airplane. There were passengers waiting to fly.

From time to time during lulls in the afternoon, Bill talked again about his field. "If you were going to make an airport out of this strip, what would you do to fix it up? For less than five hundred dollars, say."

"Wouldn't have to do much to it at all. Maybe fill that part right down at the end, though that would be a lot of fill. Wouldn't have to do that; all you'd have to do would be to mark out the levelest ground. That's the biggest problem, picking just where to touch down and roll out."

"You wouldn't say to level the place up?"

"I don't think so. Nothing better than take off downhill and land uphill. Just put down some lime or something like that, to mark where to land. Put in a gas pump later, if you wanted. With the lake there and the place to eat, this would be a nice little airstrip."

"How wide would you think it might be?"

"Oh, maybe from about here . . . over to about . . . here, would be wide enough. Be plenty wide."

He took a double-bit ax from the bed of the pickup and chopped a mark into the earth at each edge of the landing area.

"I'll just mark this off here and maybe some day we'll have something going."

As it happened to the first barnstormers, it happened to me. An ax marks the place where the first airplane lands, and someday in the future there are many airplanes landing. I didn't think till later that if this field were turned into an airstrip, there would be one less pasture in the world for barnstormers to fly from.

"I'll fly with you if you promise to fly real smooth . . ."

It was my red-Ford driver and self-styled coward, Ray.

"You want to go up in that dangerous thing," I said, "that dangerous old airplane?"

"Only if you promise not to turn her over."

I had to smile, for despite all his words of fear, the man wasn't afraid at all; he rode the airplane like a veteran, the circle over the golf course, the two circles of town, the steep spiral over the strip, looking down, looking down, like it was all a dream of flying.

"That was really fun," he said, and went back to his car, happy.

"Free ride for the owner, Bill," I said to the elder Cowgill. "Let's go."

"I think Cully wants to ride more than I do."

Cully did, and pulled his own leather flying helmet from the jeep as he ran for the airplane. "Dad got it for me at the war surplus," he explained, climbing by himself into the front seat. He liked his ride before we ever got off the ground.

With my debts paid, and the last ride flown, I poured two five-gallon cans of Regular gas into the tank. Enough to fly alone, and to check the effect of car gas on the engine. It worked just as smoothly as aviation fuel, if not a tiny bit smoother.

So, by sundown, I had flown twenty passengers and had $49 in my pocket after food and fuel. A good feeling from the hayfield noon, with a dime to my name.

I knew now, without question, that the land of yesterday does exist, that there is a place of escape, that a man can survive alone with his airplane, if only he has a wish to do so. Milan had been good to me, and I was happy. But tomorrow it would be time to move on.

CHAPTER NINETEEN

THE DAYS FOLDED one into another, and into events of August and September. County fairs, with special brushed cows and combed sheep waiting for judgment, dining only on the cleanest of polished straw.

Coins raining down on glassware with the sound of wind chimes in the night, above the song of the barker: "Nickel in the crystal glass, folks, and it's yours to take home. Toss a nickel and win a glass . . ."

Quiet streets, old towns; where the Vogue Theater had been turned into a machine shop, and finally closed.

People with memories of old airplanes flying, and of droughts and floods, the good and bad of decades.

Foot-tall jars of Mrs. Flick's Oatmeal Cookies, three for five cents.

Pioneer-dressed women in small-town celebration, and square dances in the streets.

Music amplified and echoing through the starlight, rippling across the still wings of a biplane and through the silken hammock of a barnstormer listening, watching the galaxy.

A great burly grizzled mountain of a man, Claude Shepherd, tending his monster-iron Case Steam Tractor, built 1909. Twenty tons of metal, barrels of water, bunkers of coal, giant huge bull gears driving wheels seven feet tall. "I got to love steam power from the time I was a little tad, on my grandfather's knee. Smoothest power in the world, steam. When I was five, I could set the valves . . . never got over it, never got over lovin' steam."

Passengers, passengers, men and women and children rising up to see the sky, to look down on the water towers of towns everywhere Midwest. Every takeoff different, every landing different, every person in the cockpit ahead a different person, guided into gentle adventure. Nothing happened by chance, nothing by luck.

Sunrise into sunset into sunrise. Wild clear air, rain and wind and storm and fog and lightning and wild clear air again.

Sun fresh and cool and yellow like I'd never seen. Grass so green it sparkled under the wheels. Sky blue and pure like skies always used to be, and clouds whiter than Christmas in the air.

And most of all, freedom.

CHAPTER TWENTY

THEN CAME A day when we took off, the biplane and I, into Iowa.

Chugging north, looking down. One town had a good hayfield, and we circled and landed. But the margin wasn't there. If the engine stopped on takeoff there was only rough ground ahead. There are those who say that the chances of engine failure on takeoff are so remote that they aren't worth worrying about, but those people do not fly old airplanes.

We took off again and turned farther north, into the cold air of autumn. The towns here were islands of trees, isolated by seas of cornfields ready for harvest. The corn grew right close in to town, and there weren't many possible places to work. But I wasn't worried. The question of survival had long since been answered. Some good place always showed up by sundown.

I had just discarded another small town when the engine choked, one time, and a puff of white smoke whipped back in the windstream. I sat up straight in the seat, tense as iron.

The smoke was not good. The Wright never acted strangely unless it was trying to tell me that something was wrong. What was it trying to say? Smoke . . . smoke, I thought. What could make a puff of white smoke? The engine was running smoothly again. Or was it? Listening very carefully, I thought that it was running the slightest bit roughly. And I could smell the exhaust more than I usually could. But all the instruments were pointing in their proper places: oil pressure, oil temperature, tachometer . . . just as they should have been.

I pushed the throttle forward and we climbed. Just in case something was wrong, I wanted more altitude for gliding if everything went to pieces and we had to land in the gentle hills below.

We leveled at 2,500 feet in icy air. Summer was over.

Was there a fire under the cowl? I looked over the side of the cockpit, out into the wind, but there was no sign of fire forward.

There was something wrong with the engine. There! It was running rough, now. If the engine would stop, that would be one thing, cause for definite action. But this roughness, and the smell of the exhaust, and that puff of smoke. It all meant something, but it was hard to tell what . . .

At that instant, a great burst of white smoke flew back from the engine, a solid river dragging back in a dense trail behind. I looked over the right side of the cockpit and saw nothing but smoke, as if we had been shot down, in real combat.

Oil sprayed windscreen and goggles. We are in trouble, airplane.

I thought again that we were on fire, which would not be good in a wood-and-fabric airplane, half a mile in the air. I shut down the engine and turned off the fuel, but still the smoke poured overboard, a long helpless streak across the sky. Great Scott. We are on fire.

I kicked the biplane hard up on her wing, slammed full rudder, and we slipped wildly sideways toward the ground. There was an open field there, with a hill, and if we played it just right . . .

The smoke came thinner and finally stopped, and the only sound was the quiet whistle of the wind through the wires and the faint clanking of the propeller as it fanned around.

There was a tractor working the other side of the sloping field, mowing hay. I couldn't tell whether he saw us or not, and at the moment, I didn't care.

Level out, cross the fence, slip off a little speed, catch the hill on the rising side . . .

We touched, and I forced the control stick hard back, digging the tail skid deep into the ground. We rolled across the peak of the hill, rumbling, clattering, slowed, and stopped.

I sat in the cockpit for a moment, thankful that the airplane had been under control every second. Perhaps there was only something minor wrong. A valve, maybe, or a hole in a piston, pumping oil into a cylinder.

I got out of the cockpit and walked to the engine. There was oil streaming from every exhaust port, and when I moved the propeller, oil gurgled inside. This was nothing simple.

I unbolted the carburetor and remembered one of Pop Reid's adventures. "Supercharger oil seal," he had said, years ago. "She blew three gallons of oil in two minutes flat. Had to tear down the whole engine."

In a few minutes the answer was clear. A bearing in the center of the engine had come to pieces, and oil poured with the fuel into all cylinders. That's where we got the smoke, and the oil on my goggles.

The Whirlwind, at the end of summer, was finished.

I accepted a ride from the farmer and rode into Laurel, Iowa, on his tractor. A call to Dick Willetts, and he was on his way with the Cub. Thank God, again, for friends.

I went back to the biplane and covered her for the nights ahead. There was no spare engine. I could come here with a truck and take this engine home for rebuild, or I could take the whole airplane home on a trailer. Either way, it would be a while before she flew again.

The little yellow Cub was a beautiful sight in the sky, and Dick set her down on the hilltop lightly as a feather in a pillow factory. We would leave, and the Parks would stay in her field. I climbed into the backseat of the Cub, and we lifted over the hay and homeward. The plane looked lost and lonely as she dwindled in distance.

All the hour's flight, I wondered about the meaning of the engine failure, why it stopped the way it did and where it did and when it did. There is no such thing as bad luck. There's a reason and a lesson behind everything. Still, the lesson may not always be simple to see, and by the time we landed at Ottumwa, I hadn't seen it. I had only one question about the engine failure: Why?

* * *

The only thing to do was to bring the biplane home. The first wind-storm could hurt her, the first hailstorm destroy her. She did not belong out in the weather with winter rolling down upon us.

I borrowed a pickup truck and a long flatbed trailer from Merlyn Winn, the man who sold Cessna airplanes at Ottumwa airport, and three of us traveled the eighty miles north: a young college friend named Mike Cloyd, Bette, and I. Somehow we had to find a way to take the airplane apart and lash it onto that trailer, and to do it in the five hours left before dark. We wasted no time at the job.

"She looks kind of sad, don't she?" Mike said, when the wings lay yellow and frail on the hay.

"Yeah." I agreed only because I didn't feel like talking. The machine didn't look sad to me. It looked like a bunch of mechanical parts disconnected across the ground. The thing was no longer alive, was no longer a she, no longer a personality. There was no chance of it flying now, and the only life it knew was when it was flying, or able to fly. Now it was wood and steel and doped cloth. A pile of parts to load on a trailer and take home.

At last it was done and it was just a matter of sitting in the cab and pointing the truck down the road until we reached home. I still couldn't understand why this was all happening, what important thing I would have missed if the engine had not failed.

We turned onto Interstate 80, all modern and highspeed pavement. "Mike, keep an eye on the trailer, will you, see if anything's gonna fall off, now and then?"

"Looks all right," he said.

We accelerated up to forty miles an hour, glad to be on the fast road home. It would be good to get this game over with.

At forty-one miles an hour, very slightly, the trailer began fishtail-ing. I looked in the rearview mirror and touched the brake. "Hang on," I said, and wondered why I would say that.

The trailer took ten seconds to play its part. From a gentle fishtail, it swerved harder left and right, and then it lashed sudden and wild from one side to another behind us, a whale shaking a hook from its jaw. Tires screamed again and again, and the truck was slammed heavily to the left. We were out of control.

The three of us were interested bystanders, sitting together in the cab of the truck, unable to steer or stop. We slid sideways, then backward, and I looked out the left window to see the trailer smashed against the side of the truck, glued there, while we went off the road. I could have reached out and touched the big red fuselage for a while, but then we slid into the grass valley between the two highways of the Interstate.

The dead body of the airplane lurched up on one wheel, teetered there a second in slow motion and then slowly went crashing upside down into the ditch. I sat idly and watched the centersection and its struts crush down in no hurry at all, bending, tearing, splintering away under the thousand-pound fuselage. It was all very quiet. How like a paper bag, I thought, the way it folds up.

We came to a stop, all in a neat row: truck, trailer, fuselage; like sea creatures caught and laid side by side in the grass.

"Everybody OK?" Everybody was fine.

"I can't open the door on this side, Mike, trailer's jamming it. Let's get out on your side."

I was disgusted. The lesson escaped me entirely. If there is nothing by chance, just what in God's name was this all supposed to mean?

The fuselage that we had just barely managed to strain onto the trailer through brute force was now upside down, wheels in the air. Gasoline and oil poured from the tanks. The lower wings were trapped between the trailer and the airplane body, holes torn through them. One engine rocker-box was pounded flat, where it had struck concrete. We might as well set the thing on fire, I thought, and drive home alone. It's dead, it's dead, it's dead.

"The hitch busted," Mike said. "Look, it tore right out of the bumper, tore the metal right out."

It was so. Our trailer hitch was still firmly coupled and lashed, but it had been ripped bodily from the heavy steel of the bumper. It would have taken at least five tons on the hitch to shear it free, and the complete load on the trailer was a little over a tenth of that.

What were the chances of this happening, on the one time I had ever put the biplane on a flatbed trailer, on the only time she had not been able to fly herself out of a field, with a truck and trailer that had been designed for hauling airplanes? A million to one.

Cars and trucks stopped along the roadside, to help and to watch.

A truck driver brought a heavy jack, and we lifted the pickup free of the trailer, undamaged, and drove it up to the edge of the highway. By now it was full dark, and we worked in the beams of headlights; it all felt like a Dante nightmare.

With ten men, and with a heavy rope tied from truck to fuselage, we finally dragged what was left of the biplane back onto its wheels, and forced it again onto the trailer. I wondered how we were going to tow a trailer without a hitch, or even move the trailer out of the low grass valley.

A great boxy truck stopped by the plane, and the driver got down. "Can I help you?" he said.

"Kinda doubt it; can't do too much more, I guess. Thanks."

"What happened?"

"Hitch broke off."

The man walked to look at the broken metal. "Hey, look," he said. "I have a hitch on my truck, and I don't have to be in Chicago for another couple days. Maybe I can tow you somewhere. I'm kind of interested in airplanes . . . airline pilot out of Chicago. Don Kyte's the name. Coming home from California. I'd be glad to help you, if I could."

About that time I came awake to what was happening. Again . . . what are the chances of this guy coming along this road in this month in this week in this day in this hour in this minute when I have no possible way to tow that trailer, and him coming along not only in a truck, not only in an empty truck, but in an empty truck with a trailer hitch on it, and he not only happens to like airplanes but he is an airline pilot and he has days to spare? What are the chances of a lucky coincidence like that?

Don Kyte backed his truck down into the valley, pulled the trailer straight, then hitched up to it and pulled it onto the road.

The police arrived, then, and an ambulance, red lights flashing in the dark. "Anybody hurt?" the officer said.

"Nope. Everybody's fine."

He ran back to his patrol-car radio to report this, and then came slowly out to see the trailered airplane. "We heard there was an airplane crash on the Interstate," he said.

"Sort of, yeah." I explained what had happened.

"Any cars damaged?" He began to write on a clipboard.

"No."

He held his pencil, and thought. "No cars damaged, nobody hurt. This isn't even an accident!"

"No, sir, it isn't. We're all ready to move on, now."

We unhitched the trailer by the Ottumwa hangar at midnight, and Don came to stay the night with us. We found that we had mutual friends from one coast to another, and it was past two when we finally folded the couch down into a bed for him and let him alone to sleep.

The next day I went to the airport and unloaded airplane parts, stacking them in the back of the hangar.

Merlyn Winn walked to meet me, his footsteps echoing in the giant place.

"Dick, I don't know what to say. That hitch was welded into bad iron there, and it just picked this time to go. Gosh, I'm sorry about what happened."

"It's not all so bad, Merlyn. Centersection and struts, biggest part. Engine had to be overhauled, anyway. Some work on the wings. Be a good winter job."

"Nice thing about old airplanes," he said. "You just can't kill 'em dead. Shame it had to happen, though."

A shame it had to happen. Merlyn left, and in a moment I walked out from the hangar into the sunlight. It never would have happened at all if we had stayed home, if the biplane and I had only flown on Sunday afternoons, around the airport. I'd have no smashed airplane, then, no parts awaiting rebuild in the hangar. There would have been no crash at Prairie du Chien, picking up a handkerchief with a wingtip. No crash at Palmyra, as Paul met his challenge. No crash on Interstate 80, when a trailer hitch strangely failed.

There would have been no Stu plummeting down through the air, or puzzling us with his silent thoughts, or having the most continuous fun of his life. No mouse attacking my cheese. No passengers turning in the air for the first time, no "That's great!" no *"WONDERFUL!"* no immortality in Midwest family albums. No crumpled money-piles, no proof a gypsy pilot can survive, if he wishes, today.

No Claude Shepherd, by his giant hissing monster engine, talking the wonders of steam. No country fairs, no mosquito-hum at midnight, no honey-clover for breakfast, no formation flying in the sunset or sorrow of a lone airplane disappearing in the west. No freedom tasted, none of these strange affairs I called guidance to whisper that man is not a creature of chance, pointed into oblivion.

A shame? Which would I rather have, the wreck in the hangar or a polished piece of a biplane that flew only on calm Sunday afternoons?

I walked across the concrete ramp in the sun, and for a moment I was in the biplane again and we were flying together beside the Luscombe and the Travelair, up in the wind, out over those green fields and towns of another time. I still didn't know the why of the wreck, but someday I would.

What mattered, I thought, was that the color and the time still waited for me, as they always had, just across the horizon of a special free enchanted land called America.

EPILOGUE

It DIDN'T TAKE a winter to rebuild the biplane, it took two years.

Two years of saving dollars and working on the wreck—lifting away the smashed wood and fabric, the broken struts, the remains of the engine. In that time I finished and covered a new centersection for the top wing, replaced a dozen splintered sections in the body and wings of the plane, stood guard with water while torches replaced bent fittings with hot new steel, while new struts were formed from streamlined tubing.

Bit by bit as the months turned past. Fuel tank repaired—month, month—windscreen replaced—month, month—coaming formed from wrinkled metal back into a smooth curve, and painted.

In that time one part of my being was locked there in pieces and bolts across the hangar floor, no longer free, asking, over and again, "Why?" I was glad to pay the price for the discovery of my country, yet it seemed so unnecessary, and that part of me in the hangar was a heavy sad part indeed.

Friends. What a pure and beautiful word. Dick McWhorter, in Prosser, Washington: "I still have a Whirlwind engine down in the hangar. It hasn't run since 1946, and you'd better check it, but it looks good. I'll hold it for you . . ."

John Howard, in Udall, Kansas: "Sure, I'd be glad to look at the engine for you. And say, I have some wing bolts . . ."

Pop Reid, in San Jose, California: "Oh, don't worry, kiddo. We have a collector ring for that engine, and all the connections—never been used. You might as well have it, it's just sitting around out here ..."

Tom Hoselton, in Albia, Iowa: "I have more work than I know what to do with, but this is special. I'll have the fittings welded up for you in a week ..."

Very slowly, years passing while I struggled to earn a living with a bargain-basement typewriter, the biplane changed in the square cocoon of its hangar.

Fuselage finished. Wings attached and rigged. Tail on. Engine mounted. New cowling.

And then the day came that the old propeller on the new engine jerked around in a blurred silver streak, and very suddenly the biplane, two years dead, was alive again, bouncing hard echoes off the hangar doors. Up ahead in the roar and the wind, the black rocker-arms clicked up and down, spraying new grease back from their uncovered boxes.

So long dead, and I was alive. So long chained, and I was free.

At last, the answer why. The lesson that had been so hard to find, so difficult to learn, came quick and clear and simple. The reason for problems is to overcome them. Why, that's the very nature of man, I thought, to press past limits, to prove his freedom. It isn't the challenge that faces us, that determines who we are and what we are becoming, but the way we meet the challenge, whether we toss a match at the wreck or work our way through it, step by step, to freedom.

And behind it, I thought, lifting the biplane up once again into the sky, lies not blind chance but a principle that works to help us understand, a thousand "coincidences" and friends come to show us the way when the problems seem too hard to solve alone.

True for me, true for my country America.

We turned gently about a cloud, and flashed sunlight, a mile in the air, setting course for the towns of Nebraska.

Problems for overcoming. Freedom for proving. And, as long as we believe in our dream, nothing by chance.

About the Author

Richard Bach is the author of sixteen books, including the bestselling *Jonathan Livingston Seagull* and *Illusions*. A former USAF fighter pilot, gypsy barnstormer, and airplane mechanic, he flies a seaplane today.